FACTORING LAW AND PRACTICE

AUSTRALIA AND NEW ZEALAND
The Law Book Company Ltd.
Sydney : Melbourne : Brisbane : Perth

CANADA
The Carswell Company Ltd.
Toronto : Calgary : Vancouver : Ottawa

INDIA
N.M. Tripathi Private Ltd.
Bombay
and
Eastern Law House Private Ltd.
Calcutta and Delhi

M.P.P. House
Bangalore

Universal Book Traders
Delhi

ISRAEL
Steimatzky's Agency Ltd.
Jerusalem : Tel Aviv : Haifa

PAKISTAN
Pakistan Law House
Karachi

FACTORING
LAW AND PRACTICE

BY

FREDDY R. SALINGER F.C.A.

With a foreword by Professor Roy Goode

LONDON
SWEET & MAXWELL
1991

Published in 1991 by
Sweet & Maxwell Limited of
South Quay Plaza, 183 Marsh Wall,
London E14 9FT
Phototypeset by
Apek Typesetting
Nailsea, Bristol BS19 2PH
Printed in Great Britain by
Butler and Tanner of
Frome, Somerset

British Library Cataloguing in Publication Data

Salinger, F. R.
Factoring law and practice.
1. Great Britain. Business firms. Financial management.
Factoring. Law
I. Title
344.1067

ISBN 0-421-41000-0

FOREWORD

Factoring is now a highly developed form of finance in England, yet there remains widespread ignorance both as to its basic purpose and as to the law and practice governing factoring operations. From a legal viewpoint factoring is both fascinating and complex, because it spans so many different branches of law and poses numerous questions on which the law is unclear. Additional problems arise from export and import factoring, which may necessitate reference to at least two different legal systems and to rules of private international law. Not all legal systems are as effective as English law in accommodating factoring transactions. Hence the conclusion of the 1988 Unidroit Convention on International Factoring, which is designed to remove some of the impediments to cross-border factoring created by national laws.

A comprehensive and reliable guide to factoring law and practice is therefore essential for those engaged in factoring and their legal advisers. Yet the literature on the subject remains small, for there are very few people who combine a detailed knowledge of domestic and international factoring practice with a mastery of the legal and accounting implications of factoring. Mr. Freddy Salinger is one of them. By common accord the doyen of the United Kingdom factoring industry, he combines a vast experience of all forms of domestic and international factoring with an encyclopaedic knowledge of the relevant legislation which exceeds that possessed by all but the most specialist lawyers.

Moreover, as will be known to the many readers of earlier publications, Freddy Salinger has the gift of communicating his knowledge clearly and concisely, so that even those with no prior knowledge of the subject can follow the reasoning, whilst the cognoscenti will find the more intricate aspects of the subject examined in satisfying detail. The UNIDROIT Convention itself reflects in no small degree the guidance and counsel Freddy Salinger gave throughout the progress of work on the Convention.

It is therefore with great pleasure that I recommend this book, the most up to date, reliable and comprehensive guide to the law and practice of factoring. It will be found invaluable not only by factoring companies and their legal advisers but by banks, business organisations and all others engaged or interested in this important field of finance.

Roy Goode
St John's College
Oxford

ACKNOWLEDGEMENTS

As is usual in the creation of a book of this nature I have been helped by many people: family, friends, former colleagues and practitioners in factoring and in the law.

First, I must express my appreciation of the encouragement given to me by wife, Ann, and her tolerance of my disregard of all else during many months. I am also grateful to my daughters, Rosemary and Abigail, who assisted me with the burden of the typescript.

I acknowledge with gratitude the assistance and encouragement of Edward Wilde and his partners and colleagues at Wilde and Partners and particularly of Declan Gilroy on the basis of whose notes Chapter 4 was written. I am also most grateful to:

Griffin Factors Limited for permission to publish a specimen of their client accounting and to Peter Johnson, a director, who made many useful suggestions regarding up-to-date factoring practice;
International Factors Limited for permission to publish a specimen client account;
Lombard NatWest Factors Limited and Jack Doyle a former director for help with some of the passages on accounting and V.A.T. bad debt relief;
Security Pacific Business Finance (Europe) Limited for the provision of a deed of priorities published as an appendix to the book;
Venture Factors PLC for permission to publish their standard factoring agreement as a specimen;
Brian Arculus of The Leasing Corporation PLC for the diagrams in the appendices;
The Association of British Factors and Discounters for some statistical information;
The Secretariat of Factors Chain International for a copy of the Code of International Factoring Customs and other material;
The Secretariat of UNIDROIT for the Convention published in one of the appendices;
Harvey C. Guberman, now of Kreindler & Relkin of New York, and Heinrich J. Sommeer, formerly a Managing Director of Diskont & Kredit AG of Dusseldorf, both former colleagues on the Legal Committee of Factor Chain International, for their help regarding developments in their respective countries;

D John McNeil OBE, WS of Morton Fraser Milligan who reviewed the passages on Scots law;
Tony Shea of Clifford Chance for his assistance in relation to the White Paper on Banking Services; and
Philip R Wood of Allen & Overy for his advice on some difficult points relating to set-off.

I acknowledge with very many thanks the valuable advice, particularly on some of the more difficult questions relating to security rights and priorities, which I received from Roy Goode OBE, QC.

I am sincerely grateful to Tolley Publishing Co. Limited for their having given permission for the reproduction of some passages from some of my earlier publications.

Last but not least, I must express my appreciation to the publishers for their co-operation, assistance and encouragement.

PREFACE

The subject of this book is factoring as it is practised in the United Kingdom: the selling of trade debts by businesses in order to raise finance or to relieve them from administrative functions or bad debt losses. Factoring has raised strong emotional feelings on the part of some practitioners, who regarded it as a panacea for most business problems, whilst at the same time arousing equally strong feelings on the part of some people in business and their professional advisers who have seen no good in it. There has recently been a more rational approach to the consideration of its benefits on both sides and it is hoped that, by dealing frankly with some of the unwarranted criticisms of factoring and with its limitations (particularly in Chapter 2), this book may encourage these developments.

The book is aimed at a wide audience: practitioners and their staff, both old and new, students, prospective clients and, not least, their professional advisers. Partly for this reason the book is in two parts, the Practice and the Law, so that those who are interested only in the practical applications may avoid some of the more esoteric legal problems and those who are interested in the latter may skip the matters with which they are familiar. Naturally the law creeps into the first part and the practice into the second, because the two are closely bound together and the latter is to a large extent governed by the former. It is hoped that those who dip into the book for a particular matter may be helped to find both aspects of that matter easily by the many cross references in the footnotes.

Much of the book, particularly the second part, is devoted to advising practitioners how they may structure their arrangements for the provision of finance with confidence. The apparent imbalance is somewhat redressed by some suggestions (in Chapter 5) of aspects of the proposed arrangements which prospective users of the service and their advisers should consider with care, including contractual provisions sometimes prescribed by some practitioners, by reason of over-enthusiasm, for protection.

Throughout the book it has been postulated that the legal mechanism for the provision of all forms of factoring is based upon the outright purchase of the client's trade debts by the factor. Although it would be possible to provide the finance by loans on the security of the debts and the other functions of the factor by a service agreement it now seems unlikely that any factor will consider changing from the traditional method and this is explained in Chapter 1 where the origin of the structure is reviewed. For this reason, the second part of the book is devoted to the legal background in which the outright purchase of debts takes place; the law in relation to the financing of debts by advances secured by security rights over such debts has been well documented elsewhere.

Whereas in the United States factoring by the purchase of accounts receivable had by the early 1960s become well established in usage and custom and recognised in the Uniform Commercial Code, the introduction of it into England, Wales and Northern Ireland (and to a greater extent in Scotland) rested on an insecure foundation of law which had not been designed to receive it. In spite of a few significant reported cases since that time, little has changed in this respect; as a result, there is a marked contrast between the simple concept of a sale of trade debts (as described in the first part of the book) and the complex legal problems which may, and very often do, arise in relations between the three parties: the client, the factor, and the debtor.

It is, therefore, to these difficult and uncertain areas of the law that much of the second part of the book is directed. Such areas concern mainly the debtors' countervailing rights against the factor as assignee and conflicts and competition between factors and third party claimants to the assigned debts. Naturally, no definite answers to problems can be given where uncertainty remains but a full exposition of these uncertainties may point the way to better commercial decisions by factors and their clients and, in some cases, the avoidance of later conflicts by prior agreements.

The treatises in the second part of the book (except in paragraphs 7–22 to 7–25 inclusive) relate to English law and are based upon legislation, reported cases and other material known to me at the end of August 1990. Of the changes brought about by the enactment of the Companies Act 1989, most of which are expected to be brought into effect by Order during 1990 and 1991, a few will particularly affect the business of factoring. These changes relate to the registration of charges, the effect of failure to register and the doctrine of constructive notice. The likely effect of the changes (as if they were already in effect) as regards conflicts between factors and others with interests in the factored debts is discussed in Chapter 8.

Although the factor is always and the client most usually a corporate body they should each strictly be referred to as "it" but solely for simplicity and reasons of style I have most often referred to each of them as "he". Similarly, in the discussion on conflicts of law in Chapter 12 there are several references to "English" clients and factors; naturally, as Wales is part of the same jurisdiction, it should be implicit that such expressions are intended to refer to Welsh clients and factors also. The expression has been used solely for brevity and simplicity in the text. I hope that no sensibilities will have been touched upon by the use of the pronoun and the expression.

September 1990

Freddy Salinger
West Chiltington
Sussex.

CONTENTS

TABLE OF CASES

TABLE OF STATUTES

TABLE OF STATUTORY INSTRUMENTS

TABLE OF RULES

CHAPTER 1

AN INTRODUCTION TO MODERN FACTORING OF DEBTS—ITS ORIGINS AND NATURE

1–01 To understand fully the modern practice of factoring of trade debts it is necessary to study its origins; to describe it briefly or define it is not an easy task. The reason for this difficulty is the absence of agreement among business and professional people (and not least among the practitioners of factoring themselves) as to what is and what is not factoring.

1. THE NATURE OF FACTORING

Definitions

1–02 The Concise Oxford Dictionary has a definition of factoring as buying at a discount the debts owed to another in order to profit by collecting them. In this very wide description of the activity it is seen entirely from the purchaser's point of view and not that of the seller of the debts; is he selling them to be provided with a service or with finance by being paid for them before they are due to be paid? At the other extreme is a very restricted definition generally accepted in the United States:

> "...a continuing arrangement between a factoring concern and the seller of goods or services on open account, pursuant to which the factor performs the following services with respect to the accounts receivable arising from sales of such goods and services:
> (1) Purchases all accounts receivable for immediate cash.
> (2) Maintains the ledgers and performs other book-keeping duties relating to such accounts receivable.
> (3) Collects the accounts receivable.
> (4) Assumes the losses which may arise from the customer's financial inability to pay (credit losses)."[1]

[1] See Carroll G. Moore, "Factoring—A Unique and Important Form of Financing and Service" *The Business Lawyer* (1959) Vol. XIV, No. 3.

It should be noted that the author of this definition has been careful not to infer that the services are provided *for the seller* because, having purchased the accounts receivable (or debts), the factor is collecting and book-keeping for himself. The object of the arrangement for the seller is the complete relief from the need for the service! As a result the four items would be better described as functions.[2]

A description for the United Kingdom

1–03 It is certain that few people concerned with factoring in the United Kingdom or Europe (whether as sellers of debts, buyers of them or advisers) would accept such a restrictive description. Few would even accept a definition by which, only if the factor were responsible for at least two of the functions mentioned in the last paragraph, would the arrangement be considered to be factoring.[3] There remain a few purists among the practitioners who would not regard as factoring an arrangement which provided finance by immediate cash payments but by which the factor carried out no other function; most would not consider it to be factoring unless the arrangement was disclosed to the debtors so that payments were to be made by them direct to the factor.

1–04 However, most practitioners would exclude from factoring debts incurred by individuals in their private capacity and debts payable by instalments or on long terms (*i.e.* usually considered to be more than six months from the delivery of the goods or performance of the services from which they arose). This restriction is not included in the narrow definition above but was probably implied. For simplicity in this book it has been accepted that the provision of finance alone by early payment by the factor for the debts (even if it remains confidential as regards the debtors) is included in the term. Accordingly in this book factoring is:

> The purchase of debts (other than debts incurred for goods or services purchased by a debtor for his personal, family or domestic use and debts payable on long terms or by instalments) for the purpose of providing finance, or relieving the seller from administrative tasks or from bad debts or for any two or all of such purposes.

[2] See also Chap. 12, n. 36.
[3] As contained in the Draft International Convention promulgated by UNIDROIT (see paras. 12–19 *et seq.*)

Factoring otherwise than by sale and purchase

1–05 Factoring as described in this book has been limited to the carrying out of these functions only by way of the sale and purchase of debts. Other means have been found to provide the same commercial effect but, after some excursions into other legal forms, in general, practitioners have followed the well trodden path. In particular arrangements have sometimes been made for the factor to purchase the goods themselves from his client, the supplier, to pay immediate cash for them and to effect a sub-sale of the goods to the customer through the agency of his client. In this way the client receives immediate funds for the sale of goods and is relieved from the need to provide the credit terms which his customer requires; if the arrangement is disclosed, the factor may carry out the administrative functions and collect direct and, if the client does not guarantee payment by the customer, the client is protected against bad debts. In practice the agency was normally undisclosed and the client collected on behalf of the factor and guaranteed payment; the object of the arrangement was to provide funds only.

1–06 The arrangement, the nature of which derives much from the origins of modern factoring,[4] has the merit of simplicity of concept. It was also believed to have the merit that where the client has charged its assets to a lender no arrangement was necessary to release any assets from the charge; it was believed that the sales by the client to the factor would be considered to be normal commercial transactions. However, it has been rejected by most practitioners because the factor, as principal in the sale to the customer, is a party to the contract of sale and accordingly liable for any breach and for defects in the goods themselves. Furthermore, difficulties have been encountered in devising suitable forms of documentation.[5] In the purchase of the *debts* the assignee, although being in no better position than the seller, is not subjected to liability under the contracts of sale giving rise to the debts.[6]

Another alternative

1–07 As regards the provision of funds, lending against a fixed charge on the book debts of the client might have the same practical effect as factoring by the purchase of the debts and payment on account for them by the factor on invoice date. At one time the advantages

[4] See para. 1–10 below.
[5] See for example *Welsh Development Agency* v. *The Export Finance Company Limited* F.T.L.R. April 10, 1990.
[6] See para. 9–32 below.

and disadvantages of each form would have been evenly divided.[7] Lending on security would overcome the difficulties of prohibitions of assignments in contracts between sellers and buyers of goods and services,[8] of Stamp Duty considerations[9] and of conflicts with other chargees.[10] On the other hand, a purchase and sale of the debts provided for the factor the benefit of direct recovery from the debtors (as opposed to the need to appoint a receiver), the absence of the need for the client to register a charge (where the client is a company) and payment of charges by the client without deduction of tax. From the client's point of view an advantage is that at present the finance is "off balance sheet."[11]

1–08 At one time some practitioners of factoring were considering a change to lending on security. The introduction of the administration procedure by the Insolvency Act 1986 and the advantages of the present system to a factor whose client is subject to an Administration Order[12] now appear to have caused the scales to come down firmly on the side of buying the debts. This seems likely to remain the position in spite of proposed changes in accounting standards whereby some forms of factoring may cease to be off balance sheet as far as the client is concerned.

2. THE ORIGINS AND A BRIEF HISTORY

1–09 "There are many ways of raising cash besides borrowing. One is by selling book debts . . .."[13] The selling of debts to "raise the wind" is as old as commerce itself and some writers of the history of factoring have traced the practice back to Babylonian times 5000 years ago. However, for the development of modern factoring as described in the next chapter of this book it is necessary to go back only to the last century. A brief consideration of the origins and history is of help to an understanding of factoring in all its variations and the avoidance of some of its misuse and the

[7] For a full discussion of this alternative see Salinger, "Factoring: an Alternative?" (1983) 1 *Law & Tax Review* 89.
[8] See paras. 9–30 and 9–31 below.
[9] See para. 7–07 below.
[10] See Chap. 8.
[11] See Chap. 3 and paras. 5–16 *et seq.* below.
[12] See paras. 11–26 *et seq.* below.
[13] *Chow Yoong Hong* v. *Choong Fah Rubber Manufactory* [1962] A.C. 209 *per* Lord Devlin at p. 216.

difficulties occasioned thereby. Factoring in the United Kingdom appears to have developed from two sources: from the activities of mercantile agents in the United States and of banks in continental Europe.

The start of modern factoring in the United States

1–10 The early factors, as their name implies, were mercantile agents. Up to the latter part of the last century and before the rapid advances made in systems of transport and communication it was common for any manufacturer or merchant, selling outside his immediate locality, to employ mercantile agents. Such agents (or "factors" as they were known) took their principals' goods physically and held them on consignment, marketed and sold the goods and collected payment from the customers on behalf of the principals. They were rewarded by a commission and had a prescriptive right to deduct that commission and any other charges and expenses from amounts held by them for their principals by reason of collection from customers. Some of the factors were *del credere* agents who guaranteed to the principals due payment by each customer.

1–11 It was natural that during the important period of colonisation by European countries from the sixteenth century onwards the exporters of consumer goods from the mother countries should look to the establishment of mercantile agents in the colonies to assist their exports. The exporter would have little knowledge of the market and the customers and it would be necessary to maintain stocks in the country of the customers in order to provide for prompt delivery of orders. The developments and rapidly increasing standards of living in the eastern seaboard of the United States made increasing demands on exporters from the United Kingdom and Europe. Many great factoring houses flourished there and, in time, were in a position to assist their principals with finance by making loans against the goods sent on consignment to them secure in the knowledge of the prescriptive right of a mercantile agent to reimburse himself out of the proceeds of the sale of the goods. Later such rights were validated by statute in several states by the adoption of Factors' Acts which gave the factor a right of lien on his principal's goods to secure his advances and other sums owed to him.

1–12 The factors provided in essence six services: marketing, storage and distribution, administration, collection from customers, protection against bad debts and finance. Towards the end of the 19th century the improvement in communications and in the speed of the transport of goods made it unnecessary for the manufacturers and merchants to send goods on consignment; the goods sold by sample could be despatched direct to the customer. For similar reasons the principals could also dispense with the services of marketing provided by the factors. However, the principals wished to retain the comfort of the protection that they were receiving from their factors in guaranteed collection from their customers; some also needed the finance. Thus modern factoring of debts was created by the substitution of the assignment to the factor of debts arising from direct sales by his client (formerly his principal) for the sales by the factor as mercantile agent. As owner of the debts the factor would retain the right to collect which he formerly enjoyed as a mercantile agent; as owner of the debts, the monies which he collected from customers became his property so that he was able to reimburse himself for the funds which he had laid out for the purchase of the debts to be assigned to him. The factor would no longer be required to find the customers but the details of the customer when found would be submitted to him for credit approval; the factors' knowledge of local businesses in which they had acted as agents for many years would still be invaluable to their clients.

The development of factoring of debts in the United States

1–13 The change in the function of the early factors in the United States took place in an uncertain background of law. The new relationship (formerly between the principal and agent) as assignor and assignee had to be established under the common law by judicial decisions and by the fourth decade of this century there were sufficient precedents available in New York and the New England states for the factors there to be able to provide their services with some confidence. For the most part, according to such cases, notice to the debtor was necessary to validate the assignments against the rights of third parties and any countervailing claims of the debtor. For this reason invoice discounting (or confidential factoring without disclosure to the debtor as described in the next chapter) was not feasible. Later, in response to growing demand by businesses and finance houses for a method by which the latter could finance the debts of the former, many of the states adopted statutes by which the assignment either by way of outright sale or by way of security could be validated otherwise than by notice to the debtor. In some cases the validation was by reliance on a written instrument of assignment or by the marking of the client's ledgers.

1–14 More importantly some of the states introduced the provision for the registration of the assignments. Such statutes were the basis for those parts of Article 9 of the Uniform Commercial Code which deal with the perfection of security interests in intangibles including debts.[14] Under the Uniform Commercial Code (of which Article 9 has now been adopted by every state) assignments of future debts can be perfected by registration to secure fluctuating advances. Even if the factoring is based, as it usually is, on the outright sale and purchase of debts, the arrangement must be registered, *as if it were* a security right, in order to be valid against the claims of third parties or a trustee in bankruptcy of the client. Such arrangements have created a much more certain background of law in which a factor may operate and it is significant that since the adoption of the Uniform Commercial Code by most states in the 1950s factoring and in particular "accounts receivable financing"[15] has increased rapidly. In the early 1960s factoring as practised in the United States, was transferred to England, like a tender seedling, and embedded into a basis of law and commercial practice which was scarcely prepared to receive it; and this (including the absence of any comprehensive code to cover such arrangements and security rights) accounts for the many uncertainties which are documented in the second part of this book. It also accounts for the difficulties encountered by practitioners in its early years here.

Another source of factoring in the United Kingdom

1–15 In many countries in Continental Europe it had been customary for banks who had not the advantage of the peculiarly English security right, the floating charge, to finance the trade debts owned by their customers by advancing money against the delivery of copy invoices to the banks. The exact form of documentation appears to have varied considerably but it is probable that in many cases the taking of assignments of the debts represented by such invoices would not have given the banks security against the claims of third parties or in the bankruptcy of the customer. In many jurisdictions[16] notice to the debtor in some form or another would have been necessary to have perfected the assignments for these purposes. No doubt the banks would have relied on evidence of the likely cash flow available to liquidate the advances.

1–16 By the early part of the 1950s, in the absence of interest in such business by the clearing banks, many small and several larger finance houses in London and some of the larger provincial cities had entered the market of discounting "invoices" on a similar individual basis. The banks continued to rely on their well tried practice of taking floating charges. Some of these finance houses

[14] Or "accounts" as they are referred to in the U.S.
[15] As invoice discounting on an undisclosed basis is known in the U.S.
[16] Including France until 1982 when the enactment of the Loi Dailley made provision for the "cession" of book debts to banks without notices to the debtors.

were originally manufacturing concerns with cash to spare which may have been persuaded by the higher returns apparently available from providing finance in this way than were available from the mundane activities of the manufacture of goods. Such concerns were mainly in the textile and furniture trades for which the service had been largely provided by the banks in continental Europe; at least one major furniture manufacturer sold its business entirely and turned to the discounting of trade debts.

1–17 It is probable that the discounters took their cue from the continental practice. The arrangements were similar to those practised on the continent: the trader presented his copy invoices to the discounter with a document offering the debts to the discounter for sale; no notice was given to the debtor and the trader guaranteed payment by the customers by a specific number of days after invoice date. The discounter paid a percentage (less his charges) on account and relied on his having an assignment of the debts represented by the invoices (owing to the very liberal rules relating to equitable assignments in England) and on the trader's undertaking to pass on to the discounter payments received from the customers. In practice, arrangements for the discounter to recover his investment varied and very often there would be a monthly settlement by which recoveries from customers and amounts payable by the trader for recourse were set off against advance payments to be made against new invoices.

1–18 In considering their security in these arrangements the discounters were probably influenced to some extent by a false analogy with the discounting of bills of exchange. The analogy is false because a bill, representing a sum certain in money accepted by the debtor, gives the discounter as a holder in due course the right to payment free from any defence, counterclaim or set-off which the debtor may have against the creditor as drawer of the bill. The situation with an invoice is quite different: many trade debts are the resulting balance of debits for amounts payable by the debtor for goods and services (represented by invoices) and credits for counterclaims by the debtor (whether or not represented by credit notes) and deductions for discounts and other allowances. An invoice does not tell the whole story and, in the absence of notice to the debtor of the assignment, the discounter may be faced additionally with justified deductions by the debtor in respect of equities arising after the discounting of the debt purportedly represented by the invoice.[17] Thus some of the early discounters, who discounted debts on the basis of individual invoices, were faced with losses when the net indebtedness of the

[17] See Chap. 9.

debtors emerged, on the insolvency of clients, as far less than the face value of the invoices.

1–19 The early discounter's feelings of insecurity, arising from these losses, were increased by claims by liquidators of client companies that the arrangement was in fact a disguise for the substance of the transaction: lending against the security of the debts. As an unregistered charge the discounter's rights to the debts would be void against the liquidator. These claims for the most part failed. However, discounters were advised that, to be safe in this respect, all their dealings with their clients must be consistent with the outright purchase of the debts rather than the taking of a security right over them. It was therefore, important that the sums collected from customers, being the discounter's property, should be passed on to the discounter in the original form. Unlike payments made to meet a bill of exchange on its maturity, payments on open credit terms do no always relate to particular invoices; some customers in the trades in which invoice discounting was acceptable were in the habit of paying round sums on account and, as not all invoices were discounted, payments could often not be appropriated to particular discounted invoices. Accordingly the actual payments could often not be passed on to the discounter and a weekly or monthly settlement was made.

1–20 The result of such influences was to cause a number of smaller discounters to withdraw from the provision of the service altogether. A few looked to greater security by providing their services for the whole of a client's sales and by requiring notices to the debtors for payments to be made direct to the discounter. By such means the discounter would have greater control, would avoid many cross-claims by debtors and would be seen to be purchasing the debts and not lending against them. In effect they started to provide a factoring service much as it had evolved in the United States although not many of them accepted the risk of loss by reason of the financial inability of debtors to pay.

The two sources of factoring merge

1–21 From these two sources factoring developed in the United Kingdom in the 1960s on similar lines responsive to the market which looked in the factoring services increasingly for a source of funds rather than for the administrative services of sales accounting and collection and for protection against bad debts. Most of the early practitioners who had looked to the United States for guidance still provided the full service including protection against bad debts whereas others looked to direct collection from debtors as an enhancement of their security and tended to concentrate their marketing on the provision of finance alone.

3. MORE RECENT DEVELOPMENT[18]

Developments in the United States

1–22 Whilst factoring was developing in the United Kingdom in the early 1960s on a disclosed basis with notices to the debtors and direct collection from the customers, paradoxically in the United States the financing of trade debts by way of the undisclosed discounting of invoices (without any form of administrative service or protection against bad debts) developed more strongly. The development of this type of facility, normally labelled "accounts receivable financing," had been encouraged by the adoption of the Uniform Commercial Code[19] by all states except Louisiana at that time. This trend has appeared to continue.

1–23 Factoring on a disclosed basis, without recourse to the client as regards the inability of the debtor to pay by reason of his insolvency, had developed strongly in the trades for which the early functions of mercantile agents had been traditional.[20] These were in the main businesses dealing in textiles, clothing and footwear, furniture, toys and other (mainly non-durable) consumer goods. However, by the 1960s the provision of this service in such trades was reaching a point of saturation. Attempts by United States factors to develop their services outside these trades do not appear to have been altogether successful. The reasons for this difficulty seems to be the absence of a file of credit information on debtors and prospective debtors outside the traditional trades. Whilst factors in the United Kingdom for this aspect of their services rely to a large extent on the insurance principal of a spread of risks and in some cases on credit insurance as a form of reinsurance, factors in the United States relied on a close knowledge of their customers and the receipt of financial information direct from them. In trades where most of the suppliers use factors it would be natural for the debtors to co-operate with the factors to establish and maintain credit ratings.

1–24 In breaking into other trades and industries, factors in the United States find themselves caught in an inextricable circle. In order to establish files of credit information great expense is necessary and before they have such files they are unable to market the service and achieve the income to provide for such investment. The difficulties and expense in establishing such files arises from the reluctance of debtors to provide financial information when they have no need to purchase from a client using a

[18] See table in App. 1. Care should be taken in assessing the figures in this table vecause in the U.S. only the full service is included in "factoring".
[19] See para. 1–14 above.
[20] See para. 1–10 above.

factoring service. Another difficulty, which has been met by those attempting to extend their services into other fields, is the reluctance of debtors in such other trades and industries to deal with factors direct and to make payment to them. This may seem surprising in view of the ineffectiveness of a prohibition by a debtor on the assignment of debts under the law in the United States.[21] However, it appears that for a factor to pursue such a claim through the courts would be time consuming and expensive; and the commercial considerations, such as the likely reluctance of the debtor to purchase from a supplier using factoring in the future, would probably preclude such a step. Even were the debtor to accept that payment had to be made to the factor, the factor would not have the leverage that he has in the traditional trades to obtain prompt payment: the effect on the debtor's credit standing of delayed payments.

1–25 The difficulty in breaking away from the traditional trades has been aggravated by the pressure on profit margins caused by severe competition among factors in those trades. The pressure on margins is the result of the restriction; and the reluctance to invest in the development in other areas is the result of the poor profitability. Thus the development of "accounts receivable financing" continues to be the main thrust of the expansion of factoring in its wider sense in the United States. It is unlikely that accounts receivable financing is included in the figures for the United States in the table in Appendix 1.

1–26 It may be that the provision of factoring for sales across national borders will create another impetus for the development of the service outside the traditional trades. In international factoring it is usual for the factor of an exporting client to use the services of a correspondent factor in the importers's country to guarantee and to collect the debts.[22] The developing use of factoring by exporters to United States (especially of electronic and engineering products from the Far East) may well be a compelling element in the extension of factoring to these trades; in order to provide the services expected from them by their overseas correspondents, the United States factors will need to broaden the base of their operations.

Developments in Continental Europe

1–27 In Europe factoring has developed strongly in the last three decades on the basis of a provider of finance for domestic business and for international trade as a provider of finance and the protection against bad debts. With the exception of the Federal

[21] See para. 12–27 and Chap. 12, n. 49 below.
[22] See the description of factor's "chains" in Chap. 6.

Republic of Germany, Belgium and the Netherlands the main development has been of factoring, whether disclosed to the debtors or not, on a full recourse basis whereby no protection against bad debts is provided. For the practitioners the absence of the expense of establishing a credit information base has outweighed the slightly smaller income generated by the absence of the additional service; from the point of view of the users of the service there seemed to have been little demand for protection against bad debts—probably on account of the widespread use of credit insurance. Developments have not been regular across all the countries: the early rapid development of factoring in Scandinavia (especially in Sweden) in the 1960s and 1970s has given way to faster growth in Italy where factoring volumes are now about half of the total of all continental Europe. In Germany the impetus towards non-recourse factoring was the result of decision of the courts that recourse factoring was to be considered as if it were the lending on the security of the debts; as a result the factor was at a disadvantage as compared with the non-recourse factor in a conflict, over the rights to the debts, with a supplier to his client who had reserved title to goods until paid.[23]

1–28 The demand for factoring from exporters is a demand, not only for finance, but also for an assurance of prompt payment without the risk of default. The exporter may be fully versed in the credit standing of his debtors and of the law and practices in relation to the collection of debts in his own country but in many cases wishes to rely on a factor where he is selling to another country. In some of the smaller countries, such as Belgium and The Netherlands, where the domestic markets are small, the development of international factoring has tended to be proportionately greater than in the larger markets. This has applied not only to the factoring of exports of the factor's own clients but also to their acting as correspondent factor for those factors in other countries who are exporting; in order to provide this service it has been necessary for the factors in such smaller countries to establish credit information bases and such a library of credit information is best established on the basis of a good domestic non-recourse factoring business.

Developments in Asia

1–29 It is well known that vast quantities of consumer goods are exported from countries in South East and East Asia to Europe and North America. Up to the beginning of the last decade the main instrument of payment was the letter of credit; by means of

[23] See Chap. 12, n. 16.

such an instrument the exporter was assured of payment by importers of whose credit standing he may have had little knowledge. More recent developments in communications and the handling of cargo have created situations in which letters of credit are not the most suitable terms of payment. Furthermore, many importers are reluctant to be committed to pay for goods for the inspection of which they have not had an opportunity and before they have the documents of title to the goods and thus an assurance of delivery; in some cases the importers have been able to use their bargaining position to insist on terms of payment against the delivery of documents of title or of open credit. Even the former terms appear to have become less popular. In order to provide such terms and at the same time to obtain, not only finance, but also an assurance of prompt payment exporters in such countries have turned increasingly to factors. Thus export factoring appears to have been the chief impetus to the growth of factoring there.

Developments in the United Kingdom

1–30 The early reluctance of the factors in the United Kingdom to provide their services on an undisclosed basis owed much to the feeling that against an uncertain background of law, with disclosure to the debtors, they would be less likely to be attacked in the courts as providing loans on the security of debts in disguise. As a result of requiring notice to the debtors and direct collection from them by the factor, the full non-recourse service was provided by most and, in marketing, emphasis on the administrative service and protection against bad debts had equal prominence with the provision of finance. However, the marketing of factoring in this sense was severely impeded by the widespread use of credit insurance in the traditional trades for which factoring and invoice discounting had been used and the reluctance of potential clients to agree to the disclosure of the relations with a factor to their customers. This resistance to the disclosure of the use of the service was increased by the selling by some of the early factors of the service (sometimes fully on a recourse basis) to businesses for which it was not suitable and by some smaller entrants into the field whose administration and collection functions were not up to the perceived standards. The result of this misuse of factoring (which is more fully documented in Chapter 2) was the spread of bad reports among potential users and a growing antipathy in some sections of the accountancy profession to which potential users looked for advice. Unfortunately the successful achievements of some of the factors in enabling their clients to grow rapidly and soundly by a proper use of the service were not well documented.[24] In this way factoring had a slow start in the 1960s and by the start of the next decade some of the promoting shareholders of the early factoring companies (merchant banks and confirming houses) disposed of their interests.

1–31 At about that time the clearing banks started to take an interest in factoring and either by acquisition or the starting up of a new company all of the four largest banks became an owner of a factoring company. Although these companies in the main still provided non-recourse factoring, the inclusion within the range of financial services of the banks of factoring in all its forms was seen as a form of asset based finance and not so much as an administrative service or an alternative to credit insurance. Such an emphasis in the marketing has probably arisen from the need of a bank to earn a return on its deposits rather than to be a provider of a pure service.

1–32 The interests of the banks in factoring and the establishment over the last decade of a large number of smaller factoring companies owned either by foreign banks or by companies outside the banking sphere has led to a substantial growth of factoring in all its forms. However, the smaller companies rarely provide protection against bad debts and for the most part do not provide any administrative service; it is probable that the necessary investment in a credit information base and in systems is not attractive to them. For this reason, and possibly because the banks may be more interested in putting their funds to use than in providing the other services, in the last few years invoice discounting (including agency factoring in which, although on a disclosed basis, the factor does not provide any administrative service) has overtaken all the other forms of factoring combined.

Unlike the position in some other countries in Europe and the Far East, international factoring does not appear to have increased its share of the market. Certainly the market for the factoring of exports from the United Kingdom has diminished considerably from the days of the early factors when many in the wool trade in Yorkshire used a factor for their sales to North America; the pattern of exports from the United Kingdom is now such that most of the goods and services exported are not suitable for factoring.[25]

4. THE FULL SERVICE AND VARIATIONS

1–33 An examiner of students of factoring once set the following question: "Describe and compare the two types of factoring agreement at present in general use." He should not have been

[24] See Chap. 2.
[25] See Chap. 2.

surprised that he received several different answers all of which were correct. The students may have correctly taken the question to refer to any of the following:

(1) Recourse and non-recourse factoring agreements.
(2) Agreements for factoring with or without disclosure to debtors.
(3) Agreements for factoring with direct collection by the factor or collection by the client on behalf of the factor.
(4) Agreements which include or do not include the availability of finance by way of early payment by the factor.
(5) Agreements whereby the factor pays for each purchased debt (less any earlier payments) on a fixed maturity date or when payment is received from the debtor.
(6) Agreements which themselves provide for the assignment of the debts or which merely provide for each debt to be offered to the factor.[26]

As many factoring agreements combine features of some or all of these differences, there are a large number of combinations and permutations in the forms of factoring offered by practitioners. The difficulty in the task of describing these different forms briefly is compounded by the absence of uniformity among practitioners in the labels used for the same type of factoring and the provision by different practitioners of different types under the same labels. This chapter contains a description of the complete or full service and the main variations and a table of variants at the end of the chapter may help to dispel some of the confusion caused by the differences in the labels. Any of the variations may be provided in either way described in (5) or (6) above and these differences are described in subsequent chapters.

The full service

1–34 Factoring in its full form, or old line (*i.e.* traditional) factoring, has been described earlier in this chapter[27] where a definition accepted in the United States was reproduced. However to describe it in even more precise terms, it is a continuing relationship between a factor and a supplier (the client) of goods and services to trade customers in which the factor purchases substantially all the trade debts of his client arising from such sales of goods or the provision of such services as they arise in the normal course of business. The client in return for agreed fees and finance charges is thereby relieved:

[26] See paras. 7–12 *et seq*. below.
[27] See para. 1–02 above.

(a) from the need to administer and control a sales ledger and collect amounts payable from the debtors; and
(b) from losses arising from the inability of a debtor to pay; and
(c) from the provision of trade credit to the debtors, to a substantial degree.

1–35 The transfer of ownership of the debts is normally accompanied by:

(a) the submission to the factor either of copies of invoices representing the debts sold; or
(b) the submission of originals to the factor for onward transmission to the debtors, accompanied by copies for retention by the factor.

1–36 The factor, in turn, is responsible to the client for the purchase price of the debts assigned. The purchase price is normally the amount payable by the debtor after the deduction of any discount or other allowance allowed to the debtor and after deduction of the factor's charges. The factor will credit the account of the client in his records with such purchase price of debts sold and as a corollary the client may charge all his sales to one account—that of the factor. The client will now look to the factor alone to collect the proceeds of his sales. The final date for payment of the purchase price will be either a fixed number of days after invoice date (often referred to as the maturity date) or when collection has been effected from the debtor. These alternatives are described more fully in Chapter 3.

1–37 To the extent that the factor has given approval of the debts, he purchases the debts without recourse to the client as regards the debtor's failure to pay owing to insolvency. The client thus receives full protection against bad debts provided that he does not sell to any debtor not approved by the factor or to an extent greater than the approval given.

1–38 By making an early payment (sometimes referred to as a prepayment) on account of a substantial part of the purchase price of each debt as soon as it is created and purchased, the factor provides the finance to meet the trade credit requirements of the client's debtors. Some factors make such a prepayment by way of an advance secured by their right to set it off against the full purchase price when due, whereas others provide for prepayments by part payments of the purchase price itself. The effect is exactly the same in each case. The factor will make a retention of part of the purchase price of each debt so that in aggregate he will hold a sufficient balance to provide for any debt to be charged back to the client by way of recourse for the non-payment of an unapproved or disputed debt. However, the balance credited for the purchase price of debts purchased less the retention may normally be drawn by the client by way of prepayment at short notice.

Recourse factoring

1–39 Although most forms of factoring other than the full service are provided with full recourse to the client in respect of the failure of the debtor to pay for any reason, "recourse factoring" normally describes the service by which the factor provides finance for the client and carries out the functions of sales ledger administration and collections, but does not protect the client against bad debts. The factor has full "recourse" (the right to have payment guaranteed or the debt repurchased by the client) for debts unpaid for any reason, including insolvency of the debtor. Thus, the variation is effected by the simple expedient of providing that in respect of every debt purchased by the factor he shall have the right to sell it (or part of it) back to the client for the amount for which he credited the purchase price originally (or be guaranteed payment in full by the client) to the extent that the debtor shall not have settled it by an agreed period after invoice date. The period often agreed is three months or 90 days from the end of the month in which the invoice is dated. Such a period postulates that in many trades and industries, in which the normal usage is for payment to be due at the end of the month following that of the invoice, the factor must collect payment within two months of the due date or the recourse may come into effect. It is usual to provide that the factor will refrain from exercising his right of recourse for a specified further period in payment of an additional charge by the client. In such a case, however, the factor may require that an additional retention be maintained against the purchase price of further debts purchased so that in effect the client will have repaid the amount paid by the factor against, or on account of, the purchase price of the unpaid debts.

1–40 In this way, in respect of debts that are seriously overdue, the client will remain relieved from the collection function but the finance for such debts may be withdrawn. If the debt becomes irrecoverable the recourse is then finally exercised. It is apparent that the factor, in such a case, does not have the ultimate responsibility for collection. Approvals of credit are given by the factor on debtor accounts for the purpose of specifying the amount of finance available against them or as an advisory service to the client, or for both reasons.

Agency factoring

1–41 This variant of the service is sometimes referred to as "bulk factoring" but as virtually all factoring relates to the whole of a client's sales with the submission to the factor of batches or schedules of debts in bulk, the term "bulk" could be applied to all forms. The term "agency" is now usually used to denote the form for which the Germans use the more descriptive term "Eigen-Service Factoring" ("Own Service Factoring"). This form of factoring is further removed from the full service in that the factor, although requiring disclosure to the debtors, takes no responsibility for the administration or collection of the debts and the factoring is fully on a recourse basis. In some cases directions are given to the debtor to pay direct to the factor; in others, although notice of the assignment is given to debtors, they are instructed to pay to the client as the factor's agent. In the latter cases the client is obliged to hold the monies recovered in trust for the factor and to pay them into a bank account of the factor.

In all cases the client administers the sales ledger and enforces payment from debtors as agent for the factor; thus this form of factoring is usually referred to as "Agency Factoring" or "Agency Discounting." The purpose of the arrangement is purely for financing the trade credit requirements of the client's debtors and the notice to them to pay the factor is to improve the factor's security. The service provided is, therefore, no more than that obtained by means of invoice discounting.[28]

1–42 This system is used where the client's pattern of trade consists of a large number of small debtor accounts but where he does not meet the standards of financial standing or administration required for consideration of an invoice discounting arrangement. However, although the foregoing is the usual nature of agency factoring, at least one leading factoring company provides this service on a non-recourse basis, subject to approval of debtor accounts.

Invoice discounting or confidential factoring

1–43 For those clients who need finance for the trade credit requirement of their debtors but no administrative service or protection, another service is provided extensively by factors. By the simple expedient of releasing the client from the need to notify the debtors to pay direct to the factor and by providing that all debts sold to the factor should be subject to full recourse, factoring is changed to a purely financial service sometimes referred to as "confidential factoring" or, more commonly, "invoice discounting." In the early days of invoice discounting, debts represented by individual invoices were sold to factors. This system gave rise to some difficulties: it was not always possible for the client to pass on

[28] See para. 1–43 below.

to the factor the payment for the invoice in its original form as the payment might be made after deductions for cross-claims or combined with payment of other invoices.[29] In recent years, the service of invoice discounting has more usually been provided on a "whole turnover" basis. The client maintains the sales ledger and collects from debtors on behalf of the factor to whom the ownership of the debts has been transferred, and arrangements are made for the proceeds of collections to be paid by the client direct to the factor's bank account.

Undisclosed factoring

1–44 The term "undisclosed factoring" is sometimes applied to an invoice discounting arrangement as described above; but it is usually taken to denote an arrangement for invoice discounting whereby the factor will provide protection against bad debts to a limited extent by specifying that an agreed percentage (normally 80 per cent.) of any approved indebtedness shall be without recourse as regards credit risks. The arrangement limits the protection to such a percentage so that the client, who maintains the ledger and collects from debtors, has some incentive to carry out these duties with efficiency. In some cases however a factor has been known to accept that the full amounts of approved debts should be without recourse and thus to provide the same protection against bad debts as in the full service.[30]

Maturity factoring

1–45 The above are the principal forms of factoring in which the factor provides finance by making prepayments of part of the purchase price of the debts purchased by him. Where finance is not required, an arrangement, used increasingly by small businesses as an alternative to credit insurance, comprises full administration of the sales ledger, collection from debtors and protection against bad debts. This service, often called "maturity factoring," is provided without any financial facility. The arrangement is that of the full service but without the facility for prepayment by the factor to the client and, accordingly, no finance charge is levied. Payments for the debts purchased are made either:

(1) after a fixed period based on expectation of the average period of credit to be taken by debtors (often referred to as the "maturity period") from either invoice date or the date of the transfer of the debts to the factor and the submission of copy invoices; or

[29] See also para. 1–18 above.
[30] Felicitously labelled by one leading factor as "ID Plus".

(2) on receipt of payment from each debtor or, in respect of approved debts, the earlier insolvency of the debtor.

The system in (1) above offers obvious attractions to the client in that he may calculate his cash flow in advance as soon as sales are effected to approved accounts. On the other hand the factor may tend to make a liberal estimate of the maturity period and in many cases will reserve the right to adjust it in accordance with actual experience from time to time. The second method has the advantage of flexibility in allowing for changes of terms of payment by the client and requests to the factor for allowing latitude to debtors.

Recourse factoring or invoice discounting combined with credit insurance

1–46 Apart from the forms mentioned above, co-operation with credit insurers may be used for the benefit of the client. First, almost the equivalent to the full service may be obtained by the use of recourse factoring combined with a credit insurance policy; secondly, the equivalent of undisclosed factoring may be achieved by the use of credit insurance combined with invoice discounting.

1–47 If a business prefers the protection against bad debts offered by a credit insurer (or if he is already a policy holder and does not wish to give up the policy) but is looking for the finance for the trade credit requirements of his customers this co-operation between a credit insurer and a factor may be the answer to these requirements. In the case of recourse factoring, where the client is looking for relief from administrative burdens, the factor should agree to administer the policy (making all returns and paying the premium and other charges on behalf of the client) so that the client is relieved from these burdens; otherwise the equivalent of the full service will not be achieved. In all cases the factor's position will be more secure if he carries out these functions; if he does not he will not know if the client has breached the policy conditions in these respects so that the insurer may not then be bound to meet a claim. In such a case the factor's reliance on recovering from the insurer in respect of an insolvent debtor may be ill-founded.

1–48 The combination of recourse factoring or invoice discounting with credit insurance is normally carried out by one of the following methods:

(1) By an endorsement to the client's policy, such as a "factoring endorsement" issued by the Export Credits Guarantee

Department, by which the factor is virtually joined as policyholder for most purposes and the factor's right to prove in the insolvent estate of a debtor and to collect the debts is recognised. The endorsement should be combined with an assignment of the benefits of the policy.

(2) By the issue of the policy to the factor and client as joint insured. The factor's rights to the ownership of the debts and to administer the sales ledger would thus be recognised and the factor may submit claims direct as a policyholder. However, the factor will also be liable for the responsibilities of policyholder including the declarations and returns required by the insurer and the payment of the premium; for this reason it is sometimes arranged for the factor to administer the policy and pay the premium and, if it is to be borne by the client, to debit it to the client's account.

These arrangements go most of the way to overcome the deficiencies, from the factor's point of view, of an assignment only of the benefits of the policy. By an assignment only:

(1) in most cases neither the factor (not being a policyholder) nor the client (not being the owner of the debt) would be able to make a claim unless the factor were to reassign the debt to the client and, for reasons of his security, the factor may not wish to do so;
(2) the factor cannot be certain that the client has made the necessary returns and declarations required by the insurer and paid the premium;
(3) it is normally required by the insurer that the policy holder should carry out all credit control functions and in the case of factoring some of these functions are carried out by the factor; and
(4) on the insolvency of the client the person having the duty to administer the insolvent estate may have little reason to make a claim to enable the factor to recover.

Even if the factor becomes a joint insured he cannot be absolutely certain that the client may not have done or omitted to do something which may avoid the policy. The factor should in any case obtain a warranty from the client to cover this aspect; but such a warranty will be of little avail to the factor who is relying on recovering under a credit insurance policy when his client is insolvent.

Co-operation between factors and bankers

1–49 It may sometimes be agreed between a bank and its customer that the customer should continue to use the bank's facilities for the financing of its trade debts whilst taking advantage of a factor's services. In such a case the bank's security may be improved by the factoring arrangements and the bank's reliance on the administration and the monitoring of the debts by the factor combined with certain undertakings from him. The advantage to the bank's customer (the factor's client) will be that he will keep his full relationship with his banker and, owing to the bank's improved security, may obtain a better facility. The arrangement has advantages over a guarantee from the factor to the bank based on the factor's liability to the client for the purchase price of debts which he has purchased. First, repayment to the bank by the factor does not require a formal demand; it requires only a call (which may be by telephone) to the factor. Secondly, it does not require that the factor should rely on set-off for the recovery from the client (by reason of an indemnity) of his payment to the bank. By the use of this method the bank may lend confidently on the actual level of the client's trade debts instead of relying on projections or returns from the customer which may give little indication of the quality of the debts, the likelihood of disputes or of returned goods.

1–50 An outline of such an arrangement is as follows:

(1) The factor enters into a full factoring agreement with his client (the bank's customer) and a prepayment facility is included.

(2) Arrangements are made with the client that either (i) he is paid only on payment by the debtors (so that the factor's indebtedness to the client for the debts purchased is always approximately equal to the outstanding debts owned by the factor) or (ii) that the factor may make a substantial fixed retention based on the amount for which he would have made prepayments against the debts outstanding at the start of the arrangement.

(3) In either case the amount retained (either an amount equivalent to all the debts outstanding at any one time or a fixed amount) will be held by the factor for the benefit of the bank. Such retention is a book debt owing by the factor to the client and as such it will fall within any fixed charge on book debts created by a client company in favour of the bank. Alternatively (or if the client is a partnership or sole trader) any amount payable by the factor to the client, including the retention, may be assigned by the client to the bank. In the case of a company the assignment, being by way of security, will be registrable. To support the charge or

assignment the client will have given irrevocable instructions to the factor by which all amounts payable by the factor under the factoring agreement are to be paid to the bank.

1–51 By relying on that security and certain undertakings from the factor the bank may lend to the client either the whole of the amounts which would have been available by way of prepayment or, where a fixed amount is withheld, that amount. The undertaking from the factor will be based on its obligation to pay to the bank all amounts payable by it to the client and on a special provision in the factoring agreement by which a request for a prepayment from the bank is deemed to be a request from the client. The undertaking in the case of a fixed retention will be to pay that amount to the bank whenever so requested by the bank.

1–52 The undertakings given where the amounts retained are equivalent to the full amounts of outstanding debts are based on the amount which the factor would have paid if he had been making prepayments. Such reports may include the basis of the availability: the total of the amount of assigned outstanding debts and the amounts of unapproved and disputed debts within the total. On the basis of each report the bank should be able to allow the client's borrowing to increase to the figure of the availability; in between reports the borrowing should be reduced by payments from the factor equivalent to receipts from debtors (less the factor's charges). The undertaking by the factor will be equivalent, not to the latest availability, but to the highest balance remaining of any reported availability after deducting payments made to the bank since the date of it. In this way the bank's security would not be affected by the report of an availability less than its outstanding advances; this might occur if the factor were to find that a large outstanding debt were to be the subject of recourse to the client by reason of a dispute.

1–53 On the insolvency of the client or at any time beforehand if the bank wishes to recover its advances on the basis of this arrangement, the bank may call upon the factor to make a prepayment of the amount of its undertaking. The bank may then recover its advances without incurring the expense, inconvenience and delays caused by recovery through a liquidator or receiver. The arrangement eliminates all the shortcomings of the reliance on a charge (whether fixed or floating) on the trade debts themselves. The benefits of this arrangement for a banker is to enable him to follow more closely the fortunes of a fast growing business for which the traditional means of finance may not keep pace.

TABLE: FACTORING VARIANTS

	Availability of Finance	Protection Against Bad Debts*	Notices to Debtors	Sales Ledger Administration	Collections	
Full Service	A	A	A	A	A	Any of these may be referred to as:
Recourse Factoring	A	N	A	A	A	'Notification Factoring'
Bulk Factoring	A	N	A	N	N	OR
Maturity Factoring	N	A	A	A	A	'Disclosed Factoring'
Agency Factoring	A	S	U	S	N	
Invoice Discounting	A	N	N	N	N	Alternatively: 'Confidential Factoring' OR
Undisclosed Factoring	A	S	N	N	N	'Non-Notification Factoring'

* Any form which includes this element may be referred to as *'non-recourse factoring'*.

Key: A = Always provided
U = Usually provided
S = Sometimes provided
N = Never or rarely provided

CHAPTER 2

THE APPLICATION OF FACTORING TO MODERN BUSINESS

2–01 A client of a factoring company once mentioned to an executive of that company that the client had in the past used three different factors and had never had cause to complain and had received a good service from each. The response from the factoring executive was that the experience was the mark of a well administered business of the client. The service provided by a well established factor is a reflection of the administrative competence of the factor's client and the acceptability of its products; the factor must rely on the information passed to him by the client and cannot improve the quality of the debts created by his client.

2–02 Many businesses have been disinclined to consider factoring based on anecdotal experiences. Apart from the allegation of poor service (which in many cases may indeed be an indictment of the quality of the client rather than the factor) there have been two main criticisms. First, it is said that factoring is solely a means of finance suitable only for those businesses which do not meet the criteria of traditional lenders. Secondly, it is sometimes alleged that once a business has entered into a factoring arrangement it is difficult to terminate it and it may in some cases lead to financial difficulties. The first objection is to a large extent based on the disregard of the administrative services and protection against the default of debtors which may be provided and of the benefits of a facility which follows the growth of a developing business automatically; the benefit and use of these aspects of the service are dealt with later in this chapter. The second allegation has arisen very largely from the use of the wrong service or the wrong use of any one of the variants of factoring. In this chapter, therefore, there are described not only some of the most suitable uses for factoring but some of the limitations on its use and some of the consequences of its misuse.

1. THE USE AND MISUSE OF FACTORING

Factoring to finance the movement of goods

2–03 The true historical nature of short-term trade credit is that it is the means of financing the movement of goods to buyers who, by selling them on to sub-purchasers, will be able to liquidate automatically the credit granted to them. Such onward sales may be of their goods in their original form or incorporated into others. Any short-term credit granted by a supplier of items to be used as capital equipment by the buyer is not self-liquidating; the buyer will be in little better position to pay for the equipment at the end of the credit period than at the beginning of it. The price of such equipment will be liquidated only over a period of years by the profits generated by its use and by provisions for its depreciation; as a result such short-term credit is not true credit as described above but it is often a convenience to enable the buyer to ensure that the equipment will perform the function for which it was purchased. Factoring was not designed to fill in the period before acceptance of the client's product by the customer and any credit required for the financing of such purchases should be found by leasing, hire-purchase or medium-term loans. Factoring was developed to fill the requirements of suppliers of goods for the granting of true self-liquidating short-term trade credit to their customers; therefore, the service is most suitable for the suppliers of raw materials, components and consumer goods. These goods can be made, sold and forgotten; the debts arising from their sales can stand by themselves and be fully collectable in the absence of the supplier. Such goods, unlike goods sold to a user as capital equipment, are not often subject to substantial after sales services or back-up; and the factor can be reasonably confident of their acceptance by the customers because they are likely to be of a repetitive nature so that the factor can judge the likelihood of acceptance by his experience. Only with such confidence can the factor pay out, at invoice date, a large proportion of the amount which he may expect to recover; the factor, unlike other providers of debtor finance, does not have the debtor's signature before paying out. Such confidence is essential to a successful factoring arrangement; in the absence of such confidence the factor may impose additional safeguards which may detract severely from the benefit of the service to the client.

2–04 Reference to the origins of factoring in the United States[1] should indicate that the type of business that is most suitable for the service of a factor is the type that would have been able to make

[1] See paras. 1–10 *et seq.* above.

use of the services of a mercantile agent in the absence of modern methods of marketing and distribution. In addition factoring has been used most successfully for businesses providing short-term services such as the provision of temporary staff or cleaning or inspection services except when they are provided under long term contracts. Where the full service has been applied to businesses for which factoring is suitable there have indeed been successes. An efficient factoring service, including finance automatically following the growth of sales, combined with a well managed supplier of goods and services is an unbeatable combination to bring a proprietary company to the stage of public participation.

Failure of factored businesses to achieve profits

2–05 The successes mentioned above have been masked by the more notorious failures caused by the use of factoring by a flagging, unprofitable and badly managed business. In such a case factoring will have been adopted purely for the funds generated by it. The charges of the factor may not be recovered by reduced administration in such a case and the extra cost may well increase the losses. The usual result is to defer the ultimate failure so that when it does occur the assets available for creditors have been further dissipated. Time and again recourse has been made to a factor in such circumstances for what has become known as "last resort finance." Only if it can be seen that the business is returning to satisfactory profitability should it resort to factoring; it is then that the extra breathing space may be of value.

Factoring finance used for capital expenditure

2–06 A similar situation of frustrated expectations for both client and factor may arise when factoring is used as a means of financing capital expenditure. The additional funds generated by the prepayments made available to the client become locked up in fixed assets. The business is then in the position of being paid regularly for a large part of its sales immediately on despatch of the goods but will continue to take the normal period of credit from its suppliers. If the business had strained resources before the new investment and the start of factoring, the growth will still be inhibited because the working capital has been depleted and the investment in the new fixed assets will not be able to pay for its keep. If the business was financing comfortably before the new investment any downturn in trade will now cause delays in payments to creditors; prepayments for this month's reduced level of sales will not be sufficient to cover expenses and creditors incurred at a higher level of trade in the previous months. This is a classical overtrading situation[2] in which the growth of the business must continue indefinitely (even if unprofitably) and any downturn avoided at all costs if financial difficulties are not to be met. The position can be avoided by using factoring with a financial facility for the purpose for which it was designed (to allow the more effective use of working capital) and by financing the capital investment by medium-term loans, leasing or capital.

No difficulty in terminating factoring if properly used

2–07 It is in the circumstances described above that the factor's client will find himself demanding a higher and higher level of prepayments—a level which the factor cannot safely meet. In the first case the demand will be to finance continuing losses and in the second, after a downturn in sales, to meet the high level of creditors' claims previously incurred. It is in such situations that the client will find it difficult to terminate the arrangements. Where, however, a profitable business uses a factoring service for the relief of administration and protection against bad debts no such difficulties will emerge. Furthermore, no difficulties will be encountered when the funds generated by a factoring agreement are used to finance working capital to support an increasing level of sales and to assist in producing higher profits resulting from lower unit costs. Then the finance provided will probably not be used to the full at all times, allowing creditors to be paid up to date and advantage taken of special purchasing opportunities. If factoring is so used, at no stage should there be any difficulty in terminating the arrangement when this is necessary.

Disregard of recourse by client

2–08 A difficulty may arise from a misunderstanding by the client of the nature of recourse factoring. It has been known for a concern, with the type of business for which factoring is quite suitable, to enter into such a recourse arrangement without full regard to the recourse provisions and to use the prepayments in such a way that the funds would be removed from working capital (for example by using the funds for investment in fixed assets or even to repay directors' loans in the client company). The result is that, when the factor exercises his right of recourse, no funds are available to repay the prepayments made in respect of the recoursed debt and the factor must perforce make deductions from further payments in order to recover what is due to him. Thus, the planned cash flow may not materialise and the client may find himself in difficulty.

[2] See paras. 2–11 *et seq.* below.

2–09 It is situations such as this that cause professional advisers to dissuade their clients from using factoring in any of its forms; a not uncommon complaint is that a factor will make his prepayments but that the balance of the purchase price seems to be delayed indefinitely owing to the setting off of recourse against it. However, it is not the factoring arrangement that is wrong, it is the misuse of the funds generated and the failure of the client to understand that the funds provided under a recourse arrangement are not "non-returnable cash." Such arrangements are the equivalent in substance, though not in form, of the borrowing of the money on the security of the debts and should be treated as such in financial planning. Similar disregard of the contingency of recourse is less likely to arise in the case of bulk or agency factoring or invoice discounting in which the client, and not the factor, has the responsibility for collecting the debts on behalf of the factor. With the presence in the client's offices of the sales ledger and credit control department, the impression of the managers of the business is not that (as has indeed happened) the debts have been sold, but that finance has been raised against the security of the debts. Where the factor has the appearance of responsibility to collect the client may fail to discriminate between recourse and non-recourse. It is apparent that recourse factoring should not be used where there are exposures concentrated on few debtors of relatively high value; it should be used then in conjunction with credit insurance with an undertaking from the factor not to exercise recourse whilst awaiting payment from the insurer. On the other hand such additional problems of recourse factoring may be avoided where the business has a good spread of debts owing by debtors of good credit standing.

Factoring no panacea for debtors of poor quality

2–10 Businesses that sell traditionally to trades and industries in which the expectation of bad debt losses is exceptionally high will not find a solution to this problem through factoring or credit insurance. These services can only spread the costs of such losses horizontally, across their many clients or insured, and by time over a period of years; they cannot therefore subsidise such a business in its regular high incidence of losses. Losses, other than those that are exceptional, have to be absorbed by a high margin of profit. Because the factor will need to keep his prepayments to a relatively low level so that his retention may be sufficient to cover the expected high level of bad debts the client will be disappointed with the level of finance provided and he may well have planned for more. Even where the full non-recourse service is provided the factor will be unlikely to accept, in return for a small percentage on sales values, such higher than average risks and this will be reflected in the level of his approvals.

Factoring and overtrading

2–11 The benefits of factoring, the relief from administrative burdens and bad debt losses and the availability of finance linked to sales volume without formal limit, are especially valuable to and appreciated by businesses which are growing vigorously. The service enables such a business to increase its sales rapidly, confident in the knowledge that the resulting trade credit requirements of its customers will be met. In this way, growth takes place without overtrading as might well not be the case if the business relied on traditional finance tied to a limit based on an historical financial position. On the other hand to take the view, as some have, that factoring leads to overtrading is a false syllogism; because many who are overtrading turn to factoring, factoring is not on that account a cause or encouragement to overtrade. Certainly, as demonstrated earlier, factoring in any form will not help those who are already overtrading in the classical sense: selling on shorter terms than they are buying so that growth is imperative at any cost (even at a loss) to keep the business alive. Indeed, if any form of factoring with finance is used in such circumstances and the funds generated used for investment in fixed assets, then the difficulties may be aggravated as is described above.[3]

2–12 Overtrading in its widest sense is usually taken to mean the carrying on of a business which is too large for the resources available for its support. The availability of immediate funds, without recourse, to the extent of 75 per cent. or 80 per cent. of debts created by the sale of acceptable goods to creditworthy customers, should enable a business to plan for growth with the resources automatically available. Thus, provided that the resources generated are used wisely as working capital to finance profitable sales and creditors are paid in due time, the growth may take place without overtrading. The factoring facility will provide the basis for achieving increased profits, which themselves can form the basis for the raising of additional resources. It seems that a more potent cause of overtrading is the reluctance of traditional providers of capital and lenders to provide a business with the necessary resources until profits have been earned and ploughed back and a healthy net asset position achieved. In this way businesses are tempted to try to achieve the profits without the resources to support the necessary sales volume. Factoring will break into this vicious circle, providing the necessary resources in

[3] See para. 2–06 above.

the first place so that the increased sales may be achieved and profit earned.

2–13 However, it is often overlooked that the key to the avoidance of overtrading is the non-recourse element in the full service. Only with this protection, and without the danger that the funds taken by the client may have to be repaid, may the client plan confidently for rapid growth. Otherwise the business must continually provide for the contingent liability to repay the factor (or more usually for an interruption in cash flow when the factor takes the repayment against sums currently due to the client) in the event of a debtor failing to pay after the specified period after due date.

2. THE BENEFITS OF THE SERVICES

Sales ledger administration and collection

2–14 The importance of good sales ledger administration is not always appreciated by business-people and even accountants. This may arise from the emphasis placed by members of the accountancy profession on management and financial accounts. However, it is apparent that a sales ledger is the basis for the cash flow of a business. Apart from compliance with statutory requirements, a business needs its sales ledger to know exactly how much is owed by any one customer, to enable it to send clear statements to and to collect from customers and to provide information for the control of credit. In order to achieve such aims it is essential that the ledger should be kept on an "open item" basis whereby all specific invoices, unpaid parts of invoices (representing unauthorised deductions by the debtors) and unallocated credit notes and payments are listed. Many small businesses seem unable to keep their sales ledgers on this basis even with the advent of data processing packages specially designed for this purpose; many such businesses keep their ledgers on the basis that items brought forward from previous months are shown as a balance. Such a balance may include deductions made many months previously and may be the result of the deduction of unallocated or round amount payments. The result is often the masking of disputed items whilst the debtor has been paying more recent items promptly. The longer this situation is allowed to develop the bigger is the eventual write-off for disputes which cannot be satisfactorily settled at a late stage.

2–15 An open item system will highlight such disputes; the necessity of allocating payments as they come in will create a discipline to resolve disputes and deductions promptly. Many small businesses, even with systems that provide for open item accounting, have not the time or the resources to enjoy the benefits of the system because in most cases all the appropriation of payments and credit notes to invoices cannot be carried out automatically by the system; even in some of the most advanced systems only payments which clear individual invoices without deduction can be appropriated automatically. By the use of full, maturity or recourse factoring[4] any business has the benefit of an open item system with prompt allocation of payments and credits by well trained and experienced personnel. The management of the business using such services is relieved from the burden of the supervision of these tasks and is usually provided with regular clear reports of outstanding debts analysed by the age of the invoices and highlighting disputed items.

2–16 The supervision of overdue sales ledger accounts and the collection from debtors which is vital for the cash flow for most small businesses are often part time tasks of management or personnel who have many other functions. In many small or medium-sized businesses the employment of a full time credit controller may not be justified. Often these tasks tend to be the Cinderella of the accounting function and are not given the importance which they deserve until cash flow problems remind the management of them. It may then be difficult to make the necessary allocations and bring the accounts up to date. By the use of full, maturity or recourse factoring[5] the debts purchased by the factor should be collected by personnel skilled in keeping the credit taken by customers to a minimum whilst avoiding prejudice to customer relations. In particular, in full factoring or maturity factoring, the factor has the ultimate responsibility for the collection of the debts approved by the factor in respect of which there is no recourse to the client; in providing such service the factor has the incentive to collect promptly in order to avoid the risk of the debtor's default.

The use of factoring to avoid bad debts

2–17 Insurance for merchants and manufacturers against losses caused by the default of their customers was introduced into the United Kingdom at the end of the second decade of this century. For many years credit insurance, as this type of insurance is known, did not have general acceptance. It was surprising that, although it was usual for businesses to effect insurance in respect of current assets against many risks (some of them indeed rare), it was not often considered prudent to insure debts against the risk of the insolvency of debtors which is something that is occurring

[4] See Chap. 1.
[5] *Ibid.*

every day. It was more surprising because in the circulation of working capital it is at the stage of becoming a debt that, with added value and profit margin included, an item has reached its greatest value. However, during that past decade, the higher incidence of insolvency has greatly increased the perception of the danger of the interruption of cash flow caused by such an event. Sometimes the default of a large customer has been the cause of the failure of the supplier itself; this has been referred to as the domino effect. It starts with the insolvency of a large company which hitherto appeared soundly financed and which has many independent suppliers; the failure of some of the suppliers has in turn been the cause of the insolvency of some of their own suppliers. Thus credit insurance is, in particular, an instrument for stability in a recession.

2–18 In considering the use of credit insurance some prospective insured consider the expense of it only in relation to the past incidence of bad debts. Regular small losses are part of the cost of running a business and the inclusion of them in an insurance arrangement is, in effect, a "pound swapping" arrangement with additional costs of administration. It is against the large unexpected losses that insurance is essential in many types of business; it is when such a loss occurs that management consider the loss to be bad luck whereas it is the result of bad management—the failure to effect insurance. Even if a bad debt reserve of a size sufficient to absorb the loss is held there is unlikely to be held additional liquid resources to represent such reserve and to replace the lost cash flow. The loss may be aggravated by the loss of work in progress and of a sales outlet. Such losses arrive unexpectedly and may cause considerable difficulty; on the other hand the cost of credit insurance or factoring is predictable and may be budgeted for in costing the price of products.

2–19 In spite of the recent more widespread recognition of the importance of credit insurance there is still little recognition among businessmen and their professional advisers of the benefit of this aspect of the services of the non-recourse factors. The benefit of this protection may be obtained without any finance, for those who wish to continue to rely on their traditional sources of finance, by the use of maturity factoring. For a small or medium-sized business there may be considerable advantages in the use of a factor as compared with the use of credit insurance. The principal advantage is that the money lost by the interruption of the cash flow, caused by the default of the customer, is immediately replaced in full (to the extent of the factor's approval); the business does not have to wait for the settlement of the claim and the insurer's indemnity is often 75 per cent. or 80 per cent. of the insured debt and not the full amount. Such settlement may in some cases be deferred until official insolvency, followed by the obtaining by the insured of admittance of his proof in the insolvent estate and a period for consideration of the claim by the insurer. In the case of full factoring a substantial part of the purchase price of the debt (its amount less the factor's charges) will already have been paid when the invoice was issued and the balance will be paid on the date of the insolvency.

2–20 Another advantage is the relief from the administration of the policy; in a typical credit insurance arrangement periodic returns of turnover and of overdue accounts are required and the claims procedure requires additional paper work. Furthermore factors do not often require additional fees for the approval and maintenance of credit limits; these costs are merged into the cost of providing the full administrative functions. It has on some occasions emerged that the savings engendered by the relief from administrative and collection functions by the use of the full service or maturity factoring[6] can cover the factoring administration charges so that the protection against bad debts may be provided for virtually no fee.

2–21 There are naturally many businesses for which such protection is not necessary; they may have such a wide spread of customers that the business is self-insuring in this respect or they may sell only to government departments. However, when a decision has been taken that protection is necessary then a careful review of the costs and benefit of insurance and non-recourse factoring should be made. In some respects credit insurance has advantages over the services offered by factors: cover for work-in-progress is sometimes available and some insurers will stay on risk in respect of a disputed claim against a debtor whereas a factor will normally effect recourse in respect of a debt the subject of a dispute which is not settled within a few months.

The benefit of the finance generated by prepayments

2–22 The following statement on the finance generated by factoring summarises the benefit of this aspect of factoring services and comes from a completely disinterested source:

> "Factoring is without doubt today one of the most effective ways for a small or medium-sized business selling raw materials or consumer goods or providing services to finance the trade credit it grants to its customers. True, it may rely on its own resources or on credit provided by the bank or on that provided by its own suppliers but inflation coupled with high interest rates and the current low supply of risk capital have

[6] *Ibid.*

led many businessmen to seek the alternative forms of finance such as factoring, with the many services which it offers."[7]

2–23 Before the Second World War merchants and manufacturers financed the credit to be granted to their customers partly by using their own capital resources, which were augmented by the ploughing back of profits, and partly by the credit granted to them by their own suppliers. In the years since the war high rates of taxation combined to reduce the supply of internally generated resources. The deficiency could not be filled entirely by the credit granted by suppliers (themselves often suffering from the same forces). The problem was aggravated for those near the end of the chain of supply between raw materials and retailers where the customary periods of credit tended to be longer. For these reasons there has been an increasing dependence on bank finance especially by way of overdraft. However, since banks' facilities are determined to a large extent by criteria other than the value of the prospective level of trade debts outstanding from time to time, young vigorously growing businesses have not always been able to obtain sufficient finance to realise their full productive capabilities. A bank might well expect its customer to reach a sufficient level of trade and thus of profitability and thereby produce the profits and the assets to support the required level of finance; but without the availability of the finance to support the required level of trade the business cannot reach it.

2–24 It is the function of the factor to cut into this inextricable circle. The factor's provision of finance by way of prepayment (typically 80 per cent.) of the purchase price of debts created automatically follows the growth of the business without formal limit. This enables a factor's client, without sufficient internally generated funds to support a higher level of trade, to plan for growth in the knowledge that the factor will exactly match to the extent of 80 per cent. the funds required for the trade credit to be granted to his customers. Particularly in the case of the full service the factor undertakes to buy without recourse every debt arising from the sale of acceptable goods (or the provision of acceptable services) to creditworthy customers. The client is then required to fund only the remaining part (in this example 20 per cent.) and the agreed percentage may match his gross profit margin. For a business with new products or markets to develop, such an arrangement will enable it to support the additional turnover and to produce the higher profits; in the case of a manufacturing business the extra

[7] From the report of the secretariat of UNIDROIT (see para. 12–19 below) following a second meeting of the representatives of governments for the consideration of a draft convention to harmonise the laws relating to factoring for international trade.

sales volume may well reduce unit costs. In this way the factor's charges may be easily absorbed without taking account of savings engendered by the saving of administrative tasks and the avoidance of bad debts.[8]

3. LIMITATIONS ON THE USE OF FACTORING

Post-invoice contractual obligations of client

2–25 The factor's ability confidently to provide funds at the time when goods are delivered or services completed, without the debtor's intimation that he has accepted the goods and services, depends, not only on his experience of the acceptability of the goods and services in question, but also on the absence of substantial continuing obligations of the client under the contract of sale or for services. Where there remain continuing obligations, then, in the event of the insolvency of the seller or the cessation of the business for other reasons, the factor will be faced with counterclaims from the debtor which in some cases may well have the effect of reducing the amount payable by the debtor to nil.[9] The factor will in most cases have no positive liability to the debtor, but the indeterminate amount of such likely cross-claims has the effect of limiting the use of factoring. In addition to the unsuitability of factoring to the provision of most items purchased by the debtors for use as capital equipment (in respect of which the client may be responsible for warranties and service after invoice date) factors normally find themselves unable to provide their services to contractors in the construction industry.[10] In neither of these industries is the factor able to make a confident assessment of the acceptability of the products based on previous sales; in most cases every product differs from others produced by the same supplier.

2–26 There are many other goods and services provided on the basis of contracts continuing over several months or even years. In the case of a business of which this is the normal pattern of trade, the factor may well take the view that to provide for the counterclaims, arising from claims for damages for failure to complete such a contract, should preclude the provision of any form of factoring which includes finance by way of payment on account of the purchase price of the debts on invoice date.[11] On the other hand there are cases in which the problem can be overcome by the expedient of agreements between the prospective client and his debtors by which the contracts are made divisible and the goods or

[8] See also the case histories in para. 2–30 below.
[9] For a full analysis of the effect of such cross-claims see paras. 9–12 *et seq.* below.
[10] See paras. 9–37 *et seq.* below.
[11] *Ibid.*

services represented by each invoice are regarded as provided under a separate contract.[12]

Effect on client of use beyond limitations

2–27 It may be thought that the use of factoring beyond its limitations is a matter that will affect the factor only and that, if he is prepared to accept the risks of such possible cross-claims by debtors, it should not be to the detriment of of the client. However, when it is apparent to the factor that he may be faced with such difficulties in making an early recovery, the result may well be a restriction in prepayments and even a complete interruption to the client's cash flow. The difficulties may even result in poor administration by the client and be reflected in difficulties in collection from debtors; by reason of the debtors' cross-claims, the failure of debtors to accept the goods and services or modifications (in the case of machinery for capital equipment) the required collections may be the responsibility of the client. Even in the case of non-recourse factoring the factor may no longer be responsible for the default of the debtor and the disputed debt may be subject to recourse; for it is normal for factors to have the right of recourse in respect of a debt the subject of a defence or counterclaim which is not settled within a reasonable period (sometimes defined as 60 days). To the client the resulting disservice is apparent; the restriction in the prepayments may cause an aggravation of the deficiency of working capital which may have initially caused its management to look to factoring. The business may well have embarked on planned growth on the understanding that the agreed percentage of sales would be available on despatch of its products; but, owing to its being unable to warrant that it had completed all its obligations under its contract of sale, it may then find that prepayments by the factor are withheld only because, in accordance with trade practice, there may be much to be done after invoice date.

2–28 Difficulties cannot be attributed to the services themselves but only to the way in which they are used; to blame the services would be equivalent to blaming the concept of a motor car for the cause of an accident, rather than the way in which it is driven. Factoring can only benefit by a thorough consideration of its proper use and the difficulties caused by its misuse described above. Much of the adverse comment on factoring has been caused by the acceptance by factoring companies of the wrong type of client in the wrong circumstances for the wrong reasons; this has not always been the result of any misunderstanding by the management of factoring companies but sometimes of pressure by shareholders on

[12] See para. 9–43 below.

managers to widen their marketing outside the industries that are usually considered suitable in order to increase profitability more rapidly. In most cases the factoring company has not suffered; it has been able to protect itself by reducing its prepayments. But the image of factoring has been impaired. Only by a full ventilation and discussion of the misuse of the services can the criticisms of the service be rebutted and the undoubted benefits and value of factoring and some of its variations be brought to the attention of the business community and professional advisers.

4. BUSINESSES WHICH MAY BENEFIT MOST FROM FACTORING

2–29 From the foregoing it is apparent that to be suitable for factoring the contracts of sale of the prospective client should give rise to debts which not only represent the full performance of the contract (without further or continuing obligations on the part of the supplier) but which also are strictly numerable as to value by reference to the contracts and are free from the likelihood of counterclaims. Ideally the debts should be such that they stand by themselves as fully payable without any back-up from the client. There are many businesses the sales of which give rise to such debts; for example, the sale of a specific number of tables or chairs at a specific price unrelated to any other contract for sale would give rise to such strictly computable debt. On the other hand a contract for public relations services or other consultancy based on certain performance and results over a specific period might not give rise to a strictly computable amount of debt. It is often not recognised that some invoices issued by service and contracting companies represent only the supplier's idea of what he should be paid (they have been sometimes described as the hopes and aspirations of the supplier) and do not necessarily coincide with the debtor's opinion of what he owes. In the provision of special purpose machinery the amounts payable may become the result of negotiations between engineers on each side, particularly when modifications to the machinery are necessary; in the case of shopfitting and similar work the end result may seem to the customer different based on his expectations from the specification and plans.

The benefit of factoring to businesses with good growth prospects

2–30 Within the limits of suitability there are a large number of situations in which factoring may be of particular benefit. The most usual case is that of a well managed business with a good and acceptable product of which the growing sales will outstrip the financial support of traditional lenders. The finance provided by a factor, which automatically follows the growth of the outstanding book debts, enables the business to plan for an increase of sales without having to make frequent applications to its bankers supported by cash flow forecasts, budgets and other financial information; the management of the business may concentrate on producing and selling. Furthermore the acceptance by the factor of the administration of the sales ledger, which may be greatly increased, and the credit assessment of new customers will be of especial benefit in such a case. Examples of the assistance given by a factor in such circumstances are as follows:

Example 1

A company, which had started with capital of £10,000, after two years of trading had a net worth of about £15,000 and had achieved a sales volume of £150,000. Its bankers were willing to lend on overdraft a sum which would match the net worth. The company was then introduced to a new market for its products and the exploitation of the new market would quickly result in an increase of sales to £400,000 and outstanding book debts of about £65,000. The banker suggested to the company that it should use factoring and as a result of the use of a factor the additional funds were found to finance the book debts; the use of the full service enabled the company to sell into the new market without increasing its accounts staff and gave it confidence in the avoidance of bad debts in a market in which it had little experience. Ten years later the company's annual turnover was £7,000,000 and net pre tax profits about £350,000. The principal director was sure that this could not have been achieved without factoring, but his successful use of it was based on his never having used all the resources available from his banker and his factor to the full at any time.

Example 2

A holding company owning subsidiaries in several different trades owned a company selling products to the building industry. At a time of rapid expansion of the subsidiary's sales, the holding company's chairman was looking for some way of funding the subsidiary's growth automatically. At the time the subsidiary's outstanding book debts amounted to £80,000 and, on enquiry at its bankers as to how much would be available on overdraft when the book debts reached £500,000, it was suggested that the chairman should not ask hypothetical questions. To a similar question a factor replied that, provided that the debts arose from the sale of acceptable goods to reasonably creditworthy customers, then the factor would provide £400,000 by way of prepayments for those book debts. The management of the subsidiary could not see any saving in the factor's administration of the sales ledger which was a function performed by personnel with other duties; but they decided on the full service for the protection against bad debts. After several years, when outstanding book debts had risen to well over one million pounds, the finance by way of prepayments was no longer required; but the company decided to continue to use the factor's services, not only for the protection against bad debts, but also because the sales ledger and collection functions had grown to such an extent that to carry out such tasks themselves would cost the company more than the factor's charges.

The benefits of factoring in the development of new products

2–31 A business person may be very well versed in the credit standing of customers in his or her own trade or industry. However, when a new type of product is developed or the business diversifies by the purchase of other businesses, there may be a completely different type of customer to be served. It has been known for businesses to be restrained from diversification by fear of the unknown credit risks. Such uncertainties may even arise from the simple change in the pattern of trade so that sales which hitherto had been made to a relatively small number of wholesalers are to be made to a large number of small retailers. In all such cases the use of a factor will enable the business to exploit its new opportunities with confidence. In the case of a switch of sales from wholesalers to retailers the acceptance of the administrative function by the factor will also assist this development. Factoring was used in such circumstances by a company dealing in precious metals the sales of which were for the most part to a small number of customers in the jewellery business well known to the company and its executives. A development in the electrical and electronic industry created a demand for the company's products there so that it had the potential to sell to any company in these industries. The number of actual customers increase by many times the original number and the sales volume would develop substantially. For these two reasons alone factoring would have been justified but the main impetus was the factor's approval of customers in the new fields in which the factor was experienced; in this way the company was able to develop its business with confidence in relation to finance, administration and protection.

Factoring and seasonal trades

2–32 In businesses which have most of the sales concentrated in one or two short periods during any year the working capital requirements during those short periods may be quite out of proportion to the capital resources of the business and consequently to the amount of finance available from traditional sources which are looking at balance sheet ratios. Such a disproportion applies particularly to the trade debts of manufacturers who may attempt to spread their sales by offering long credit outside the peak selling period. For example, a lawn mower manufacturer may offer terms of payment to its customers by which payment for all sales from December through to May are to be made at the end of June; in this way the distributors would have an opportunity to sell the products at the start of the grass cutting season before being obliged to pay. The resulting high value of debts, which may be well out of line with other balance sheet items, may be safely financed by the purchase of the debts by a factor relying on experience of the acceptability of the product and on the profitability of the supplier without regard to the balance sheet ratios.

2–33 There are many other examples of such seasonal peaks of outstanding book debts in consumer goods trades, particularly in the clothing industry which traditionally experiences two seasons: Spring and Autumn. An importer of such goods may have the goods which he imports financed largely by a bank's opening letters of credit on his behalf and releasing the goods to him for onward sale on a letter of trust; but the bank may require repayment of the amounts laid out for the purchase of the goods as soon as they are sold. The employment of a factor in such circumstances may enable the importer to finance the goods right through to the ultimate payment from the customers of the sub-sales.

Factoring and the relief of administrative burdens

2–34 Maturity factoring has often been adopted for the protection it offers against bad debts together with the relief from the tasks of sales accounting and collections from debtors by businesses which have no need of the financial benefit. It has sometimes been found advantageous for a business to accept the administrative function alone and the savings together with the protection against bad debts have outweighed the cost of the service. The following is an example of such a saving:

Example 3

> A small company in the foundry industry, watching his competitors invest in expansion in the late 1970s, expected a recession in the industry. In view of the growth of capacity in the industry and the expected fierce competition together with a recession, he decided to cut his overheads to the minimum and to reduce his office staff from three to one; he expected to be able to cope with some of the additional work himself. Unfortunately he had just not enough time for all the administrative tasks and, naturally, the following up of overdue accounts and collections from debtors fell into arrears because there was no particular deadline for these tasks. He considered the alternatives of a new member of staff or maturity factoring; the cost of each was about equal when the overheads were taken into account. The advantage of factoring was that the factor was always there to carry out these tasks, whereas there would have to be cover for the extra member of staff during absence for vacation and sickness. After several years of the use of maturity factoring it emerged that the cost had been no more than the cost of the additional personnel would have been; additionally the factor had absorbed some bad debts so that the protection against bad debts had been provided for him at virtually no expense.

The choice of a suitable service

2–35 When it is considered that factoring might be suitable to assist in the financing or administration of a business or both it is important that the business should choose the right service to meet the particular situation. Finance for growth alone may be achieved by invoice discounting if it is used by a well established company with adequate reserves and efficient accounting procedures. A company exploiting new markets or a new product may be better served by the full service so that it is relieved from unfamiliar risks and trade usages. A business that is growing fast on a small capital base also needs the full service. In addition to the finance and administrative function it needs the assurance that it will not be set back by an interruption to its cash flow by customer defaults.

CHAPTER 3

THE FACTOR'S RELATIONS WITH HIS CLIENT

3–01 This chapter deals with the relations, the communication and the accounting between the factor and the client. The factor's main requirement from this aspect of factoring is that it should be ensured that the debts which he has purchased are payable at the value at which they are notified or offered to him without his need to enlist the support of the client. The factor will also wish to rely on the client's support in collecting the debts should this be necessary by reason of the debtor's defence or counterclaim or because there remain after invoice date further obligations of the client to the debtor; and in the case of invoice discounting and in some cases of agency factoring[1] he must have confidence in the sales ledger administration of the client. The factor also needs to specify the rates at which he is to be remunerated for the functions which he carries out. From the client's point of view, the procedures should provide for payment in accordance with his perception of the finance to be generated by his sale of the debts to the factor; and he will wish to have confidence in the factor's reports and accounting with him so that he may have sufficient information for the proper conduct of his business. The client will also need to know the exact circumstances in which he will be required to repurchase any debt from the factor by reason of the exercise of recourse by the factor. The legal relationship by which these matters are regulated is described in the second part of this book[2]; here the administrative procedures of a typical factoring arrangement are described.

3–02 Any of the types of factoring described in Chapter 1 may be provided under an agreement which simply provides for the offer of each debt to the factor as it arises (a "facultative" agreement) or under an agreement which itself binds the debts as being assigned to the factor without further formality (a "whole turnover"

[1] See paras. 1–43 and 1–41 respectively.
[2] See, in particular, Chap. 10.

agreement).[3] In the former case each debt must be the subject of an individual offer normally evidenced by the delivery of copy invoices, by which such debts are represented, to the factor; in the latter case the invoices are merely "notified" to the factor as an accounting function because the debts will have already vested in the factor upon their coming into existence.[4] In order to avoid prolixity in this chapter, the sending of invoices or copies to the factor by the client will in all cases be described as a notification whether the sending of them constitutes an offer or not.

1. PROCEDURES IN FULL, RECOURSE AND MATURITY FACTORING

The start of factoring

3–03 When the agreement between the factor and his client has been executed and the factor and the client are ready to start the arrangement, it is first necessary for the two parties to prepare for the details on the client's sales ledger at the prospective starting date to be entered into the factor's records. It is usual for the factor to purchase the debts outstanding at the starting date; if he does not there will be confusion among debtors as to whom to pay until the outstanding debts are cleared. Furthermore, subsequent credits allowed to or deductions made by debtors relating to the outstanding debts may be applied by the debtors against amounts owing to the factor for later invoices.

3–04 If the arrangement is for non-recourse factoring (*e.g.* full or maturity factoring) then, at the earliest opportunity, the factor must make a review of the debtors currently served by the client in order to assess their credit standing and to determine the level of his approvals. The approvals are usually based on a credit limit for each debtor and, in respect of debts at any time within that limit, the factor will have no recourse if the debtor fails to pay by reason of his insolvency.[5] For this purpose the client is usually expected to prepare a list of all his debtors paying meticulous attention to names and addresses in view of the number of concerns whose names tend to be similar. The factor will then make his assessment of each debtor on the basis not only of the information available to him from his own files or from status reports and files at the Companies Registry but also relying to some extent on the client's own experience of payments from the debtors. As this exercise sometimes takes place a few weeks before the debts themselves

[3] For a description of the two types and an explanation of the difference between them see Chap. 7 and especially paras. 7–12 and 7–13 below.
[4] As to when a debt comes into existence for this purpose see para. 7–14 below.
[5] See paras. 3–10 *et seq.* below for a description of the methods by which approvals are given.

are taken on by the factor (in order to allow the factor time to make his assessments) it is important that the client should *from that time* send in to the factor applications for credit approvals and not wait until the starting date. It has not been unknown for the starting date to be delayed with a consequent change in the make up of the outstanding debtors, whereupon the factor may not be in a position to give immediate approval to some of the debts; if prepayments[6] are to be made only in respect of approved debts then the initial cash flow expected by the client may not be forthcoming. For this reason, among others, many factors start the non-recourse arrangement with sales after the start of factoring and accept the initial outstanding debts with full recourse to the client; in this way it is often hoped to arrange for an earlier start.

3–05 In order to transfer the existing debts to the records of the factor and to make the first arrangements for payments to be made direct to the factor the client must bring his ledger up to date to the close of business on the day before the starting date and prepare statements for his debtors. The statements are prepared in duplicate and one copy is sent to each debtor with a notice of the assignment and instructions to pay to the factor; the statement is often accompanied by an introductory letter the legal effect of which is analysed in Chapter 8. The other copy may be sent to the factor as a notification of the initial outstanding debts, but in some cases the factor may require copies of the individual invoices not least so that he may be in a position to send any copies required to debtors. In any event, if the sales ledger has not been kept on an open item[7] basis by the client the ledger will need to be analysed so that each balance represents only specific invoices before it can be taken on by the factor. On the basis of the statements, the copy invoices or the analysis the factor will create his own sales ledger accounts and credit the client with the purchase price of the debts which is the total invoice value (less any outstanding credit notes) less the factor's charges.

3–06 If prepayments[8] are to be provided (*i.e.* otherwise than in maturity factoring) the client will be at liberty to draw against the credit less the agreed retention; that retention is naturally a percentage of eligible debts which is inverse to the prepayment percentage in addition to the equivalent of any debts not eligible for prepayments. Such ineligible debts will include those disputed or seriously overdue and, although in some cases the factor will be prepared to make prepayments in respect of debts whether

[6] See para. 1–38 above.
[7] See para. 2–14 above.
[8] See para. 1–38 above.

approved for credit or not, in others ineligible debts will include those not approved for credit.

Continuing arrangements

3–07 From the start of factoring the client will invoice his customers in the usual way but the invoices are to bear a notice that the debts represented by them have been purchased by and assigned to and are payable only to the factor. It is considered that the notice should refer to the "purchase" by the factor in order to make it clear that the debt has been the subject of an outright assignment by way of sale and purchase; in the words of a well-known judgment the debtor should be made aware that the debt has been "made over" to the factor.[9] The invoices are to be notified to the factor in convenient batches, but only after delivery of the goods or completion of the relevant service. Such notification is normally by the submission of copies of the invoices but some factors require to have the originals sent to them for onward transmission to the debtors so that they may ensure the delivery to debtors of the assignment notices. The notification normally constitutes a warranty that the debt is then a legally binding obligation of the debtor without the possibility of any defence or counterclaim.[10] The notification will also constitute other warranties; in particular that the debt has arisen from a contract of sale providing for payment on terms approved by the factor, in a currency approved by the factor and otherwise as approved by the factor. The factor and the client must agree on such terms at the outset so that the factor's terms on which he purchases the debts are properly assessed.[11] In particular it is important that the maximum settlement discount to be allowed to the debtor should be approved by the factor at the outset so that the factor's retention[12] may be fixed at a level to absorb such a reduction in the amount recoverable from debtors.

3–08 The amounts of the invoices are debited to the particular debtors' accounts by the factor and the client is credited. As a corollary, the client will notify the factor of credit notes issued which have the effect of reducing the amount payable by the debtors. The amounts of these credit notes will be credited to the relevant debtor accounts and debited to the client's account,

[9] *Wm. Brandt's Sons & Co.* v. *Dunlop Rubber Co. Ltd.* [1905] A.C. 454 *per* Lord Macnaghton at p. 462.
[10] See para. 10–07 below.
[11] See paras. 10–09 *et seq.* below.
[12] See paras. 5–36 and 10–02 *et seq.* below and 3–06 above.

thereby reducing *pro tanto* the amount payable by the factor to the client. Most factors now expect that the client should place a debtor's account number on each invoice and credit note so that the input to the factor's data processing system can be effected without delay; this assists the factor in updating the accounts daily and in providing up-to-date feedback of information to the client. There are also likely to be future developments by which the factor's debtor accounts for a particular client may be updated by input from a terminal in the client's offices.

3–09 The client may continue to draw the agreed prepayment percentage of the value of notified invoices less the factor's charges and less the value of any notified credit notes; in addition the factor will also pay the balance of the purchase price of debts which have been settled by payment by the relevant debtors. In effect the client may draw up to the balance credited to him less the retention as described in paragraph 3–06. If a payment is made by a debtor, the outstanding debts are reduced by the same amount; the retention, which includes a percentage of the outstanding debts eligible for prepayment and the full amount of ineligible debts, is then automatically reduced and that releases the unpaid purchase price of the debt which has been paid. Some factors will pay the balance of the purchase price, not on payment of the debt, but a fixed number of days after the invoice date or after the end of the month in which the debt has been invoiced. This latter system which normally only applies in the case of non-recourse factoring (full or maturity factoring) has the advantage to the client that he can budget his cash flow more exactly.

Approvals

3–10 Approvals of debts in full and maturity factoring are given for the purpose of specifying debts which the factor will accept without recourse as regards the failure of the debtor to pay by reason of insolvency. In recourse factoring approvals are not given for this purpose because every debt is purchased by the factor with full recourse; they may be given as an advisory service as regards the credit standing of the debtor or to determine the eligibility of the debt for prepayments. This difference and the fact that, whilst some non-recourse factors will make prepayments only in respect of approved debts, others may prepay in respect of approved and unapproved may have caused some confusion; as a result the term "eligible" is now sometimes used to label a debt in respect of which a prepayment will be made leaving the term "approved" to denote "without recourse".

3–11 Whichever the reason for the approvals they may be determined in any of the following ways:

(a) by establishing in respect of each debtor a credit limit within which the total indebtedness of that debtor at any time is deemed to be approved;
(b) by specifically approving debts arising from individual contracts of sale;
(c) by the establishment of limits in respect of each debtor for monthly deliveries whereby any deliveries in excess of such a limit will rank as unapproved;

or by a combination of any two or all the above methods.

3–12 The advantage of method (a) is its flexibility in that it allows for irregular deliveries and for invoices in respect of deliveries, that have been made whilst the limit is full or exceeded, to drop into the limit to the extent that a debtor payment or credit note creates an availability within it; on the other hand under method (c), to the extent that any invoice exceeds the periodic delivery limit, such invoice remains unapproved. Each of the methods has a disadvantage as compared with the others. Method (a) will only enable the client to ensure that all the outstanding debts are protected if he has sufficient information to know the up-to-date state of all the debtor accounts at all times[13]; only with this information can he control the deliveries so that the outstanding debts remain within credit limits. Method (b) imposes an undue administrative burden on both parties unless the business of the client consists of a relatively small number of orders of large amounts. Method (c) has the advantage of allowing the client to make his deliveries without reference to the state of the account. However, it has the disadvantage of inflexibility: if deliveries are not spread regularly there may be unapproved debts arising from one month's sales whilst the outstanding is less than the factor would in total be prepared to approve.

3–13 It is necessary for the factor to protect himself from a deteriorating financial position or impending insolvency of a debtor by reducing or cancelling a credit limit of either type referred to above but naturally such cancellation or reduction should not affect deliveries of goods made or services completed before receipt by the client of notification of it. If this were not so the client could not confidently effect his deliveries or perform services in the certainty of protection against a bad debt. In this respect it is unfortunate that some factors, in their agreements, take the right to refuse to accept any debt offered to them (or to have any debt repurchased by the client on its notification under a whole turnover type of agreement[14]); a client might make a delivery within a limit only to find that, because the debtor had called a meeting of

[13] See para. 3–14 below.
[14] See para. 7–13 below.

creditors between the delivery and the raising of the invoice, the factor had declined to accept the invoice and that consequently the client was not protected. With the use of specific approval of individual orders (method (b) above) the factor should have no need to have the right to withdraw an approval; he will normally stipulate that the approval is conditional on delivery within a period (for example 60 days) and it will naturally be expected that the client will not release any goods on notification of any official insolvency of the debtor.

Reports and feedback of information to client

3–14 Whereas in the United States factors tend to take the view that the client should not be concerned with the state of the sales ledger provided that they are obtaining approval in respect of every invoice and are looking to the factor alone for payment, factors in the United Kingdom have been constrained by market forces to furnish their clients with the fullest up to date information regarding customer accounts. This applies notwithstanding the fact that it is to the factor's account with the client that the client must look for his incoming funds because the factor has become the client's only debtor as regards that part of the client's business within the scope of the factoring arrangement. This feedback of information is particularly important if approvals are given by means of limits of outstanding indebtedness.[15] Accordingly most factors in the provision of the full service or recourse or maturity factoring, whereby the client is relieved from the administration of the sales ledger, provide at the minimum monthly lists of outstanding debts analysed by the due dates for payment of the items. Such lists often provide additional information regarding disputed items, the current credit limit for each debtor and a note of how much is unapproved and consequently with recourse to the client. Although such a list will be invaluable as guide to the pattern of the client's sales and the payment habits of the customers and will allow the client to locate the problems of slow payments where these are indicated generally by an increase in the value of debts in relation to sales, the sending of such a list once a month or even once a week may in many industries not provide the instant information necessary to enable the client to decide whether or not to release a delivery. As a result several factors now provide a terminal in the client's office by which the client may have access, among other things, to any account on the sales ledger.

3–15 It has often been suggested that a factor in carrying out the sales ledger function is in an unrivalled position to provide the client

[15] See paras. 3–12 and 3–13 above.

with any sales analysis which the client might require; such an analysis might be of sales each month by product or area. Such analyses have in fact been provided by factors for many years. However, the provision of such information has been on the basis of the inclusion in the factor's accounting period (which is normally a calendar month) of the invoices of which notifications are received during that period. On the other hand, the client's requirements are for information on the basis of invoices *dated* during a calendar month or other accounting period which might vary between four and five week periods. Owing to the delays in the raising and notifying of invoices and the varying cut off dates for invoicing in any period it does not seem that a satisfactory solution to this problem has yet been found. As a result such an additional service does not appear to have a high priority among factors.

2. PROCEDURES IN AGENCY FACTORING AND INVOICE DISCOUNTING

The start of the arrangement

3–16 In the case of undisclosed factoring (or invoice discounting without recourse)[16] or some cases of agency factoring in which the factor is accepting debts without recourse the procedures described in paragraph 3–04 above must be adopted to enable the factor to make detailed credit assessments of all but the smallest debtors. In the usual case of invoice discounting or agency factoring with full recourse to the client, many factors do not assess individual debtor accounts but protect themselves against the insolvency of debtors by relying on a good spread of the business and a provision to protect themselves against undue concentration of a large proportion of sales on individual debtors.[17] In such a case the procedures for a detailed examination of each individual debtor account is not required. Other factors will expect to establish credit limits for all the debtors over a certain size in order to provide for the eligibility of debts for prepayments or the factor may rely on a credit insurance policy and the limits approved under it.

3–17 In no case however will it be necessary for the ledger to be transferred to the factor's records because it is the essence of these arrangements that the client retains the sales ledger function

[16] See para. 1–44 above. This variation of the service has been labelled concisely but descriptively by one factor as "ID Plus" (invoice discounting with protection against bad debts).
[17] See para. 3–24 below.

carrying it out as agent for the factor who has become the owner of the debts. The factor will nevertheless expect the ledger to be kept on an open item system so that he may ensure that the administration of it and the control of credit are up to the standards which he requires; in some cases this may entail an analysis of the ledger and a change of system to enable the client to qualify for the service and this alone may be of benefit to the client! In most cases the factor will rely, for the notification of the debts outstanding at the start, on a copy of the client's sales ledger control account showing the position in total together with an aged list of debtors; that is a list of balances on the sales ledger analysed by the due dates of the invoices. The aged list will assist the factor in determining which debts may be disputed and which debtors need examining from the point of view of credit assessment. The factor will credit the client with the full value of the debts outstanding at the start of factoring and allow the client to draw the agreed percentage of that credit after deducting from it the total of ineligible debts (*i.e.* disputed debts, debts in excess of any specified credit limit or more than specified number of days overdue). In effect the amount of the ineligible debts becomes a part of the factor's retention; the remainder of it is the percentage of the aggregate amount of eligible debts that remains after deducting the prepayment percentage from 100 per cent.

Continuing arrangements in invoice discounting and agency factoring

3–18 In most such arrangements the factor will not expect to be notified by the provision of the individual invoices. The client will usually send a notification of total sales, returns, discounts allowed and other adjustments each week and the factor will make available the agreed percentage of the net amount of such notification (less his charges) and the equivalent of the remaining percentage of the debts settled by customers during that week. At the end of each month the factor will be furnished with an up to date aged list of debtors on the basis of which he will be able to adjust that part of the retention representing ineligible debts; for example, this enables the client to have the benefit of a drawing against any disputed amount in respect of which the dispute has been settled in his favour but it creates a new retention against any new dispute. The factor will also be furnished with a copy of the client's sales ledger control account at the end of each month so that he may reconcile these figures with his own records and most factors arrange for occasional visits to the client's offices by members of the factor's staff in order to be reassured of the correctness of the records and the effectiveness of the control of credit.

Recovery of payments from the debtors

3–19 In invoice discounting, notices to the debtors of the assignments of the debts is not required except in the case of a serious breach of the agreement by the client or its insolvency. Accordingly, unlike the position in disclosed factoring, the proceeds of the debts do not flow automatically to the factor. In order to enable the factor to make recoveries from the debtors it is provided that collections by the client are held in trust for the factor and are made available to the factor either by being paid into a trust account, in the name of the client but for the benefit of the factor, or by being paid in by the client direct to the factor's own account through the branch of the factor's bank nearest to the client. In both methods the charges for the collection of cheques are borne by the client either by inclusion in the factor's charges to the client or, in the case of a trust account, by instructions to the bank to debit such charges to the client's normal account. In order to enable the client to pay direct to the factor's account cheques made payable to client without the task of endorsing them, the bank will normally accept an indemnity and instruction from the client or an indemnity from the factor. Such an indemnity is also usually given in the case of disclosed factoring in view of the number of debtors who persist in sending their cheques made payable to the client. However, if the government adopts the proposal in the White Paper on Banking Services,[18] whereby cheques crossed "a/c payee" should not be transferable, the device of a trust account, as referred to above, will have to be used by the factor.

3–20 There are two methods by which the factor may recover payments from the debtors in agency factoring. Often, although the client is administering the sales ledger and sending out statements and reminders to debtors, the notices by the client to the debtor may be in the usual form by which the debtor is instructed to pay to the factor direct; in this method the factor will recover direct from the debtors as in the case of full or recourse factoring. Alternatively, if the factor wishes not to carry out the function of processing the incoming remittances, the debtor may be sent a notice of assignment but be instructed to pay the client as agent for the factor; the funds are then passed to the factor in the same way as in invoice discounting as described above. The disadvantage of the first method is that, in order to enable the client to administer the sales ledger and follow up for payments, the factor must keep the client constantly informed of payments; this is normally done by the daily sending of copies of remittance advices from debtors. In the second method the notice must be somewhat equivocal and

[18] Cmnd. 1026 (1990).

it detracts considerably from the benefits to the factor of such notices.[19] As such notice must mention the agency of the client it is important that it should include a notice that the client is not authorised to bind the factor in any way.

3. DISPUTES AND CONCENTRATION IN ALL TYPES OF FACTORING

The disposal of disputes

3–21 It is important that both the factor and the client should be aware at the earliest stage of any failure of a debtor to accept the goods or service and the invoice by which it is represented giving rise to a debt sold to the factor. A factor normally has the right to include the amount of any such disputed or queried debt in his retention and ultimately to have the debt repurchased by the client. If the client fails to inform the factor at the earliest time of such disputes or queries the factor may lose confidence in the debts notified to him and may require some increase in his retention and this may lead to the factoring arrangement as a whole being subject to criticism as not providing the amount of finance which was envisaged at the outset. On the other hand, if the client is not informed of any dispute notified by the debtor to the factor, but not to the client, there will be a delay in the resolution of the disputes and such delays often impede such resolution; furthermore, in the case of any form of non-recourse factoring, it is not unusual for the agreement to provide for the factor to be no longer responsible for the credit risk in respect of a debt which is or has been disputed even if it is approved. For these reasons, and because disputes may hamper collection efforts in respect of undisputed debts on the same account, the importance of early disposal of disputes is of prime importance to the satisfactory working of the factoring arrangements.

Dispute notices

3–22 In the full service or recourse or maturity factoring it is very often only on a demand for payment being sent by the factor that the debtor notifies that he has not accepted the goods or service or the invoice. In such case it is a normal procedure for the factor to send to the client a notice specifying the debtor, the invoice and the reason for the withholding of payment together with a copy of any relevant communication from the debtor. The factor will expect then to be kept informed regularly of the progress of the

[19] See para. 8–07 below.

efforts of the client to settle the matter. If payment is not made by the debtor or a credit note is not issued by the client within a reasonable period, normally in domestic trade a matter of months, then the debt will be the subject of recourse.

The exercise of recourse

3–23 Even when a debt becomes the subject of the right of recourse it is not advisable for any factor who has accepted the sales ledger function to give effect to the recourse and reassign the debt to the client until such time as it is clear that it should be credited out of the sales ledger. Although retaining the debt on his records and refraining to give notice of any reassignment, the factor will in most circumstances be fully protected. In the full service or maturity factoring it is normal for disputed debts, even if previously approved, to become unapproved and consequently the factor will no longer be responsible for the credit risk; and where prepayments have been made he will normally have the right to make a retention in respect of the disputed item against the next debts notified to him. The early exercise of recourse in respect of disputes means that until the disputed items are to be credited the factor is not performing the whole sales ledger function which may have been a reason for the acceptance of factoring by the client. More important to the factor is the aggravation caused to debtors who, having received an introductory letter by which they are informed in strong terms that *all* payments for the client's supplies must be made to the factor, are then given notice that certain invoices are to be paid to their supplier, the client. Such aggravation is believed to have been the cause of the prohibition of assignments in the purchase orders of some large and powerful buyers of goods and services. It has then been known for such concerns to agree to make payments to a factor only on terms that *all* payments must be made to the factor until the arrangement comes to an end. The right of recourse in respect of debt, which should still be kept on the ledger account, naturally arises more often in the case of recourse factoring in which recourse may be exercised at a specified time related to the date of the invoice whether the debt is disputed or not.

Concentrations

3–24 Closely allied to the problem of disputed debts is any concentration of a large proportion of the client's sales to one or a few debtors; it is likely to be a problem to a factor who is making prepayments. If a dispute arises in relation to a substantial part of the indebtedness of a debtor which constitutes as much or more than the retention held by the factor, the factor may consider the need to withhold payments against further invoices notified to him by the client. Such a step may put the client into acute difficulty by virtually stopping the cash flow of the business. In most cases the matter would be settled by a compromise allowing the client sufficient resources to carry on his business but the factor has to make a difficult decision as to whether the dispute may or may not indicate that all the products of the client are subject to some fault. Sometimes the withholding of payment by a large debtor may arise from an extraneous disagreement between the debtor and the client unconnected with the debt owing to the factor; or the debtor may hold up payment of the whole account on the grounds of one faulty delivery. In all such cases the factor may find himself in the awkward position of having to make a judgment on the merits of the case and in having to decide between his own and his client's interests.

3–25 It is usually considered advisable for a factor to avoid finding himself in such a position by providing at the outset of the factoring arrangements that he will not be obliged to make prepayments in respect of any indebtedness of any one debtor which exceeds a specified percentage of the aggregate of outstanding debts purchased by him from the client. Such arrangements are referred to as "concentration limits" and are becoming more usual, particularly in recourse and agency factoring and invoice discounting; in full factoring or undisclosed factoring without recourse the factor can protect himself by not making prepayments in respect of debts over credit limits.

4. SOME NORMAL EXCLUSIONS FROM THE ARRANGEMENTS

3–26 Although factoring is normally arranged to include the whole of a client's sales (or in some cases the whole of the sales in a particular market or of a particular branch or division of the client) and although this applies whether the agreement is on a whole turnover or facultative basis,[20] there are certain debts which the factor may wish not to have notified to him. The principal type of debt of which the factor does not require notification comprises debts in respect of which the client cannot give all the warranties and undertakings required by the factoring agreement[21]; such debts include:

[20] See para. 3–02 above.
[21] See Chap. 10.

(1) debts arising from sales to the client's own suppliers which may result in a set-off available to the debtor against the factor[22];
(2) purported debts arising from contracts for delivery on sale or return;
(3) debts arising from sales on terms more liberal than those approved by the factor.

Other debts which are normally excluded from the arrangement include debts arising from sales to associates of the client and sales of goods to individuals for their personal or domestic use.

3–27 The exclusion of such debts from the factoring arrangements where the agreement is on a facultative basis[23] is a simple matter; the factor either requires that they should not be offered to him or he declines to accept them. In the case of an agreement of the whole turnover type[24] a paradox arises: the agreement itself effects the transfer of ownership to the factor of all debts existing at the starting date and arising thereafter and the client is required to notify every debt. If the client notifies any such debts, he is deemed to have warranted that which he cannot warrant; if he does not notify them he is in breach of the agreement in that respect. The problem may be overcome by providing that any such debt shall be notified separately from other debts, that such separate notification shall not be deemed to constitute any warranties and that the factor shall have no obligation to make prepayments but shall have the right of recourse in respect of the debts included in them.

5. THE FACTOR'S CHARGES

3–28 The factors charges to his client in most cases consist of an administration charge (or service or factoring charge or commission) and a discount for prepayments. In most cases the factor will endeavour to cover all the functions which he performs, except for the finance by way of prepayments, in the administration charge. However in some cases additional charges for specific aspects are made; in particular in the case of export sales, any bank charges for the collection of cheques or for the exchange of currencies into sterling are usually charged additionally to the client. Where a client's pattern of business is such that he needs to apply frequently for the opening of new accounts or credit approvals on them and the number is out of proportion to a relatively small

[22] See Chap. 9.
[23] See para. 7–12 below.
[24] See para. 7–13 below.

volume of sales the factor may charge for the maintenance or opening of such accounts.

There is, however, an important exception to the absorbing by the factor (within the administration charge) of the cost of all the functions of and related to sales accounting. It is normal that the costs of legal proceedings for the recovery of a debt or part of a debt, which is subject to recourse, should be borne by the client.

The administration charge

3–29 By whatever expression the charge is labelled, it is normally calculated *ad valorem* as a percentage on the notified value of the debts included in the factoring arrangements before the deduction of any discounts, credit notes or other allowances granted to the debtors. The charge is usually to cover the functions undertaken by the factor (*e.g.* sales accounting or the acceptance of the risk of bad debts) and as a commitment fee for the provision of finance following the growth of the business without formal limit. As a result, the charge will vary widely according to the nature of the factoring service provided.

3–30 In the case of invoice discounting or agency factoring with full recourse, whereby the client retains the accounting function as agent for the factor, in addition to acting as a commitment fee, the charge will often cover only the additional bank charges which the factor may bear by the collection of cheques into his own bank account. However, some factors have arranged for global insurance to cover them and their clients against the loss of the debts by reason of the destruction of the records by fire or other perils. Such insurance is necessary to protect the factor against the loss of documentary evidence of the debts (orders and delivery receipts) even if there is adequate back up for the data. It also protects the client because the debts lost in such circumstances would be the subject of recourse. The cost of such insurance is sometimes included in the administration charge. In invoice discounting or agency factoring the percentage charge is often a fraction of 1 per cent.

3–31 Where any form of non-recourse factoring is provided the administration charge must include an element to cover the risk of bad debts and this element is related to the appropriate credit insurance premium and thus varies according to the industry, the spread and quality of the debtors and the average period of credit taken by debtors. This element in the charge may be kept down by the expedient of providing that only the excess over a fixed small amount in respect of any one bad debt loss will be accepted by the factor without recourse; by this means there will be avoided the "pound swapping" of a higher administration charge against the factor's acceptance of the normally expected small losses. For the full service, recourse factoring or maturity factoring, in which the factor carries out the sales ledger function, the charge must cover the administration of the sales ledger and the collection of payments; this element will vary according to the number of invoices, credit notes, payments and debtor accounts for a given volume of sales. For the full service the charge typically varies between 0.5 per cent and 2.5 per cent according to the variables mentioned above and the total volume of sales of the client; the charges for any variation of the service (such as recourse factoring) where the client retains some of the functions should be somewhat less.

Minimum and additional administration charges

3–32 It is natural that the cost to the factor of carrying out the sales ledger administration and collection functions as well as providing finance by way of prepayments is to some extent reduced proportionately to the sales volume by the scale of the operation. It is much less expensive for the factor to provide his services to five clients each with a sales volume of £10 million than to 50 whose turnover is only £1 million each. For this reason two variations of the strict application of an *ad valorem* method of calculation are often used. The first is the agreement of a minimum aggregate charge; by such a provision if the aggregate value of debts sold to the factor during any specified period (month, quarter or year) should not produce a specified aggregate of charges then the client is obliged to pay an additional fee to make up the difference. Normally such charge would be based on an annual turnover but charged on account monthly and adjusted at the end of the year. Secondly, in order to provide a downward sliding scale of total charge as the client's volume of sales increases, it is sometimes arranged for the client to pay a fixed fee each month and for the *ad valorem* charge to be fixed at percentage less than normal. The latter method of charging is more usual in invoice discounting where the factor takes on no administrative function; indeed there are factors who will charge a fixed administration charge only for that service or rely only on the discount charge and waive any administration charge. Any such fixed charge must naturally be by way of debit to the client's account and not, as is the case with the *ad valorem* charge, a deduction from the purchase price of each debt.

Refactoring charges

3–33 In many recourse factoring arrangements it is provided that the factor will normally exercise his right of recourse in respect of any debt which remains outstanding a specific number of days after invoice date or after the end of the month in which the invoice is raised. In this way the factor is obliged to carry out the sales accounting function and collection for a limited period. In many such cases in order to relieve the client of all these functions the factor will be prepared to continue to account for any debt and his efforts to collect it after the date when recourse is due and, for the continuation of the acceptance of these functions, the factor will make an additional *ad valorem* charge in respect of each such debt retained for each month in which it remains outstanding.

The discount charge

3–34 The business of purchasing debts payable *in futuro* with the immediate payment or payment of part or all of the purchase price has on several occasions been distinguished by the courts from the lending of money on the security of the debts.[25] Such discounting of debts postulates that the purchaser will be recompensed for his providing finance for the period from early payment until settlement of the debt by deducting a discount in the calculation of the purchase price of the debts. The courts have also recognised that "the amount of the discount is no doubt often calculated by reference to the amount of interest which the payer calculates his money would have earned if he had deferred payment to the due date."[26] However, it has also been considered that, as opposed to interest which accrues from day-to-day, a discount is fixed as a deduction from the purchase price at the time of the purchase.[27] As it is important to the factor that all his procedures should be consistent with the purchase of debts[28] some of the early factors in the United Kingdom, also taking their cue from American practice, calculated the discount to be applied to the purchase of every debt in advance to a fixed maturity date. The maturity date was established by reference to the average period of credit taken by the debtors of the client over the previous one or two years. The discount was deducted from the notified value of each batch of invoices by reference to the weighted average of the invoice dates; the client was then allowed back interest on the undrawn part of the purchase price. This method of calculating the discount

[25] See paras. 7–18 and 7–19 below.
[26] *Chow Yoong Hong* v. *Choong Fah Rubber Manufactory* [1962] A.C. 209 *per* Lord Devlin at p. 217.
[27] *Ibid.* See also *Welsh Development Agency* v. *The Export Finance Company Ltd.* F.T.L.R. April 10, 1990; in that case, although not having a direct bearing on the distinction between purchasing debts and lending, some cases in which interest and discount were distinguished were reviewed.
[28] See paras. 7–18 and 7–19 below.

provided certainty for the client and a discipline for the factor to keep his collections within the agreed maturity date.

3–35 The system was found to create a certain amount of conflict between the client and the factor. It did not allow for flexibility to the client in the granting of terms; the client gained no benefit from sales on shorter terms and the factor would be reluctant to agree to latitude to a favoured customer of the client. Furthermore it meant that in order to keep the ledger as a whole within the limits of the maturity date the factor needed to exercise recourse in respect of a disputed debt as soon as the dispute was notified with the disadvantages outlined in paragraph 3–23 above. Some clients considered that their factors were using undue pressure on their customers for early payment (in order to obtain payments before the maturity dates) and were thereby causing them loss of business. For these reasons and owing to the difficulty of making an accurate forecast of the payment habits of debtors in the business environment of the United Kingdom (as opposed to the more disciplined payment habits of debtors in the United States), the discount charge is now normally calculated on a day-to-day basis at a rate per cent per annum on the amount of each prepayment until it is recovered by settlement of the debt by the customer. For practical purposes the charges are normally calculated in aggregate. According to the accounting method used[29] the calculation may be on the balance on a current account or on the difference between the aggregate of outstanding debts and the unpaid balance of the purchase price of those debts owed by the factor to the client; the amount on which the charge is calculated is often referred to by factors as the "funds in use." Although the charge is specified as a discount to be deducted in calculating the purchase price of the debts, it cannot be calculated in advance. For administrative purposes the purchase price is credited to the client's account before the deduction of the charge and the charge is normally debited monthly.

3–36 From a review of the cases, in which discounting has been distinguished from lending,[30] it seems reasonable to infer that apart from the method of calculating the finance charge there are other distinguishing features. Of these a principle test is whether or not (as there must be in the case of lending on security) there is an equity of redemption[31]; and in this respect and in every other respect most factoring arrangements are consistent with the purchase of the debts. In view of the practical and commercial convenience of charging the discount on a day-to-day basis most

[29] See paras. 3–39 *et seq.* below.
[30] See Chap. 7, n. 42 and *Welsh Development Agency* v. *The Export Finance Company Ltd.* F.T.L.R. April 10, 1990.
[31] This is explained in para. 7–19 below.

factors now charge their finance charge in this way relying on the other distinguishing features of their activities to ensure that they are in practice purchasing debts.[32]

3–37 The method is acceptable to the client in its providing flexibility for him in the granting of credit. The factor does not need the discipline of a fixed maturity date to encourage him to obtain early settlement of debts; competition and the additional risk of the debtor's default are two spurs to the factor's performance in this respect. The factor also wishes to keep his funds in use in each client's business to the minimum in order that he can provide his services as widely as possible for the investment of a given amount of funds.

Collection date or maturity date

3–38 Although most factors now calculate the discount charge on a day-to-day basis there are two separate methods of determining the "funds in use" on which the charge should be calculated. The two methods derive not from a difference as to the concept of funds in use; in both cases this is the difference between the aggregate notified value of outstanding debts and the unpaid balance of their purchase prices. It is the amount paid on account by the factor in addition to any charges to his client less his recoveries from debtors. The different methods of calculation derive from two separate concepts as to when a debt ceases to be outstanding for this purpose. The first concept is that a debt remains outstanding until it is paid by the receipt of cleared funds into the bank account of the factor (the collection date). The second concept is that a debt ceases to be outstanding on a maturity date; such maturity date is normally calculated in the manner referred to above[33] and it might be expected that this method would have the disadvantages of that early method of charging.[34] However, the difference is that factors who now employ the maturity date system of charging reserve the right to make additional discount charges on any excess of outstanding debts and to make an allowance for any shortfall; it is often also provided that the factor should be able to adjust the maturity period during the currency of the agreement. Furthermore although the initial amount of the discount could be calculated in advance it is often calculated on a day-to-day basis to avoid the need to credit back interest in respect of undrawn funds. Closely allied to this question is the date for the payment of the balance of the purchase price of debts, that is the purchase price after

[32] See also paras. 7–18 and 7–19 below.
[33] See para. 3–34 above.
[34] See para. 3–35 above.

allowing for any prepayment. Such payments are made either on the collection date or the maturity date to coincide with the method used for the calculation of funds in use.[35]

6. CLIENT ACCOUNTS AND PAYMENT BY THE FACTOR

3–39 There are two methods of accounting between the factor and his client which are in use and which are consistent with the factor's purchase of and ownership of the debts. One of these methods is normally used where payment of the balance of the purchase price of each debt is to be made on the collection date[36] and the other where it is to be made on a maturity date.[37] The importance of a system of accounting between the factor and the client which is consistent with the purchase of debts as opposed to lending on the security of them is apparent from the remarks in paragraph 3–34 above.

Accounting: payment on collection date[38]

3–40 In this system there is one account between the factor and his client and this is kept strictly in accordance with the purchase of debts by the factor. The account, normally labelled the "current account",[39] is kept in the same way as a purchase ledger account kept by a purchaser of goods which would have entered on it credits for the goods purchased and debits for payments by the purchaser for the supplies and which would show a balance representing the amount owed by the purchaser. The current account therefore has credited to it the purchase price of the debts purchased by the factor; the purchase price is the notified invoice amount of debts less any settlement discount or other allowance to the debtor and less the factor's charges. As the amount of any discount or allowance and the amount of the factor's discount charge cannot be ascertained until some time after the notification of the debt, the credit on notification is usually of the notified amount less the administration charge only and the other items to be deducted are debited as soon as ascertained. Also credited is any other amount payable by the factor to the client; for example, any amount recovered by the factor in relation to a debt which has been repurchased by the client by reason of recourse.

[35] See above.
[36] See para. 3–38 above.
[37] *Ibid.*
[38] See App. 2.
[39] For the advantage in law of keeping the accounts by this method, see paras. 10–02 and 10–03 below and *Re Charge Card Services Ltd.* [1986] 3 W.L.R. 697.

3–41 The following items are debited to the current account:

(1) Any payments (including prepayments) made by the factor to or on behalf of the client.
(2) The amounts by which the purchase price of any debts are to be reduced or extinguished whether such amounts are represented by credit notes or not; such amounts may arise by reason of recourse or discounts or other allowances granted to debtors.
(3) Any part of the factor's charges which have not been deducted from the notified amount of any debt in making the credit to the account.
(4) Any other amount payable by the client to the factor (for example, amounts payable to the factor for supplies to the client by another client of the factor and consequently assigned to the factor).

The balance in credit on the account at any time represents the unpaid balance of the purchase price of the debts notified to the factor. The client will be at liberty to draw that balance subject to the agreed retention (a percentage, inverse to the prepayment percentage, of the debts eligible for prepayment in addition to the equivalent of the full amount of any that are not eligible).

Availability reports

3–42 The current account is normally submitted to the client once a month and the amount of the approximate balance may be made known to him more frequently; some factors will now make arrangements for the client to interrogate their current account at any time by use of a computer terminal in the client's offices. However, the up-to-date balance on the current account will not indicate to the client the amount which he may draw unless he knows the amount of the retention; and, as in most cases some debts will be ineligible for prepayment (for example disputed debts or those not approved for credit), he will not be able to calculate the retention unless he knows the make up as well as the total amount of the outstanding debts. For this reason the factors using this system of accounting usually make arrangements for their clients to know the availability from time to time; this means their knowing (in addition to the balance in credit on the current account) the total of the outstanding debts, the total amount disputed, the total amount otherwise ineligible and the amount retained in respect of each category.[40] As such information is required frequently by the client there is a trend towards on line

[40] See App. 3.

access by the client to the factor's computer data for this purpose also.

The memorandum account

3–43 This account which may be labelled "the discounting account" or (perhaps more aptly) simply "funds in use" is referred to as a memorandum account because it is not an account in the accepted sense of the term showing the position between two parties and arising from the transactions between them. The current account shows the position between the factor and his client; the individual debtor accounts show the position between the factor and the debtors. The memorandum account is debited with payments by the factor to or on behalf of the client and with the factor's charges and credited with payments from debtors. There should be entered on the account any entry in the factor's records which does not affect the current account with the client *and* an account with a debtor; consequently no credits for invoices or debits for credit notes or discounts or for the recourse of debts are entered on it. The balance should represent the difference between the net total of the sales ledger for the particular client (*i.e.* after deduction of any credit balances) and the credit balance on the current account. The account represents the extent to which the outstanding debts are financed by the factor while the credit balance on the current account represents the amount which remains to be financed by the client. The purpose of the account is for the calculation of the discount charge on the daily balance. If a credit balance emerges on the account the factor may credit to the client a discount allowance.

Accounting; payment on a maturity date[41]

3–44 Payment of the balance of the purchase price of each debt on a fixed maturity date provides the client with the advantage of the ability to forecast his cash flow more accurately than where payment is made on the collection date. A typical system of accounting between the factor and the client, where this method of payment is used, consists of three accounts and is as follows:

(1) A sales ledger control account:

This is not part of client accounting; the debts purchased by the factor are owned by him and the sales ledger comprises the accounts between the factor and the debtors. However the

[41] See App. 4.

account is used as part of the accounting information provided to the client in place of the memorandum account used in the system described above and partly also in place of availability reports. All entries on the factor's sales ledger in relation to the business of the particular client (comprising in the main invoices and credit notes notified to him and payments received by him) are entered on the account in aggregate. The balance on the account at any time represents the net total of the factor's sales ledger in respect of debts purchased from the client.

(2) Debts purchased account

The gross notified invoice value of debts is credited to this account as soon as they are notified to the factor; the corresponding debit will have been to the sales ledger control account. There are no other entries on this account except for the transfer to the credit of the current account described below by debit to this account of the notified value of each batch of invoices on their maturity date. The balance in credit on the account represents the aggregate notified value of debts purchased by the factor from the client which have not reached their maturity dates irrespective of any payment by the debtors or credit note issued by the client.

(3) The current account

The notified value of the debts purchased by the factor is credited to this account when they have reached their maturity date. The account is debited with any payments (including prepayments) to or on behalf of the client. It is also debited with all the other items chargeable to the client as are listed in paragraph 3–41 above. It is apparent that, as payment of the balance of the purchase price of debts (after deducting prepayments) is payable under this system on their maturity dates, a nil balance on this account would indicate that no prepayments had been taken in respect of the outstanding debts; any debit balance will represent the aggregate amount of prepayments drawn against the debts remaining outstanding.

3–45 If the aggregate value of outstanding debts as notified to the factor and represented by the balance on the sales ledger control account is larger than the balance on the debts purchased account (representing the total of notified unmatured debts) then collections are being made on average after the maturity date. As a corollary, if the balance on the sales ledger control account is less than the balance on the debts purchased account, the collections are being made, on average, before the maturity dates. It is therefore possible to determine the actual funds in use by putting the three accounts together. By adding to the current account balance the difference between the sales ledger control account balance and the debts purchased account balance (if the former is larger) or deducting the difference (if the former is smaller) the result will be the amount of funds in use. For this purpose the accounts may be combined as follows:

Example 1:

	£
Current account balance—debit (prepayments and charges uncollected)	100,000
Sales ledger control account—debit (net total of sales ledger)	350,000
Debts purchased account—credit (total of unmatured debts)	325,000
	£125,000

In the above example the client has been paid £100,000 before the maturity of the debts and the funds in use have been increased by £25,000 because this is the extent to which the client has been paid on maturity for debts not paid by the debtors.

Example 2:

	£
Current account balance—debit (prepayments and charges uncollected)	100,000
Sales ledger control account—debit (net total of sales ledger)	310,000
Debts purchased account—credit (total of unmatured debts)	325,000
	£85,000

In this example the actual total of the sales ledger is less than the aggregate value of notified debts as they would have been if they had remained, on average, outstanding until the maturity dates; they are being collected on average faster than had been estimated and the amount of funds provided by the factor is to that extent less.

Calculation of discount charge

3–46 In the system by which payment of the balance of the purchase price is payable on maturity, the discount charge may be calculated on the balance on the current account which represents the aggregate of prepayments in respect of debts whose maturity dates have not arrived (whether they have been paid or not). However in order to provide for flexibility, many factors using this system will make an adjustment for average payments earlier or later than the maturity dates. The combination of the accounts under this system provides an equivalent to the memorandum account[42] under the arrangements where the balance of the purchase price is to be paid on the collection date. Therefore, in order to avoid separate adjustments the discount charge is often calculated on a day to day basis on the balance of the combined account; thus the client will gain the benefit of fast collections and suffer the penalty of delays in debtor payments as he does when payment is made on collection. If the current account had been in credit to a greater extent than any excess of the sales ledger control over the debts purchased account then the funds in use are a negative amount. In such case it is not unusual for the factor to allow the client a discount allowance on the negative balance.

Availability

3–47 By reference to the current account and the debts purchased account the client using this system will be able to ascertain the extent to which he has drawn prepayments and the amount of the unpaid balance of the purchase price of debts. But, in order that he may be able to determine the retention and thus the amount available to him from time to time, he will need to know the balance on the sales ledger account; in most cases it will be necessary for the client to have a report as described in paragraph 3–42 above because he will need to know the amounts of ineligible debts outstanding in respect of which there may be a full retention.

Accounting; in other jurisdictions

3–48 In other jurisdictions, where it is not essential to differentiate so clearly between purchasing debts and lending on security, a very simple method of accounting now appears to be in common use among factors providing recourse or agency factoring or invoice

[42] See para. 3–43 above.

discounting. The factor maintains two accounts. First, the mirror image of a sales ledger control account (sometimes referred to as the "collateral account") to which he credits the value of all notified debts and to which he debits the value of all transactions which have the effect of reducing the debts including payments from debtors and the value of credit notes and allowances to debtors and of debts the subject of recourse. The other account is the "current account" to which are debited payments made to or on behalf of the client and the factor's charges; to this account are credited payments from the debtors notwithstanding that they are factor's recoveries. As a result, the current account will reflect the same balance as the memorandum account described above[43] but in this case it is regarded as an account between the factor and his client. It is apparent that to determine the amount owing at any time in respect of the unpaid balance of the purchase price of debts it is necessary to deduct the balance on the current account from the balance on the sales ledger account. As is the case in both the other accounting systems described above, in order to know the availability of funds which he may draw, the client will in most cases need an availability report based on the total of eligible and ineligible debts outstanding.[44] In this system the discount charge is normally calculated on the balance on the current account which represents the funds in use. However although the method of accounting is simple, for its use in England and Wales (or any country whose law in relation to these matters is based on English law) it should be viewed in the light of the comments in paragraphs 7–18 and 7–19 below.

Methods of payment

3–49 For many years after the introduction of factoring into the United Kingdom the usual method of payment (whether a prepayment or a payment on the maturity or collection date) was by cheque direct to the bank account of the client. In the early days most factoring companies calculated the discount charges from the dates of the cheques sent in payment to the client (not the dates when they were presented to the factor's bank) until the clearance of the debtors' cheques. As interest rates increased this question of the value dating of the cheques was of concern to the clients and prospective clients. As a result several of the factors changed their practice and began to allow for the value dating of the cheques sent in payment to the client in the calculation of the discount charge. Others overcame the problem to some extent by paying by telegraphic transfer to the client's bank; however, this was not

[43] *Ibid.*
[44] See para. 3–42 above.

entirely satisfactory owing to the cost of such method of transferring funds and the limit below which such method is not acceptable to the banks. At present practices vary[45] but many of the leading factors will now transfer funds electronically and ensure that their discount charge is calculated from the date of receipt of funds by the client. Telegraphic transfers are now used mainly for emergency transfers of funds and the cost is usually covered by a specific charge to the client.

[45] See para. 5–08 below.

Chapter 4

THE FACTOR'S RELATIONS WITH THE DEBTORS

4–01 In most circumstances there are no contractual relations between the factor and the debtors. The factor's rights to collect payment from the debtors derives purely from the purchase of the debts by the factor and their assignment to him. It would be possible for the factor to become a party to the client's contracts of sale with a debtor by means of a novation (an agreement among the client, the debtor and the factor) substituting the factor as a party in place of the client; but such an arrangement would be administratively impracticable because it would require the debtor's execution of the novation agreement in each case and the factor has no wish to become a party to the contracts of sale and thereby accept responsibilities as well as rights under them. Such considerations also influenced some early factors in changing from factoring arrangements by which, instead of buying the debts, the factor bought the goods (the subject of a sale by his client) from his client and resold them through the client as the factor's agent. In a few cases such an arrangement had been used to provide a commercial effect similar to factoring; by paying 80 per cent. of the price of the goods immediately to the client and allowing credit to the debtors, the factor relieved his client from the need to provide trade credit.[1]

4–02 The factor's rights, deriving from his purchase of the debts, and the debtor's countervailing rights are analysed in Chapter 9; this chapter deals with the usual procedures for the collection of payment of the assigned debts from the debtors in any case in which the factor has responsibility for this function (*i.e.* full, recourse or maturity factoring).[2] These procedures start in the client's office with the acceptance of orders and the production of the source documents (invoices and credit notes), continue in the factor's office with the sales accounting and collection and, if such collection procedures fail, may finally end in legal proceedings.

[1] For a case in which the transactions covered by such an agreement were held to be loans on security, see *Welsh Development Avency* v. *The Export Finance Company Ltd.* F.T.L.R. April 10, 1990.

[2] See paras. 1–34, 1–39 and 1–45 above respectively.

1. NORMAL COLLECTION PROCEDURES

The client's terms and conditions of sale

4–03 Provided that there is no agreement between the client and the debtor, whether in the contract of sale or otherwise, by which any debt arising from a contract of sale between the client and the debtor should not be assigned,[3] the factor obtains, by the assignment of the debts to him, the absolute right to be paid without the need for the consent of the debtor.[4] However, the factor obtains no rights better than those of the client under the contract of sale. The factor may collect only according to the agreed terms. Accordingly it is necessary for the factor to examine carefully his client's standard terms of sale, particularly as regards the due dates for payment and maximum settlement discounts to be allowed, and to be advised of any variations. It is normal for the factor to have stipulated in his factoring agreement the most liberal terms to be allowed by the client and for the right to approve any other terms; as a purchaser the factor should be able to determine precisely the rights that are to be assigned to him.

4–04 Many large buyers, such as mail order houses, department stores and government departments will purchase only on their own standard terms of purchase and it is essential that these should be examined in respect of customers existing at the outset of factoring and arising thereafter. Unfortunately where the buyer purchases on his standard terms and the seller (the factor's client) considers that the sale was on his own standard terms of sale it is not always an easy matter to determine whose terms prevail. This has been referred to as the "battle of the forms".[5] It must depend very much on the circumstances of the case. If the order is placed by the buyer on his terms and the seller acknowledges them on his own and if nothing more is said before the goods are delivered and accepted by the buyer, it is likely that in English law the seller's terms would prevail. The original order constituted an offer which was not accepted by the seller because he did not accept the terms in every particular (and this would apply even if the buyer's terms provided that they were to apply notwithstanding anything to the contrary in seller's terms)[6]; the seller's acknowledgement would be likely to be considered to be a counter-offer which had been accepted by the buyer by conduct. However, in many cases the events would not have followed this pattern and, ideally, the client

[3] For the effect of such a ban on assignments see paras. 9–30 and 9–31 below.

[4] See para. 7–06 below.

[5] *Butler Machine Tool Co. Ltd.* v. *Ex-Cell-O Corporation (England) Ltd.* [1979] 1 All E.R. 965, C.A.

[6] See Goode, *Commercial Law*, p. 96.

should obtain the customer's signed acknowledgement of his standard terms of sale before trading begins. It might well be possible for such a document to be included in any new customer's application for credit terms so that such terms would be granted only if the acknowledgement were to be signed.

The raising of source documents

4–05 At the outset, and during the currency of the factoring agreement on the opening of any new debtor account by the factor, it is essential that he should ascertain the exact legal name of the debtor (*i.e.* the name of the sole proprietor, partners or company where a trading name is used). Such information should be readily available to the factor's client; in accordance with the provisions of the Business Names Act 1985 the full names of the partners or individual owning the business and an address for the service of legal proceedings must be shown on most forms of business communication from the debtor and be exhibited at its principal place of business. Similar provisions apply to the registered name of any company and its registered office whether or not it is using a business name other than the name under which it is registered.[7] In view of the probable clog on recovery proceedings, which may be caused by the absence of the identity of the owner or owners of a debtor's business, factors should not accept as approved for credit or eligible for prepayment any debt in respect of which these details are not made available to him by the client. It is also important, not only from the point of view of the factor, but also for the client's benefit that the exact terms and conditions of any sale should be determined and that any invoice (and the copy sent to the factor) should accord with those terms. If meticulous attention is not paid to these matters aggravation may be caused to debtors by incorrect due dates on the factor's statements and requests for payment of items which are not due and this may result in damage to customer relations. Such errors may also result in delays in collection procedures and ultimately in a defence on the part of the debtor when proceedings for recovery are taken. The invoices (and the copies sent to the factor as notifications of the debts purchased by him) will bear a notice of the assignment of the debts to the factor and instructions to pay the factor direct. Such notices should be printed on the invoice forms or, in the case of computer produced invoices, printed by the computer. It has been the practice of some factors to arrange for the notices to be placed on the invoices by means of sticky labels but this procedure may lead to omissions.

[7] Companies Act 1985, ss.348, 349 and 351.

4–06 The client should also ensure that credit notes for agreed allowances and returned goods are promptly sent out to debtors and notified to the factor. It is also important that on any such credit note that relates to a specific invoice the invoice in question should be identified so that the credit note may be properly allocated by the factor on the open item system. If items that should be credited are left on the ledger, and thus on any statement sent to the debtor, payments may be delayed by queries from the debtor.

Collection from the debtors

4–07 The debtor, having been notified by the invoice (and in most cases by an introductory letter from the client) of the factor's ownership of the debts, will then expect to receive a statement and requests for payment from the factor. Having been notified the correct details of the dates and amounts of the invoice and their due dates for payment, the factor will include these details in the input to his computer. The resulting sales ledger accounts, kept on an open item system as described in Chapter 2, will produce clear statements listing the individual invoices and their due dates. It is advisable for the factor to include on each debtor statement a notice of assignment, not only as a reminder to the debtor, but also as some support for evidence of the debtor's receipt of notice. If the debtor denies receipt of notice, naturally the burden of proof of its actual receipt is on the factor and without an acknowledgement or, in the absence of its despatch by recorded delivery or by hand, evidence of the receipt of the invoice bearing a notice may not be a simple matter. The sending of such regular, prompt and correct statements is the foundation of the factor's procedures for the collection of payments by debtors; although some large concerns disregard statements and pay against invoices most business concerns still expect to receive a statement each month before making payments.

4–08 From the data taken from the copy invoices and the input of cash receipts and credit notes, lists of overdue accounts may be produced for the factor's staff from which they will be able to determine the next stage in the collection procedure. Such procedures, comprising several letters of increasing severity, are very often determined by agreement with the client at the outset and revised from time to time. Such agreement may cover the form of the letters and their timing and any special treatment to be given to particular customers. In this way it is possible to ensure that such procedures are not out of line with normal practices in the particular trade; and by this means the client may be able to influence to some extent the keeping of the funds in use (and consequently the discount charges) to a minimum without damaging customer relations. In the case of some larger buyers of goods and services the factor may have to follow up for payment for a number of clients; in such cases it may be that letters will not be effective and the client's staff may build up a relationship with the purchase ledger department of the buyer by telephone calls for payment of the supplies of several clients. By the creation of such relationship queries and disputes, which are often the cause of delays in payments, may be cleared up rapidly. Requests and demands for payment by telex very often have more effect than letters; telexes are often seen by senior executives who may not be aware or even countenance serious delays in payments.

4–09 Where, as is sometimes the case, standard letters are produced by the factor's computer at the prescribed number of days overdue it is advisable that hard copies should be kept in case it is necessary, in subsequent legal proceedings, to show exactly what demands have been made. At the minimum there should be a record of the text of the standard letter and evidence of the addressee and the date on which it was sent. For a similar reason careful notes should be kept of any telephone calls. The answer code should appear on the copy of any telex message and, in the case of any letter sent by facsimile, evidence of its transmission should be available; such evidence of transmission to the right debtor is particularly important if the letter includes a notice of the assignment.

4–10 It is well known that many debtors resent demands (or even polite requests) for payment after the date when payment is due. Such an attitude seems illogical particularly from buyers who would be more than a little upset if the seller was late in delivering the goods and would make their feelings known to the seller in blunt terms. The due date for payment of supplies is part of the contract terms and by paying late in breach of his obligations the buyer inflicts the damage of increased finance charges on the seller. As such feelings do in fact exist it is of the utmost importance that the factor's records show details of every invoice, correct in accordance with the contract of sale, so that no unjustified demands are made on the debtors. Such meticulous correctness must be founded on first class administration in the client's office as well as that of the factor and on close co-operation between the two. If any such unjustified demand is sent the reputation of both client and factor may suffer.

4–11 The delays in paying suppliers by large and powerful buyers has been the subject of much publicity in recent years and attempts have been made to introduce a statutory right of the seller to interest on overdue payments. However it seems that such legislation would be unlikely to be a remedy for the problem. The cost of credit to be granted to a customer must be reflected in the price of the goods sold; if the buyer has the bargaining power to delay payment without being met with a refusal of the supplier to supply further at the same price, then the buyer would have the power to reduce the price paid if he were to be obliged by statute to pay interest. Alternatively most buyers with such bargaining power would seek to contract out of the statutory obligation. A better influence on the payment habits of the customers, for a supplier with an acceptable product at an attractive price, is for the supplier to make it clear at the outset (*i.e.* when the order is taken) that supplies will continue only if payments are made promptly. In the case of such a supplier who is the client of a factor, the factor should be requested to remind the buyer's accounts payable department of this requirement at the earliest stage and that the client's invoices are to be given priority for payment.

The next steps

4–12 When persuasion, cajolery or threats have failed to produce payment, then it is quite usual for the client to be consulted. For administrative convenience the client may waive consultation and, except in relation to certain specified debtors, leave it to the factor to take legal proceedings in such circumstances. However, in many cases consultation with the client may serve to avoid legal proceedings and the mark of a good collection system is the ability to obtain payment without resort to solicitors. The client may assist recovery at this stage by:

(1) holding up delivery of further supplies; and/or
(2) adding his own persuasion to that of the factor.

4–13 Although the courts deprecate the use of petitions for the winding up of companies or for the bankruptcy of individuals for the purpose of debt collection, the threat of such a petition may often bring payment without the need for the factor to have recourse to legal proceedings. It seems reasonable that a creditor faced with persistent refusal to pay without reason on the part of a business of some substance should not remind the debtor of the creditor's rights in this respect. A petition for the winding up of a company may be founded on an inability to pay its debts[8] and it is deemed to be unable to pay its debts if it has neglected to pay or secure or compound to the reasonable satisfaction of the creditor a debt exceeding £750 for three weeks following the service at its

[8] Insolvency Act 1986, s.122(f).

registered office of a demand in the prescribed form.[9] Inability to pay debts may be based on other evidence[10] and it may well be that an unsatisfied demand for payment within a shorter period (especially if preceded by persistent reminders) may suffice for such evidence. In the case of an individual, who is domiciled and then present in England and Wales and has carried on business there within the previous three years, a petition for bankruptcy may be founded on the individual's inability to pay (or his having no reasonable prospect of paying) a liquidated debt of more than £750.[11] As in the case of a company, inability to pay may be based on the failure to pay or secure or compound within three weeks after the serving of a statutory demand.[12] In either case therefore the issue of a statutory demand may be used in suitable cases as pressure to bring about payment.

The use of bills of exchange to settle factored debts

4–14 In some trades it is normal practice for the credit granted by suppliers to their customers to be covered by bills of exchange drawn by the buyer and accepted by the debtor. Naturally if the bulk of the sales of a supplier of goods is to be sold on such terms, the supplier may be able to obtain the funds which he requires for the trade credit granted to customers by discounting the accepted bills and it is unlikely that he would use a factor for the other functions. However it is not uncommon for a factor's client to have some customers who will accept bills. The use of bills will largely avoid the time-consuming debt collection procedures outlined above and such convenience will outweigh the additional administrative tasks in the obtaining acceptance of the bills in the first place; if a bill is not met on first presentation, in the absence of a request by the debtor for an extension (normally by the replacement of the old bill by a new one with a later maturity), then more often than not it is a case for immediate legal proceedings to obtain payment.

4–15 According to the terms agreed between the client and the debtor the bill will be drawn either at invoice date or at the end of the month in which the invoice is raised. In factoring arrangements the bills are sometimes drawn by the factor who would then have the task of sending the bill to the debtor and procuring the debtor's acceptance of it; and the client may regard these tasks as being the

[9] *Ibid.* s.123(1)(a). The demand is known as a "statutory demand" and for its form and content see Insolvency Rules 1986 (S.I. 1986 No. 1925) r. 4.5.
[10] *Ibid.* s.123(1)(e).
[11] The amount may be changed by statutory instrument.
[12] Insolvency Act 1986, s.268(1)(a). For the form and content see Insolvency Rules 1986 (S.I. 1986 No. 1925) r. 6.1.

proper functions of the factor. However, in many cases the client himself draws the bill, obtains the debtor's acceptance of it and sends it to the factor duly endorsed in his favour. In some cases the factor will expect not to make a prepayment of the purchase price of a debt, arising from a contract of sale which provides for payment by a bill, until he has received the accepted bill endorsed in his favour; the factor, having taken the bill in good faith and for value, will then be a holder in due course[13] and protected against the debtor's defences and counterclaims of which he had no prior notice. If the client omits to endorse the bill the factor may do so on the client's behalf in accordance with a power of attorney which is usually given by the client in the factoring agreement.[14] However, although the factor may have arranged with his bankers to collect for him negotiable instruments made payable to the client without endorsement,[15] in the case of bills of exchange (other than sight drafts) it is as well for the factor to arrange for their endorsement in order that he may have the rights of a holder in due course.[16] For this reason many factors arrange for the endorsement of all cheques and sight drafts also if the insolvency of the client is pending; by becoming a holder in due course the factor expects to mitigate the impact of disputes and counterclaims of the debtors.

The practice of "self billing" by buyers

4–16 An increasing number of large buyers including most mail order houses and "catalogue" sellers have adopted a practice by which the seller's invoice is disregarded and payment is made on short terms on the basis of the buyer's own orders and records of goods received and accepted against the orders. The buyers raise their own internal document to take the place of a seller's invoice and their remittance advices, consequently, makes no reference to invoice numbers. Where there are a large number of relatively small transactions relating to consumer goods, rejections and deductions are not infrequent; then it is often almost impossible for the factor to reconcile the remittance advices to the debtor account based on his client's invoices. There have been attempts to overcome the difficulties by the use of notifications by the client to the factor of delivery notes or other documentation of which the

[13] Bills of Exchange Act 1882, s.29(1).
[14] See paras. 10–34 and 10–35 below.
[15] See para. 3–19 above. But see the *White Paper on Banking Services*, Cmnd. 1026 (1990) para. 5.6 in which it is proposed that, where the words "a/c payee" appear in the crossing of a cheque, the cheque should not be transferable.
[16] See n. 13 above.

reference numbers may be quoted by the buyer. However, it seems that no satisfactory solution has yet been found. Certainly the advantage of having a large debtor of satisfactory credit standing will be outweighed by the additional administrative burden incurred by the factor in dealing with this problem. Furthermore, in order to avoid the accumulation of a large number of unallocated deductions or disputed items on such an account, which in view of the short terms may be a high percentage of the outstanding balance, the factor should make arrangements whereby his client will promptly accept a charge back of the buyer's deductions and debit notes. If such accounts are included in invoice discounting or agency factoring it is advisable for the factor to monitor carefully the client's handling of the appropriation of payments, deductions and debit notes from the buyer.

A final step before legal proceedings

4–17 It is apparent that efficiency in the collection function, which is of benefit to both the factor and his client, depends on efficiency not only in the factor's office but also in the client's; unless the basis on which the sales ledger is constructed is correct and the terms are clearly agreed between the client and the debtor, even the most efficient factor may have difficulty in collecting. Inefficiency or negligence on the part of the client may also cause difficulties at a later stage. The failure of the debtor to pay may appear to the factor to be without reason but it may have nothing to do with dilatoriness or shortage of liquid resources; it may arise from a reason (either justifiable or not) known to a client which has not been communicated to the factor. For example, the debtor may have paid the client by reason of a prohibition of assignments in the contract of sale or because he had overlooked the assignment notice; or the debtor may not have accepted the goods. In such circumstances, if the client is negligent and has failed to inform the factor, legal proceedings (or a threat of them) may be a cause of much aggravation and unnecessary expense. In order that the position should be clarified it is often advisable, especially in the case of a large creditworthy debtor, to bring the matter to the notice of a senior official by telephone or telex or by a letter sent by facsimile for his attention. If the telephone is used the call should be confirmed by one of the other means. It may be that the accounts-payable department of the debtor had not thought it necessary in such circumstances to respond to the factor's pressing letters or calls and the management may be quite unaware that the company may be considered a slow payer. In many cases the unpleasantness of unnecessary proceedings has been avoided by these means.

2. MATTERS TO BE CONSIDERED BEFORE LEGAL PROCEEDINGS

Who may sue

4–18 In Chapter 7 arrangements for transferring the ownership of debts to the factor from the client, who creates them by the supply of goods or services, are described. It was there predicated that such debts were not normally transferred to the factor by assignments in statutory form[17] (normally referred to as legal assignments) but by assignments in equity only; and the reasons for this normal procedure are also explained there. However, although the absence of a legal assignment in no way detracts from the factor's rights of ownership there is a procedural difference when it comes to legal proceedings for the recovery of the assigned debts.[18]

4–19 In the case of a legal assignment completed by notice to the debtor the factor as assignee may sue in his own name alone[19] but where the assignment is valid in equity only, even when notice of that assignment has been received by the debtor, then the client as assignor and the factor as assignee should be joint plaintiffs. The purpose of the rule appears to have been founded on the requirement of the courts to have all three parties before them following the merging of the administration of the courts of equity and common law.[20] Such a requirement would certainly be necessary where only part of a debt has been assigned and that is possible in equity but not if the assignment is to be in accordance with the statute. Accordingly it has often been the practice for a factor who wishes to avoid the complication of joining his client in any proceedings for the recovery of debts to have the transfer of the ownership to him of the debts perfected by a legal assignment; in most factoring agreements the factor would have the right to such perfection and indeed to execute the form of assignment himself by virtue of a power of attorney in the agreement.[21] Often, however, a factor, having only an equitable assignment of a debt but of the *whole* of it, will take the proceedings in his own name alone relying on the rules of the court procedures by which no action should fail for want of a joinder.[22] This procedure may avoid the delay and the cost (including the possibility of the

[17] In accordance with the provisions of the Law of Property Act 1925, s.136; and see para. 7–05 below.
[18] See para. 7–06 below.
[19] Law of Property Act 1925, s.136 and see para. 7–05 below.
[20] See para. 7–04 below.
[21] See para. 10–34 below.
[22] R.S.C., Ord. 15, r. 6 and C.C.R., Ord. 15, r. 1.

incidence of stamp duty[23]) of the legal assignment; but the factor runs the risk that the case may be put back if the Court orders the client as assignor to be joined as a party to the proceedings.

Further steps before proceedings—identification of the debtor

4–20 By the time that solicitors have been instructed, whether the factoring is on a disclosed or undisclosed basis,[24] notice of the assignment of the debt will have been given to the debtor. If the assignment is to be perfected in statutory form a further notice will have to be given to complete that assignment. The advantage of early notice is that the notice fixes the rights of the three parties (particularly as regards the debtor's rights of set-off and counterclaim[25]) and prevents the debtor from discharging the debt by a subsequent payment to the client. In the case of disclosed factoring, where notice is carried on the invoice, for evidential purposes such notice should be confirmed as often as possible in subsequent communications to the debtor (*e.g.* on statements and requests for payment).

4–21 The full details of the case to be passed to the solicitor for the purpose of proceedings must include the amount of the debt, the invoice date and the date on which payment was due according to the contract of sale or service as well as the client's and the debtor's full legal name and address.[26] Where either of them is a company the registered office should be included. The use by a debtor of a trading name, as opposed to the name or names of the natural person or persons or the company owning the business, may cause problems and delays. If the trading name only is given then there may be an error in identifying the person to be sued with consequent delay and further aggravation. Furthermore, if the trading name only is the subject of the proceedings then on an attempt to execute on goods after judgment the debtor may avoid the execution by claiming that the goods are owned by a company. Accordingly, to avoid delays in establishing the correct legal name of the debtor, it is important that this should be established when the account is opened.[27] It is also advisable for the factor to check once again the details of the order, particularly as to the due date for payment and delivery, before instructing solicitors to avoid as far as possible any defence by the debtor in relation to these matters. It is also important that the factor should be aware that

[23] See paras. 7–07 *et seq.* below.
[24] See "Table of Factoring Variants" at end of Chap. 1.
[25] See para. 8–07 below.
[26] See para. 4–05 above.
[27] *Ibid.*

there are no trade customs or a course of dealing indicating that the credit to be allowed has not been exceeded.

4–22 Although there is no legal requirement for the solicitor to send a letter of demand before issuing proceedings there are several practical reasons why in many cases such a letter should be sent. In many cases a solicitor's letter, indicating to the debtor that the factor is serious regarding the threat of proceedings, will elicit payment from the debtor without the cost of such proceedings. Furthermore if proceedings result in immediate payment by the debtor the Court may refuse to award to the factor legal costs up to the prescribed amount if no such letter has been sent.

Payment by instalments

4–23 Sometimes in order to avoid legal proceedings, on receipt of a demand from the factor or the solicitor, the debtor may offer to pay by instalments. If the factor wishes to consider accepting such an offer he should carefully bear in mind the following:

(1) The agreement for instalments should always be in writing.
(2) The agreement should contain an admission and precise details of the debt to which it relates including the exact amount and references to the invoices by which the debt is represented. In some cases, particularly when there have been arguments regarding the amount of the debt or any counterclaim, it may be advisable to obtain the debtor's agreement to submit to judgment on an undertaking by the factor not to enforce it whilst the instalments continue to be paid promptly. Such a procedure will obviously avoid delay in enforcement if there is any breach of the instalment arrangements.
(3) It is important that the precise amount of the instalments, the intervals and the date of the first payment should be stipulated (for example: first payment on December 10, 1990, and thereafter on the 10th day of each subsequent calendar month).
(4) For the benefit of the client, where the discount charges are calculated until the collection date,[28] and otherwise for the benefit of the factor the agreement should provide for interest at a rate at least matching the discount charge.
(5) It is essential that the agreement for instalments should provide for the full unpaid amount to become immediately due and payable on any default by the debtor. Otherwise the factor may be left in a position of having to sue for each instalment as it becomes due.

[28] See paras. 3–34 *et seq.* above.

(6) If the debtor is a limited company then instalment arrangement should be guaranteed personally by the directors, shareholders or other interested third parties. If the debt is substantial, the possibility of taking a charge to secure it over assets of the company or any property of the guarantors should be considered. In the case of individuals or partnerships a charge on property should also be considered.

(7) Finally it is advisable to have the instalments represented by post-dated cheques or accepted bills of exchange. If the latter are taken and drawn by the client and endorsed in favour of the factor, the factor's position as a holder in due course may serve to avoid any further dispute being raised by the debtor.[29]

4–24 A statutory demand sent by the factor[30] may well bring about an offer of payment by instalments and in any case the three week period following the issue of the demand should be used for negotiations towards a settlement of the debt without resort to a petition for winding up (or bankruptcy in the case of an individual) or other proceedings.

Winding up or bankruptcy proceedings

4–24 If a statutory demand has been made on a company, or if a petition for winding up of a company or bankruptcy of an individual has been threatened and there are other grounds for showing that the company or individual is unable to pay its debts, then consideration should be given to whether or not to proceed with the petition. In any circumstances, if there has been an advertisement of another creditor's petition for the winding up or bankruptcy of a debtor who owes to the factor an overdue account, it is advisable for the factor to give notice of support[31] to the petition. In the absence of such notice, if the petitioning creditor's debt is settled, the factor will be left to start his own proceedings; but in the case of the factor's notice of support the debtor will have to settle with the factor as well as the petitioner in order to avoid the possibility of a winding up order or bankruptcy as the case may be. An acknowledgement of the notice of support should be obtained from the petitioner or his solicitor together with an undertaking not to agree to the dismissal of the petition without consulting the factor.

[29] See para. 4–14 above.
[30] See para. 4–13 above.
[31] Insolvency Rules 1986 (S.I. 1986 No. 1925) r. 4.16 and r. 6.23 respectively.

4–25 If on the petition for winding up or bankruptcy (as the case may be) or on giving notice of support to another's petition the debtor offers to settle the debt then the factor should also insist on his costs being paid in order to settle the matter. Furthermore there are advantages in arrangements for payment in settlement to be made by a third party (for example: a director of a corporate debtor). In the case of the factor's petition there may be supporting creditors or in the case of the factor's notice of support there may be still further supporting creditors; if settlement is not made with all of these the winding up or bankruptcy order may well be made. Now, where a company is being wound up by the court, any disposition of its property made after the date of the petition (the commencement of the winding up[32]) is void; similarly all such dispositions of a bankrupt's property after the date of the bankruptcy petition are void.[33] Consequently the liquidator or trustee in bankruptcy may claw back any such payment made by the debtor after the petition, notwithstanding that it was made for the purpose of avoiding winding up or bankruptcy respectively, if an order is made on the petition of the substituted supporting creditor. On the other hand it is doubtful if any payment by any third party in such circumstances could be rendered void.

3. LEGAL REMEDIES

Where to take proceedings

4–26 A winding-up or bankruptcy order will not bring about payment of the debt but only the factor's right to participate ultimately *pari passu* with other unsecured creditors. Therefore if all other efforts to obtain payment as described above have failed, and if the factor knows of no reason why the debt should not be paid, then the factor will have no alternative but to resort to legal proceedings for its recovery. Consideration must then be given as to the court in which proceedings should be taken. The County Courts have jurisdiction in respect of claims up to £5000 and in the High Court, which has jurisdiction over all cases without financial limit, proceedings are not normally commenced for claims under £600 because no recovery of legal costs may be made in such small cases. Accordingly the factor as an alternative forum in respect of proceedings to recover debts over £600 and not exceeding £5000. If a dispute is envisaged and the debt has not been the subject of recourse to the client then it may be advisable for the case to be started in the name of the client in the County Court in the district

[32] Insolvency Act 1986, s.129.
[33] *Ibid.* s.127 and s.284 respectively.

of which the client's business is located; proceedings for a disputed debt in the High Court might be the subject of considerable delay. However, in the case of undisputed debts it is usually considered advantageous for the factor to seek to obtain judgment in the High Court for the following reasons:

(1) The High Court is more used to dealing with commercial matters as opposed to claims against individuals in respect of goods purchased for personal or domestic use.
(2) In the County Court interest ceases to accrue once judgment has been obtained; in the case of a High Court judgment interest accrues until payment.
(3) Judgments in the County Courts are executed by bailiffs and those in the High Court by sheriffs who are, to some extent, paid by results, and tend to be more efficient.

However, there is now a procedure whereby a judgment for over £2000 may be transferred from the County Court to the High Court and, on the sealing of the judgment by the High Court, interest starts to accrue again and the creditor may use the services of a sheriff.

4–27 An acknowledgement of the High Court Writ or County Court summons may indicate that a defence is to be entered. If the factor believes that the defence is entirely without merit then he may be advised to proceed immediately for summary judgment.[34]

The enforcement of judgments

4–28 With an unsatisfied judgment, apart from proceedings for winding up or bankruptcy of the debtor, the factor has a number of choices open in order to enforce the judgment. The procedures open to him include the following:

(1) Execution may be levied on the debtor's goods by a writ *fieri facias* in the High Court or a warrant of execution in the County Court. If the debtor trades in more than one place, it may be advisable for the sheriff or bailiff to attend at more than one or all; in this way delays, in starting again after finding premises to be empty, may be avoided. If more than one sheriff or bailiff is instructed each must know of the other's taking part in the proceedings.
(2) As a judgment creditor the factor may obtain a garnishee order on a person (referred to as the garnishee) who is indebted to the debtor. The object of the order is an attachment of monies owed to the judgment debtor. An order nisi is made on the application to the court by the

[34] R.S.C., Ord. 14 and C.C.R., Ord. 9, r. 14.

judgment creditor (who can show that there is a sum owing by the garnishee to the debtor) and is served upon the garnishee; the order has the effect of restraining the garnishee from parting with any money owed to the debtor and orders his appearance in court on a given day (normally not less than eight days later). Unless the garnishee can show reason why he should not pay the attached debt to the judgment creditor the order will then be made absolute and the debt must be paid over to the judgment creditor. Such orders are often served on banks in respect of a credit balances on debtors' bank accounts but to be effective the account must be in credit when the order nisi is served. It is also possible for a factor to garnishee a debtor's own trade debtors if the factor is able to ascertain who they are and what they owe. Attempts have been made to garnishee factors who provided factoring services for debtors of other factors, but usually these attempts fail; either there is no availability on the debtor's account with the factor because the debtor has drawn up to the hilt or in some cases the debtor's factoring agreement provides that such an order is one of the events that gives the factor the right to withhold payments. There was even an attempt to garnishee a receiver of a company who, having discharged all the indebtedness to the secured creditor who appointed him, held funds of the company by reason of his realisations of its property. However in that case the receiver managed to arrange for a petition for the winding up of the company between the order nisi and the date of the hearing; no order absolute will be made in respect of a company in liquidation and the commencement of the winding up of a company by the court is the date of the petition.[35]

(3) The factor with a judgment against a debtor may apply to the court for a charging order on any real property of the debtor. In this way the factor will become a secured creditor. The application accompanied by an affidavit that certain property is owned by the debtor is lodged with the court which then makes an order nisi pending a hearing some weeks later. Then, on being satisfied with the facts of the case including evidence of the debtor's interests in the property, the court will make an order absolute. A statement in any document signed by the debtor (for example in a guarantee if he is a guarantor) of the debtor's interest in the property in which he resides would be useful evidence for this purpose. Any such charge should be registered.

[35] See para. 4–29 below.

4–29 The steps to be taken will naturally depend upon the factor's assessment of the property of the debtor available to satisfy the judgment but whichever route he chooses he should act quickly. The intervention of winding up or bankruptcy of the debtor may well forestall the factor's efforts at self-help. If another creditor of the debtor hears of the impending execution, attachment or charging order, feeling aggrieved that all creditors are not to be treated on a *pro rata* basis, he may take steps for winding up or bankruptcy. Any creditor who has issued execution against any goods or land of a company or has attached any debt due to it may not retain the benefit of the execution or attachment unless it is completed before the commencement of the winding up of the company or the court in its discretion orders otherwise.[36] In the case of a winding up by the court the commencement is the date of the petition[37]; in voluntary winding up the commencement is not until the member's resolution to wind up but, if the creditor has received notice of a meeting at which a resolution to wind the company up is proposed, the date on which he had notice is substituted for the commencement of winding up for this purpose.[38] For the purpose of these provisions the completion of the execution or attachment is as follows:

(1) in relation to goods, the seizure or sale or the making of a charging order;
(2) in relation to a debt, receipt of the debt; and
(3) in relation to land, seizure, the appointment of a receiver or the making of a charging order.

In most cases of the bankruptcy of an individual the factor, attempting to levy execution on or attach the property of the debtor, will be met by a similar bar to his recovery once a petition for bankruptcy has been presented. At any time while proceedings on the petition are pending the court may stay any action, execution or other legal process against the property of the debtor.[39]

Partnerships

4–30 Although in English law a partnership has no corporate existence the Insolvency Act 1986 has introduced provisions for the winding up of insolvent partnerships as if they were companies and

[36] Insolvency Act 1986, s.183.
[37] *Ibid.* s.129.
[38] *Ibid.* s.183(2)(a).
[39] *Ibid.* s.285(1).

these rules are discussed in Chapter 11.[40] Therefore the factor's rights in relation to execution of the property of a partnership must be viewed not only in relation to the partners as a collection of individuals but also in relation to the partnership as a whole in a case in which it is to be wound up as if it were a company.

4. INSOLVENCY OF THE DEBTOR

4–31 The effects of the most usual forms of insolvency on the rights of the parties with whom the insolvent company, partner or individual has contracted are described in Chapter 11. These forms are:

(1) administrative receivership of a company;
(2) an administration order in relation to a company;
(3) the winding up of a company or partnership by the Court;
(4) the voluntary winding up of a company;
(5) the bankruptcy of an individual or the partners of a partnership; and
(6) a voluntary arrangement in the case of a company or individual.

It will be noted from the discussions of these effects in Chapter 11 that the rights of a creditor to obtain payment are in all cases obstructed.

The appointment of an administrative receiver

4–32 If, as is usual, the charge under which an administrative receiver has been appointed covers all the property of the debtor company, the factor will be unable to enforce any judgment against it because all its property will be in the possession of the receiver. In such circumstances virtually the only remedy that is open to the factor is to petition for the winding up of the company. This course will not bring about any prospect of payment of the factor's debt nor, indeed, of an earlier distribution (*pro rata* with other unsecured non-preferential creditors) because any liquidator appointed by virtue of any winding up will be unable to take possession of the property of the company until the receiver has been discharged. However such a petition may be considered for the following purposes:

(1) to obtain early bad debt relief in respect of Value Added Tax in a case where the receiver is unable to give the requisite certificate for that purpose[41];

[40] See paras. 11–52 *et seq.* below.
[41] See para. 10–41 below.

(2) where it may seem possible for the charge to be avoided in the winding up of the company,[42] to enable a liquidator to investigate such a course of action; or
(3) where the directors have taken no steps to wind the company up voluntarily and the discharge of the receiver is impending, to ensure a *pro rata* distribution of assets available to unsecured creditors.

In any such circumstances careful consideration must be given to the position of the company because a winding up order may be prejudicial to the ultimate return to unsecured creditors by hampering the receiver's efforts to carry on the company's business and to sell the business as a going concern.[43] Since the enactment of the Insolvency Act 1986 and the provisions therein for an administrative receiver to consult with and provide information for unsecured creditors,[44] such decisions may be taken in the light of the best available information.

4–33 Unconnected with the question of recovery from a debtor company in receivership but related to it in time is the consideration by the factor of approving credit for a receiver who is carrying the business of the debtor company. In carrying on such a business a receiver will often require supplies from the source previously available to the company. Unless it is otherwise provided in the contract for the purchase of goods an administrative receiver is personally liable on it.[45] Accordingly if there is no exclusion of liability the factor may look to the standing of the receiver personally, as well as the availability of assets of the company to the receiver, in assessing the request for approval. If, as is now often the case, the receiver excludes personal liability the factor will be able to consider only the position of the business of the company in receivership.

Voluntary arrangements

4–34 The effect on creditors' rights of recovery under a voluntary arrangement will depend on the terms of the arrangement. When the arrangement becomes effective[46] the terms of it are binding on every person who had notice of and was entitled to attend the meeting of creditors at which the proposal was approved; and this would normally include the factor as a creditor. Such arrangements may provide for no immediate payment or payment by

[42] For example pursuant to the provisions of the Insolvency Act 1986, s.245 or as a transaction at an undervalue (see para. 11–51 below).
[43] See para. 11–25 below.
[44] ss.46–49 (incl.)
[45] Insolvency Act, s.44(1)(b).
[46] See para. 11–60 below.

instalments over a period or for payment of part only of each debt; but it is likely that all unsecured non-preferential creditors will be treated rateably. It is likely also that having been bound by the terms of the arrangement the factor would be unable to take any further proceedings for recovery whilst it remained in force; in any case on a report of the decision of the meeting by the supervisor[47] the court is likely to stay any winding-up proceedings which have already been commenced.

Administration orders

4–35 On and after the issue of a petition for the appointment of an administrator in relation to his debtor (until the dismissal of the petition or the coming to an end of the administration) a factor as an unsecured creditor will have no remedies available to him for recovery of his debt.[48] He will, however, be able to petition for the winding up of the company up to the time when an administration order is made; thereafter no winding-up order will be made.[49]

Winding up and bankruptcy

4–36 From the time of a petition for the winding up or bankruptcy of a debtor and, in most cases, following the notice of a meeting of creditors of a debtor company the factor will be unable to enforce any judgment.[50] After a winding-up or bankruptcy order in relation to his debtor the factor will be unable to start or continue any proceedings for the recovery of his debt.[51] In the case of a voluntary winding up the property of the company must be applied, after payment to preferential or any secured creditors, to a *pari passu* distribution to unsecured creditors[52]; furthermore following notice of the meeting no execution or attachment may be enforced.[53] Therefore the factor will have no further remedy available to him except to petition for winding up by the court; such action may be taken if the factor is dissatisfied with the prospective conduct of the voluntary winding up. However, the court is likely to take into account the views of all unsecured creditors, who appear at the hearing, in coming to a decision whether to make an order or to let the voluntary winding up continue.

[47] *Ibid.*
[48] See para. 11–27 below.
[49] See para. 11–28 below.
[50] See para. 4–29 above.
[51] See paras. 11–36 and 11–44 respectively.
[52] Insolvency Act 1986, s.107.
[53] See para. 4–29 above.

5. RECOVERY FROM GUARANTORS

4–37 If a debt owing to a factor is guaranteed by a third party, such as a director of a debtor company, amounts recovered from the guarantor do not have to be deducted from the factor's proof of debt in the bankruptcy or winding up of the principal debtor until the position has been reached that by reason of payments from the guarantor and dividends from the insolvent estate the factor has received payment in full.[54] The reason for this is that, until the guarantor has paid the guaranteed debt in full, he has no right to be subrogated to the factor's right to prove in the estate of the principal debtor and there can, therefore, be no double proof for the same debt. For this reason it is important that when taking a limited guarantee the factor should ensure that the form of guarantee covers the *whole* debt (subject to a limitation of liability on the part of the guarantor) rather than *part of the debt.* In the latter case the guarantor would be subrogated to the right to prove on payment of the whole of the part guaranteed and this would result in the inability of the factor to maintain his proof for that part.

4–38 In the event of the bankruptcy or winding up of a guarantor the factor will be able to submit proof in the estate of the guarantor for the amount of the debt as reduced by any payment made by either the guarantor or the principal debtor *before* the submission of that proof; but he will not be required to reduce his proof in respect of sums received from the principal debtor afterwards.[55] In the event of the bankruptcy or winding up of both principal debtor and guarantor the factor will be able to maintain his proof for the full amount, notwithstanding any dividend from either. Naturally, the factor will be unable to maintain any proof in either of the foregoing situations once he has received 100 pence in the pound. As a result of these rules it is as well for the factor to get his proof in to the insolvent estate of a guarantor at the earliest possible stage in his recovery proceedings.

6. A RECENT DEVELOPMENT

4–39 In recent years there has been a tendency for some large buyers of goods and services to require that their suppliers should send invoice data electronically for entry in the buyers purchase ledger

[54] *Re Sass* [1896] 2 Q.B. 12 and see also Goode, *Legal Problems of Credit and Security* (2nd. ed.), pp. 196 *et seq*.
[55] *Re Amalgamated Investment & Property Co. Ltd.* [1985] 1 Ch. 349 and see Goode, *op. cit.*, p. 204.

records without any hard copy invoice. This poses two problems for the factor. First, the factor's client on whom this system has been imposed will be expected to accept electronic input to his records instead of the usual copy invoices and credit notes for notifications or offers of debts. Such a system should pose no problem as regards the assignments which are almost invariably equitable[56] but postulates a high degree of trust on the part of the factor.

4–40 Secondly, the factor will have a problem of ensuring that the notices of assignment will be conveyed to the buyers; it is unlikely that the buyer's system would provide for the notice to be received and recorded. Some factors have considered reliance on introductory letters[57]; but it is likely that such letters are not effective as notices except for debts in existence at the dates of the letters.[58]

[56] See para. 7-06 below.
[57] See paras. 8-08 *et seq.* below.
[58] *Ibid.*

CHAPTER 5

MUTUAL REVIEWS: THE FACTOR AND THE CLIENT (AND THE ROLE OF THE PROFESSIONAL ADVISER)

5–01 The use of factoring, the relations between the factor and his client and the operational procedures have been described in previous chapters; the legal relations between the parties are described in the second part of this book. This chapter discusses the considerations to be taken into account by the factor and the client before entering into an agreement. In reviewing any proposal for factoring the prospective client's professional advisers, accountants and solicitors, have an important role. It has been said that factoring is like a marriage whereas other forms of business finance, such as leasing or hire purchase, are more like flirtations. A business is likely to have only one factor and the relationship should last a long time; it may have several leasing or hire-purchase agreements in place at the same time. Accordingly, great care must be taken by both parties before a decision is made to enter into the agreement; the wrong decision made in haste may be the cause of some of the difficulties described in Chapter 2.

1. THE PROSPECTIVE CLIENT'S ASSESSMENT

Businesses seeking additional finance

5–02 First, it is important that a business that is looking solely for additional finance should look critically at its own financial position with the independent advice of a professional accountant to ensure that the finance generated by a factoring arrangement will be a suitable answer. It is important that such finance should not be used for capital expenditure; it should be used to provide the additional working capital required for any increase in trading generated by additional capital expenditure.[1] If the business is unprofitable or heading for insolvency, factoring will be unlikely to assist; in most such cases it will merely postpone the final failure

[1] See para. 2–06 above.

whilst assets available for creditors are further dissipated.[2] Only if there are good prospects for the business to return to profitable trading within a short period will factoring be of assistance. In order to ensure the positive use of the finance to be provided by a factoring arrangement, cash flow forecasts and extrapolations of revenue accounts should be prepared comparing the likely position over the next one to three years with and without the assistance of a factor. Then before considering the use of factoring it should be seen that the business will be profitable, with a positive cash flow, after absorbing the costs of the factoring arrangements.[3] In an ideal situation the funds provided would enable the factor's client to achieve an increase in sales volume and thus reduce unit costs. Furthermore in making projections of cash flow and profitability it should not be assumed that the maximum allowable prepayments should always be drawn. The most successful use of factoring has rarely been based on using funds to the full at all times; reliance on such full use may be a cause of some difficulty if planned sales are not achieved or if a substantial debt does not rank as eligible for the prepayment of a part of its purchase price.

The factor's other functions

5–03 A business with adequate credit insurance or a pattern of debtor portfolio that makes it self-insuring may not require the credit protection afforded by full or maturity factoring[4]; and if it is efficient in sales accounting and credit control then it may not require to hand these functions over to a factor. In such a case invoice discounting or agency factoring[5] will provide the finance which it is seeking from factoring. However, in many cases it is likely that one of the other variants of factoring may be more beneficial by relieving the client from the bad debts and the administrative functions. Examples of such use of factoring (for example by a business exploiting new products or markets which may result in unfamiliar risks[6]) are described in Chapter 2. If the factoring is to be used to finance rapid growth it is as well for the prospective client to consider a form of non-recourse factoring[7] or to use credit insurance in conjunction with invoice discounting or recourse or agency factoring. In this way the danger of a setback to

[2] See para. 2–05 above.
[3] See para. 3–28 above.
[4] See paras. 1–34 and 1–45 respectively above.
[5] See paras. 1–43 and 1–41 respectively above.
[6] See para. 2–31 above.
[7] See "Table of Factoring Variants" at end of Chap. 1.

the plans for expansion, or even financial difficulty, by reason of a substantial bad debt may be avoided.[8]

5–04 The use of factoring otherwise than for the provision of finance is not often considered, particularly by professional advisers. However, there are many cases in which it may be fully justified and beneficial; neither the prospective user nor the adviser should be deterred from considering such use only on account of the general view that factoring is just another means of "raising the wind." Such considerations should particularly apply in the case of small businesses which need protection against bad debts; businesses with sales volumes of less than several million are often not attractive to credit insurers and their terms may not compete with those of a factor when due allowance has been made for the factor's relieving the business from administrative tasks.[9] The handing over to a factor of the functions of sales accounting and collection from customers and the acceptance by the factor of bad debts has been proved to be of economic benefit by the examples of many businesses which, having accepted full factoring for the finance provided, continued to retain it when they no longer required the finance. All these considerations should be taken into account in choosing the right variant.

Choice of factor

5–05 Having decided on the type of factoring that will meet his needs, a prospective client will then have a choice of factoring companies. Although there are a number of good factoring companies offering their services throughout the United Kingdom, surprisingly many prospective users enter into agreements after negotiations with one only. In some cases this failure to look further afield arises from the recommendation by a bank to its customer that a factoring company owned by the bank should be used; in such a case the customer may believe that his relations with the bank may be impaired if he looks elsewhere. However, even if ultimately the bank's own factoring company is to be used, it is advisable for the prospective user to check the terms offered by at least one other factor and its method of operation to ensure that what is offered is as suitable as can be obtained elsewhere. The apparent terms offered by factoring companies for the same business vary widely; and, more significantly, even if the apparent terms are identical the resulting cost may vary owing to differing methods of calculation of the charges and, in some cases, the addition of other charges.

[8] See para. 2–13 above.
[9] *e.g.* as described in para. 2–34 above.

5–06 In most circumstances the prospective client should select two or three likely factoring companies and investigate their terms, method of operation and the provisions of their agreement in detail. The proposed arrangement will be likely to include the whole of the sales of the business and consequently its cash flow; accordingly a great deal of care in the selection will not be out of place. At an early stage a specimen of each factor's standard contract should be obtained. Many businesses which are seeking a factoring service leave this consideration until they have made up their minds which factor to use; they may then pass the standard form to their solicitors for a review almost as a formality. This is a mistake; factoring agreements vary widely and at that late stage it may be difficult to procure an amendment to a standard document. If, however, the factor is aware that there are still competitors in the field the amendment of a provision, unacceptable to the prospective client, may be more readily forthcoming. In particular the matters mentioned in the succeeding paragraphs *together with the normal operational procedures* should be carefully examined. The operational procedures may often be considered at a visit to the factor's offices; most reputable factors are prepared to show a prospective client their systems at first hand and, if required, to refer the prospective client to an existing client for an impartial view of the effect of that particular factor's methods of operation.

The factor's charges[10]

5–07 Many businesses, which have adopted factoring in the past, have, even with the guidance of their professional advisers, chosen purely on the basis of the apparent cost of the administration charge as a percentage of turnover and the finance charge as a percentage of funds used. The choice is not so simple. It is necessary to look at the basis of the calculation of the charges. For example, some factors, in providing recourse factoring, make an additional charge in respect of any debt which remains unpaid a specific number of days after due date. This is sometimes referred to as a refactoring charge[11] and it is often not taken into account by the client in assessing the cost. There are often cases, especially for small businesses, where a minimum annual administration charge[12] is pitched at a level which, when compared with the achieved sales volume, will make the arrangement quite uneconomic for the business in question. However, in view of the unbounded optimism of most small businesses such a minimum charge may have been compared at the outset with a sales level quite unlikely to be

[10] See also paras. 3–28 *et seq.* above.
[11] See para. 3–33 above.
[12] *Ibid.*

achieved. It is here that the professional adviser should counsel caution.

5–08 The method of calculation of finance charges[13] varies considerably. Whether the basis of ultimate payment by the factor for debts purchased is when collection is made from the debtors or on a fixed maturity date, it is important that it should be made clear to the prospective client when the finance charge will start to run. Some factors have started the calculation of the finance charge on the date on which a cheque is sent to the client; as it is natural for the factor to allow several days for clearance of cheques received before the finance charge ceases to run, the result is that the client is charged for a period during which he has no use of the funds. This may be the case even where ultimate payment of the purchase price is on a maturity date, because the factor will normally have the right to charge his finance charges for the extra days beyond the maturity date taken on average by the debtors and, in making this calculation, the maturity date will be extended by a period for the clearance of cheques. The best practice, now very often followed, is for cheques sent by the factor to be value dated for clearance, in the same way as cheques received, or for funds to be transferred electronically so that the client does not start paying a finance charge until cleared funds are at his disposal. Where finance charges are levied on the extra days a comparison solely of the percentage charge may be entirely misleading.

5–09 The simple percentage of the administration charge may also not give a correct estimate of the cost; it is necessary for the prospective client to know which of the administrative functions are to be accepted by the factor for that charge and which are to be charged for separately. Nobody would decide on the purchase of a motor car, for example, by simply comparing prices and not quality and performance or, in particular, which of the accessories are optional extras and have to be paid for separately. However, many business people have chosen a factor simply on price; not only have they not considered the basis of calculation of the charges, but also they have not taken into account (for example) that, whilst most factors which provide non-recourse factoring will absorb debt collection costs on approved debts, in recourse factoring such costs are normally an additional charge to the client.

The factor's right to variations

5–10 The original basis of the factoring arrangement may on the face of it seem attractive, but a close examination of the standard factoring agreement may disclose that the factor has the right in

[13] See paras. 3–34 *et seq.* above.

certain circumstances, or even at his entire discretion, to alter certain elements in the arrangement. These elements may include the percentage of prepayments and, in the case of final payment on a maturity date, the maturity period. In both cases if alterations are made during the course of the agreement to the detriment of the client, then the main reason for which he may have entered into the agreement, a guaranteed cash flow, may be impaired. Some factors even take the right to alter, at their entire discretion, the administration and discount charge during the currency of an agreement.

Arrangements for termination

5–11 In Chapter 2 above it was suggested that the reluctance of some people in business to use factoring was based on their experience that, once a business had adopted it, there might be some difficulty in terminating the arrangement when it was no longer required. It was pointed out that these experiences were probably based on the use of the wrong variant of the service or the use of the service in the wrong circumstances. In all circumstances, however, it is most important at the outset for the prospective user to find out exactly what arrangements may be made for termination. It has been known for a factor to provide for a long period of notice (up to six months or more) by the client if he wishes to terminate. If such a period of notice is stipulated and provision is made for no prepayments during that period, then obviously the client may have some difficulty in arranging for termination; to obtain a replacement of the finance provided from a bank or another factor the debts must be freed immediately from the existing agreement by which they are bound. A reputable factoring company, which is confident in the excellence of its service should not need to incorporate into its factoring agreement draconian provisions for termination in the absence of insolvency or a serious breach of the agreement on the client's part; such a factoring company will be confident that the client will not wish to cease using his services merely to seek another similar arrangement.

Method of dealing with credit approvals

5–12 If protection against bad debts is sought by the prospective client or it is considered advisable as a precaution against overtrading, the factor's method of providing this protection should be examined. A comparison with usual credit insurance practice as regards this aspect will be instructive. For example, many factors follow credit insurance practice in providing that cancellation of a credit limit will not affect deliveries already made by the client, even if a copy of the relevant invoice has not yet been received by the factor at the time of the cancellation. On the other hand, in some factoring contracts, the factor takes the absolute right to refuse to purchase any debt until such time as the copy invoice has been received and accepted. In such circumstances, the client may have made a delivery of goods in the knowledge that it is within an approval given by the factor, but may be faced with a refusal by the factor to accept the debt on the subsequent submission of the copy invoice. The method of division of any recoveries after the insolvency of the debtor is also a matter which should be considered; although most factors take the right to appropriate payments by solvent debtors to debts approved for credit in priority to those that are not approved, once the debtor is in liquidation or bankruptcy, dividends and other recoveries should be shared rateably.

Disputed accounts

5–13 A factor cannot take responsibility for dealing with disputes with and rejections by the client's customers, whether they arise from the goods or services themselves or from the invoices or the terms of the contract of sale or service. A factor will have the right of recourse to the client in respect of any debt which cannot be collected for such reasons. Such a right of recourse postulates the obligation of the client to repurchase the debt; the prospective client and his adviser should ensure that the factor will allow adequate time for such difficulties to be settled by the client before such right of recourse is exercised. Some factors now take the view that, even if a dispute is not settled within a reasonable time, recourse should not be exercised but that the factor should await settlement of the debt by payment or the issue of a credit note or a combination of both. If the factor adopts this course he may protect himself by stipulating that, at the time when the factor had the right to exercise recourse, the disputed debt becomes unapproved, even if it has previously been approved, so that it is no longer eligible for credit protection or prepayment. The advantage of this system is that it avoids the need to tell the debtor that the debt has been reassigned; some large buyers from factored suppliers have objected to the position arising whereby certain invoices are to be settled direct to the supplier whilst most others are to be paid to the factor.[14]

[14] See para. 3–23 above.

Guarantees and indemnities

5–14 Not infrequently when a factor is requested to provide his services, including prepayments, for a company in a group, he may require guarantees and indemnities from other group companies; and in the case of an independent company he may require them from directors or shareholders in a personal capacity. The main purpose of such requirements is to provide for the factor to be reimbursed in the event that, on the insolvency of the client company, he is unable to recover from the debtors the prepayments which he has made. Many such guarantees and indemnities are very widely drawn and would even cover the factor against inability to recover if his loss arises from the failure of the debts to vest in him owing to a defect in his documentation. On the other hand, a usual practice now is for the factor to be satisfied with an indemnity covering losses arising only from breaches of the factoring agreement by the client company. Such losses, for example, might be occasioned by the banking by the client company in its own bank account of debtors' cheques, purportedly in settlement of debts purchased by the factor, or from the failure of the client to deliver to the debtor goods which conform to the details on the copy invoice notified to the factor. The rationale of the requirement for such a restricted form of indemnity is that the events, which may give rise to the factor's losses and are covered by the indemnity, are within the control of those who manage the business of the client company; they are naturally quite outside the control of the factor. However, if a wider form of indemnity is expected then the prospective guarantor or indemnifier may well consider if he is prepared to be responsible for the factor's losses arising from:

(1) the failure of the debts to vest in the factor owing to a defect in the factoring agreement;
(2) a claim to the debts by a receiver owing to the failure of the factor to have obtained a waiver from a bank holding a charge on the debts[15]; or
(3) the insolvency of any debtor.

In the case of any form of non-recourse factoring it is apparent that (3) should be excluded; the whole object of a non-recourse arrangement is for the factor to accept the credit risks in respect of approved debts and, in respect of unapproved, he should avoid loss by declining to make any prepayment. Even in the case of factoring with full recourse to the client it is arguable that in some circumstances the factor, being an expert in matters of trade credit

[15] See paras. 8–44 *et seq.* below.

should be in a better position than the guarantor to protect himself.

2. THE CLIENT'S AUDITOR

5–15 All the considerations mentioned above in this chapter should be taken into account by a professional adviser to a prospective user of factoring. The standard documentation should be reviewed at an early stage and the actual operational procedures and accounting arrangements should be seen at first hand. If the person advising a prospective client is also the auditor, an examination of the factor's accounting procedures at this stage may well be a help later on when the audit of the client's annual accounts is to be undertaken. Most factors are quite willing to demonstrate to professional accountants the factoring systems, the returns made to clients and the accounting procedures. The auditor may then be able to assess whether the systems, returns and accounts will be satisfactory to him as an auditor.

The accounting conventions

5–16 Present factoring practice postulates the transfer of the ownership of the debts to the factor whichever variant of the service is used. As a result, in accordance with the accounting conventions, as they are at present,[16] those debts appear in the balance sheet of the factor and not that of the client. There appears as a debt, in the balance sheet of the client, the unpaid balance of the purchase price of the debts purchased by the factor; this is the amount of the purchase price of the outstanding debts (*i.e.* the amounts payable by the debtors less the factor's charges) less the amounts already paid on account of the purchase price by way of prepayment. This balance remains as a debt owing to the client subject to the factor's rights of retention and set-off. The auditor must satisfy himself as to the extent that the debt is recoverable; and the role of the auditor of the client in relation to the debts factored is to assess whether sufficient provisions have been made in the accounts of the client to provide for a diminution of the factor's debt to the client by reason of set-off for the recourse of uncollectable debts. Such recourse may arise in the case of factoring on a recourse

[16] *I.e.* before the implementation of any proposals based on the Exposure Drafts of the former Accounting Standards Committee relating to this type of "off balance sheet financing" as referred to below.

basis[17] if the failure to collect arises from any reason; in the case of non-recourse arrangements[18] it may arise, in respect of an unapproved debt, from the insolvency of the debtor or, in respect of any debt, from the rejection by the debtor of the goods or the invoice. Where the factor is to take over the functions of sales accounting and collection as in full, maturity or recourse factoring,[19] most factors provide full and clear returns to the client and, as these will normally include an analysis of debtor balances by age and details of disputed items, the auditor may be able to make his assessment of the potential recourse on the basis of such returns as at the balance sheet date. Where agency or undisclosed factoring or invoice discounting is used, the client keeps the sales ledger and collects as the factor's agent and, consequently, the auditor's duty may extend to the sales ledger itself although the debts represented by it are the property of the factor; only by extending his duty to the sales ledger in such case may the auditor be able to satisfy himself as to the likely recourse to be set off against the factor's debt to the client.

5–17 The accounting conventions, by which the ownership by the factor of the debts the subject of a factoring agreement are recognised in the accounts of the factor and his client, have been challenged in the case of any form of factoring which provides for recourse to the client of all debts at a specified time. Such provisions are normal in recourse factoring, agency factoring and invoice discounting.[20] The challenge is based on the premise that, as the factor in such cases is looking ultimately to the client for the funds which he has laid out in purchase of the debts, the substance of the arrangement (in order to show a true and fair view in the balance sheets of factor and client) requires that the debts should remain in the balance sheet of the client and should not be shown in that of the factor.[21] Such a treatment is entirely at variance with the true legal and factual position and, for that reason, has been vigorously opposed by some in the factoring industry. However the treatment of items in accounts otherwise than in accordance with the strict legal position as to ownership is not unusual; major examples of such treatment are:

(1) the inclusion in the balance sheets of purchasers of goods on terms by which title to the goods has remained with the supplier at the date of the balance sheet; and
(2) the treatment of equipment the subject of finance leases.

[17] See "Table of Factoring Variants" at end of Chap. 1.
[18] *Ibid.*
[19] See Chap. 1.
[20] See paras. 1–39, 1–41 and 1–43 respectively above.
[21] See, for example, Exposure Draft (ED 42) of the former Accounting Standards Committee.

At least one factoring company which provides predominately recourse factoring has in recent years shown as a current asset in its balance sheet, not the purchased debts, but the amount of unrecovered prepayments on account of the purchase price of those debts.

5–18 A more recent publication by the former Accounting Standards Committee[22] takes an entirely different line. In that publication it is predicated that the absence of recourse is not relevant to the treatment of the debts in the client's balance sheet; it is argued there that a non-recourse arrangement is the equivalent to credit insurance, the adoption of which would not affect the treatment of the debts in the balance sheet of the insured. Instead it is suggested that the principal matter to be considered is whether or not the discount charge (and thus the purchase price of the debts) may be determined at the date of their transfer to the factor; only if the purchase price can be determined then, should the debts be treated as the property of the factor. Otherwise the debts should be shown in the balance sheet of the client, notwithstanding their having been sold to the factor, and the part payments of the purchase price of those debts made before balance sheet date should be shown as a liability.[23] As virtually all factors calculate their discount charges up to the date of payment of each debt, the adoption of this proposal would mean a change in the accounting conventions in relation to nearly all businesses using factoring. The earlier proposal[24] seemed to look more closely at the substance of the transactions; it looked at the source from which the factor was ultimately to recover the funds which he had laid out in the purchase of the debts. Furthermore those proposals are in line with the treatment accorded to factoring in other countries, particularly in Germany. However, the latest proposals seem to be based on false premises. First, the outright purchase of a debt, although superficially appearing to provide a protection equivalent to credit insurance, may be distinguished from it; in credit insurance the insured cannot be absolutely certain of his protection until he has shown that he has made reasonable efforts to collect the debt which is the subject of the claim and the insurer is in a position analogous to a surety. In non-recourse factoring, on the other hand, by the purchase of the debt the factor has become the principal debtor to the client and he alone is responsible for collection. The adjustment of the purchase price at a time after the ownership of the debts has been transferred would not appear to be relevant to the nature of the transaction; there are many

[22] "Proposed Statement of Accounting Practice—Reflecting the substance of transactions in assets and liabilities" (May 1990 ED 49).
[23] *Ibid.* para. C.16.
[24] See para. 5–17 above.

examples in commerce of such later adjustments and these do not appear to have affected the treatment of the transaction in the balance sheets of the purchasers. A common example of such an adjustment is the giving by a seller of quantity discounts related to the volume of goods purchased over a period which may not have ended until after the balance sheet date and thus cannot then be determined. Furthermore the publication seems to have based its proposal on examples of factoring practice which are by no means typical among the leading factoring companies.

3. THE FACTOR'S ASSESSMENT OF THE PROSPECTIVE CLIENT

5–19 Some of the mischief caused by the use of factoring for an unsuitable business or at the wrong time was described in Chapter 2; in Chapters 3 and 4 it was demonstrated that a successful factoring operation depends not only on the efficiency of the factor but also on that of the client's own office administration. It is therefore important for the factor to make a thorough review of every prospective client's business before offering any variant of factoring. If the factor does not, he runs the risk that the arrangement will not be successful; and the blame for the unsuccessful outcome will probably be laid at the door of the factor's own operations (which may be impeccable) or even of "factoring" in general. For the purpose of such a review it is normal for a first exploratory discussion to take place between a new business executive of the factor and an executive director or principal of the prospective client.

The survey

5–20 If, as a result of such a meeting, a prima facie case can be made out on both sides for the proposed factoring arrangement then the factor will normally expect to carry out an investigation of the prospective client's business; this is referred to as a "survey." Apart from determining the suitability of factoring in the particular case the purposes of the survey, combined with the initial and any other meetings, are as follows:

(1) to assess the quality of the debtors and thus the likely risks of the failure by the factor to collect in the purchased debts and, in the case of non-recourse factoring, to determine how much to include in the factor's charges for this risk in relation to approved debts;

(2) to assess the administrative function to be taken over by the factor and how much the factor should charge for this element;
(3) to assess the strength of the client's business and the prospect of its profitable operation whilst the factoring arrangements are in place;
(4) to ensure that the factor will obtain ownership of the debts purported to be sold to him free from any charge or other encumbrance or claim by any third party[25]; and
(5) to determine the extent to which the factor's ability to collect the debts purchased by him will be frustrated by disputes, returns and allowances and other cross-claims by debtors.

The best practice is for terms to be quoted only after the survey has been carried out because, even if there is a clear indication of suitability on both sides, suitable terms can be arrived at only after an in depth study of the nature and pattern of the prospective client's business. Unfortunately severe competition and pressure on management to produce fast growth in recent years appear to have reduced the survey to something of a formality for some factoring companies who have consequently entered into agreements with unsuitable businesses or at the wrong time; the result has been some of the unhappy events described in Chapter 2. The matters to be studied are described in the succeeding paragraphs of this chapter. Some of them may be considered at the initial meeting or on the survey or at other times before an offer is made; the timing depends on the factoring company's own organisation and new business strategy.

Independent enquiries

5–21 Naturally the factor will make the normal independent enquiries regarding a prospective client. In relation to a company such enquiries have in the past included a search at the companies' registry regarding the capital and constitution of the company, its shareholders and officers and any charges on its property. The question of whether this practice as regards charges should continue following the coming into force of the provisions of the Companies Act 1989 relating to the abolition of "deemed notice"[26] is discussed in Chapter 8.[27] In all cases the factor is likely to obtain status reports on the prospective client and, in the case of a newly established business, to make extensive enquiries regarding the

[25] The encumbrances most often met are described and their effect is analysed in Chap. 8.
[26] By the insertion into Companies Act 1985 of new ss.416 and 711(A).
[27] Para. 8–12.

previous business activities of the directors and shareholders or principals. The examination of financial accounts of the past few years and up-to-date management accounts will assist the factor in assessing the financial strength and future prospects of the business.

The product

5–22 Possibly the most important condition for a successful factoring operation is that the client's product should be acceptable to its customers, in good demand and of such a nature that there will be little (or ideally nothing) in the way of post-invoice contractual obligations on the part of the client. The nature and acceptability of the product will affect, not only the degree to which the factor will be faced with credits and allowances granted to the debtors by the client and claims for set-off and abatement by the debtors,[28] but also the credit risk as regards the debtors. There is little doubt that debtors will pay more promptly for goods that are essential to their businesses and cannot be obtained elsewhere than for goods or services which are widely available; furthermore, a supplier with a product which is competitively priced and in good demand should be able to command customers of good quality. Where the business of the client is more than usually liable to disputes or is liable to substantial contractual obligations after the delivery of the goods,[29] payments by debtors may well be delayed pending testing of the product or completion of the further obligations. Any such delays in payment will increase the credit risk.

5–23 In Chapter 2 there are described the difficulties that may result both for the factor and the client from the provision of factoring to certain types of business. It is not possible to list the types of business that are suitable and those that are unsuitable because even within the same trade or industry there are considerable variations of practice. There are also many areas in between complete suitability and unsuitability and, although of prime importance, the product is not the only matter to be taken into account. There are however two important principles to be considered:

(1) the nearer the product is to being simple and repetitive without any post-invoice contractual obligations, the more likely is the factor to be able to avoid disputes and cross-claims; and
(2) the greater the competition in the trade or industry the more likely is the factor to be faced with poor credit risks.

[28] The effect of such claims on the ability of the factor to collect is analysed in Chap. 9.
[29] See paras. 2–25 *et seq.* above.

As regards the first of these principles, many factors in the United Kingdom and Europe have disparaged their counterparts in the United States for not developing factoring widely outside the traditional industries: textiles, clothing, footwear, toys and similar consumer goods. However, that may be the result of long experience and there is little doubt that some outside the United States have become overconfident as regards the suitability of certain types of business; there have certainly been examples of factors' inability to collect from debtors on the insolvency of their clients solely by reason of the type of product or service provided by the client.

5–24 A particular difficulty has been experienced where the client's business includes the sale of products made from special tooling (or moulds) produced and retained by the client. In some cases the client will recover the cost of the special tooling by including an element to cover it in the price of the products and in such a case the tooling will probably remain the property of the client and there will be no problem as regards the factoring arrangements. However, in most cases the tooling is invoiced separately and becomes the property of the debtor. If the debt for the mould or tooling is accepted by the factor then it is advisable that no payment on account of the purchase price of that debt should be made until some of the products have been accepted by the debtor. Even when the mould or tooling has been paid for by the debtor difficulties may be met on the insolvency of the client if other debts are then owing by the debtor: the debtor may well decline to pay unless the tooling is delivered to him and the person charged with the administration of the client's insolvent estate may decline to release it. It is likely that the debtor would have no right in the liquidation or bankruptcy of the client to set off his claim to the tooling against a debt for goods sold and delivered to him[30] but the debtor may not be easily persuaded to pay promptly in such circumstances.

The terms and conditions of sale or service

5–25 Closely allied to the consideration of the goods or service provided by the prospective client is a review of the client's terms and conditions of sale. The importance of such a review in relation to collections from the debtor has been referred to in Chapter 4 and the question of the debtor's countervailing rights is dealt with fully in Chapter 9. It will be apparent from a study of Chapter 9 that the factor must be particularly vigilant in those cases where

[30] In order that set-off should apply in the bankruptcy or liquidation of the debtor both claims must be claims as will result in payment of money and not claims for the return of goods in specie; see para. 9–10 below.

because of competitive pressures the prospective client must accept the debtor's terms and conditions of purchase in place of his own terms of sale. The following are some of the matters to which special consideration often has to be given:

(1) A prohibition on the assignment of debts arising from the contract of sale or service[31] will enable the debtor to obtain a good discharge by paying the client. If sales to a debtor who includes such a term in his purchase contract constitute a large part of the total then it may be advisable for the factor to procure a waiver from the debtor.
(2) Contractual set-off provisions that are wider than those arising in equity[32] are often included in such terms.
(3) Where orders constitute more than one delivery the factor should consider whether the contracts are entire or divisible[33] and it may be necessary to procure the inclusion of a"cut-off clause".[34]
(4) The reservation of title to goods sold until payment has been received may well assist the factor in his assessment of the credit risk but he should ensure that such terms do not detract from his right to payment on due date for which provision is made.
(5) If goods are delivered on consignment or terms of sale or return or sale or exchange and debts are notified to the factor on delivery, the factor will not have a definite due date on which he can recover from the debtor. The factor may be able to accept the debts when a firm sale has been effected but such arrangements call for additional monitoring by the factor in order to ensure that the debts which he has purchased are in fact collectable and not subject to return or exchange.

The factor as assignee cannot be in a better position than the client as regards his relations with the debtors; it may, therefore, be necessary for the prospective client's standard terms to be amended before factoring starts.

5–26 The factor should also consider the following special classes of debtor:

[31] See paras. 9–30 and 9–31 below.
[32] See paras. 9–07 *et seq.* below.
[33] See para. 9–38 below.
[34] See paras. 9–43 and 9–44 below.

(1) Government departments including agents for the government such as area health authorities.[35]
(2) Debtors closely associated to or under common control with the prospective client. Such associates, including directors or employees of the prospective client, do not effectively provide for an independent source of recovery for the factor.
(3) Individuals purchasing for their own personal, domestic or family use.

Debts incurred by any such debtor and those arising from some of the special terms mentioned above (in particular any debts arising from sales on a sale or return basis) are often excluded from the factoring arrangements. Furthermore, where a debtor is also a regular supplier it may well be advisable to exclude such debts unless an agreement between the *factor* and the debtor not to effect set-off can be concluded.[36] However, the factor whose agreement is of the whole turnover type[37] should consider whether it would not be to his advantage not to exclude them but to release the client from the obligations to notify them to the factor and to give notice to the debtors. By such means the factor may own the debts and the release of the obligation to notify is based on the rationale that the client cannot give the factor the requisite warranties in relation to them.

Encumbrances on debts

5–27 In Chapter 8 it is argued that a factor should not be concerned with the terms on which the client is purchasing from its suppliers[38]; unlike his complete information regarding the debtors the factor has no information regarding the suppliers from whom the client may purchase from time to time. In this respect he must rely on the warranties in the factoring agreement that the debts notified to him will be free from any counterclaim in respect of purchases by the client from the debtor and that such debts will not be held in a fiduciary capacity on behalf of any supplier. However, it is as well for the factor to examine the purchase ledger to assess as far as he can the degree to which cross trading giving rise to claims by debtors to set-off may be endemic in the particular business. Where there may be a significant incidence of set-off it may be advisable to stipulate that the client should provide periodically lists of creditors for comparison with the debtors.

[35] See paras. 9–27 and 9–28 below.
[36] See para. 9–17 below.
[37] See para. 7–13 below.
[38] Paras. 8–25 *et seq.*

5–28 In spite of the provisions of the Companies Act 1989 in relation to the doctrine of deemed or constructive notice[39] it is considered advisable for the factor to make a search at the Companies Registry to determine whether there are any registered charges affecting the debts to be factored. He should search again after the factoring agreement has been executed and before any money has been paid to the client and ideally such search should be 21 days after the execution of the agreement to ensure that no charge created before the execution of the agreement has been registered within the requisite 21 days; the factor may well be in a stronger position in a conflict with a chargee if his agreement was entered into before the creation of the charge.[40] Enquiries should also be made as to whether any debts are likely to represent the proceeds of goods released to the prospective client on the strength of a letter of trust by which such proceeds are held in trust for a banker or other financier. If in the course of these enquiries any encumbrances on the debts to be factored emerge then the factor's rights to the debts should be settled by a waiver from the other party or by a priority agreement.

Management and administration

5–29 The factor's administration of the sales ledger and his ability to collect from the debtors depends to a large extent on the reliability of the client in sending the right goods to the right customers and in producing invoices that are meticulously correct. It is therefore important that the factor should carefully review the administrative arrangements in the client's offices. In particular it should be ensured that there are adequate controls to deal with:

(1) the acceptance and processing orders;
(2) in the case of manufacturing the putting of the ordered products into production;
(3) the raising of invoices;
(4) disposal of disputes and claims by debtors;
(5) the approval and issue of credit notes; and
(6) the retention and availability of evidence of the delivery of goods and the completion of services.

4. THE FINANCIAL STRENGTH OF THE PROSPECTIVE CLIENT

5–30 It is probable that before the survey the factor will already have examined audited accounts of the business for its last completed

[39] See para. 8–12 below.
[40] For a review of such conflicts see Chap. 8.

and previous two or three financial years. However, such accounts may not give an absolute indication of the up-to-date position and prospects of the business. There are some in the factoring industry who consider that a factor, in his consideration of a new client, should not be too concerned with this aspect; their view is that, if the factor's rights to collectable debts owing by creditworthy debtors are secure, the failure of the client will not be the cause of a loss. It is therefore sometimes considered that the detailed investigation of the viability of the business of a prospective client will cause them to miss a great deal of new business which will not be outweighed by the saving of the additional expense of a fast turnover of clients. The general view, however, is that:

(1) the acceptance of businesses that are likely to fail increases the factor's expenses, by reason of the cost of setting up new sales ledgers and the recovery of the debts on old ones; and
(2) such increase in costs may be reflected in the charges of the factor to all clients; and
(3) such an attitude tends to lend credence to the allegations that a factor is a relatively expensive financier of last resort.

As a result most factors consider that an examination of the up-to-date financial position of the prospective client, his prospects, the viability of the business and the benefits which will accrue to it from the use of factoring is of the highest importance. For this purpose, apart from financial accounts, the examination will often include:

(1) up-to-date management accounts; and
(2) an analysis of trade creditors by age; and
(3) the checking that amounts payable for PAYE, VAT and national insurance have been settled satisfactorily; and
(4) a consideration of cash flow forecasts.

5. ASSESSMENT OF DEBTORS

The quality and spread of debtors

5–31 Unless the number of debtors is unusually small, it is not normally possible or commercially acceptable to make a detailed investigation of all the debtors at the stage when a survey is conducted. To check the credit standing of several hundred debtors is expensive in staff time and in the cost of information. At this stage, therefore, the factor will obtain an indication of the general quality of the debtors by examining:

(1) the quality of the largest 12 or 20 regular customers; and

(2) the incidence of the placing of accounts for collection with a debt collection agency or solicitor; and
(3) the average period of credit taken by the debtors (usually referred to by factors as the "debt turn") over a period of at least one year and the comparison of this with the debt turn normally expected in the particular trade or industry.

The debt turn

5–32 The debt turn—the average period of credit taken by debtors—may also be an indication of acceptability or otherwise of the product. It may, however, be the result of the absence of good collection procedures by the prospective client—the very reason for his seeking the assistance of a factor. An allegation that a poor debt turn is the result of the lack of diligence should not be accepted by the factor at face value; a careful investigation may reveal some serious disputes, poor credit risks or even special arrangements such as consignment sales or long credit terms. The calculation of the debt turn may be carried out in a number of ways; but the most usual is to compare the average of month end totals of debts outstanding with the gross sales value:

$$\frac{AD \times 365}{S} = \text{Debt turn in days}$$

Where AD = average total debts at each month end over one year and S = gross sales value for the year.

The calculation can however, conceal distortions caused by the inclusion of:

(1) large disputed accounts;
(2) bad debts which have not been written off;
(3) accounts on which special terms have been agreed; or
(4) associated company current accounts.

If possible these distortions should be eliminated by excluding such accounts from the sales value and the totals of debts. The calculation may also be somewhat distorted by any delay in the issue of credit notes. In spite of the drawbacks of this method of calculation, it has the advantage of simplicity. It may not give a true absolute figure owing to the taking of the average of outstanding debts on the basis of end of month figures, because in many cases these are regularly the highest each month; if terms are monthly account, payments usually come in early in the second month after invoice date. It does, however, give a reasonable though crude indication of a trend and a comparison with others in the same type of business. By other methods the details are more difficult to extract and may also be distorted by special circumstances.

6. ASSESSMENT OF THE FACTOR'S TERMS

The discount charge

5–33 Having come to the conclusion that the business is suitable for the particular variant of factoring under consideration, the factor must assess the discount and administration charge to be quoted. The discount charge will be based on the cost of funds to the factor, the attractiveness of the business to him and the risk of any loss which he may suffer if the client becomes insolvent. His assessment of the risk of loss will depend on the strength of the prospective client's financial position, the quality of its management and the likelihood of disputes and cross claims from debtors; in the case of any recourse arrangement the quality of the debtor portfolio will also be germane to this assessment.

The administration charge

5–34 In the case of invoice discounting or agency factoring[41] in which the factor does not take over any administrative function the administration charge will reflect only the factor's requirement for remuneration as a commitment fee for making available the funds in addition to the cost of administration of the client's accounts, the reconciliation of the sales ledger control and his periodic visits to inspect the accounting records. In any case where the factor carries out the sales accounting function the charge must include element to cover this and the collection from the debtors. In order to be able to assess the appropriate charge at his survey of the prospective client's business the factor will extract some statistics relating to these functions. The most usual figures considered for this purpose are:

(1) the number of invoices and credit notes issued for a given volume of sales;
(2) the number of remittances received from debtors for that volume of sales and, in particular, the proportion of remittances that may be appropriated automatically to invoices;
(3) the number of active debtor accounts and the number of new debtor accounts opened (or old ones reopened) each month;
(4) the incidence of settlement discounts; and

[41] See paras. 1–43 and 1–41 respectively above.

(5) the incidence of any other special features such as carriage charges or returnable pallets.

The non-recourse element

5–35 If the factor is providing any form of factoring without recourse as regards the failure of approved debtors to pay by reason of their insolvency then he must include within his administration charge a percentage to cover the risk to him of the insolvency of approved debtors. Unlike a banker who tends to avoid the risk of loss by taking adequate security except in the case of businesses of first class standing, the factor providing non-recourse factoring seeks to accept the risk of loss but to be adequately remunerated for doing so. He will avoid unusually high risks by declining to approve the debtor concerned but he will expect to accept the credit risks which are normal in the trade and industry. His assessment of this element in the charge will depend on his knowledge of the expected percentage of losses in the particular trade, the record of losses sustained by the prospective client over the past three to five years and his review of the general quality of the debtors and his calculation of the debt turn.[42]

The prepayment percentage

5–36 At this stage the factor must also consider what percentage of the purchase price of the debts sold to him he should withhold until payment by the debtors; this retention is to provide for the set-off of recourse. The converse is his maximum prepayment or early payment on account of the purchase price. In order to assess a reasonable percentage for this purpose the factor must take into account to what extent the invoiced amount of sales is not recovered from debtors (otherwise by reason of bad debts) in the normal running of the sales ledger. This unrecovered percentage will include settlement discounts, returns and allowances, quantity discounts and disputed accounts to be credited. On his survey the factor will take out figures to calculate the percentage of these items to sales over a period of at least a year; he will then need to add to that percentage for the risk that, if the client becomes insolvent, there may well be an increase in the rejection of goods, particularly if the client's business includes an element of post-invoice contractual obligations.

5–37 The matters described above are those that a factor will usually review before offering any variant of factoring; in particular types of business there may be others that the client will need to take into account. In the case of some of the variants less emphasis may

[42] See paras. 5–31 and 5–32 above.

be placed on some aspects but in most cases all should be taken into account; even if the factor is not taking on the sales ledger function he should be aware of the workload because he may have to accept it if the client's administration deteriorates or if the client gets into financial difficulties. At all times when considering the client's business the factor should keep in his mind's eye the possibility of having to collect the debts without the assistance of the client.

CHAPTER 6

INTERNATIONAL FACTORING

6–01 A factoring arrangement will normally be designated by practitioners as "international" if the client (as supplier of goods or services) and the person responsible for the payment for the goods and services are situated in different States. Such a designation is virtually in accordance with scope of the application of the UNIDROIT convention[1]; the application of that convention is limited to receivables arising from contracts of sale of which the parties are in different States. For the purpose of determining that factoring transactions are international in character the situation of the factor does not appear to be relevant: the factor may be in the State of the client or the debtor (or there may be a factor in each) or it may be in a third state. Even in the rare case of a factoring contract between a factor in one State and the client in another in respect of domestic sales of the client it is probable that the factoring contract would be considered to be domestic. The special legal aspects to be taken into account in international factoring are described in Chapter 12; in this chapter the principal methods of dealing procedurally with international factoring transactions are considered.

6–02 The requirement in international factoring of procedures different from those in domestic business arises from differences in language, law and business practice. Among the most important of these matters are the law and practice relating to the collection of debts and those relating to the financing of businesses. Although there are many overseas States where English is the language of communication and commercial law and practices are almost identical with those in England, the factoring of exports to or imports from such countries is treated by English factors as international. On the other hand in spite of the marked difference between English and Scottish law relating to factoring

[1] See paras. 12–19 *et seq.* below and App. 5.

transactions[2] it is natural that business between England and Scotland should be treated as domestic business.

1. THE TWO FACTOR SYSTEM

6–03 In the early days of modern factoring, whilst its practice was virtually limited to the United States and Canada, little thought had been given to the special difficulties that might arise in the factoring of debts arising from sales across national borders. Special difficulties do not even appear to have arisen in the factoring by factors in the United States of debts rising from exports to that country from the United Kingdom; and this probably arose because these difficulties often arise from the factor's lack of knowledge of the law and practice relating to the collection of debts in another country and the factor in such cases would have been collecting in his own country. However, when factoring was introduced into Europe, factors in the United States saw the opportunity of developing factoring for export transactions by using a correspondent factor in the importers country. At the same time factors in Europe where international trade consisted of a larger part of the sales of typical prospective clients were faced with the problems mentioned above together with need to obtain fast and reliable credit information. These needs gave rise to the "two factor system" and the creation of worldwide groups of correspondent factors normally referred to as "chains".

The use of the two factor system

6–04 By the two factor system the client enters into an agreement, to include his export sales, with a factor in his own country so that for his domestic and export business he has to deal with only one factor. The client's factor ("the export factor"), having made arrangements with correspondent factors ("the import factors") in the countries of the client's customers to accept the credit risk on the debtors and to be responsible for collection, then sub–assigns the purchased debts to the import factors. The export factor remains responsible to the client for all aspects of the service and will normally provide finance by way of prepayments. The import factor, dealing with debtors in his own country, will be responsible for the credit risk in respect of approved debts and for collection; having no contractual relations with the client, he will be responsible for these matters to the export factor who in turn will be responsible for them to the client. Naturally the export factor will

[2] See paras. 7–20 *et seq.* below.

be responsible to the import factor for the acceptance of recourse (*e.g.* for a disputed debt) and will look for it in turn to the client.

The establishment of chains

6–05 Chains of correspondent factors were established for the purpose of promulgating common rules to cover the relations between import and export factors[3] and for the accounting arrangements between them. The rules normally cover such aspects of the business as:

(1) the acceptance by the import factor of a new client;
(2) the acceptance of the credit risk by the import factor and cancellations of approvals for future shipments;
(3) the settlement of disputes and recourse;
(4) warranties by the export factor regarding the value and validity of the assigned debts and of the validity of the assignments; and
(5) the time and method of payment by the import factor for the assigned debts.

The export factor must ensure that his own factoring agreement with his client is consistent with these rules to the extent that he has no liability to the import factor for which he cannot look to the client and that he is not exposed to risks as regards failure of the import factor to collect for which he cannot look to the import factor. The accounting rules should include the provision of frequent accounts by the import factor to the export factor showing the position between the two parties and frequent returns showing payments received, disputed items and the state of the debtor accounts.

6–06 In order to provide wide coverage for exports the chains have made vigorous efforts to expand their operations. There are now members of chains in about 40 countries including most countries of Western Europe, the United States, Canada, many countries in Central and South East Asia and on the Pacific rim and some countries in South America and in Central and Eastern Europe. Some of the chains (known as "Closed Chains") limit their membership to one factor in each country and the members of such chains tend to be associated by common shareholders. On the other hand the membership of Factors Chain International is open to a number of factors in any one country and, although some members have common shareholders, this is not a prerequisite of membership. The wide membership allows for competition by

[3] See App. 6.

factors for import business in any country in which there is more than one member.

Procedures under the two factor system

6–07 A typical two factor system works like this[4]:

(1) At the outset, the export factor obtains from the client the normal information obtainable on a survey[5] of the client's business.
(2) The export factor passes to each import factor the following information relating to the client's business in the import factor's country:
  (a) nature of goods or services provided;
  (b) estimated sales volume;
  (c) terms of payment;
  (d) number and type of debtors;
  (e) expected number of invoices and credit notes for the stated volume of sales.
(3) Each import factor considers the information and indicates his terms (administration charge for his part of the service).
(4) On receipt of all quotations from import factor's the export factor will be able to determine his own terms.
(5) When the arrangement starts, the procedure for the client is exactly the same as for sales within the United Kingdom[6] except that:
  (a) the notice of assignment on his original invoices directs the debtors to pay to the appropriate import factor; and
  (b) the client must supply an extra copy of each invoice to the export factor for onward transmission to the import factor.
(6) On notification or acceptance of each debt the export factor transfers it to the appropriate import factor who is supplied with a copy invoice.
(7) The import factor is then responsible for collections and accounts to the export factor who, in turn, accounts to the client.
(8) Where the arrangements are for factoring without recourse details of the debtors, together with required approvals, are submitted by export factor to import factor. The import factor gives his approvals either by credit limits or approval of specific orders according to the arrangements in force between the factors. The export factor gives the equivalent

[4] See App. 7.
[5] See paras. 5–20 *et seq.* above.
[6] See Chap. 3.

approval to the client. In such a case it is often arranged that the import factor will pay at the latest 90 days after due date for any unpaid approved debt except:

(a) if the failure to pay arises from a denial by the debtor of his liability to pay or a counterclaim by the debtor; or
(b) if the debt is subject to a breach of warranty by the seller or import factor.

(9) The import factor will take no responsibility for disputes, but will assist in their settlement if required.

Naturally, on a reciprocal basis factors in the United Kingdom act as import factors for overseas factors in respect of sales by their clients to customers in the United Kingdom.

Advantages and disadvantages of the two factor system

6–08 The advantages for the parties in the use of the two factor system are as follows:

(1) In spite of having indirectly handed over the function of sales accounting and collection to an expert in the law and business practices of the country of the debtor, *the client* has only one factor to whom to look for his factoring services. Even if his exports are spread among a number of countries, he will receive only one account and the communications from his factor in his own language and according to the business practices of his own country.
(2) It may also be possible for *the client* to receive the benefit of a lower discount charge if this is generally available in the country of the debtor. This result may be achieved by arranging for the import factor to make prepayments for the debts sub–assigned to him at the rate of discount charge in effect in his own country; the benefit would then be passed on by the export factor to the client. In such a case, as the export factor is responsible for his client it would be necessary for the export factor to give the import factor an indemnity against failure to recover owing to disputes or breach of warranty on the part of the client.
(3) *The export factor* is in a position to offer expert collection in a large number of countries without having to obtain experience of the law and practice of those countries. He is relieved from the need to deal with debtors in their own language and of the misunderstandings which sometimes arise from translations. He may rely on credit approvals given by factors who are experts in the credit conditions of their own countries. Furthermore, although it is not the responsibility of the import factor to resolve disputes

between the client and the debtor, he would normally be expected to help with their disposal; in the absence of a correspondent in the debtor's country this may be difficult for a factor particularly in the insolvency of his client.

(4) There is also the advantage to *the debtor* in his being able to pay to a person in his own country and to receive communications from his creditor in his own language. It is also helpful for a debtor to be able to communicate with such a person regarding any disputed item.

6–09 There are also disadvantages in the system. The overall cost will probably be more than if a single factor[7] (whether in the country of the exporter or of the debtor) is used because the two factors must share the administration charge and, however efficient the system, there must be some duplication of records. The transmission of funds from the debtor may be slower than if the export factor is paid direct by the debtor because the import factor may await cleared funds in his bank account before paying the export factor; and for smaller items settlements may be made weekly or two weekly.

6–10 For *the import factor* such business is often not attractive. The exports of the client may be scattered over a large number of countries so that the sales volume to each is relatively small and the cost to the import factor of dealing with a client account for such small volume may be disproportionate. He may have to deal with only a few accounts and may not receive sufficient remuneration to accept the exposure of the credit risks. This disadvantage of the two factor system has sometimes been aggravated by the practice of direct import factoring which has been used in some cases of substantial sales to an individual country.

Mitigating the exchange risk by the two factor system

6–11 The risk to a client, selling in the currency of the debtor's country, by reason of the fluctuation of exchange rates between the dates of shipment and payment may be largely eliminated by the use of the two factor system and prepayments by the import factor. If, in reliance on an indemnity from the export factor in respect of any recourse, the import factor makes prepayment of the *whole* of the purchase price on shipment of the goods in the currency of the invoice (in which he should be reimbursed by collection from the debtor) then the export factor may sell that currency immediately upon receipt. The client would then have available to him the sterling equivalent of the invoice value at the spot rate ruling shortly after shipment date.

[7] See paras. 6–14 to 6–20 (incl.) below.

Prospective improvements in the two factor system

6–12 The disadvantage of the two factor system caused by the duplication of records has been aggravated by the reluctance of export factors to rely fully on the returns from import factors of the sales ledger records. In theory the export factor should not need to keep the sales ledger because the debts have been sold to the import factors and the export factors should rely on the import factors' accounting and reports. However, export factors often feel the need to maintain a sales ledger updated by the reports of payments which they receive from the import factors in order to be in a position to provide prompt feedback of information to the clients. Such a need is particularly relevant when the factor offers on line access to his records through a terminal in the client's offices.[8] Considerable efforts have been made to overcome this problem: systems have been evolved for message switching through a satellite by which invoices and credit notes may be notified to the import factor and instant updating of debtor accounts by the import factor may be relayed to the export factor. When such systems shall have been adopted by at least one member in every country in which a chain is represented the problem may be largely overcome.

6–13 Although reports of receipts from debtors may be made instantaneous by such advanced systems the problem of the receipt by the import factor of cleared funds (so that he may credit his client for the purpose of accruing discount charges) remains intractable. The most obvious remedy for this problem is a multi-party, multi-currency, set-off arrangement similar to that adopted by the world's airlines many years ago. The matter appears to be under study by at least one of the chains.

2. OTHER SYSTEMS FOR INTERNATIONAL FACTORING

The single factor system

6–14 This system, which has been sometimes more aptly described as the "one-and-a-half factor system," was designed as a solution to some of the defects in the two factor system. The intention of its protagonists is to modify the two factor system in order to avoid the delay in payments to the client of the purchase price of debts where such payment is to be made by the export factor on receipt of payment from the debtor; such delay may arise in the two factor system by reason of the debtor's payment having to pass additionally through the hands of the import factor.[9] The system may also

[8] See para. 3–14 above.
[9] See para. 6–09 above.

have the effect of overcoming some of the duplication of administrative tasks which is a feature of the two factor system.[10]

6–15 By the single factor system the use of the import factor is dispensed with for normal routine collections from and payments by the debtor. However, the import factor acts to protect the export factor against the risk of the insolvency of the debtor, to collect seriously overdue debts and to assist with the resolution of disputes. The inception of the arrangement is exactly the same as under the two factor system.[11] There is however a difference in the operation of the arrangement as follows:

(1) There is at the date of shipment of the goods no sub-assignment to the import factor; the debts for the time being remain in the ownership of the export factor. As a result, the notice on the invoices is for payment direct to the export factor who is responsible for collection.
(2) The import factor, having given credit approvals,[12] will be responsible for the failure of the debtor to pay an approved debt by reason of his financial inability to do so.
(3) If any debt remains unpaid for an agreed number of days after its due date for payment (or in respect of an approved debt on any earlier insolvency of the debtor), that debt will be assigned by the export factor to the import factor. The import factor will thereafter be fully responsible for collection of that debt (if approved) and will use his best efforts to collect it (if unapproved).
(4) As in the two factor system the import factor will be responsible to pay in respect of any approved debt unpaid 90 days after the date on which it is due for payment except in the case of a dispute or counterclaim or a breach of warranty.

The period mentioned in sub-paragraph (3) above is sometimes specified as 60 days; this period will give the import factor an opportunity of 30 days in which to collect before becoming liable to pay the import factor. If the period is specified as 90 days the import factor will have the invidious duty of having to pay before having had an opportunity to communicate with the debtor and to ensure that there is no reason, other than financial inability, for the non-payment.

6–16 Although by the single factor system the import factor's tasks are limited to the acceptance of the credit risk and the collection of difficult accounts, there are some disadvantages. First, the normal

[10] See paras. 6–09 and 6–12 above.
[11] See para. 6–07 above, sub-paras. (1) to (4).
[12] *Ibid.* sub-para. (8).

collection procedures by a factor, who may not fully understand the business practices of the debtor's country and who may have some difficulties with the language, are less likely to produce results of the standard of collections by the import factor. Secondly, the debtor may be confused by his receiving two notices of assignment: the first to the export factor on the invoice and the second after the agreed period when the import factor takes over. If proceedings for recovery are necessary, such double notice may induce the debtor's lawyer to require evidence of the assignments. Thirdly, the import factor may be less liberal in the giving of approvals than when he has the responsibility for collection from invoice date.

Direct import factoring

6–17 It has often been arranged for a client with a substantial volume of export business with one country to factor his debts with a factor in that country. This was the method of factoring used by the early factors in the United States.[13] Naturally it would not be a good solution for an exporter whose exports are spread among a number of countries because it would then result in a multiplicity of agreements according to different laws and a multiplicity of factors using different systems of operation. Its advantages are simplicity and the use by the client direct of a factor who has the knowledge and experience to deal efficiently with credit approvals and collections in his own country. Provided that there is no problem of communication between the client and the factor and the client is competent to deal with a foreign factor, it is an almost ideal solution where the client is looking for collection and protection against bad debts only without any finance by way of prepayments. Indeed, in some cases members of chains[14] have made arrangements with a correspondent factor to take on a direct basis the client's business in the correspondent's country in return for an introductory commission. The purpose of such an arrangement is to avoid delays in the transmission of information and funds.

6–18 Where the client is looking for finance for his export sales the factor may find it difficult to monitor the operations of his client without a correspondent in the country of the client with the knowledge of local law and business procedures. This would be the case especially in the event of the insolvency of the client where the factor's ownership of the debts might be challeged by a creditor or the person charged with the task of administering the insolvent estate of the client. It is also necessary for the factor to consider all the legal problems of the assignments of debts across

[13] See para. 1–13 above.
[14] See para. 6–05 above.

national boundaries which are described in Chapter 12; he should ensure that his agreement is binding on the client and third parties and, in the insolvency of the client, according to the law of the client's country as well as that of his own. It is possible also that there may be regulatory impediments in the factor's country to the giving by him of finance by way of prepayments.

Direct export factoring

6–19 Before the establishment of the international chains,[15] it was normal for factors, whose clients wished to include exports within the factoring arrangements, themselves to handle those functions delegated to the import factor under the two factor system. Some factors still handle exports on this basis and the system has the advantage of simplicity for the client; he has to deal with only one factor with one system of procedures and accounting and that factor is in his own country. There is no problem of communication and the information on the state of debtors' accounts does not have to pass through two hands; payments are received direct by the factor and not through an import factor. A factor experienced in export documentation may even assist with this aspect of exports and with collections against shipping documents and letters of credit.

6–20 For the factor, however, there are a number of problems in direct export factoring. First, he must give careful consideration to all the problems relating to conflicts of law in relation to his purchase of the debts free from encumbrances.[16] In this connection he would be well advised to ensure that his assignments and the procedures for them conform to the laws of the debtor's countries as well as those of his own; this is not a light task if his client's business is spread among a large number of countries. Secondly there are the following commercial matters to be considered:

(1) *Credit risks:*

> The assessment of credit risks in relation to debtors outside the United Kingdom is difficult without a detailed knowledge of the country of the debtor and its business practices and accounting conventions. The usual answer to this problem is credit insurance. However, the assignment of a credit insurance policy to the factor is not a complete answer to the problem. Unless the factor is named in the policy as joint insured he may not be aware that the policy has been avoided owing to the client's default in making declarations

[15] *Ibid.*
[16] See Chap. 12.

under the policy or in the payment of premiums. In some cases only the first named of joint insured is given notices by the insurer so that it may be necessary for the factor to be named first in the policy. Even if the factor is so named he may not be aware of other breaches of the policy by which it may be avoided (*e.g.* non-disclosure to the insurer of a material fact). It may be a better solution for the factor to take out cover itself in respect of any debt which is not recoverable from the debtor *or* the client (by way of recourse) by reason of the insolvency of the debtor and for the client to rely on its own policy.

(2) *Collections from debtors:*

Collection by a factor in a country other than that of the debtor may be impeded by the following difficulties:

(a) Letters in a language foreign to the debtor may be disregarded or sent to be translated while payments are still withheld.
(b) It might be difficult to deal with general correspondence relating to the collection procedures.
(c) In countries which still maintain exchange control the regulations are often used as an excuse for delays in payment; these delays may be genuinely aggravated by a change in the payee and the channel of payment.

(3) *Disputes:*

There is little doubt that the incidence of disputes and of the non-acceptance of invoices is higher in international trade than in domestic business. This arises (*inter alia*) from misunderstandings regarding contract terms owing to language problems, misunderstandings regarding trade customs and damage and loss of goods in shipment by sea and air. There is less inclination on the part of debtors to report such disputes to a factor in another country; if the dispute has been notified to the seller it does not seem necessary to go to the length of reporting it to another organisation in the same country. If it is reported then it may be in a language that is not understood and, by the time it is translated, valuable time in which to recoup from the client may be lost. It has been known that, without the intervention of a correspondent factor in the country of the debtor, only at the stage of legal proceedings was the factor made aware of the dispute.

Foreign correspondents

6–21 From the foregoing it should be apparent that in order to operate direct export factoring successfully a good correspondent in each country in which a debtor is located must be available to effect collection when any debt becomes seriously overdue and such correspondent must be familiar with the extra difficulties which arise when collection is on behalf of an assignee. The correspondent must be familiar with developments in the legal concepts relating to the protection of the assignee against the claims of third parties including those arising in the insolvency of the client. In this connection it should not be overlooked that these matters will probably fall to be considered according to the law of the debtor's country. Such correspondent must be available at short notice to assist with the resolution of disputes arising from contracts of sale. Attempts have been made to establish a chain of such correspondents outside the factoring industry; but owing to the specialised knowledge required and the economics of establishing procedures for a few *ad hoc* problems from time to time it is doubted if any solution can be found better than membership of a chain and the use of a correspondent within the chain.

3. CURRENCY RISKS IN INTERNATIONAL FACTORING

6–22 There are necessarily some currency risks associated with exporting. Exporters are often obliged by the force of competition to quote prices and to invoice in the currency of the country of their debtor's domicile. An exporting client of a factor may be protected against the risk of fluctuations in the currency in which he has invoiced between invoice date and payment in one of three ways:

(1) He may arrange with his bank to sell the currency forward and with his factor to remit to him, on payment by the debtor, in the currency of the invoice.
(2) He may arrange for the factor to credit him in sterling at the rate of exchange ruling on the date when he notifies or offers the currency debt. The exchange risk will then be the factor's responsibility.
(3) He may arrange with the factor, under the two factor system, that the correspondent factor in the debtor's country will make a prepayment immediately upon receipt of the copy invoice so that the proceeds may be sold immediately by the export factor and the client paid in his own currency.[17]

[17] The procedure is explained in para. 6–11 above.

4. INVOICE DISCOUNTING

6–23 In view of the rapid growth of the demand for and the provision of invoice discounting and other forms of factoring on a confidential basis without notice to the debtors in many countries of the world, serious consideration has recently been given to the extension of these services to export sales. In the past, several invoice discounters in the United Kingdom have extended this service to the exports of clients without any special precautions; but they have done so on a limited basis whereby the export sales are a small proportion only of total sales. In this way debts that are difficult to collect may be recoursed to the client and absorbed by the retention held by the factor.[18] If it is proposed to offer factoring or invoice discounting where exports are all or a large proportion of the sales of the prospective client then all the considerations mentioned above[19] in connection with direct export factoring should be considered very carefully; the difficulties will be magnified by the absence of notice. It is likely that notice to debtors to pay the factor direct would be given only when the client is in financial difficulty or insolvent. Experience in domestic discounting and factoring has demonstrated that a client's difficulties are likely to be known to customers who will then be more reluctant to pay promptly and may delay until they have ensured that they will have no cross-claims against the client. Such difficulties may be compounded in the case of a factor giving notices for the first time; the factor will need to act quickly and notices in his own language may not be understood immediately so that the debtors may continue payments to the client whilst a translation is being obtained. This problem may be partly overcome by the holding of the factor, from the start of factoring, of a stock of letters signed by the client giving notice of the assignments in the languages of the debtors.

5. BACK-TO-BACK FACTORING

Back-to-back arrangements between two factors

6–24 Back-to-back factoring is usually an extension of the two factor system: its object is to overcome the difficulty created by the channelling by an exporter of all his sales to one country through a distributor. Very often the distributor is a subsidiary or associate of the exporter; in those and other cases the result is often that the amount of credit required by the distributor is far higher than can

[18] See para. 3–06 above.
[19] At paras. 6–19 and 6–20.

be granted by the import factor on the normal unsecured basis. In many cases the import of the client's products is the only business of the distributor. The difficulty of accepting the credit risk is overcome by the entry into a factoring agreement by the distributor with the import factor and the use of the balance owing by the import factor for debts purchased as security for the credit granted.

6–25 A typical back-to-back arrangement works like this:

(1) The export factor enters into a factoring agreement, covering the full service, with the client (exporter) and makes arrangements with import factor to act as his correspondent factor.

(2) The import factor enters into a factoring agreement with the distributor for his domestic sales. This agreement may be for any form of factoring in which prepayments are available. However, the normal arrangements will be varied as follows:

(a) prepayments are not normally taken; they may, however be limited to a very small percentage to cover the distributor's overhead expenses.

(b) the import factor and the distributor agree that, at any time at the discretion of the import factor, the amount due to the import factor for the supplies by the client (indebtedness assigned to him by the export factor) may be set off against amounts due to the distributor under the domestic factoring arrangements.

It is thought that the right of set-off would be available to the import factor in the insolvency of the distributor.[20]

(3) The approvals given to the export factor by the import factor will be made in one of two ways:

(a) on the basis of the position on the distributor's account with the import factor; or

(b) on the basis of firm orders from approved debtors received by the distributor for goods to be shipped. Alternatively, the import factor may accept all debts from the export factor with recourse but undertake not to exercise any recourse to the extent that he has available rights of set-off.

(4) The exports from the client to the distributor will then be factored through the two factor system in the usual way except that settlement by the distributor to the import factor (and consequently the import factor to the export factor)

[20] See para. 9–10 below.

will depend upon his sub-sales and the position on his account with the import factor.

It will be appreciated that the system may be difficult to bring into operation when the distribution arrangement is just starting. Until goods have been imported and sold the import factor has no basis for his approvals as he has nothing owing to the distributor. This lacuna can be overcome only by the exporting client accepting that his first sales will be with recourse.

Back-to-back arrangements by a single factor

6–26 An arrangement similar to back-to-back factoring is sometimes entered into without the assistance of an export factor. In such a case the factor enters into a domestic factoring agreement with a distributor and agrees to accept instructions to pay a percentage of the purchase price of each invoice to the supplier. The supplier may or may not be in the same country as the distributor. Difficulties have been encountered by factors in accepting such instructions and confirming them to the supplier. The percentage to be paid to the supplier will be the invoice value (less VAT for imports) less the importer's mark-up. The balance payable to the importer may not be sufficient to cover the importer's overheads owing to a high incidence of recourse for returned goods. The importer may allege that the recourse arises from deficiencies on the part of the supplier and should be deducted from payments to him.

6–27 The purpose of such arrangements is to give the supplier confidence in the granting of credit to the distributor; the factor may, therefore, not be in a position to make such deductions owing to the form of his confirmation to the supplier. If it is part of the proposed arrangements that such confirmation should be given to the supplier, then it is advisable that the instructions should be for all payments to go to the supplier (or to an account under the joint control of the supplier and the distributor). It will then be up to these two parties to divide the amounts so paid. As such difficulties may be compounded when there is more than one supplier these arrangements should be made only with a distributor of the goods of one supplier.

CHAPTER 7

THE LEGAL STRUCTURE OF FACTORING AND TRANSFER OF OWNERSHIP OF THE DEBTS

7–01 In its simplest form, which is the provision of funds by way of invoice discounting without any form of service or protection to the client, factoring is in substance no different from lending against the security of debts. However, the judiciary has on several occasions distinguished in law the provision of funds to a business by a purchase of debts (which is the method almost invariably used by factors in the United Kingdom) from the lending of money.[1] This chapter and the next cover the legal relations between the factor and his client; and in this chapter the legal structure of the arrangement for the transfer of ownership of the debts is described.

1. TRANSFER OF OWNERSHIP BY ASSIGNMENT

7–02 The factor's principal demand of the law is that he should obtain unencumbered ownership of the debts which he has purchased in such a way that he may have the sole right to collect them in full; in this way he should be able to recoup the funds he provides to the client for the purchase price of the debts. Naturally the principal requirement of the client from the factoring agreement is that he should be paid the full purchase price (the amount payable by the debtor less the factor's charges) at the time stipulated according to the particular variation of the service to be provided.

7–03 Debts which are the subject of factoring arrangements belong to a class of property known as "choses in action", the ownership of which cannot be enforced by possession as is the case with chattels. In a small proportion of cases the debt may be represented by a bill

[1] "There are many ways of raising cash without borrowing. One is by selling book debts . . . ." *Chow Yoong Hong* v. *Choong Fah Rubber Manufactory* [1962] A.C. 209. See also, for example, *Re George Inglefield Ltd.* [1933] Ch. 1 and Lloyds and Scottish Finance Ltd. v. *Cyril Lord Carpets Sales Ltd.* (1979) 129 N.L.J. 366.

of exchange or other negotiable instrument (a documentary intangible) the ownership of which may be transferred by endorsement and delivery; but most factored debts are not so covered and are pure intangibles. As a result, in order to enforce his ownership of the debts, the factor must have transferred to him the sole right to collect from the debtor using, if necessary, legal proceedings. Such transfer is effected by an assignment which is an agreement by a creditor to transfer his rights in relation to a debt to a third party and the latter's agreement to accept those rights without necessarily the consent of the debtor.

Historical background to assignments

7–04 Common law has never recognised the transfer of ownership of pure intangibles except by means of a novation requiring the consent of the debtor. Before the Judicature Act 1873 the common law courts were influenced by (1) the personal character of the obligation of the debtor and (2) the fear that the purchase of dubious claims at a large discount by wealthy people might flood the courts with contentious litigation. Although courts of equity recognised such assignments, proceedings for the recovery of debts had to be pursued in the common law courts. As a result it was necessary for the assignee to recover from the debtor by using the assignee's name and, if the latter refused to co-operate, to obtain an order for the assignor to do so from the court of equity before starting proceedings in the common law court. Since 1873 when the Judicature Act combined the administration of the courts of equity and of common law this cumbersome procedure has been unnecessary provided that all three parties, the debtor, the assignor and the assignee, are before the court. If the assignor co-operates in the action the assignor and assignee will be joint plaintiffs in the action; if he does not, then the assignee must proceed against the debtor and assignor as joint defendants[2]

Assignments in statutory form

7–05 Section 25(6) of the Judicature Act 1873 gave statutory recognition to assignments of debts provided that they conformed with its requirements. The provisions were substantially re-enacted by section 136 of the Law of Property Act 1925. A formal assignment in accordance with the statute is normally referred to as a "legal assignment" to distinguish it from other assignments still recognised in equity. The requirements of the statute are that it should

[2] *Holt* v. *Heatherfield Trust Ltd.* [1942] 2 K.B. 1.

be in writing under the hand of the assignor, it should be an absolute assignment of the whole debt (and not by way of charge only) and written notice of it should be given to the debtor. An assignment, complying with these requirements and being completed when notice has been received by the debtor,[3] has the effect (subject to equities having priority[4]) of transferring to the assignee:

(1) the legal right to the debt;
(2) all legal and other remedies for the debt; and
(3) the power to give a good discharge for the debt without the concurrence of the assignor.

Therefore, providing that there are no equities having priority (either by way of countervailing rights of the debtor[5] or third party claims[6]) a legal assignment would give the factor what he requires: the unencumbered sole right to collect from the debtor.

Equitable assignments

7–06 Any assignment of a debt or other legal *chose in action* which does not fulfil these requirements will be valid in equity provided that the intention of the parties is clear and value is given. Such an equitable assignment need not be in writing. Notice to the debtor is not a necessary prerequisite to the transfer of ownership; but notice is important in relation to competing interests.[7] It is probable that notice to the debtor alone, provided that it was made with the knowledge of the assignee, would constitute an equitable assignment. An equitable assignment may be of part of a debt only or by way of a charge.

However, whether an assignment is legal (in statutory form) or equitable, provided that the substance of the transaction is for the outright sale and purchase of a debt, such assignment will have the effect of transferring ownership absolutely. The statute has in no way detracted from the efficacy of equitable assignments and the position in relation to them remains exactly as it was before 1873.[8] The difference is purely procedural: the assignee has the right to sue in his own name alone for recovery from the debtor only if the

[3] *Ibid.*
[4] See para. 8–03 below.
[5] See Chap. 9.
[6] See Chap. 8.
[7] See paras. 8–06 and 8–07 below.
[8] *Wm. Brandts Sons & Co.* v. *Dunlop Rubber Co. Ltd.* [1905] A.C. 454 at p. 462.

assignment is legal. Otherwise proceedings should be in the joint names of the assignor and the assignee.[9]

2. STAMP DUTY CONSIDERATIONS

7–07 In spite of the procedural advantages to the factor of legal assignments, factoring agreements normally provide in the first instance for equitable assignments only. In the case of any form of undisclosed factoring the absence of notice would preclude a legal assignment. In all cases the form of documentation (or absence of it) is dictated largely by the incidence of stamp duty. However, the factoring agreement will usually provide for the right of the factor to perfect his rights to any debt by taking a legal assignment of any particular debt should he find it requisite to do so.

7–08 Stamp duty, a charge to which is imposed by the Stamp Act 1891 as amended by subsequent Finance Acts, is a duty on instruments and not on transactions. Accordingly, if a transaction can be conducted without an instrument, then there can be no liability to the duty. Mortgages and most deeds and agreements under hand, other than those for which specific provision is made in the statutes, are not liable. An assignment of a debt is a conveyance or transfer on sale of property and any instrument evidencing such a conveyance or transfer is liable under the Act to *ad valorem* duty.[10] The duty is levied according to the consideration which, in a factoring transaction, will normally be the amount payable by the debtor less the factor's charges (*i.e.* not substantially less than the amount invoiced). With effect from March 20, 1984, the rate of duty has been 1 per cent. subject to an exemption which relates to any independent transaction whereof the consideration does not exceed £30,000. However, in order to qualify for the exemption, the instrument must include a certificate of value; the certificate is to the effect that the transaction represented by the instrument does not form part of a larger transaction or series of transactions in respect of which the aggregate consideration is of value greater than the exemption limit. Thus, all linked transactions must be aggregated for the purpose of qualification for the exemption. The signature on the certificate is that of the assignor.

7–09 It is apparent that, if it is necessary that an assignment should be in writing in order that it should be recognised as a legal assignment, in relation to every legal assignment there will be an

[9] See para. 7–04 above. However, in practice it is not unusual for factors to take proceedings in their own name alone under an equitable assignment which has been notified to the debtor; unless the debtor objects the action should not fail for want of a joinder (see, for example, R.S.C., Ord. 15, r. 6).

[10] Stamp Act 1891, s.54 and Sched. I.

instrument which (subject to the exemption referred to in paragraph 7–08 above) will be liable to stamp duty. Attempts have been made in the past to provide for legal assignments to be effected on every sale by the client as soon as goods are delivered or services completed without the incidence of stamp duty, but these arrangements are of doubtful validity. The method usually adopted was to structure the agreement to provide for the client to offer the debts to the factor as they arose and for the factor to have the absolute right to accept or decline each debt offered. By this method the agreement does not provide for the actual transfer of ownership of the debts; the transfers are effected by the individual offers and acceptances. The agreement thus becomes a master agreement giving effect to the terms by which all the prospective assignments will be regulated. By arranging for each offer to cover debts of an aggregate value of an amount less than the exemption limit then in force and to include a certificate of value, it was hoped to apply the exemption to every written assignment. The doubt about the exemption from stamp duty of this arrangement arises from the premises that, as the master agreement provides that all trade debts arising in the business of the client must be offered, the factor has an option to purchase every such debt and, accordingly, the master agreement links all the transactions.[11]

7–10 It is now generally considered that in order to avoid the incidence of *ad valorem* stamp duty in an arrangement for factoring, one of two methods of vesting the debts in the factor must be adopted. Both methods avoid the use of a document to evidence the assignment. The methods are:

(1) An agreement, by which debts are offered to the factor and accepted or declined by him on a "facultative" basis[12] is used; but it is provided that, in the absence of a written rejection within a stipulated period, the offer is deemed to be accepted and the assignment of the debt is complete in equity. The offer document by itself does not evidence the assignment.[13]

(2) An agreement on a "whole turnover" basis[14] is entered into by which *inter alia* every trade debt of the client in existence on the starting date or which comes into existence subsequently during the currency of the agreement is to be sold by the client to the factor and vests in the factor as soon as it

[11] For an analogy see *Attorney General* v. *Cohen* [1937] 1 K.B. 478 which case related to the grant by a vendor to a purchaser of options to buy individual plots of land instead of a sale of the whole land in one conveyance.

[12] See para. 7–12 below.

[13] See Nock, *Monroe and Nock on the law of Stamp Duties* (6th ed., 1986), para. 1–16.

[14] See para. 7–13 below.

comes into existence without further formality or any document evidencing the assignment.

7–11 Even in the absence of a written instrument to give effect to the assignment of each individual debt in "whole turnover" type of agreement, consideration must be given to the stamping of the factoring agreement itself. A contract or agreement providing for the sale of any equitable estate or interest in any property whatsoever is chargeable to *ad valorem* duty.[15] On the face of it, such an agreement would appear to be liable. However, an instrument is stampable on execution and, if at that time the consideration is entirely uncertain (without any stipulation as to minimum or maximum) and in consequence *ad valorem* duty cannot be calculated, the instrument will not attract such duty.[16] At the date of the execution of a factoring agreement (provided that this date precedes the starting date) the value of the debts to be assigned and, consequently purchase price of them as consideration, cannot be known. Accordingly in such circumstances *ad valorem* duty on a whole turnover type of factoring agreement cannot be claimed and the agreement as a deed no longer attracts the former fixed 50 pence stamp.

However in some cases in order to obtain a minimum income from a factoring agreement factor's have stipulated in their agreements a minimum aggregate value of debts to be assigned in each year for which the agreement is in existence; in such circumstances it is possible that duty of 1 per cent. could be claimed on the purchase price of that minimum aggregate of debts. Accordingly, if *ad valorem* duty is to be avoided, a factor should eschew such a device.

3. TYPES OF AGREEMENT COMMONLY USED

Facultative agreements

7–12 Of the two types of agreement almost invariably used by factors, owing to stamp duty considerations, the most commonly used has hitherto been the facultative type. It is termed facultative because, although the client is bound by the agreement to offer every debt arising from sales in the normal course of its business (or of a particular division of the business or in a particular market), the factor may accept or decline to accept any debt. Thus as far as the factor is concerned the arrangement is purely optional. This type of agreement was based on long usage in the block discounting of hire purchase and instalment credit debts and on the practice in

[15] Stamp Act 1891, s. 59.
[16] See Nock, *op. cit.*, para. 1–67.

the United States. The absolute right to decline any debt was thought to give the factor better security; if the prospects of recovery from the debt were doubtful he need not have the responsibility of paying for it. However, the same protection can be effected, in an arrangement in which the factor buys all debts, in other ways.[17]

It was also considered at one time that by using such an agreement the factor could have assignments in statutory form in respect of every debt and avoid stamp duty by using the exemption limits as described above.[18] Now the normal arrangement is for the factor to be deemed to have accepted the offer and purchased the debt either by not declining the offer within a stipulated period or by paying an amount on account of the purchase price on receipt of the offer. The factor will obtain ownership of the debts in equity by such an informal assignment.[19] The facultative agreement itself gives the factor no real rights as regards the debts; but, apart from containing the factor's contractual right to have the debts covered by the agreement offered to him, the agreement also includes the rights and obligations of the parties in relation to every debt upon its being assigned to the factor by a separate act.

Whole turnover agreements

7–13 Common law has never recognised a present assignment of property not yet in existence or in the ownership of the assignor. Therefore, were it not for the assistance which equity provides for the factor, a whole turnover agreement by which the client agrees to sell and the factor agrees to purchase all debts arising in the client's business would require a new act of transfer by the client when each debt arose. However, by the equitable doctrine by which that which ought to be done is done, the ownership of future property can be transferred by a present agreement. Once consideration has passed such an agreement is effective to assign debts as they come into existence without further formality or act of transfer.[20] There is but one other stipulation for such an agreement to be effective: the subject matter, as it comes into existence, must be identifiable from and bound by the agreement itself.[21] The inclusion within the scope of the agreement must not be based on a later act of appropriation. The agreement need not cover *all* debts

[17] See para. 7–14 below.
[18] See para. 7–09 above.
[19] See para. 7–06 above.
[20] *Holroyd* v. *Marshall* (1862) 10 H.L.Cas. 191.; *Tailby* v. *Official Receiver* (1888) 13 A.C. 523.
[21] *Tailby* v. *Official Receiver* (1888) 13 A.C. 523.

of the client; it may apply to a certain division or product or market (as long as the debts are clearly defined) but not (for example) to debts owing by such debtors as the client may wish to include from time to time.

A whole turnover type of agreement is not effective upon execution but only on the payment or credit by the factor of the purchase price of a debt falling within its scope. Equity will not decree specific performance of such a contract so that for the contract to be enforceable the consideration must be executed[22]; one credit or payment is sufficient for this purpose because this type of agreement is a single indivisible contract for the sale of all debts to which it relates.

Advantages of whole turnover

7–14 From the Factor's point of view the advantages of a whole turnover type of agreement are as follows:

(1) The agreement will define the class of debts to which the agreement applies and all those debts vest in the factor whether or not they are notified to him. The factor may protect himself against paying early on account of the purchase price of debts, of which he has doubt, by either or both of the following:
  (a) a provision by which debts are approved for early payment and by which payment for unapproved debts is made only upon their collection;
  (b) the right to require the client to repurchase any debt in relation to which the client is in breach of any warranty (*e.g.* if the debt is disputed or subject to set-off).

  In a situation in which the factor's client is insolvent and the factor has doubts about the collection of all the funds laid out by way of early payment, it is better for the factor to own additional debts for which he has not paid (even if such debts are disputed or encumbered or doubtful of collection) than to own no such additional debts at all.

(2) Debts created up to the time of the appointment of a receiver or administrator to a client or the commencement of the bankruptcy or winding up of a client vest in the factor

[22] *Holroyd* v. *Marshall* (1862) 10 H.L.Cas 191. and see Goode, "Some Aspects of Factoring Law" (1982) J.B.L. at p. 242.

whether or not such debts have been notified to him and, more importantly, whether or not they have been invoiced. In this connection an existing debt is a debt arising out of an existing contract, whether or not it has been earned by the performance of the contract by the supplier.[23] However this prinicple does not apply to any debt arising out of the delivery of goods or the performance of services by a trustee in bankruptcy or liquidator of an insolvent client even if the debt arose from a contract in existence at the date of his appointment.[24] It also seems likely that, based on the analogy of the position in bankruptcy, the principle would not apply to debts earned by performance by an administrator or administrative receiver.

(3) Once an agreement of this type has started and the first credit or payment by the factor has been made, in the absence of compliance by the client of his obligations to notify the debts to the factor and to give notice to the debtors, the factor may himself give such notice and collect the debts. This would assist the factor if the client fraudulently discounted the same debts elsewhere without the factor's knowledge.[25] On the other hand a facultative type of agreement, constituting a series of independent transactions, does not bind the subject matter as it comes into existence and, in the absence of offers and notices to the debtors, the factor has no such right *in rem* but only a personal right against the client for damages; and he has no right for specific performance. The factor would, therefore, only have a personal right against the client for breach of warranties and undertakings if, instead of offering the debts to the factor, the client charged them to a bank or sold them to a third party.

(4) As a whole turnover agreement is a *present* assignment of future debts, upon the creation of any debt falling within the scope of the agreement (provided that some part of the consideration for which the agreement provides has passed) the rights of the factor to the debt take effect as from the

[23] *Hughes* v. *Pump House Hotel Co. Ltd.* [1902] 2 K.B. 190.

[24] *Re Jones (ex p. Nichols)* (1883) 22 Ch. D. 782; *Re Collins* [1925] 1 Ch. 556; *Wilmot* v. *Alton* [1897] 1 Q.B. 17, C.A.; and see Wood, *English & International Set-off*, paras. 7–173 to 7–176 (incl).

[25] The factor relying on the rule in *Dearle* v. *Hall* (see para. 8–02 below) would be able to defeat the claims of the other discounter.

date of the agreement.[26] Accordingly the factor with this type of agreement is in a strong position to rebut the claims of any person who seeks to encumber the debts of the client after the agreement has become effective by the first payment or credit by the factor. The factor, whose agreement is of the facultative type, is often in a much weaker position. For example, such a subsequent encumbrancer might be a bank in whose favour the client creates a fixed charge on book debts and, in the case of a facultative agreement, the factor, in many cases, would be unable to accept any further offers of debts except subject to the charge.[27]

7–15 It is sometimes claimed that an agreement of the whole turnover type, the existence and effect of which is notified to the client's customers at the outset, will give the factor advantages in relation to the preclusion of the set-off of certain of the debtor's countervailing rights and in the factor's claim to priority under the rule in *Dearle* v. *Hall.*[28] It is unlikely that these advantages exist in the present state of the law and the questions are discussed in detail in chapter 8.[29]

A disadvantage to the factor of the facultative type of agreement arises from the factor's need to control the timing of assignment notices to debtors.[30]

4. SOLE TRADERS AND PARTNERSHIPS

7–16 The only disadvantage of a whole turnover type of agreement is that, if it is entered into with a sole trader or partnership, it should be registered under the Bills of Sale Act 1878. It is provided by the Insolvency Act 1986[31] that a general assignment of existing or future book debts or any class of them made by a person, who is subsequently adjudged bankrupt, is void against the trustee in bankruptcy as regards book debts not paid before the bankruptcy petition unless the assignment has been so registered. An agreement of the whole turnover type described in paragraph 7–13 constitutes a general assignment for this purpose; as a result, in the absence of registration, the factor with an agreement of this type

[26] "The rule of equity which applies to the assignment of future choses in action is, as I understand it, a very simple one . . . . As soon as they come into existence, assignees who have given valuable consideration will if the new chose in action is at the disposal of the assignor, take precisely the same right and interest as if it had actually belonged to him, or had been within his disposition and control at the time when the assignment was made." "*Tailby* v. *Official Receiver* (1888) 13 A.C. 523 *per* Lord Watson at p. 533.

[27] See para. 8–18 sub-para. (2) below.

[28] (1823) 3 Russ. 1 and see para. 8–02 below.

[29] See paras. 8–08 to 8–10 below.

[30] See 8–06 below. A specimen of a whole turnover type of agreement is contained in App. 8.

[31] s. 344.

may expect, in the bankruptcy of his client, to lose all the debts purchased by him and outstanding at the date of the petition. It is further provided by the section that the expression "general assignment" does not include an assignment of book debts due at the date of the assignment from specified debtors or of debts becoming due under specified contracts. As a result there is no need for the registration of an agreement of the facultative type.

7–17 The section re-enacts in substance section 34 of the Bankruptcy Act 1914 with a re-arrangement of the text and an amendment of the effective time (for the debts to be paid in order to escape the provisions) consequent upon the abolition of the concept of acts of bankruptcy. The insolvency of partnerships is provided for under the subordinate legislation—The Insolvent Partnerships Order 1986.[32] Under the order the normal method of dealing with an insolvent partnership is by winding it up as if it were an unregistered company and the provisions as to winding up[33] apply with necessary amendments. There is no provision, for the avoidance of a general assignment of book debts, in the Insolvency Act 1986 in relation to the winding up of companies whether registered or unregistered. However the provisions for winding up a partnership appear to be permissive and not mandatory and an insolvent partnership may in some circumstances be administered in bankruptcy; in particular, where all the partners are individuals and none is a limited partner and bankruptcy orders are made against *all* of them *on their own petitions* then the trustees of the various estates administer the partnership property and this procedure is not a winding up as an unregistered company.[34] Furthermore, although the section refers to an assignment by "a person", by the Interpretation Act 1978[35] "a person" includes "a body of persons corporate or unincorporate". Accordingly a factor's assignment of the whole turnover type with a partnership must be registered under the Bills of Sale Act 1878 in order to avoid the risk of a claim by a trustee in bankruptcy to debts outstanding at the date of the petition.

5. LENDING ON SECURITY DISTINGUISHED FROM PURCHASE

7–18 It is important to distinguish the normal basis for factoring by the outright purchase of debts from the lending (as by bankers) on the

[32] S.I. 1986 No. 2142.
[33] Under Pt. V of the Insolvency Act 1986.
[34] The Insolvent Partnership Order 1986 (S.I. 1986 No. 2142) Introductory Note 4–002(c) and Pt. 4.
[35] s. 5 and Sched. 1.

security of debts. Although, as mentioned in the introduction to this part of the book, it would be possible to provide the full service and its variants with financial facilities by means of lending money on the security of a fixed charge on the client's book debts, normal factoring arrangements in the United Kingdom are based on the sale and purchase of the debts and the vesting of them in the factor. As a result of the outright sale and purchase, the debts cease to be the property of the client and, in the case of a client incorporated under the Companies Acts, there is, at present, no way of registering a security interest in them such as there is in the United States under the Uniform Commercial Code.[36] The arrangement certainly does not constitute a charge because the ownership has passed to the factor; consequently no registration is necessary or would be acceptable to the registrar under Part XII of the Companies Act 1985.

In view of this absence of registration and as the lending on security of book debts and the purchase of them, together with prepayments, appear to be very similar in substance, it is most important that the distinction should be kept firmly in mind by the factor when dealing with an incorporated client. If an agreement for prepayments on account of the purchase price of debts sold to the factor were to be held by the courts to mask a true transaction of lending on the security of book debts it would be registrable.[37] In such an event, not being protected by registration, the factor would be unable to recover in competition with the rights of:

(1) an administrator (appointed pursuant to the Insolvency Act 1986) or liquidator of his client; or
(2) any person who for value acquires an interest in the debts;

where the event occurred at any time after the date of the creation of the charge[38] which in such a case would be the date of the agreement.

Where invoice discounting or agency factoring are the services provided and the client not only guarantees payment of the debts sold to the factor but also collects them for him, there is, in particular, a very fine line between the purchase and a loan on security. It is therefore as well for the factor to ensure that, not only his documentation and communications both with the client and the outside world, but also his procedures and accounting are compatible with the outright purchase of debts.

[36] U.C.C., s.9 401/408.
[37] Companies Act 1985, s.396(1)(c) (from June 1991 when the amendments made by Companies Act 1989, s.93 come into effect).
[38] Companies Act 1985, s.399(1) (from June 1991 when the amendments made by Companies Act 1989, s.95 come into effect).

7–19 Where an agreement for the sale and purchase of debts or of goods has been challenged as being in substance lending on the security of such debts or goods two questions have been considered by the Courts: do the documents represent the true intention of the parties and does the substance of the transactions differ from their form.[39] From a study of the relevant cases[40] it seems possible to extract three main tests to be applied in any such challenge in order to determine whether or not an agreement for the purchase of debts is, in substance, a charge on book debts. These are as follows:

(1) *Equity of redemption:*

In the case of a charge (including a mortgage) the borrower has "an equity of redemption"; that is the the right to the ownership of the charged assets free of the charge on the discharge of his obligations to the lender. This is certainly not the same as the right which factor may take in his agreement to have the debts repurchased by the client on the happening of certain specified events. It is possible (but not certain) that it is not the same as a right of the client as seller of the debts to repurchase them at their full original purchase price. However, if the client were to have the right to have the debts transferred back to him free of any encumbrance on repayment of all prepayments plus charges, that is almost certainly an equity of redemption.

(2) *Rights on realisation of the charged property:*

In the case of a loan on security the lender, on ralising the charged assets, has to account to the borrower for any excess over the amount of the borrower's obligations to him; and as corollary, if the asset does not realise the amount of the obligations, the borrower is still liable for the shortfall. In the case of an outright purchase, the purchaser is owner and any profit or loss on realisation attaches to him. The profit to the factor as purchaser should be the difference beween the amount paid for the debt and its realisation; from this point of view the definition of the purchase price as "the amount payable by the debtor less the factor's charges" and the immediate credit of the purchase price are consistent with

[39] See *Curtain Dream plc* v. *Churchill Merchanting Ltd.* [1990] B.C.C. 341, 349.

[40] For example *Olds Discount Co. Ltd.* v. *John Playfair Ltd.* [1938] 3 All. E.R. 275; *Re George Inglefield Ltd.* [1933] 1 Ch. 1; *Chow Yoong Hong* v. *Choong Fah Rubber Manufactory* [1962] A.C. 209; *Lloyds and Scottish Finance Ltd.* v. *Cyril Lord Carpets Sales Ltd.* (1979) 129 N.L.J. 66; and more recently: *Curtain Dream plc* v. *Churchill Merchanting Ltd.* (1990) B.C.C. 341 and *Welsh Development Agency* v. *The Export Finance Company Ltd.* F.T.L.R. April 10, 1990.

purchase. A factor is unlikely to realise any other profit. On the other hand, in the cases of debts purchased with recourse, he is protected by the client against any loss by reason of short payment (or no payment) by the debtor; but such arrangements have been present in cases where the purchase of debts was upheld as such.[41] It is clear that the factor's protection is the obligation of the client to repurchase the debt or to guarantee payment; neither of these are the same as the obligation to repay the money paid to the client by the factor to the extent that it is not recovered by collection of the debts. It also seems clear that a non-recourse factoring agreement should undoubtedly pass this test.

(3) *Discount or interest:*

A discount charge has been said to be fixed and paid once and for all in advance and interest to accrue from day to day. To be consistent with the purchase of a debt, the debt should be "discounted" by the application of a fixed discount to the purchase price at the outset.[42]

Administrative convenience has dictated that most factors now calculate or adjust their discount charges on a day to day basis.[43] It is therefore important that the substance of the arrangement (as well as the form) in all other respects should be consistent with the sale and purchase of debts and demonstrate that it is the true intention of the parties. It is likely that the most important test of a security right (as opposed to outright purchase) is the inclusion of an equity of redemption.[44] Accordingly, the factor should never give his client the absolute right to have reassigned to him any of the debts sold to the factor. It should also be noted that a provision in an assignment by which all rights in respect of the subject matter of the assignment remained with the assignor until certain events occurred was an influence in a decision of the Court that the assignment was not an absolute assignment, but by way of charge[45]; even where the client is appointed agent to administer

[41] See for example *Olds Discount Co. Ltd.* v. *John Playfair Ltd.* [1938] 3 All. E.R. 275 and *Lloyds and Scottish Finance Ltd.* v. *Cyril Lord Carpets Sales Ltd.* (1979) 129 N.L.J. 366.

[42] *Chow Yoong Hong* v. *Choong Fah Rubber Manufactory* [1962] A.C. 209; *Lloyds and Scottish Finance Ltd.* v. *Cyril Lord Carpets Sales Ltd.* (1979) 129 N.L.J. 366. However, this test does not appear to be decisive; see *Re George Inglefield Ltd.* [1933] Ch. 1 where the calculation of the finance charge does not appear to have been considered.

[43] For an analysis of this aspect of factoring practice see paras. 3–34 to 3–38 (incl.) above.

[44] *Curtain Dream plc* v. *Churchill Merchanting Ltd.* (1990) B.C.C. 341 *per* Knox J. at p. 351.

[45] *"The Halcyon the Great"* [1984] 1 Lloyds Rep. 283.

the sales ledger and collect the debts[46] it should be specified in the factoring agreement that the right to collect remains with the factor.

Words such as "advance", "loan" or "interest" should be eschewed in favour of "prepayment", "early payment" or "discount". However, it would appear that the word "finance" would not be an influence because finance may be provided equally by selling assets.

There appears to be no recently reported case in which a liquidator or creditor has upset an arrangement for the sale by a trading company of its book debts to a financier as being in substance to be loans on the security of the debts. Indeed there are several cases in which such an attempt has failed[47] and the courts accepted that the agreements between the parties reflected the true nature of the transactions in spite of the compatibility of certain of the practical arrangements with the lending of money. However, recently the judiciary appear to have looked more critically at agreements relating to security rights with reference to the substance of the transactions.[48] Consequently it may well be that in some future case arising from factoring (particularly invoice discounting or agency factoring) the court may make its decision on the basis of the substance of the arrangement as evidenced by internal and external communications of the factor and its procedures and accounting arrangements with its client. If commercial expediency dictates preocedures and accounting which are more consistent with lending on security the mischief cannot be cured by the agreement itself.

6. SPECIAL CONSIDERATIONS FOR SCOTLAND

Where Scottish law may apply

7–20 Although this book in the main is confined to a description of the law in England and Wales a note on the position in Scotland may serve to remind practitioners that they should not assume that their standard agreement drafted for use in England and Wales

[46] See paras 1–41 to 1–44 (incl.) above.

[47] For example *Re George Inglefield Ltd.* [1933] Ch. 1; *Olds Discount Co. Ltd.* v. *John Playfair Ltd.* [1938] 3 All. E.R. 275; *Chow Yoong Hong* v. *Choong Fah Rubber Manufactory* [1962] A.C. 209; *Lloyds and Scottish Finance Ltd.* v. *Cyril Lord Carpets Sales Ltd.* (1979) H.L. (unreported).

[48] See *Re Brightlife Ltd.* [1986] 3 All E.R. 673 at p. 677 where Hoffman J describes the ability of the chargor to collect in and deal with the proceeds of the charged book debts as the "badge" of a floating charge; *Curtain Dream plc* v. *Churchill Merchanting Ltd.* (1990) B.C.C. 341; and *Welsh Development Agency* v. *The Export Finance Company Ltd.* F.T.L.R. April 10, 1990.

will be effective for use in Scotland. For that purpose it is advisable to take advice of a Scottish legal adviser. What constitutes business in Scotland is itself a difficult question; it is certainly normally recognised that the winding up of a company registered in Scotland and the sequestration of a sole trader or partnership, established under Scottish law and whose business was mainly in Scotland, would be governed by Scottish law; thus in order that the factor may have ownership of debts, which cannot be impeached in the insolvency of his client, in such cases it will be necessary that the transfer of title to the debts takes place under Scottish law.

7–21 The question of the applicable law also arises if the client is English and the majority of the debtors are domiciled in Scotland. It is sometimes considered that the effectiveness of an assignment of a debt (as opposed to its validity as a contractual right) and the rules relating to the countervailing rights of the debtor are governed by the law of the country which governed the contract of sale from which the debt arose; but the rule is not free from uncertainty and it is not certain that the rule would apply in relation to a conflict between a factor and an administrative receiver, liquidator or trustee in bankruptcy. In the only reported case of such a conflict[49] the question was avoided by the agreement of counsel for all parties that, as most of the debts had been incurred by Scottish customers of the client, the debts were situated in Scotland and that Scottish law should be applied to determine the ownership of the debts; this was agreed in spite of the English domicile of the factor and the fact that the factoring agreement was expressed to be governed by English law. Indeed it seems that there is a general rule that the *situs* of a debt is where the debtor resides[50] and it is usually accepted that in a winding up or bankruptcy property in another jurisdiction should be dealt with in accordance with the law of that jurisdiction. In any case of doubt it is suggested that, in view of the very tolerant rules regarding the validity of equitable assignments in England and the more difficult position in Scotland, an agreement giving unimpeachable beneficial ownership of the debts to the factor under Scottish law should be used.

Transfer of ownership of debts in Scotland

7–22 Equitable doctrines relating to the assignments of debts are unknown to Scottish law. In Scotland the ownership of a debt may be transferred by a written assignation intimated (notified) to the debtor in writing. Therefore it is not possible to rely on the whole

[49] *Tay Valley Joinery Ltd.* v. *C.F. Financial Services Ltd.* 1987 S.L.T. 207.
[50] *Re claim by Helbert Wagg & Co. Ltd.* [1956] Ch. 323 at p. 342.

turnover type of agreement whereby an agreement to assign future debts creates an actual assignment of them as they come into existence without further formality; nor may the factor rely on the deemed acceptance of offers by the client in the absence of written acceptance. As each assignation must be in writing they would in most cases attract stamp duty; as a result, a factoring arrangement based on written assignations would be likely to be uneconomic.

Creation of trusts in respect of book debts

7–23 For these reasons efforts have been made to find ways of vesting debts in the factor without the need for assignations and intimations. One method which has been successfully adopted is to provide that in relation to every debt sold by the client to the factor the beneficial ownership should vest in the factor but that, in the absence of an assignation, the client should hold the debt on trust for the factor. The factor, under a power of attorney in the factoring agreement, will have the right to execute an assignation of any debt and intimate it to the debtor on behalf of and in the name of the client. However, he will do this only if it is absolutely necessary (*e.g.* to take proceedings against the debtor in his own name). The principle was approved in the Second Division of the Court of Session in *Tay Valley Joinery Ltd* v. *C.F. Financial Services Ltd.*[51] as was a textbook model of documentation and procedure for the establishment of the trust.[52] That model agreement provided:

> "Upon payment by the Factor of the whole or any part of the purchase price of any receivable the Client shall hold such receivable and the rights, instruments and securities relating thereto on trust for the Factor."

The case confirmed the view that debts may become the subject matter of a trust without the owner's divestment of them by means of an intimated assignation.[53] It also confirmed that it was possible for a person to make himself trustee of his own property for another provided that the property was dedicated to the trust by a properly constituted instrument of trust and, in relation to the trust property, by some physical act which is the equivalent to the delivery, conveyance or transfer to an independent trustee.[54]

[51] 1987 S.L.T. 207.
[52] Halliday, *Conveyancing Law and Practice in Scotland*, Vol. 1, pp. 284–294.
[53] *Ibid.* notwithstanding the dictum *E.C.G.D* v. *Turner* S.L.T. 286 at p. 290.
[54] *Allans Trustees* 1971 S.L.T. 62 and *Clark Taylor & Co. Ltd.* v. *Quality Site Development (Edinburgh) Ltd.* 1981 S.L.T. 308.

7–24 Until the *Tay Valley* case[55] there was doubt as to the nature of the act necessary to evidence the dedication of each debt to the trust. Although there was a view that all that was necessary was the submission of copy invoices to the factor and his crediting the client with their purchase price, the view was not free from doubt on the grounds that the act might well need to include a notice to the debtor to pay to the factor (*i.e.* the equivalent of the intimation of an assignation). As a result there was doubt if invoice discounting or undisclosed factoring would vest the beneficial ownership in the factor notwithstanding that the agreement provided for the establishment of trust of the debts; and some factors restricted their business in Scotland to disclosed factoring.

7–25 The *Tay Valley* case[56] was itself concerned with invoice discounting and all three judges concluded (for somewhat different reasons) that the agreement together with the normal invoice discounting procedures had the effect of investing beneficial ownership of the debts in the factor. The procedures comprised the sending of notifications of the debts by the client to the factor at frequent intervals, the crediting and payment by the factor of the purchase price of the debts, the sending of monthly aged lists of debtors by the client to the factor and the recording of the proceeds as being the property of the factor and the payment of such proceeds into an account in the name of the factor. The agreement itself did not purport to create a trust of the debts because it was a whole turnover type[57] in English form. As the agreement was expressed to be governed by English law it seems that the judges were influenced by the fact that it would in England have had the effect of transferring beneficial ownership of the debts by equitable assignments and that to achieve this result in Scotland, in the absence of the doctrine of equitable assignments, the trust would of necessity be created. It is probable that to adopt the trust device in Scotland by an agreement governed by Scottish law a more robust style of agreement, specifically appointing the client as trustee of the debts both present and future, will be necessary[58]; but there is little doubt now that factors may adopt procedures which do not necessarily include disclosure to the debtors.

[55] See n. 51 above.
[56] *Ibid.*
[57] See para. 7–13 above.
[58] For example, see Halliday, *op. cit.*

CHAPTER 8

THE EFFECT OF NOTICE TO THE DEBTOR AND CONFLICTS WITH THIRD PARTIES

8–01 In Chapter 7 the methods by which ownership of the debts, which are the subject of a factoring agreement, is transferred to the factor were explained. It was there asserted that the factor's most important demand of the law is that he should be able to obtain that ownership unfettered by claims of other parties to rights or interests in the debts purchased by him; any such rights or interests of third parties may well prevent the factor from collecting the full amount (or even any amount) from the debtors so that he may be unable to recover the monies he has laid out in the purchase of the debts.

Questions of the priorities of such rights and interests in choses in action are some of the most difficult in English law. These difficulties appear to have arisen from the development of non-possessory forms of consensual security in equity over personal property without any comprehensive statutory regulations relating to priorities such as is to be found in the Uniform Commercial Code in the United States. Such claims of others to rights or interests in the debts may be based on assignments, security rights (such as charges on the property of companies) or equitable tracing rights. In this chapter the effect of notice to the debtor, which has an important bearing on such conflicts, and factor's position in relation to such claims is considered.

1. THE RULE IN DEARLE v. HALL

8–02 The general rule which regulates the priorities between competing assignees of the same debt is based on the case of *Dearle* v. *Hall*[1] and has stood the test of time for over 160 years. The rule is that

[1] (1823) 3 Russ 1.

the assignee whose notice of assignment is first in time has priority provided that at the time of the assignment to him, which he took in good faith, he was not aware of any earlier assignment to a competing assignee[2]; and an assignee, having after the time of his assignment become aware of an earlier assignment, may still obtain priority by giving notice first.[3] In order to determine the first in time the relevant date is that on which the notice is received by the debtor and not that on which it is sent.[4] If a debtor receives, on the same day, notices from each of two independent assignees of the same debt then the earlier assignment will be preferred; it appears that the law does not take notice of a portion of a day for this purpose.[5] The case of *Dearle* v. *Hall* related to equitable assignments of equitable interests; and it appears to have statutory recognition, as regards equitable interests, owing to a reference to it in section 137 of the Law of Property Act 1925.

8–03 In a conflict between an assignee under an equitable assignment, which has been notified to a debtor, and a subsequent assignee whose assignment is in statutory form where the later assignment was taken in good faith, for value and without notice of the earlier equitable interest the rule will come to the assistance of the first assignee. This is so in spite of the usual rule that an equitable interest is subordinated to a subsequent legal interest obtained in good faith and without notice; it is the consequence of the statutory provision for the requisites of an assignment whereby the rights of an assignee are "subject to the equities having priority over the right of the assignee."[6]

8–04 Where the conflict is between two assignees who have both taken valid assignments in statutory form there can be little doubt that the first to complete his assignment by notice to the debtor must have priority. It is the date of the notice with effect from which the following are transferred to the assignee:

(1) the legal title to the debt;
(2) all legal and other remedies for the debt; and

[2] For the failure of a subsequent assignee, who was aware of a prior assignment at the time of his assignment, to obtain priority by giving notice first see *Re A D Holmes* (1885) 29 Ch.D. 786. For the failure of a receiver under a floating charge to obtain priority (on behalf of the chargee) by giving notice of the crystallisation of the charge in similar circumstances see *Re Ind, Coope & Co. Ltd.* [1911] 2 Ch. 223.

[3] "It is not a question of what a man knows, when he does that which will better or perfect his security, but what he knows at the time when he took his security and paid his money." *Per* Cotton L.J. in *Mutual Life Assurance Society* v. *Langley* (1886) 32 Ch.D. 460 at p. 468.

[4] *Johnstone* v. *Cox* (1881) 16 Ch.D. 571 affirmed 19 Ch.D. 17 and in relation to the notice of an assignment in accordance with Law of Property Act 1925, s. 136 see *Holt* v. *Heatherfield Trust Ltd.* [1942] 2 K.B. 1.

[5] *Johnstone* v. *Cox, supra.*

[6] Law of Property Act 1925, s. 136(1); see also *E. Pfeiffer Weinkellerei-Weineinkauf GmbH & Co.* v. *Arbuthnot Factors Ltd.* [1987] B.C.L.C. 522 at p. 533.

(3) the power to give a good discharge for the debt without the concurrence of the assignor.[7]

For the same reason he will prevail in a conflict with an assignee whose assignment is equitable and has not been notified to the debtor. However, in both cases the rule will apply only if the claimant under it has acted in good faith and taken his assignment without knowledge of the earlier assignment. If this is not the case the first assignee must succeed.

8–05 It appears, therefore, that in all cases of conflicts between assignees, whose assignments are either equitable or in statutory form, the priority rule is the same: the first (acting in good faith without knowledge of an earlier assignment) to procure receipt by the debtor of notice of his assignment has the right to collect and give a good discharge for the debt. It seems that part of the reasoning behind the rule is that notice to the debtor is a deterrent to the fraud of multiple assignments of the same debt; accordingly it is considered that an assignee who fails to give notice promptly is somehow negligent and deserves to be displaced by a later assignee who gives notice first.[8] As physical possession of an intangible is not possible notice is considered to be the nearest equivalent to it. The rule is also logical and commercially sound; if the priorities followed any other rule the debtor, on receipt of notice of an assignment, would be put on enquiry in every case to ascertain that there was no other assignment having priority.

2. THE EFFECT OF NOTICES OF ASSIGNMENTS IN FACTORING ARRANGEMENTS

8–06 The foregoing description of the effect of the rule in *Dearle* v. *Hall* emphasises the importance to the factor of getting out his notice as early as possible after the assignment of each debt. In the case of a factor who uses the whole turnover type of agreement[9] for any form of disclosed factoring the notice may be sent by means of a legend on the invoice direct by the client to the debtor; in normal commercial practice the debt will be in existence before the invoice is despatched to the debtor and the assignment will already have been effected automatically on the coming into existence of the debt.

[7] *Ibid.*

[8] See *Re Dallas* [1904] 2 Ch. 385 from which it also appears that a notice received by a bank after business hours is considered to have been received on the following day.

[9] See para. 7–13 above. But see also para. 4–40 above regarding difficulties in relation to the sending of notices caused by the electronic transmission of invoices.

On the other hand, where the factor uses a facultative type of agreement,[10] the assignment of each debt takes effect only when the offer of it has been made by the client and accepted (or deemed to be accepted) by the factor. Unless, therefore, the factor arranges for originals of invoices, bearing the assignment notices, to be sent to him for onward transmission to the debtor he cannot be certain that the notice has been received by the debtor *after* the assignment has been made. An assignment according to the statute[11] cannot be completed by notice before it is made and it seems doubtful if the notice of an equitable assignment, received by the debtor before the assignment has been made, would be valid for the purposes mentioned above or in Chapter 9.

8–07 In addition to assisting the factor in his claims to priority against competing interests in the debts receipt of notice by the debtor also:

(1) fixes the rights of the parties in relation to the debtor's countervailing rights[12];
(2) prevents the discharge of the debtor by subsequent payment to the client[13];
(3) avoids changes in terms in the contract of sale (which have not been authorised by the factor) being enforceable against the factor[14]; and
(4) enables the factor to take proceedings for recovery of the debt in his own name.[15]

It is therefore apparent that it is in the interests of the factor's security to ensure that notices are received by the debtors at the earliest possible time after each debt is assigned. In invoice discounting or undisclosed factoring the factor is in greater danger of detractions from his security; an invoice discounter may well lose the proceeds of debts the subject of his discounting agreement to an assignee who was unaware of that agreement but who gave notices to the debtors first. The requirement that the client should

[10] See para. 7–12 above.
[11] Law of Property Act 1925, s. 136.
[12] See Chap. 9.
[13] *Wm. Brandts Sons & Co.* v. *Dunlop Rubber Co. Ltd.* [1905] A.C. 454.
[14] *Brice* v. *Bannister* (1878) 3 Q.B.D. 569. This case related to a stop order on monies held in court; but such a stop order is usually considered analogous to a notice to a debtor for such purposes. See also para. 9–13 and the dictum of James L.J. in *Roxburghe* v. *Cox* (1881) 17 Ch.D. 520.
[15] Although strictly the assignee under an equitable assignment must join the assignor as co-plaintiff, in view of the rules of the courts that an action should not fail for want of a joinder (see for example R.S.C., Ord. 15, r. 6), it is often effective for the factor to take proceedings in his own name alone, without the formality of an assignment in statutory form, provided that notice has been given to the debtor. However, the court may require all three parties to appear and this is likely if the debtor takes the point that the assignment is not in statutory form.

mark all the records relating to the discounted debts to the effect that they have been assigned is, for this reason, an important safeguard; it is usual for a prospective purchaser of debts to inspect these records.

Introductory letters

8–08 An interesting question arises regarding notices to debtors and prospective debtors of the existence and effect of an agreement of the whole turnover type[16]; the question is whether such notices are effective (for any of the purposes mentioned in paragraph 8–07 above) as regards all future debts. It is usual practice for the factor at the outset of such an agreement to send out (or to procure that the client should send out) to all the customers (and to each prospective customer during the currency of the agreement) a letter giving notice in such terms. Typically such a letter, which is often termed an introductory letter,[17] would give notice to the customers that from the date of the letter and until further notice all debts arising from supplies by the client are automatically assigned and become payable to the factor; such a letter might also remind the customer that consequently no new claim by the customer against the client may be set off against any such assigned debt.

8–09 There are a number of reported cases which are considered to be authority for the view that a notice of assignment to a debtor is effective for the purposes of determining priorities only as regards debts in existence at the time of receipt of the notice by the debtor. These cases[18] related to multiple assignments by army officers of amounts payable to them by the government on their having resigned their commissions. The sums payable were made available through the army agents; and any notice received by the agents before receipt of the funds *and* their becoming payable by the gazetting of the officer's resignation was considered to be ineffective for this purpose. The notice to be effective had to be to some person "bound by some contract or obligation, existing at the time when the notice reaches him, to receive and pay over, or to pay over, if he has previously received, the fund."[19]

8–10 It seems possible, however, that the facts of the cases quoted above appear can be distinguished from a factor's claim to priority against a competing assignee on the grounds of an introductory

[16] See para. 7–13 above.
[17] Or sometimes termed a "switch on letter."
[18] See, for example, *Johnstone* v. *Cox* (1881) 16 Ch.D. 571; the cases were reviewed in *Re Dallas* [1904] 2 Ch. 385.
[19] *Per* Lord Selborne L.C. in *Addison* v. *Cox* (1872) 8 Ch. App. 76 at p. 79.

letter on the principle of the rule in *Dearle* v. *Hall*.[20] The position might appear to be entirely different particularly in the case of a running and continuing account. An agreement binding the debts as they come into existence is a *present* assignment (albeit of future debts) and notice of the agreement, once it is effective, is notice of an assignment already made[21]; the assignment is made by the agreement itself but is inchoate until each debt to which it refers comes into existence. It seems also that such an agreement together with such a notice may be one of the equities referred to in section 136(1) of the Law of Property Act 1925.[22] However, in the present state of the law, a factor may not rely on an introductory letter as notice for the purpose of the rule except as regards debts in existence at the time of receipt of the letter by the debtor.

3. CONFLICTS WITH CHARGEES

(a) Some general points and changes arising from Companies Act 1989 affecting conflicts with chargees

8–11 Most companies which are looking to factoring as a means of financing their businesses are likely to have, at some time, bank or other borrowing; and any such facility is likely to be granted on the security of a debenture comprising a general charge covering all the assets of the borrower including its debts. It is natural therefore that a factor, providing his services for a company and requiring that the debts which he purchases should be free from such an encumbrance, should consult any such chargee to arrange for a waiver or priority agreement at the outset; and the factor is likely to know of any valid charge affecting any debts of his prospective client (otherwise than in the circumstances described in paragraph 8–13 below) by reason of his enquiries made before the start of factoring.

It is expected that the following changes in relation to the registration of charges included in Part IV of the Companies Act 1989 wil come into effect by Order in June 1991:

(1) Particulars of a charge on book debts or a floating charge including debts other than book debts created by a company will have to be delivered to the Registrar of Companies[23] (within 21 days of its creation) if the charge is not to be void against a liquidator, an administrator (appointed pursuant

[20] See paras. 8–02 *et seq.* above.
[21] *I.e.* it is *not* a notice relating to an assignment not yet in existence; see para. 8–06 above.
[22] See para. 8–03 above.
[23] Companies Act 1985, ss. 396(1)(c)(iii) and 396(1)(e) respectively (amended by Companies Act, 1989, s. 93).

to section 13 of the Insolvency Act 1986) or *any person who for value acquires an interest in or right over property subject to the charge.*[24] Such persons consititue a new class benefitting from the provisions; until the changes come into effect the statute refers to *any creditor* of the company which has created the charge. This change will be of benefit to a factor who under the unamended Act could not always rely on the provision by which an unregistered charge was invalid as against the rights of a creditor; in most circumstances he would not be a creditor.

(2) There will be a provision for late registration; late registration will not avoid the charge, as described above, in relation to any relevant event occurring after the particulars of the charge have been delivered to the Registrar. However, to prevent abuse a late registered charge will be avoided (as described above) unless the company is solvent at the time of registration and survives for one year (in the case of a charge in favour of an unconnected person) and two years (in the case of a connected chargee).[25]

8–12 Before considering the factor's conflicts with chargees there are three special points to be considered in connection with a factor's knowledge of a duly registered charge over the debts of a prospective or existing client. First, there are two provisions in the Companies Act 1989 which, in the one case, abolishes and, in the other, limits the doctrine of constructive (or deemed) notice in relation to documents kept by the registrar and matters disclosed on the register respectively. The Act introduces a new section into the Companies Act 1985 (section 711A(1) which is expected to come into effect in November 1990) by which a person shall not be deemed to have notice of any matter solely because of its being disclosed in any *document* kept by the Registrar of Companies or made available by the company for inspection. As regards a factor, if it were not for subsection (2) of this clause, this provision combined with that a new section 416 of the Act (described below) would mean only *actual* notice of a charge would have effect in relation to questions of priority. However subsection (2) of section 711(a) provides that:

> "This does not affect the question whether a person is affected by notice of any matter by reason of a failure to make such enquiries as ought reasonably to be made."

The answer to the question as to what enquiries ought reasonably to be made is likely to depend on the circumstances of each case

[24] Companies Act 1985, s. 399 (amended by Companies Act 1989, s. 95).
[25] Companies Act 1985, s. 400 (inserted by Companies Act 1989, s. 95).

and, until there has been some judicial interpretation of the provision, it must be a matter of subjective consideration.

The other provision is in Part IV of the Act and it is expected to come into effect in June 1991. It introduces into the Companies Act 1985 a new section[26] which provides that a person (other than a person taking a charge over a company's property):

> ". . . shall not be taken to have notice of any matter by reason of its being disclosed on the register of by reason of his having failed to search the register in the course of making such enquries as ought reasonably to be made."

This provision would seem to abolish except for those taking charges, not only the doctrine of constructive notice of matters requiring registration and disclosed on the register, but also the doctrine of inferred knowledge[27] otherwise than by reason of other enquiries that ought to be made. However, this section relates to matters disclosed on the register and not (as is the case with the new section 711(a) of Companies Act 1985 referred to above) to documents. The section includes a proviso[28] that any other statutory provision, as to whether a person is to be taken to have notice of any matter disclosed on the register, is not affected; but it is unlikely that this proviso is intended to refer to section 711(A), a provision in the same statute.

It seems most likely that both provisions were intended to clarify the law and not to change it; there is academic support for the view that constructive notice of matters disclosed on the register (as it previously existed) affected only those who would be likely to search at the Companies' Registry in the normal course of dealing.[29] The provisions of the new section 416 go further because such constructive notice will affect only prospective chargees and not factors (except as chargees). Therefore, as regards the question as to whether a factor is taken to have notice or knowledge of a duly registered charged created by his prospective client one must look:

(1) as regards section 416, to the question of what enquiries (other than searches at the Companies Registry) the factor should make; and
(2) at the new section 711(A) which relates to matters disclosed in documents whether or not on the file at the Companies Registry.

[26] s. 416(2).
[27] By reason of his shutting his eyes to what is obvious.
[28] s. 416(3).
[29] See Goode, *Legal Problems of Credit and Security* (2nd. ed.), p. 44.

It would be reasonable to assume that, as the question of charges over debts of a prospective client is of material importance to a factor, the enquiries which he ought to make (for the purposes of the new section 711(A)(2)) before entering into a factoring agreement should include enquiries (by inspecting documents either at the prospective client's registered office or at the Companies Registry) as to charges created by a prospective client. Thus, it is arguable that the amendments in this respect should not change the position of a factor in questions of conflicts with chargees; and it may well be that the only change is that "deemed" or "constructive" notice of a matter disclosed at the registry will be replaced by "inferred knowledge" of a matter which would be elicited by enquiry. The discussions that follow have been based on this assumption.

Secondly, for the purpose of the rule in *Dearle* v. *Hall*[30] the holder of a charge on debts of a company is usually considered to be in a position analogous to that of an assignee notwithstanding that a charge, unlike a mortgage, does not constitute a transfer of ownership of the charged property;[31] but the rule may not assist the factor against the holder of a duly registered earlier charge because, if the factor has inferred knowledge of the charge, he is not then acting in good faith without knowledge of the prior right of the chargee.

Thirdly, the doctrine of constructive notice (as it existed before the Companies Act 1989 was enacted) has usually been considered to relate only to the existence of the charge but not to the contents of the instrument.[32] Thus, where an instrument of charge included a covenant by the chargor not to discount or factor its debts, the factor was not fixed with constructive notice of the covenant in the absence of actual knowledge of it[33]; and this appeared to be the case even if the particulars of the covenant where shown on the file at the registry, because such particulars have not been included in the matters which by law have to be shown. In this respect the law does not appear to have been changed by the Companies Act

[30] See para. 8–02 above.

[31] See, for example, *Business Computers Ltd.* v. *Anglo African Leasing Ltd.* [1977] 1 W.L.R. 578 in which Templeman J. (as he then was) describes the floating charge created by the plaintiff as an "incomplete assignment to the Debenture Holders of the assets" of the plaintiff.

[32] *Wilson* v. *Kelland* [1910] 2 Ch. 306 and *Siebe Gorman & Co. Ltd.* v. *Barclays Bank Ltd.* [1979] 2 Lloyds Rep. 142. See also Gough, *Company Charges*, pp. 355 *et seq.*

[33] Such actual knowledge might be by way of sight of the instrument of charge or by actual sight of a note on the file at the Companies Registry by reason of a search.

1989; the covenants, which may be included in the prescribed particulars for registration by the section 415(2)(a) introduced into the Companies Act 1985, are covenants against the creation of *charges* ranking *pari passu* with or ahead of the charge in question but not covenants against the factoring or discounting of debts. On the other hand there was an academic view that, as such a covenant is usual now in any charge over book debts, the factor may be deemed to have inferred knowledge of it by reason of failing to make such enquiries as he should reasonably be expected to make.[34] By analogy with that view, it seems more likely that the factor could be held to have inferred knowledge of restrictions on the dealing with debts and their proceeds in the case of a *fixed* charge on debts and their client; a fixed charge of itself postulates such restrictions if the charge is to be established as such and not merely so termed.[35] If these arguments are accepted then such inferred knowledge of the covenants or restrictions in a charge may be attributed to a factor whether his knowledge of the charge is actual or inferred.

8–13 Circumstances may arise in which the factor is unaware of the charge affecting the debts which are the subject of the factoring agreement and, on the insolvency of his client, a conflict may arise. For example, a registrable charge may be created by the client before the start of factoring but be registered after the start within the requisite 21 days of its creation and it is the date of creation of the charge, and not its registration, that governs its priority.[36] Other circumstances in which a factor may well not know of a charge on the debts which he is factoring are as follows:

(1) The charge may be on debts other than book debts (which, if not a floating charge or for the purpose of securing an issue of debentures, is not subject to registration) and it is conceivable that a debt, which is not a book debt,[37] may be included in a factoring agreement.
(2) A negotiable instrument given to secure a book debt of a company and deposited to secure advances to the company

[34] *I.e.* by his having wilfully shut his eyes to the obvious. See Farrar, "Floating Charges and Priorities" (1974) 38 Conv. 315. For a contrary view see Gough, *Company Charges*, p. 357, n. 12.
[35] *Re Brightlife Ltd.* [1986] 3 All E.R. 673; and see Goode, *Commercial Law*, p. 774.
[36] See Goode, *Legal Problems of Credit and Security (2nd ed.)*, p. 40.
[37] A book debt is usually considered to be a debt of such a nature as it would normally be entered in the books of a company even if it is not so entered. See, for example, *Paul & Frank Ltd.* v. *Discount Bank Overseas Ltd.* [1966] 2 All E.R. 922.

is not to be treated as a charge on that book debt for this purpose.[38]

(3) A shipowner's lien on subfreight which has been held to be a charge on book debts will no longer be registrable as a charge by section 396(2)(g) of the Companies Act 1985 (introduced by section 93 of the Companies Act 1989 and expected to come into effect in June 1991).

In the following paragraphs the priorities in any conflict between a factor and a chargee in relation to charges created both before and after the start of factoring are examined.

(b) Prior floating charge (duly registered)

8–14 A floating charge has been described as a present security over a fund of assets which the chargor may manage in the normal course of business[39] and by which it is contemplated that, until some step is taken by the chargee or some event provided for in the charge document occurs (usually referred to as crystallisation), the chargor may carry on its business in the usual way.[40] This means that the company may (subject to any covenants in the instrument of charge) dispose of its assets in the normal course of business free of the charge. Therefore, in the now unlikely event of the creation by a company of a floating charge containing no covenants against the discounting or factoring of its debts, the factor would be at liberty to buy the company's debts free from the charge until crystallisation of it in spite of knowledge of the charge whether actual, inferred or constructive; it seems likely that the sale of debts to a factor would be considered "in the normal course of business." At one time it was considered that any activity of a company, provided that it was not *ultra vires* its memorandum, was in the normal course of its business[41]; now that the doctrine of *ultra vires* is ineffective as regards third parties dealing in good faith with a company[42] it would seem even more likely that factoring would be considered to be in the normal course of a company's business. However, in the typical case in which the chargee is a bank and the charge contains the usual covenants, it would be unwise of the factor to rely on his lack of actual knowledge of those covenants owing to the possibility of his inferred knowledge of them.

[38] Companies Act 1985, s. 396(2)(f) which will replace Companies Act 1985, s. 396(2) (by Companies Act 1989, s. 93).

[39] See Goode, *op. cit.*, p. 49.

[40] *Evans* v. *Rival Granite Quarries Ltd.* [1910] 2 K.B. 979; *Re Yorkshire Woolcombers Association* [1903] 2 Ch. 284 at p. 295.

[41] *Re Borax Company* [1901] 1 Ch. 326 and see also *Re Ind, Coope & Co. Ltd.* [1911] 2 Ch. 223.

[42] Companies Act 1985, s. 35 and amendments thereto (including new ss.35A and 35B) by Companies Act 1989, s. 108 which is expected to come into effect in November 1990.

Whether or not knowledge of the restrictive covenants would impeach the factor's proprietary rights to the debts which he has purchased for full consideration is not certain; but, at the very least, the factor would be liable to the chargee for procuring the chargor's breach of the covenant and the courts are likely to restrain a person from enforcing his rights so as to cause a breach of a prior agreement of which he had knowledge.[43] Therefore, if in such a case the factor had entered into an agreement without any waiver or consent from the chargee, it is possible that the breach of a purely contractual provision in the charge may not prevent a valid transfer of proprietary rights by the assignments to the factor; but the factor may well be restrained from enjoying the proceeds of the debts contrary to the interests of the chargee whose covenants have been breached.

(c) Prior fixed charge (duly registered)

8–15 The concept of a fixed charge on book debts attaching to each debt as it comes into existence has gained recognition in recent years in spite of the fact that book debts comprise a class of assets which are changing from time to time. The concept had judicial recognition in the *Siebe Gorman* case[44] which has a bearing on a possible conflict between a factor and the holder of a prior fixed charge on debts. In that case it was held that the assignee of certain choses in action (the proceeds of bills of exchange) of a company, which were covered by a prior duly registered fixed charge in favour of the bank of which the assignee was aware at the time of the assignment, took the choses subject to the charge as regards sums owing to the bank as at that time. The bank had neither ruled off the account of its customer (the chargor) nor opened a new one at the date of the assignment and credits to the account since the assignment had almost extinguished that debt; consequently the assignor was at liberty to collect the proceeds of the bills subject to the payment of a modest amount to the bank. The question of the restrictive covenants in the charge document was considered; but the judge held that the assignee had no actual or constructive notice of them.

8–16 Although, by its very nature, such a charge should preclude the chargor from disposing of the charged debts and from dealing with the proceeds otherwise than under the control of the chargee, it must be presumed that awareness of the nature of a fixed charge

[43] *Encyclopaedia of Banking Law*, 4124.4 (from which it appears that, for the purpose of the assignee's liability to the beneficiary of the covenant, actual, or possibly inferred knowledge, is necessary but that constructive knowledge will not suffice) and *Manchester Ship Canal Co.* v. *Manchester Racecourse Co.* [1901] 2 Ch. 37.

[44] *Siebe Gorman & Co. Ltd.* v. *Barclays Bank Ltd.* [1979] 2 Lloyds Rep. 142.

was not imputed to the assignee which was a trading company. However, now that the nature of fixed charges is more widely known and as factoring companies may be considered to be more aware of these matters, it may be that a factor with actual or inferred knowledge of a fixed charge created before his agreement was entered into, but ignorant of any covenants in the instrument of charge, would be considered to have inferred knowledge of the restrictions which arise from the nature of the charge itself. If in such circumstances the factor were to purchase debts, covered by the charge, without a waiver or release from the chargee, it is possible that on the insolvency of the client/chargor he might be restrained from enforcing his agreement and ownership of the debts against the interests of the chargee.[45] In such circumstances he might well be unable to recover any of the proceeds of the debts until the satisfaction (from such proceeds) of *all* amounts owing by the chargor to the chargee at the time of the conflict (subject to the limitation of the charge) and not only such amounts (still outstanding at the time of the conflict) as were owing to the chargee at the dates of the assignments; and, if the factor had actual or inferred knowledge of the restrictions on the charger, his client, he may well be liable to the chargee for assisting the chargor to breach the covenants.[46]

(d) Subsequent registered charges

8–17 Factoring agreements invariably provide that the client should not create any charge which affects or may affect the debts included in the agreement. Nevertheless it frequently happens that whilst a factoring agreement is in operation the client will give a debenture including a charge on its debts to its bankers without any consultation with the factor. One must presume that the absence of consultation in such circumstances is the result of a misunderstanding of the nature of a factoring agreement on the part of both the client and the bank. If the client becomes insolvent and both the bank, by reason of its charge, and the factor, by reason of its prior agreement, claim the proceeds of the debts, the rule in *Dearle* v. *Hall*,[47] although not assisting the factor owing to actual or inferred knowledge of the charge, may possibly assist the bank: if the bank were quite unaware of the factoring agreement and the factoring was on an undisclosed basis it is possible (but unlikely) that the bank might through a receiver get notices to debtors first and obtain priority. It is therefore important that a factor, particularly in an undisclosed arrangement,

[45] See para. 8–14 above.
[46] See n. 43 above.
[47] See para. 8–02 above.

should ensure that any bank or finance company providing facilities to the client is aware of the factoring agreement.

8–18 Unless the bank is able to rely on *Dearle* v. *Hall*[48] the result will depend to some extent on the nature of the factoring agreement and the position is likely to be as follows:

(1) In the case of a whole turnover type of agreement[49] the agreement itself constitutes a present assignment binding the debts as they come into existence. Therefore it seems that there will be no debts to which the charge, whether fixed or floating, may attach other than the debt owing by the factor to the client and the debts (if any) outside the scope of the agreement. Furthermore, as the charge must take effect in equity, it must be subject to the prior equitable rights of the factor; and this would seem to apply whether the bank was aware of the factoring agreement or not.

(2) Less certain is the position of the factor with a facultative type of agreement.[50] Certainly in the case of a subsequent fixed charge the factor, having inferred knowledge of the charge, might be precluded from buying any more debts except subject to the charge if the bank was unaware of the factoring agreement when the charge was created. This is because the agreement itself gives the factor no real rights to the debts but only a personal right against the client to have the debts offered free from encumbrances; the factor's real proprietary rights arise only as regards each debt when it has been offered to the factor and accepted. In the case of a floating charge the position seems even more uncertain. Even if it could be shown that with inferred knowledge of the charge the factor had inferred knowledge also of the usual restrictive covenants, he would not have known of them when he entered into his agreement because they did not then exist. Until crystallisation the charge does not attach to the debts. As a result the conflict is between two personal contractual rights: the rights of the chargee (not as such) but under the covenants (as negative pledges) and the rights of the factor to have the debts offered to him. In such circumstances if neither one was aware of the other's rights when he entered into his own contract, it seems that the first in time (the factor) should prevail provided that his notices reached the debtor before those of the crystallisation of the charge.

[48] *Ibid.*
[49] See para. 7–13 above.
[50] See para. 7–12 above.

Naturally, if the bank had knowledge of the factoring agreement when it took its charge, there seems little doubt that the factor's ownership of the debts, which he has purchased, should not be flawed by the charge. It seems clear that the bank, having taken its charge on the debts which it knows to be the subject of contractual rights, may be restrained from exercising its own rights under the charge in such a way as to interfere with those contractual rights.[51] This principle would apply to both types of factoring agreement but it would be unnecessary to rely upon it in the case of a whole turnover type[52] as the debts are already bound by that earlier agreement.

(e) Unregistered charges

8–19 The priorities in a conflict between a factor and a chargee, whose charge was not registrable, would in most cases be governed by the rule in *Dearle* v. *Hall*.[53] However, where either one was aware of the other's prior rights, then it seems that the prior right must succeed and the giving of notices to debtors first will not assist the one whose rights have arisen later in time.[54] If the charge is registrable, but unregistered then on the liquidation of the client/chargor the chargee's claim to the debts will fail as against the factor.[55]

4. CONFLICTS WITH HOLDERS OF NEGOTIABLE INSTRUMENTS

8–20 A bill of exchange accepted (or a cheque drawn) by a debtor in discharge of a debt is a payment conditional upon the instrument being met; but the creditor's rights of action and remedies are suspended, when the instrument has been taken by the creditor,

[51] *Swiss Bank Corporation* v. *Lloyds Bank Ltd. and others* [1979] Ch. 548 at p. 573 where Browne-
Wilkinson J. (as he then was) reviewed the case of *De Mattos* v. *Gibson* (1858) 4 De G. & J. 276. The decision *Swiss Bank* case was reversed in the court of appeal but the principle appears to remain.

[52] See para. 7–13 above.

[53] See para. 8–02 above.

[54] See n. 2 above.

[55] By reason of the provisions of Companies Act 1985, s. 399 (see para. 8–11 above sub-para. (1)) and, until that new provision is in effect, in any case in which the factor is a creditor of the client; see *E. Pfeiffer Weinkellerei-Weineinkauf GmbH & Co.* v. *Arbuthnot Factors Ltd.* [1987] B.C.L.C. 522 at p. 533.

until its maturity.[56] Thus, if a cheque is given or a bill accepted by the debtor before notice of the assignment of the underlying debt has been received by the debtor (even if the assignment took place earlier), then the holder of the instrument would have the right to payment and the debtor would have no liability to the assignee; until notice the debtor is at liberty to settle with the assignor and, once the instrument has been taken by the creditor, his rights against the debtor other than in the bill, being suspended, cannot be assigned.

However, when notice of the assignment of a debt has been received by the debtor, no cheque given or bill accepted thereafter by the debtor will detract from the rights of the assignee of the debt. Notice of an assignment in statutory form completes the transfer to the assignee of all rights to the debt including the power to give a good discharge[57]; and in the case of an equitable assignment after receipt of notice the debtor is unable, either by payment or in any other way, to detract from the rights of the assignee.[58]

8–21 If such an instrument taken by the creditor in discharge or purported discharge of a debt owing to him is negotiated to a third party, who takes it before it is overdue (complete and regular on the face of it) in good faith and for value without notice of any defect in the title of the drawer (*e.g.* by reason of a previous assignment of the underlying debt), then the person to whom the instrument has been negotiated will have the right to have the instrument paid on presentation.[59] This will be so even if the bill was accepted (or the cheque given) after receipt of notice of the assignment of the underlying debt to another person; as the assignee in such a case would have the right to payment[60] the debtor would have to pay twice for the same debt. Naturally if the bill was accepted or the cheque drawn before the notice of the assignment was received the assignee would have no right to payment. The same considerations (as apply to a person to whom a negotiable instrument has been negotiated) would appear to apply to the position of a person who has advanced money on the security of a negotiable instrument deposited with him in any conflict with an assignee of the debt to which the instrument relates. As such a security right created by

[56] See Goode, *Payment Obligations in Commercial and Financial Transactions*, p. 20.
[57] Law of Property Act, s. 136.
[58] See para. 8–07 above and *Wm. Brandts Sons & Co.* v. *Dunlop Rubber Co. Ltd.* [1905] A.C. 454.
[59] Bills of Exchange Act 1882, s. 29(1).
[60] See para. 8–07 above.

a company is exempt from registration[61] a factor should make searching enquiries, before starting a factoring agreement, regarding the practice of his prospective client in dealing with negotiable instruments.

Furthermore, although most agreements for factoring or invoice discounting provide for the automatic assignment to the factor of any such instruments taken by the client in respect of the assigned debts, during the whole period of any such agreement which is on an undisclosed basis the factor must be on his guard against the discounting or pledging of negotiable instruments by his client.

5. NEGATIVE PLEDGE *SIMPLICITER*

8–22 It is now quite common for lenders to companies, whose creditworthiness is at the higher end of the scale, to take, instead of security, a covenant from the borrower that it will not, until the loan is discharged, create any form of security over its property. Such covenants, often termed "negative pledges" sometimes include a restriction on the disposal of assets of the borrower otherwise than in the normal course of business. Such a restriction might well include an undertaking by the borrower specifically not to sell its debts or accounts receivable by way of factoring or discounting. If it does not, the question arises as to whether factoring or discounting would be considered to be in the normal course of business; it seems likely but not certain that it would.[62] However, assuming that the covenant is a clear prohibition of factoring or discounting what is the position of the factor who enters into a factoring agreement with the covenantor?

8–23 It seems clear that if the factor, with knowledge of the covenant, enters into a factoring agreement with the person who has given the covenant then the position would be similar to that where the covenant was in an instrument of charge: at the minimum the factor as assignee would be liable to the beneficiary of the covenant for assisting in or inducing its breach.[63] For this purpose it would be necessary for the factor to have actual knowledge; constructive notice is not enough[64] and it is difficult to see how the factor could have inferred knowledge in such a case. In the case of

[61] See para. 8–13 and n. 38 above.
[62] See para. 8–14 and n. 41 above.
[63] See para. 8–14 and n. 43 above.
[64] *Encyclopaedia of Banking Law*, 4124.4.

a facultative type of agreement[65] each debt is offered to the factor as it comes into existence and the factor has no real right to any debts until he has accepted it. Thus, if the factor entered into such an agreement in ignorance of and after the date of the covenant but subsequently became actually aware of its existence, the conflict would be between two purely contractual rights. It is arguable that in such a situation the factor would be unable to accept any further debts without becoming liable to the beneficiary of the covenant; it seems that the rights of the one whose equity was earlier in time must prevail. In the case of a whole turnover type of agreement,[66] for the factor to be liable his knowledge would have to have arisen before he entered into his agreement because that type of agreement is indivisible.

8–24 As regards the possible impeachment of the factor's proprietary rights in such circumstances, similar considerations appear to apply as in the case of a prior floating charge which includes such a covenant.[67] It is indeed clear that a negative pledge does not create any consensual security interest in favour of its beneficiary; he will have no real rights over any of the assets of the covenantor when a conflict arises with the factor and he cannot be in a better position than he would have been but for the breach of the covenant.[68]

However, as an assignment is often considered analogous to a security right for the purposes of resolving such conflicts[69] it might be thought that the *De Mattos* v. *Gibson* principle[70] would be applied if the interest of the beneficiary of the covenant were to be affected by the factoring agreement; if this were to be so the factor might be unable to enforce his agreement and effect recoveries to some extent. However, if the detrimental effect on the beneficiary was by way of his receiving a smaller dividend in the liquidation of the covenantor than would otherwise have been the case (the most likely scenario), then it is difficult to see how this principle could be applied without benefiting *all* unsecured creditors of the covenantor; as the covenant bestows no security or real right on the beneficiary, any proceeds of the debts, which did not go to the factor, would be claimed by the liquidator. As a result, in those circumstances, the remedy for the beneficiary of the covenant would perforce be by way of a claim for damages.

[65] See para. 7–12 above.
[66] See para. 7–13 above.
[67] See para. 8–14 above.
[68] See Goode, *Legal Problems of Credit and Security* (2nd ed., 1988), pp. 18 *et seq.* (and particularly at p. 22) to which reference should be made for an analysis of negative pledges.
[69] See n. 31 above.
[70] (1858) 4 De G. & J. 276 and n. 51.

6. RESERVATION OF TITLE

(a) The background

8–25 Of all such potential conflicts, that which has probably given factors most concern is the conflict with a client's supplier who is claiming the proceeds of the sub-sales of the client because ownership of the goods has been reserved to the supplier until payment for them has been made. Such concern has arisen not because the supplier is likely to derogate from the the factor's unencumbered ownership of the proceeds as debts purchased by the factor under the factoring agreement (and such improbability may be apparent from the discourse in the succeeding paragraphs); the concern seems to have arisen from the conceptual difficulties relating to equitable tracing rights in commercial transactions and the absence of a case law bearing directly on such a conflict where the supplier is relying on such a right.

The facts in *E. Pfeiffer Weinkellerei-Weineinkauf GmbH & Co.* v. *Arbuthnot Factors Ltd.*[71] might appear to have dealt with such a conflict; but in that case the supplier's claim was based on a term in his contract of sale by which the proceeds of the sub-sales by the buyer (the factor's client) were assigned to the supplier. The assignment, being by way of security and unregistered, was void as against the factor who was considered to be a creditor of the buyer.

8–26 The practice of reserving title to goods sold until payment for them has been received by the seller, in its simplest form without any stated term by which the proceeds of any sub-sale are to be held by the buyer for the seller, has long been established in commerce and industry in England and Wales; but it did not appear to come to the general notice of grantors of trade credit or to members of the accountancy and legal professions until attention was drawn to it by reports of the *Romalpa* case[72] and commentary on it in the late 1970s.

This case broke new ground, not because the terms in the sale contract were effective to retain in favour of the seller ownership of goods still held by the buyer in their original state, but because the Court of Appeal, upholding the decision of the judge in the court of first instance, recognised that the buyers, being in a fiduciary position in relation to the sellers, were under a duty to account to them for the proceeds of sub-sales. Such proceeds were, accordingly, not available to the receiver of the buyer. However, in that case it was conceded on behalf of the defendants that they held the goods as bailees; and this seems to be one of its unique features.

[71] [1987] B.C.L.C. 522.
[72] *Aluminium Industrie Vaassen B.V.* v. *Romalpa Aluminium Ltd.* [1976] 1 W.L.R. 676.

8–27 Terms reserving ownership of the goods in their simplest form, without any attempt to attach proceeds or goods other than those for which payment has not been made, are usually referred to as "simple reservation of title." More comprehensive terms purport to reserve to the supplier, until payment has been received for all goods supplied, any of the following:

(1) any goods supplied by the supplier to the buyer (even those for which payment has been made) or any work in progress or finished goods into which the goods supplied have been incorporated ("extended reservation of title"); or
(2) the proceeds of the sub-sales of the goods or even of goods into which the goods supplied have been incorporated ("prolonged reservation of title").

(b) The effect of prolonged reservation of title on factors

8–28 In the consideration of a conflict between the unpaid supplier who is claiming the debts created by the sub-sales by his buyer and the factor who has purchased such debts by way of outright assignment from the buyer (his client), the first question is whether the buyer has given his customer (the factor's debtor) a good title by the sub-sale. If the sub-sale did not give the debtor a good title then the debt purchased by the factor would be of little value to him because the debtor under the sub-sale would be unlikely to pay for goods which might be claimed from him by the unpaid supplier. The position would in most circumstances be covered by the statutory exception to the normal rule that *nemo dat quod non habet*.[73] This provides *inter alia* that, where a buyer in possession of goods with the consent of the true owner delivers them, under a contract of sale, to another who receives them in good faith and without knowledge of the rights of the true owner, that other person obtains a good title. Therefore, provided that the buyer has been in possession of the goods before delivery under the sub-sale and the debtor had no knowledge of the supplier's reservation of title the debtor would obtain a good title.

Furthermore, many such terms in sale contracts specifically authorise the onward sale of the goods by the buyer as principal *as between himself and the ultimate customer*. Where the terms are silent on this matter such authorisation must surely be implicit because the contracts are contracts of sale, and not straightforward bailment contracts, and, except in the case of capital equipment or goods to be consumed by the buyer in the course of his business, it must usually be envisaged that the goods are to be sold on in their original form or incorporated in other goods. In this connection it

[73] Sale of Goods Act 1979, s. 25(1) and Factors Act 1889, ss. 2(1), 9.

is of interest to note that in the *Pfeiffer* case[74] Phillips J. remarked that it seemed to him inappropriate to describe the relationship of a seller and a buyer in possession to whom title has not yet passed as that of bailor/bailee, and he added that such relationship would not have the same incidents as a classic bailment.

8–29 On the premise that the supplier cannot recover his goods from the ultimate customer under the sub-sale (the factor's debtor) because the ownership has passed to the latter (which, as explained in paragraph 8–28, is most likely), it seems that the supplier will have two hurdles to overcome in order that he may have a valid claim to the proceeds of the sub-sale. However, before considering these two hurdles there are two points to be considered in relation to any such conflict. First, there are the practical matters. In the normal course of businesses of the nature of those that might be likely to use factoring services, there is very often a stream of a large number of relatively small transactions and it is rare that such detailed terms can be agreed at the time when an order is placed by the buyer; very often such orders are placed and accepted orally and the endorsement of the reservation of title provisions on the invoice is likely to be ineffective. Furthermore, in such a stream of transactions it is very often not possible to trace into a sub-sale the particular goods for which payment has not been made.

8–30 Secondly, there has been much discussion and disagreement between lawyers as to whether a factor, who is unaware that his client has been purchasing goods on terms including a reservation of title provision and effecting sub-sales of such goods and including the proceeds as debts within the factoring agreement, may be deemed to have inferred knowledge of such terms of purchase. This may be relevant where the factor is relying on the rule in *Dearle* v. *Hall*[75] by which, in a competition between two assignees of the same debt, priority goes to the one whose notice has been received first by the debtor; for that rule is subject to the qualification that he must have been unaware of any earlier assignment at the time when he made his commitment.

There may be rare cases in which the factored client is known to be a distributor for one or a few suppliers of whose long term contracts the factor is likely to be aware. However, in most cases the factor could hardly be expected to examine every one of his client's purchase contracts in the continuing stream of transactions. Even if he might be aware from his initial survey that such terms have been agreed with one or more of the suppliers, he is

[74] *E. Pfeiffer Weinkellerei-Weineinkauf GmbH & Co.* v. *Arbuthnot Factors Ltd.* [1987] B.C.L.C. 522.

[75] (1823) 3 Russ 1 and see para. 8–02 above.

not to know from whom, and on what terms, his client may subsequently make purchases. Most factors rely on warranties given by the client in the factoring agreement that such terms do not apply; and on these grounds it was accepted in the *Pfeiffer* case[76] that the factor had no inferred knowledge of the reservation of title provisions of the client's supplier.

8–31 In order to lay claim to the proceeds the supplier must first show that the goods themselves remained in his ownership until title passed to the customer under the sub-sale either by reason of the statutory provisions[77] or in accordance with a term in the supplier's contract of sale. Since the *Romalpa* case[78] there have been a number of cases in which suppliers whose terms of sale included reservation of title provisions in their extended form have sought to establish their ownership of goods into which the goods, which they supplied, have been incorporated[79] or to goods supplied by them which had been worked on in the course of manufacture.[80] In all such cases the supplier has failed in his claim except where the goods supplied had not been irretrievably mixed with other goods and could be simply traced and detached from the other goods.[81]

It seems from a review of the cases concerned that it would be virtually impossible to construct conditions of sale which would reserve to the seller ownership of the products into which his goods had been incorporated without either creating a charge (which, unless registered, would be void as described in paragraph 8–11 above) or by giving the seller the free benefit of the buyer's labour and other materials; it is doubtful if any buyer could agree to the latter.[82] As a result of the foregoing it is most unlikely that a supplier on such terms in practice will be able to justify a claim to the proceeds of his buyer's sub-sale unless the goods are sold on in their original form or, if incorporated into other products, retain their original form and are separable and clearly identifiable.

8–32 Assuming that the goods are so unchanged or separable and identifiable, the supplier must then show unequivocably that the buyer has been placed in a fiduciary capacity as regards the

[76] *E. Pfeiffer Weinkellerei-Weineinkauf GmbH & Co.* v. *Arbuthnot Factors Ltd.* [1987] B.C.L.C. 522.
[77] See para. 8–28 and n. 73 above.
[78] *Aluminium Industrie Vaassen B.V.* v. *Romalpa Aluminium Ltd.* [1976] 1 W.L.R. 676.
[79] See, for example, *Borden (UK) Ltd.* v. *Scottish Timber Products Ltd.* [1981] Ch. 25; *Re Bond Worth Ltd.* [1980] Ch. 228; *Clough Mill Ltd.* v. *Martin* [1985] 1 W.L.R. 111.
[80] *Re Peachdart Ltd.* [1984] Ch. 131.
[81] *Hendy Lennox Ltd.* v. *Graham Puttick Ltd.* [1984] 1 W.L.R. 485.
[82] For a full exposition of this aspect of reservation of title see Goode, *Proprietary Rights and Insolvency in Sales Transactions*, pp. 83–86. See also *Tatung (U.K.) Ltd.* v. *Galex Telesure Ltd.* (1989) 5 B.C.C. 325 in which it was held that the provisions in the conditions of sale, by which the proceeds of the buyer's subsale were to be held for the account of the seller, constituted a charge because in the circumstances of the case the buyer could not be considered to be a bailee.

proceeds. It seems that the courts will not import such terms into the contract of sale where no such terms exist.[83] However, a proceeds clause alone will in all probability not invest in the supplier an equitable right to trace; such a contractual arrangement appears to be the creation by the buyer of a security right in favour of the supplier. It must be shown from the circumstances of the transaction and the whole of the terms that such a fiduciary relationship exists; for example, in the *Romalpa* case it was accepted on behalf of the buyer that it was a bailee.[84] In such a case the contract terms merely confirm the fiduciary position of the buyer as regards the proceeds which has already existed by reason of the nature of the transaction.

In *Re Andrabell Ltd.*[85] the supplier's claim failed because:

(1) there was no provision for separate storage of the goods before they became the subject of a sub-sale;
(2) there was no acknowledgement by the buyer of a fiduciary relationship; and
(3) the terms did not provide for a duty to account for the whole of the proceeds of the sub-sale but only an amount equivalent to the amount owing by the buyer to the supplier.

It seems, therefore, reasonably certain that in order that a right to trace should be upheld, the transaction must clearly be that of bailment or agency,[86] and in view of the inconsistencies between such relationships and the relationships under contracts of sale this is difficult to achieve by the supplier. Furthermore it should not be overlooked that in a number of recent cases (particularly those concerning the confirmation of charges on book debts as fixed charges) the courts appear to be reluctant to uphold terms and conditions which are not operative in practice; it is doubtful if it would be commercially possible, other than in rare cases, for the supplier to ensure the separate storage of the goods and the payment of the proceeds into a special bank account.

Finally, even if in rare cases the supplier can establish his rights to the proceeds of the sub-sales by the factor's client, a strong argument that the proceeds to be attached are the monies paid to the client by the factor, by way of payment of the purchase price of the debts assigned to him, is as follows:

(1) It must be envisaged by the supplier that the client (his buyer) would effect a sub-sale of the goods (even if it is not explicitly provided for in the supplier's terms);

[83] *Hendy Lennox Ltd.* v. *Graham Puttick Ltd.* [1984] 1 W.L.R. 485.
[84] *Aluminium Industrie Vaassen B.V.* v. *Romalpa Aluminium Ltd.* [1976] 1 W.L.R. 676.
[85] [1984] 3 All E.R. 407.
[86] *Tatung (U.K.) Ltd.* v. *Galex Telesure Ltd.* (1989) 5 B.C.C. 325.

(2) The client would have given the debtor a good title and would, as between himself and the debtor, have the right to collect payment; and
(3) It is quite normal commercial practice to arrange for collection of trade debts by receiving payment from a factor in return for the transfer to the factor of the right to collect payment from the debtor.[87]

(c) Position of factor summarised

8–33 From the foregoing it seems that, in order to ensure that his rights to debts purchased should not be encumbered by claims to the debts by suppliers to his client, the factor should in all cases ensure that his client has given him a warranty that the debts falling within the scope of the factoring agreement are not the result of sub-sales of goods purchased on the basis of prolonged reservation of title. In the event of the client breaching this warranty it seems that the factor has little to fear in those cases in which his client is a manufacturer unless the goods purchased by the client are identifiable after the sub-sale and can readily be returned to their original form.

8–34 If, on the other hand, the goods are passed on in their original form, in most cases the supplier's claim to their proceeds will constitute an assignment by way of security or some other form of security right created by the client as buyer. In the case of a corporate client the supplier's claim will normally fail as against the factor because its rights will rest upon an unregistered charge void against the factor as a person who has acquired for value an interest in the charged property.[88] It is likely that notice of the assignment by the factor will have been given first, in the case of disclosed factoring, on the invoice and, in the case of confidential factoring, at the first signs of financial difficulties. In the absence of knowledge of the supplier's claim,[89] the factor would be able to

[87] In this connection it may be of interest that in Germany, where these practices have been in general use in commerce far longer than in England and Wales, in such a conflict these arguments were adduced in favour of the factor to whom the court awarded priority (BGH WM 1977, 1198; 1982, 37 and 1350); see Klaus Bette, "Factoring and Prolonged Retention of Property Title" in *Factoring Handbuch* (2nd ed., edited by Prof. Dr. K. F. Hagenmuller and Herr H. J. Sommer; published by Fritz Knapp Verlag).
[88] After June 1991 when Companies Act 1985, s. 399 is expected to come into force; until then if he is a creditor.
[89] See para. 8–30 above.

rely on the principle of *Dearle* v. *Hall*[90] and obtain priority over the supplier's assignment or charge.

8–35 There remain those cases, in which the supplier's claim is based on an equitable tracing right, and for reasons explained above these are likely to be rare. In such cases the application of the rule in *Dearle* v. *Hall* is not certain. There appears to be no reported case on the question of a conflict between a supplier, claiming by way of equitable tracing the proceeds of a sub-sale by his buyer, and an assignee of those proceeds where the assignee is seeking to rely on the rule in *Dearle* v. *Hall*. Academic opinion seems to be divided as to whether the rule would apply, although there are strong arguments that it does.[91] Therefore in such cases the factor may be at some risk, as regards debts still outstanding when the conflict arises, even in the absence of knowledge of the terms agreed between the supplier and his client.

8–36 As regards debts already paid to the factor by the time when the supplier asserts his claim, it appears that the factor should obtain priority provided that the factor has received the payments in good faith without knowledge of the supplier's terms. It appears that money passes into the legal ownership of a purchaser in good faith and the legal ownership displaces the equitable right of the supplier.[92]

8–37 Naturally, whether the supplier's rights constitute an assignment or charge or is based on equitable tracing, if the factor has actual or inferred knowledge of them (*e.g.* where the client is a distributor for the supplier under a long term contract) the factor's priority may be in doubt; this is particularly so if the reservation of title terms were concluded before the consideration is passed by the factor for the purchase of the debts in which the proceeds are comprised. In this respect a whole turnover type of agreement[93] may be an advantage to the factor; the disposition of all the debts under such an agreement takes place at the time of the first payment or credit of the purchase price of any debt under the agreement by the factor because the contract is indivisble.[94] Where the factor has knowledge of the earlier rights of the supplier, to be safe, he should obtain a waiver from the supplier.

[90] (1823) 3 Russ 1 and see para. 8–02 above.
[91] See Goode, *Legal Problems of Credit and Security* (2nd ed., 1988), p. 121. See also McCormack, "Effective Reservation of Title and Priorities" J.B.L. (July, 1990) 314 where he arrives at the conclusion that the factor has little to fear from such a conflict.
[92] *Ibid.*
[93] See para. 7–13 above.
[94] See Goode, "Some Aspects of Factoring Law" (1982) J.B.L. 242.

7. OTHER CONFLICTS

(a) Goods released on trust receipt

8–38 In order to finance the movement of goods, especially for the import of goods, banks and other financiers often take security by means of a pledge by the trader of the documents of title to the goods which is treated in law as a pledge of the goods themselves. The pledge, if it does not depend on a document but is purely a possessory security, does not require registration at the companies registry (if the trader is a company) nor as a bill of sale (if it is not). It is usually necessary for the trader to take physical possession of the goods and to sell them in order to repay the advances made by the lender. So that the lender's security should not be lost before the advances have been repaid, the lender will often release the documents to the trader against the provision of a trust receipt by the trader. By the trust receipt the trader undertakes to hold in trust for the lender, not only the goods until sold, but also the proceeds of their sale. It has been held that a trust receipt for such purposes constitutes a continuation of the pledge and that, furthermore, the lender's rights to the proceeds do not require registration at the companies registry or as a bill of sale (as applicable).[95]

8–39 It is, therefore, apparent that if a factor's client has made such an arrangement and either offers to the factor or notifies the factor of the proceeds to which such a trust receipt relates the factor may well take the assignment of the proceeds as debts falling within the scope of the factoring agreement. He might be completely unaware of the pledge or the trust receipts. On the insolvency of the client the lender might well claim that the assignment to the factor was invalid on the basis that the proceeds, being held by the trader in trust, were not property of the trader capable of being assigned by it. On the other hand, as it is probable that the factor will have given notice to the debtor first, he might claim priority on the basis of the rule in *Dearle* v. *Hall.*[96] However, as in the case of a conflict between a factor and a supplier to the client on *Romalpa*[97] type

[95] *Re David Allester Ltd.* 2 Ch. 211; *North Western Bank Ltd.* v. *John Poynter Son & MacDonalds* [1895] A.C. 56. It seems that the absence of a requirement to register at the Companies Registry in such cases will be unchanged after the coming into effect of the provisions of Companies Act 1989, s. 93 (specifically the new ss. 396(1)(b) and 396(2)(c) of Companies Act 1985).

[96] (1823) 3 Russ 1 and see para. 8–02 above.

[97] *Aluminium Industrie Vaassen B.V.* v. *Romalpa Aluminium Ltd.* [1976] 1 W.L.R. 676.

terms[98] (claiming by way of equitable tracing) it is not clear that the rule applies because it is not a conflict between two assignees.

8–40 Although there are similarities in the positions of a lender in such a case and the supplier who has reserved title to the goods sold to the factor's client, the position is in most cases not exactly the same. In the case of the trust receipt, the trust relating to the proceeds of sale is based on a well established principle (and does not require registration) whereas, in the case of the *Romalpa* type terms,[99] the existence of a trust may well not be established.[1] Although conflicts between factors and holders of trust receipts have arisen in practice, it appears that they have in all cases been resolved without recourse to litigation (possibly by compromise); as there appears to be no reported case on the point and nor any authoritative published comment on it, a resolution of the problem remains a matter of uncertainty.

(b) The liens of a carrier

8–41 The question of a carrier's lien on goods, despatched by a client to a debtor, is not strictly a question of conflict between the factor and the carrier relating to rights to debts purchased by the factor. On the insolvency of the client there may well be an unpaid carrier who has a general lien on such goods in respect of which the client had responsibility for delivery to the debtor's premises. Such a claim to the goods will obviously impair the factor's right to recover any related debt. Factors often accept notifications or offers submitted as soon as goods have been placed in transit in the United Kingdom to debtors. If the carrier seized the goods, the debtors would not pay and the client would be in breach of his warranty that the debts were bona fide obligations of the debtors.

8–42 This aspect may not be too serious a problem in the case of domestic sales in relation to which delivery may take only two or three days. Even if the carrier's charges for all his sales are the client's responsibility, the aggregate of unpaid debts may well be fully absorbed by any retention made. Indeed in many cases in the event of insolvency and an insufficient retention it may sometimes be worthwhile for the factor to settle with the carrier in order to release the goods to the debtors and recover the indebtedness. However, in the case of export sales in circumstances in which the client is responsible for carriage and freight charges, the amounts payable may be considerable and, in view of the longer transit time, the aggregate of the outstanding invoices represented by

[98] See paras. 8–25 *et seq.* above.
[99] See nts. 97 and 98 above.
[1] See para. 8–32 and n. 86 above.

goods which have not reached the debtors may be a large proportion of the whole. Furthermore, this aspect needs to be considered carefully in the case of an importing client whose business is such that the goods are despatched from his overseas supplier direct to the customers. In such a case the factor should accept responsibility for the debts only when the underlying goods have been placed in transit to the debtors in the United Kingdom.

(c) The rights of a mercantile agent

8–43 A mercantile agent (or factor in the original sense) has a prescriptive right, born of long usage in the law merchant, to a lien on his principal's goods in his possession and on the proceeds of the sale of those goods effected through his agency. As a result, if a client sells to the debtors through a mercantile agent it is likely that the agent's lien would attach to the proceeds (*i.e.* the debts) in priority to the factor's rights to debts resulting from the agent's sales on behalf of the client. The factor's rights to any such debt under the assignment to him cannot be better than the client's rights at the time of the assignment. This question does not appear to have been decided in the courts in the United Kingdom and it would not appear to be a serious matter for factors in their domestic businesses because few businesses employ mercantile agents in this country. To be a mercantile agent, for this purpose, the agent must sell in his own name without disclosing that of his principal.[2] However, the priority of a mercantile agent in these circumstances has been accepted in international trade in Europe. A factor should be on his guard if his client factors his exports and is likely to use a mercantile agent. Agreement between the factor and the agent should be reached at the outset. Obviously, if the agent is adamant about retaining his rights and the client persists in using him, then the client will be unable to warrant that these debts are free of encumbrances and they will have to be excluded from factoring.

8. WAIVERS AND PRIORITY AGREEMENTS[3]

8–44 In the foregoing paragraphs of this chapter indications have been given of some of the cases in which the factor should obtain at the outset from a third party, who may have a security right or interest in the factored debts, a waiver of such right or interest. In view of the difficulties and uncertainties in certain aspects of the law having a bearing on these potential conflicts, whenever a factor knows that a prospective client has agreed to give to a third party a

[2] *Per* Lord Denning in *Rolls Razor Ltd.* v. *Cox* [1967] 1 Q.B. 552.
[3] See App. 9.

right to purchase its debts or a security right over them, or is under an obligation to do so, the factor should obtain a waiver from that third party. It may be that the factor has been advised that in the event of a conflict his rights will prevail; but in view of these uncertainties, it is as well to obtain agreement in advance. Even the winner of such a conflict may well suffer from the anxiety, invidiousness and expense of the conflict. In the case of a facultative agreement[4] such agreement should be sought even if the third party's rights or interest arises during the currency of the agreement because under that type of agreement the factor's real rights to each debt come into existence only when the debt has been offered to and accepted by him. On the other hand in the case of an existing whole turnover agreement and the creation of a new charge (or a new assignment) by the client in favour of a third party a waiver is in most cases not necessary because the factor's rights should have priority.[5] However, in such a case, in order to avoid any misunderstanding and invidiousness, the factor should on notice of the charge immediately seek acknowledgement from the third party that it is aware of the factor's prior rights. The difference between a waiver and an acknowledgement has practical significance: in the case of a request for a waiver the third party may seek to impose some conditions. Indeed it has not been unknown for a bank, on being asked to confirm its understanding of the position in such circumstances, to offer a waiver in which a limitation is imposed on the aggregate amount of the factor's prepayments outstanding at any one time or to stipulate its ability terminate the waiver by notice. The bank would thus cause a breach by the client of the pre-existing factoring agreement!

8–45 Such waivers (or letters of release as they are sometimes termed) will normally specify that the third party:

(1) confirms that it is aware of and consents to the factoring agreement;
(2) agrees that the debts sold to the factor under the agreement shall be free from any security right in the third party's favour;
(3) stipulates that the waiver does not preclude its taking security rights over any amount that may become payable by the factor to the client (or that for avoidance of doubt an existing charge on book debts attaches to such amounts payable)[6];

[4] See para. 7–12 above.
[5] See paras. 8–17 and 8–18.
[6] Some of the banks have recently been anxious to take a specific charge on the factor's indebtedness to the client because it may be construed that, having waived *all* its rights to the debts, the bank may have no claim under its existing charge to any balance available after the factor has recovered his prepayments.

(4) reserves the right to terminate the waiver in certain circumstances (for example, crystallisation of its charge or on notice to the factor).[7]

It is important that the factor should understand the significance of the stipulation in (3) above. As the charges taken on book debts (and the factor's indebtedness to his client is undoubtedly a book debt[8]) are now almost invariably fixed, actual notice to the factor of such a charge may well preclude set-off by him, against his indebtedness to the client, of certain of the client's subsequent liabilities.[9] The notice has the same effect on the rights of the factor (as debtor) as notice of the assignment of his indebtedness.[10] The most important of such rights of set-off relates to recourse and it is probable that, as any recourse would in most circumstances arise from the same agreement as that giving rise to the indebtedness (and be closely connected with it) or be dealt with as an item on a current account,[11] the right to set off such recourse would not be affected by notice of the charge. To avoid any doubt the factor would be well advised to make certain that the stipulation in (3) above is hedged by the following proviso:

> ". . . but the chargee's rights under any such charge shall at all times be subject to all rights of defence and set-off which the factor may have against the company, whether arising before or after notice of such charge."

Factors should also not overlook the need to have included in the waivers consents to their purchasing the related rights referred to in paragraph 10–16 below and the release of such rights from any charge.

Form of waiver

8–46 Waivers are sometimes in the form of agreements between the parties. This is necessary where, as is not uncommon now, the factor takes a charge in conjunction with its factoring agreement either to catch those debts purportedly assigned to the factor, which fail to vest in him for technical reasons, or over other assets as collateral security or for both reasons. In the case of debts

[7] But see Goode, *Legal Problems of Credit and Security* (2nd ed., 1988), p. 93 where he argues that, in the case of factoring with an element of service, a waiver should be permanent; but in any case whether or not this condition is to be included depends upon the nature of the security right of the third party and the strength of its bargaining position *vis-à-vis* the factor.
[8] See n. 37 above.
[9] See Lightman and Moss, *The Law of Receivers of Companies*, para. 16–13.
[10] See para. 9–18 below.
[11] See paras. 9–14 and 10–02 below.

charged to the factor the bank cannot simply waive or release its rights to the debts and attach any surplus by charging the factor's indebtedness to the client; it must retain its charge on the debts and agree with the factor as to priorities. The effectiveness of a waiver in the form of an agreement will depend upon the presence of consideration flowing from the factor unless it is under seal. The usual consideration would be based on the fact that the factor had entered into the factoring agreement at the request of the third party which was to give the waiver; the provision of factoring service would be presumed to improve the fortunes of the client and consequently the security of the third party. Alternatively, the factoring agreement may have enabled the third party to reduce his exposure to risk.

8–47 More often, however, a waiver is drafted not as an agreement but as a letter informing the factor of a fact. The fact is the consent given to the client by the third party for the client to enter into the factoring arrangements by which the debts are to be sold to the factor free from any encumbrances in favour of the third party. If the factor were to make the arrangements to his detriment and be met by a demand from the third party that the factor give up his rights to the debts, it would seem that the third party would be estopped from denying the consent.

Waivers and assignees of security rights

8–48 The question has arisen as to whether or not an assignee of a security right would be bound by a waiver given by the original holder of the security right. For example a finance company holding a fixed charge on book debts of a company to secure a fixed sum debenture, might after having given a waiver to a factor, assign the debenture together with the security right for value; this might occur if a guarantor of the liability of the company paid off the indebtedness under the debenture and took the assignment. Would the assignee who had taken the assignment in ignorance of the waiver be bound? There appears to be no case giving direct authority on the question, but the view of a leading academic is that the assignee would be bound.[12] However, as a precaution the factor should take steps to have included in the waiver an undertaking by the third party not to assign its security rights without first informing the factor; thus giving the factor an opportunity to inform the assignee of the waiver.

[12] Goode, *op. cit.*, p. 94.

Chapter 9

SET-OFF AND THE DEBTOR'S COUNTERVAILING RIGHTS

9–01 There are few more important principles of law in commercial and financial dealings than the principle of set-off. Debts and other intangibles make up a large part of the assets of most businesses many of which rely on set-off to protect themselves as if it were a security right. It is not a security right; but its effects are in many circumstances analogous. Certainly to a factor these principles are (with the exception of the rules relating to assignments) the most important elements of the law. The factor is affected by these principles in two ways: they provide him with a method safely to recover amounts payable to him by his client, in particular in relation to recourse,[1] and they may detract from his rights to recover from debtors' funds that he has provided to his client by way of prepayments.

1. THE NATURE AND CLASSIFICATION OF SET-OFF

9–02 Unfortunately the importance of the subject is matched by its difficulty and complexity. This is demonstrated in Philip Wood's recently published massive book[2] in which he identifies seven different heads of set-off. The grey areas in the law and the conceptual difficulties, aggravated by differences in terminology, have created a subject too vast to be dealt with in this book otherwise than by way of a synopsis and those who require a more detailed analysis are referred elsewhere.[3]

[1] See Chap. 10.
[2] Wood, *English & International Set-off.*
[3] Derham, *Set-Off* and Goode, *Legal Problems of Credit and Security* (2nd ed.) and see n. 2 above.

The nature of set-off

9–03 Set-off is a means by which a debtor who has a monetary cross-claim against his creditor may use that cross-claim to discharge or reduce *pro tanto* his admitted liability to the creditor. Set-off should be distinguished from a substantive defence such as is available to a buyer where the seller has not earned payment by delivery of goods in conformity with the contract of sale; a substantive defence may be available, for example, to a defendant who claims that payment has already been made or that a condition precedent to the creditor's right to payment has not been fulfilled. Set-off should also be distinguished from the common law doctrine of abatement. This doctrine allows the defendant, who has purchased goods or contracted for work, to defend himself in an action against him for the full price by showing that what the plaintiff has delivered or performed is worth less, *at the time of delivery or performance*, than was provided for in the contract by reason of the plaintiff's breach of the contract.[4]

The relations of parties to a current account, although often included in the doctrine of set-off, may be distinguished from it because in the case of a true current account the parties have no claims on each other for the items individually debited and credited; there is only a single claim, one way or the other, for the resulting balance from time to time. This differentiation is important for the factor in relation to his ability to recover the repurchase price of debts the subject of recourse in the insolvency of his client.[5]

9–04 It is generally considered that set-off, other than where it is effected by agreement between the parties (contractual set-off), takes effect only as a procedural shield against the claim of a creditor.[6] This means that there remain in existence two independent debts but that, for convenience, claim and counterclaim are heard in the same proceedings. The two debts remain separate

[4] *Mondel* v. *Steel* (1841) 8 M. & W. 858; *Gilbert-Ash (Northern) Ltd.* v. *Modern Engineering (Bristol) Ltd.* [1974] A.C. 689; and see Goode, *Legal Problems of Credit and Security* (2nd ed.), p. 148 and Derham, *Set-Off*, pp. 54 *et seq.*

[5] See Chap. 10 and *Re Charge Card Services Ltd.* [1986] 3 W.L.R. 697 in which the factor's right to withhold amounts due to his client in liquidation (owing to *prospective* charge backs for recourse) was supported by the fact that his relations with his client were the subject of a running account.

[6] Goode, *op. cit.*, p. 138.

until judgment is given or an account is taken in insolvency. However, as regards equitable set-off,[7] the contrary view has been expressed by Derham[8] who argues that it operates as a substantive defence and may be set up, outside any court or analogous proceedings, as an immediate answer to a creditor's claim. The difference is not purely academic; it has practical implications. If set-off is purely a procedural matter then the consequences will be as follows: it will not prevent a creditor against whom the cross-claim is to be set off using any self-help available to him in respect of his whole claim. The most usual nature of such self-help is the reliance on default provisions in a contract such as the right to terminate the contract or recover goods or other chattels; the existence of a cross-claim (which may be set off only in proceedings) would not prevent a creditor, to whom only the balance between the claim and cross-claim had been tendered, relying before proceedings on any such default provisions.

The classification of set-off

In spite of the many differing circumstances in which the rights to set-off arise the doctrine is usually considered under four heads.

(a) *Statutory or independent set-off*

9–05 As the statutes of set-off have been repealed[9] and presumably to avoid confusion with set-off in insolvency[10] (which is itself governed by statute and statutory instruments) the expression "independent" has recently been coined for this category of set-off.[11] The statutes were introduced to avoid a multiplicity of actions and in spite of their repeal their effect, which is procedural, remains.[12] Set-off under these procedural rules may apply to claims and cross-claims which have no connection and are entirely independent. However, for the rules to apply both the claim and cross-claim:

[7] See para. 9–06 below.
[8] Derham, *Set-Off*, pp. 47–52.
[9] Civil Procedures Acts Repeal Act 1879, s. 2.
[10] See paras. 9–10 and 9–11 below.
[11] Wood, *English & International Set-Off*.
[12] Supreme Court Act 1981, s. 49(2) and R.S.C., Ord. 18, r. 17.

(1) must be monetary claims[13];
(2) must be ascertained liquidated claims representing debts accrued due (but not necessarily due for payment) at the time of the pleadings; and
(3) must lie between the same persons in the same right.[14]

Although the importance of independent set-off has declined since the development of the doctrine of equitable set-off it remains important where claim and cross-claim are not connected to the extent that the latter doctrine would apply.

(b) *Equitable set-off*

9–06 Equitable set-off is normally considered wide in scope, in that it is not a condition of its application that the cross-claim should be for a liquidated sum which has accrued or become due. On the other hand, it will only be applied where the claim and cross-claim arise out of transactions which are closely connected; it is not essential that they should arise out of the same contract and the closeness of the connection has been the subject of judicial consideration in a large number of cases in which the decisions fall on either side of a line which is difficult to define.[15] It will not be available in every case where the claim and cross-claim arise from the same contract; for example, it is regarded as an established rule of law that set-off is not available to the owner of a cargo in respect of his claim for damages (against the shipowner for breach of contract) and his obligation to pay for freight.[16] In an early case[17] it was said that for the doctrine to apply the cross-claim must "impeach" the claim to the effect that it would be inequitable to allow the plaintiff to obtain judgment for it in full. Although some more recent cases seem to have somewhat widened the scope of the availability of the remedy it appears that for it to apply the following requirements remain:

(1) whether or not the claim and cross-claim arise out of the same contract they must be closely connected and the cross-claim must be such that it would be inequitable not to allow credit for it;
(2) in most circumstances the cross-claim must be a monetary claim; and

[13] There is an exception to this requirement which does not seem relevant to a treatise on factoring; see Derham, *Set-Off*, pp. 52 and 53 and Goode, *Legal Problems of Credit and Security* (2nd ed.), p. 153.
[14] See Goode, *op. cit.*, pp. 153–155.
[15] For a full review of the cases see Wood, *English & International Set-Off*, paras. 4–51 *et seq.* and Derham, *Set-Off*, pp. 11–26.
[16] *"The Dominique"* F.T.L.R. February 14, 1989.
[17] *Rawson* v. *Samuel* (1841) Cr. & Ph. 161, 178.

(3) the claim and cross-claim must be between the same persons in the same right.[18]

(c) *Contractual set-off*

9–07 By agreement two parties may extend almost without limit the right and availability of set-off in respect of their respective claims against each other. Such an agreement may be relied on by either party not merely as a procedural defence against the claims of the other; the cross-claim will operate in a substantive manner to reduce or extinguish the claim of the other party *pro tanto* before any judgment or analogous proceedings. In effect the dealings of the two parties, which are the subject of the set-off agreement between them, are considered to give rise to only one debt after a merger of the opposing claims. If the agreement extends the right of set-off to contingent claims then to give effect to the right, a two stage process is necessary. First, the party setting up the contingent claim will be able to suspend payment until his cross-claim becomes liquidated; then he will be able to set off the liquidated sum.

9–08 Such contractual arrangements may include the combination of accounts between the parties which for accounting convenience have been kept separately; although a banker has a prescriptive right to combine all the current accounts of a customer,[19] for others (such as a factor) to have such a right, it would seem necessary to provide for it in a contract.

9–09 As a corollary to contractual set-off it is possible to exclude set-off by agreement between the parties; but such an agreement will not be effective in the bankruptcy or winding up of either party when the rules of insolvency set-off are effective because these statutory provisions cannot be waived or renounced by contract.[20] Furthermore, until the rules relating to insolvency set-off apply between the debtor and the assignee, a provision in the assignor's contract with the debtor that the debtor will not raise claims against an assignee is enforcible.

[18] See Goode, *Legal Problems of Credit and Security* (2nd ed.), pp. 155 *et seq.*

[19] *Garnett* v. *McKewan* (1872) 27 L.T. 560 which was approved in *Halesowen* (see n. 20).

[20] *British Eagle International Airlines Ltd.* v. *Compagnie Nationale Air France* [1975] 1 W.L.R. 758; *National Westminster Bank Ltd.* v. *Halesowen Presswork and Assemblies Ltd.* [1972] A.C. 785. For confirmation that a debtor and creditor may by agreement exclude set-off (until the winding up or bankruptcy of one or the other intervenes) see *Hong Kong & Shanghai Bank* v. *Kloeckner* [1989] B.C.L.C. 776.

(d) *Set-off in insolvency*

9–10 The rules of set-off to be applied in the bankruptcy or winding up of either of the parties are contained respectively in the Insolvency Act 1986[21] and The Insolvency Rules 1986.[22] The rules cannot be excluded nor modified by agreement between the parties[23] nor by any multilateral arrangement among a group of traders for the netting of debit and credit balances.[24] They provide that, as between the person in bankruptcy or winding up and a creditor claiming in the estate, only the balance (if any), after an account has been taken of what is due from each to the other, is provable or payable to the trustee or liquidator. The rules apply when:

(1) there have been mutual credits, mutual debts or other mutual dealings between the creditor and the insolvent person before the commencement of bankruptcy or the company goes into liquidation (as the case may be)[25];
(2) the claims on both sides are such as would be provable in an insolvent estate and as would result in a claim for payment of money (*e.g.* as opposed to a claim for the return of goods in specie)[26]; and
(3) the sums due from the insolvent person to be included in the account taken must have been *due* before the other party had notice of a bankruptcy petition (or, in the case of a company, a winding up petition or the calling of a meeting of creditors) of the insolvent person.[27]

The mutuality of the dealings mentioned in (1) above means that the debts must be due to and by the parties in the same right and, for example, the rules will not apply where the claim on or by one of the parties only is as trustee.[28]

[21] s. 323.
[22] S.I. 1986 No. 1925, r. 4.90.
[23] See n. 20 above.
[24] *British Eagle International Airlines Ltd.* v. *Compagnie Nationale Air France* [1975] 1 W.L.R. 758; however, the Companies Act 1989, ss. 158–165 will make provision for the modification of the law relating to insolvency in respect of default in certain financial markets and it is probable that some netting arrangements may then remain valid in the insolvency of a member of the market (and in some cases of a client of the member). These provisions are expected to come into effect in November 1990.
[25] Insolvency Act 1986, s. 323(1) and Insolvency Rules 1986, r. 4.90(1).
[26] *Rose* v. *Hart* (1818) 8 Taunt. 499.
[27] Insolvency Act 1986, s. 323(3) and Insolvency Rules 1986, r. 4.90(3) and see para. 9–11 below.
[28] See, for example, *Barclays Bank Ltd.* v. *Quistclose Investments Ltd.* [1970] A.C. 567.

9–11 The provisions substantially re-enacted section 31 of the Bankruptcy Act 1914 and its extension to the winding up of companies.[29] However, the new act and rules provide that the debt on which the solvent party is claiming must be "due" before he had notice of certain events portending the insolvency; and this replaced the old provision by which the credit from which the debt arose must have been granted before notice of the specified events. Consequent upon the enactment of the 1986 Act and the making of the Rules there has been much uncertainty and disagreement among lawyers as to the precise meaning of these provisions. Certainly the word "due" does not mean due for payment, but due in the sense of "in existence"; but the uncertainty, in particular, relates to the question as to whether a contingent liability of the insolvent party could be set off against an actual liability to the trustee or liquidator. The question had been a matter of controversy before the Act, notwithstanding the view of the Insolvency Law Review Committee that there was no doubt that set-off in such circumstance was available[30]; but the question in relation to most problems in relation to factoring seemed to have been settled in affirmative by the judgment of Millet J. in *Re Charge Card Services Ltd.*[31] in which he made a thorough review of the authorities in relation to this matter. That case[32] related to events which took place before the enactment of the Insovency Act 1986 and the coming into effect of the Insolvency Rules 1986[33] and it seems that some uncertainty must remain. However, there are strong arguments to support the view that set-off against an estate in bankruptcy or winding up should not be disallowed solely because the claim against the estate is contingent provided that it is in existence and capable of being quantified, as for proof of debt, at the time *when the account is taken.*[34]

2. THE DEBTOR'S DEFENCES AND COUNTERCLAIMS

9–12 In Chapter 10 the warranties normally given by the client are described. One of the most important of these is that, by which the client undertakes that every debt sold by him to the factor shall be

[29] Companies Act 1985, s. 612.
[30] *Insolvency Law and Practice* (Cmnd. 8558 (1982) para. 1356).
[31] [1986] 3 W.L.R. 697.
[32] *Ibid.*
[33] See nts. 21 and 22 and Wood, *op. cit.*, paras. 7.235 and 7.236.
[34] See Goode, *Legal Problems of Credit and Security* (2nd ed.), pp. 183 *et seq.*

payable by the debtor as a valid collectable debt free from any defence or cross-claim. Accordingly, if the factor is unable to collect any debt that he has purchased, by reason of such a claim by the debtor, he will have the right to be indemnified by his client or to exercise his right of recourse. However, reimbursement from the client can normally only be obtained by set-off against the balance owing to the client in respect of other debts purchased.[35] In a continuing agreement the level of the factor's retention, as a minimum balance, may well be sufficient to absorb any debts which are subject to recourse for this reason. It is in the situation of the insolvency of the client, when the debtors are likely to look more closely at their rights, that the level of these defences and claims for set-off increases. Such difficulties on the insolvency of clients have been the cause of many significant losses to factors since the service was introduced into this country. It is therefore important that a factor should be fully aware of the rights of the debtor in such a case. In the event of the insolvency of the client it may well be possible that a debtor may raise a defence or cross-claim that he may consider commercially justifiable but which, on examination, is not tenable in law.

9–13 The general rule is that the factor, as assignee, can be in no better position as regards his right to recover from the debtor than the client was at the time when the debtor had received notice of the assignment; as assignee, he takes the assignment subject to equities. An example of this principle is contained in the words of James L.J. in *Roxburghe* v. *Cox*[36]:

> "Now an assignee of a chose in action . . . takes, subject to all rights of set-off and other defences which were available against the assignor, subject only to this exception, that after notice of an assignment of a chose in action the debtor cannot by payment or otherwise do anything to take away or diminish the rights of the assignee as they stood at the time of the notice."

Accordingly, if a defence relating to defects or deficiencies in the very goods or service, that give rise to the debt in question, is raised by a debtor, the factor will be in no better position than the client (against whom, in the case of goods, a defence would be available to the debtor under Sale of Goods Act 1979, s. 53(1)(a)). The defects or deficiencies must have been in existence at the time when the debt was assigned.

[35] See para. 10–20 below.
[36] (1881) 17 Ch. D. 520.

Equitable and independent set-off by debtor against factor

9–14 As regards any counterclaims, the general view is that the debtor will be able to set off, in reduction or cancellation of the factor's claim for payment, any cross-claim arising out of the same contract as that which gave rise to the factored debt or out of a contract that is "closely connected" with the contract which gave rise to the assignee's claim.[37] The close connection does not appear to extend to a cross-claim arising from the creditor's tort; for in *Stoddart* v. *Union Trust Ltd.*[38] it was held that the debtor could not set off his cross-claim, which was for damages for fraudulently inducing his entry into a contract, against an assigned debt arising out of the very contract.

9–15 In respect of a counterclaim arising out of any other contract or on any other grounds (where independent set-off is claimed as available to the debtor) the generally accepted rule is that the notice of the assignment fixes the rights of the parties. As a result, after receipt of the notice, the debtor cannot set off against the factor a debt which comes into existence subsequently, even though it arose out of a liability that existed before the notice; but the debtor may set off against the factor a debt that accrued before the notice even if not payable until after it.[39] For a thorough review of the law relating to the rights of a debtor in respect of set-off against an assigned debt, reference should be made to the judgment of Templeman L.J. (as Templeman J.) in *Business Computers Limited* v. *Anglo-African Leasing Limited.*[40] After a detailed review of the authorities he summarised the position thus:

> "The result of the relevant authorities is that a debt which accrues due before notice of an assignment is received, whether or not it is payable before that date, or a debt which arises out of the same contract as that which gives rise to the assigned debt, or is closely connected with that contract, may be set off against the assignee. But a debt which is neither accrued nor connected may not be set off even though it arises from a contract made before the assignment."

It is apparent that, apart from the question of defences raised on account of defects in the goods or services supplied, the factor must be on his guard in relation to some ancillary transactions between the client and his debtors. The most common cause of

[37] *Business Computers Ltd.* v. *Anglo-African Leasing Ltd.* [1977] 1 W.L.R. 578; *"The Nanfri"* [1978] 2 Lloyds Rep. 132; *"The Raven"* [1980] 2 Lloyds Rep. 266 at p. 272.
[38] [1912] 1 K.B. 181.
[39] *Re Pinto Leite & Nephews* [1929] 1 Ch. 221.
[40] [1977] 1 W.L.R. 578.

such counterclaims are claims for set-off for goods supplied by the debtor to the client; if these goods were supplied before the assigned debt on which the factor is claiming arose, the debtor may well be able to set off notwithstanding that the two claims arose from entirely independent contracts.

The effect of contractual set-off on the factor as assignee

9–16 The factor's rights as assignee of a debt will not be affected in any way by any contract between the client and the debtor extending the common law or equitable rules of set-off where that contract has been entered into *after* the debtor received notice of the assignment of that debt.[41] The position where the client and the debtor enter into such a contract *before* notice has been received by the debtor is not so clear. The normal equitable principles, that an assignee takes subject to the equities and cannot be in a better position than the assignor is at the time of notice to the debtor, would appear to indicate that the factor would be fully bound by such contract terms.[42] In *Watson* v. *The Mid Wales Railway Company*[43] set-off of a cross-claim relating to rent not accrued due was not allowed against the assignee of a bond although the contract giving rise to the rent was in existence at the time of notice of the assignment to the debtor. However, the dicta in the case indicate that, had the payment of the rent been made a charge on the bond (*i.e.* if by contract payment under the bond could be applied to discharge the rent) before notice of the assignment, then the set-off might have been allowed. Where an assignor and a debtor had agreed, before the debtor had received notice of the assignment, to set off future claims, it is considered that the assignee would not be affected by transactions arising between the debtor and the assignor *after* the debtor had received the notice; but there appears to be no reported case on the point.[44]

9–17 If the contract between the client and the debtor is to exclude or restrict the application of set-off[45] the client's rights under such an agreement are unlikely to be available to the factor unless the debtor specifically agrees (*i.e.* by a new contract or a novation). It is possible, but not certain, that the debtor might be deemed to have waived his right of set-off if he had received and not demurred at notice implying that the factor had taken his interest

[41] *Roxburghe* v. *Cox* (1881) 17 Ch. D. 520.
[42] *Mangles* v. *Dixon* (1852) H.L. Cas. 702; see also Derham, *Set-Off*, p. 317.
[43] (1867) L.R. 2 C.P. 593.
[44] See, for example, Goode, *Legal Problems of Credit and Security* (2nd ed.), p. 174 and Wood, *English & International Set-off*, para. 16–36.
[45] See para. 9–09 above.

in the debt for value relying on the agreement not to set-off.[46] Therefore, if the factor wishes to protect himself against the countervailing rights of the debtor as described below, it is advisable for him to make an independent agreement with the debtor not to set-off any cross-claims against the assigned debts. Such an agreement would not stand up in the insolvency of the debtor,[47] but it would do so in the insolvency of the client (if the debtor were not insolvent); and it is when the client is insolvent that the factor most needs this protection because he may not then be able to recover from the client in respect of the client's breach of the usual warranty that the debt is free from encumbrance.

3. THE EFFECT OF NOTICES ON THE DEBTOR'S COUNTERVAILING RIGHTS

9–18 In paragraph 8–07 the effect of notice to the debtor was described and it was demonstrated that the ability of the factor to collect from the debtor would be assisted by procuring notice as early as possible. From the preceding paragraphs it is apparent that the sooner the notice is received by the debtor the more likely is the factor to be able to defeat any claim of the debtor to independent set-off or set-off in insolvency; receipt of notice by the debtor fixes the rights of the parties in these respects. It should not be overlooked in this connection that where an assignment is purportedly made in breach of a contract term prohibiting the assignment of a debt arising from that contract, then the assignment is invalid[48]; accordingly any notice given in such a case will be of no effect and the debtor will have available to him all rights of set-off as if there had been no notice.

Introductory letters and the debtor's countervailing rights

9–19 The effect of the usual method of notice by procuring the endorsement of it on the invoice has been described in paragraph 8–06; and the effect of letters informing debtors of the automatic assignment to the factor of all future debts of the client (introductory letters) in relation to an agreement of the whole turnover type[49] was discussed in paragraphs 8–08 to 8–10. It was there concluded that, in the present state of the law, such letters may not be of any effect in respect of debts not in existence at the time

[46] See also paras. 9–22 and 9–23 below.
[47] See para. 9–09 above.
[48] *Helstan Securities Ltd.* v. *Hertfordshire County Council Ltd.* [1978] 3 All E.R. 262 and see paras. 9–30 and 9–31 below.
[49] See para. 7–13 above.

when they are received by the debtor for the purpose of the factor's claim to priority under the rule in *Dearle* v. *Hall.*[50] There remains to be considered if such a letter would be effective in respect of future debts as regards the countervailing rights of the debtor. The cases which have a bearing on the matter[51] support the view that a notice to be effective must be of a debt in existence at the time when the notice is received by the debtor. However, most of the cases related to conflicts between competing assignees; and in one case in which the question of the debtor's countervailing rights were concerned the set-off by the debtor was allowed because his claim was in existence before he received notice.[52]

9–20 Furthermore none of the reported cases related to trade debts and the circumstances of a Canadian case[53] may seem persuasive to the contrary. In that case, at the start of a factoring agreement the client sent to the debtor, the defendant in the case, a letter informing the latter of the existence of the factoring agreement (and incidentally giving notice of the assignment of the debt then owing to the client). Notwithstanding the admitted receipt of that letter, following the subsequent insolvency of the client the debtor, in paying the factor, deducted from his debt to the factor amounts owed in respect of the debtor's supplies to the client. The factor claimed that by reason of the notice given in the letter the debtor was not entitled to impair the factor's right to payment in full by a claim to set off an independent debt unconnected with the contract which gave rise to the debt assigned to the factor. The trial judge gave judgment in favour of the factor and this was upheld in the Ontario Court of Appeal. However, the decision was reversed in the Supreme Court, but only on the grounds that the factoring agreement did not bind the debts as they came into existence but merely provided that each debt of the client should be offered to the factor; thus when each debt came into existence there was no automatic assignment arising from the agreement itself.

9–21 In this connection there might also be considered the analogy between this type of agreement, binding the debts as they come into existence without any further formality, and a present fixed charge attaching to future book debts as they come into existence. It seems likely that actual notice to a debtor of such a fixed charge created by his creditor on present and future book debts would have the same effect, as regards set-off by the debtor, as notice of

[50] See para. 8–02 above.
[51] See Chap. 8, nts. 18 and 19.
[52] *Roxburghe* v. *Cox* (1881) 17 Ch. D. 520.
[53] *Canadian Admiral Corporation Ltd.* v. *L. F. Dommerich & Co. Inc.* S.C.R. 1964, p. 238.

an assignment of such indebtedness as it came into existence.[54] However, it is generally considered that, whilst logic seems to be on the side of the full effectiveness of such notices, the law in England has not developed beyond reliance on the cases quoted above[55] and it is probable that the effectiveness is restricted to debts in existence at the time of the notice. In any event, if a factor considers it worth while relying on the possibility that the law may have developed so that such notices may be effective as regards future debts, he should ensure that the notices are clear and brought to the attention of a responsible official of the debtor.

Notices and the debtor's implied waiver

9–22 It occurs not infrequently that a debtor will not raise the question of set-off (particularly in relation to an independent cross-claim) until some difficulty emerges in his relations with his creditor or the latter appears to be in financial difficulties. A debtor may continue for many months to pay to a factor the exact amount of assigned debts without raising the question of a debt owed to the debtor by the client which may have been in existence for some time past. When the debtor finally applies the set-off and deducts the indebtedness of the client to him from his payment to the factor, the factor may well consider that the debtor has impliedly waived the right of set-off. By the debtor's silence the factor has been led to believe that the debts which he had purchased would be free from encumbrance and he has thereby been induced to make prepayments against their purchase price which he may not be able to recover in full; if the client then becomes insolvent the factor may be unable to recover from the client in respect of the latter's breach of warranty.

9–23 It seems, on the analogy of an estoppel, that silence can only be considered as having induced a change of position if the silent party had, in the particular case, a duty to speak[56] and there is good authority for the proposition that it is the duty of the assignee, in a situation as described in the preceding paragraph, to make enquiries and not of the debtor to volunteer the information.[57] However, if it is clear that the assignee has been deceived and is making a financial commitment based upon a misunderstanding then the debtor may lose his right to take

[54] See Lightman and Moss, *The Law of Receivers of Companies*, paras. 16–12 to 16–14.
[55] See Chap. 8, nts. 18 and 19.
[56] See Goff and Jones, *The Law of Restitution* (3rd ed., 1986), p. 700.
[57] *Mangles* v. *Dixon* (1852) 3 H.L. Cas. 702.

advantage of the equities available to him against the client.[58] As a result, it seems that a factor may be helped in such a situation if his assignment notices have included words on the lines of the following: ". . . and [name of factor] should be advised immediately of any claim or dispute affecting this debt."

4. INSOLVENCY SET-OFF AND THE FACTOR

(a) The debtor's insolvency

9–24 If a debtor is bankrupt or in liquidation the insolvency set-off provisions[59] will not operate as regards the factor's claim on the debtor and any cross-claim which the debtor may have against the client because there is no mutuality. However, the factor will be met with such cross-claims as would have been available to a solvent debtor; these may affect the factor's right of proof of debt and consequently the amount of any dividend to which he may be entitled from the debtor's estate. The cross-claims of a debtor in bankruptcy or liquidation which will be applied to reduce (or extinguish) the proof of the factor as assignee are all those which would be available (by way of equitable set-off or independent set-off) to a solvent debtor against an assignee.[60]

9–25 In any case where the debt is subject to recourse, the factor will be affected by an impairment of his proof (by reason of a cross-claim by the liquidator or trustee in bankruptcy) if he is unable to recourse the shortfall to the client; this would happen if the client is insolvent and there are insufficient sums owing by the factor to the client against which the recourse may be set off. If the debt is not subject to recourse (otherwise than by reason of the cross-claim) the factor would in any event have the right to recourse the amount of the debt on his books for which proof is not accepted; in such a case the application of the set-off may be of positive benefit to the factor in not having to accept a bad debt loss for the full amount of the debt.

(b) The client's insolvency

9–26 If the debtor is not insolvent the bankruptcy or liquidation of the client will not directly affect the rights of the factor and the debtor *inter se*; the rules of insolvency set-off apply only to the mutual indebtedness of a party in bankruptcy or liquidation and his creditor or debtor. However, it is in such a situation that the debtor is most likely to rely on any equitable or independent set-

[58] *Ibid.*
[59] See paras. 9–10 and 9–11 above.
[60] See paras. 9–13 *et seq.* and Wood, *English & International Set-off*, para. 16–132.

off available to him against the factor as assignee. It is probable also that any pre-existing agreement between the client and the debtor not to set off their mutual claims on each other will be ineffective to prevent the debtor exercising those rights. The set-off rights available to the debtor are those which would have been available to him against the assigned debt if the client had been solvent.[61]

(c) Set-off by and against the Crown

9–27 The rights of set-off between the Crown and a solvent person are governed by the Crown Proceedings Act[62] and the Rules of the Supreme Court[63] the general effect of which is *inter alia* that without leave of the court set-off is not available to or against the Crown:

(1) if the claim and counterclaim relate to different government departments; or
(2) the Crown is sued or sues in the name of the Attorney General.

However, where the other party is in bankruptcy or liquidation the insolvency provisions[64] apply. They are mandatory; they apply where the claims by and against the Crown are through different departments and they also apply in relation to a claim under a statutory provision (*e.g.* for taxes) and a contractual claim.[65] An attempt was made in Scotland by a liquidator of a Scottish company to obtain payments from the Ministry of Defence free from cross-claims by the Department of Trade and Industry and the Inland Revenue. But that attempt failed and the court held that the Crown was an "indivisible entity" and applied the insolvency rules of set-off then in force in Scotland.[66] The Insolvency Law Review Committee[67] recommended that there should be no set-off by and against different government departments, nor between contractual and statutory claims by and against the same department; but the law remains as stated above.

9–28 It has usually been considered that a factor whose client's customers include government departments must watch carefully the liabilities of his client for taxes and other sums owing to the Crown. The rationale behind this view has been that, in the banktruptcy or liquidation of such a client, any debt owing by a

[61] See Wood, *English & International Set-off*, paras. 16–122 to 16–131 (incl.).
[62] s. 35(2).
[63] R.S.C., Ord 77, r. 6.
[64] Insolvency Act 1986, s. 323 and Insolvency Rules 1986, r. 4.90.
[65] *Re D. H. Curtis (Builders) Ltd.* [1978] Ch. 162; *Re Cushla* [1979] 3 All E.R. 415.
[66] *Smith* v. *Lord Advocate* 1981 S.L.T. 19.
[67] *Insolvency Law and Practice* (Cmnd. 8558 (1982), paras. 1342 to 1347 and 1362).

government department and vesting in the factor would be subject to insolvency set-off in respect of amounts accrued due to the Crown before the assignment of that debt had been completed by notice to the department concerned. However, this view is open to rebuttal: in order that insolvency set-off should apply there must be mutuality in relation to the claim and cross-claim[68] and the assignment destroys the mutuality.[69] It therefore seems that any claim for set-off by the Crown in such a situation would be by way of independent set-off. In that case the provisions of section 35(2) of the Crown Proceedings Act 1947 and the R.S.C., Ord. 77, r. 6, will apply.[70] It is, therefore, probable that where, in proceedings, the Crown claims to set off amounts due from a factor's client for duties and taxes against the claim of a factor for an assigned debt due by another department of the govenment, the set-off must be subject to leave of the Court.

9–29 However, in many cases a factor will be faced with a valid claim by the Crown to exercise its rights in respect of insolvency set-off; and this will apply to debts accruing due to the Crown *after* as well as before notice of the assignment to the factor of any debt due by the Crown. This difficulty for the factor arises from the practice of some government departments to include, in their purchase contracts, the terms forbidding the assignment of claims against then under such contracts.[71] Unless the factor had obtained a waiver of the prohibition the notice to the debtor of an assignment in breach of such a term would be ineffective.

5. CONTRACTUAL TERMS PROHIBITING ASSIGNMENTS

9–30 Closely connected with the question of the debtor's countervailing rights is the right of a debtor to refuse to deal with the factor where the purported assignment to the factor arises from a contract in which there is a prohibition of the assignment of the right to payment under it. Such a purported assignment will be void[72] and the debtor may refuse to deal with the factor. As a result, the debtor's payment to the client in such circumstances will give him a good discharge and he will have the same rights of set-off as if the debt had not been subject to the factoring agreement. It appears

[68] See para. 9–10 above.
[69] See para. 9–24 and n. 61 above.
[70] See para. 9–27 above and Wood, *English & International Set-off*, para. 12–179.
[71] See para. 9–30 below.
[72] *Helstan Securities Ltd.* v. *Hertfordshire County Council Ltd.* [1978] 3 All E.R. 262.

that the effect of the judgment in the *Helstan*[73] case was as follows: not only was the assignment invalid as regards the debtor so that he was able to disregard it, but also it was wholly void so that, as between the assignor and assignee, the ownership of the debt had not been transferred.

9–31 This more serious mischief to the factor (that he may have made a payment to his client and received no debt in return) may be mitigated[74] but, as the notice of a void assignment is of no effect, the factor is in the position of having rights to a debt which at any time may be impeached by payment by the debtor to the client, by subsequent changes in the contract of sale or service or by the coming into existence of subsequent claims by the debtor against the client. The factor's ability to recover from debtors, who have contracted with the factor's client on these terms, may in some cases be restored by the debtors' sometimes overlooking their contract terms and making payment to the factor. There seems little doubt that, if the debtor has established a pattern of paying the factor in respect of invoices bearing a notice of assignment, the debtor would be deemed to have waived the prohibition.

6. POSITIVE LIABILITY OF THE FACTOR TO THE DEBTOR

9–32 Although a factor may have his own claim against a debtor reduced or extinguished by the debtor's countervailing rights, he incurs no positive liability to the debtor under the contract that gave rise to the assigned debt. As the bare assignee of the amount payable by the debtor he is not a party to the contract. Furthermore, it is also generally accepted that in most circumstances, once the debtor has paid the assigned debt to the factor, any claim by the debtor against the client, whether arising out of the contract that gave rise to the assigned debt or not, must be against the client. The factor is considered in most cases to have no liability to repay to the debtor; it has been said that although an assignee takes subject to equities he is not subjected to them. The burden of performance of the client's contract with the debtor can be shifted on to the shoulders of the factor only by a novation accepted by all three parties; but this has the effect of cancelling the old contract between the client and the debtor and creating a

[73] *Ibid.*
[74] See paras. 10–25 to 10–28 below.

new one between the factor and the debtor. Such an arrangement is not part of the functions of a modern factor.

Position of the factor arising from total failure of consideration

9–33 A difficult and uncertain question of law arises when the debtor has paid to the factor in respect of a transaction in which there has been a total failure of consideration on the part of the client. This might occur if an invoice had been issued and either no goods or services had been supplied or the goods or services supplied had been lawfully rejected by the debtor for non-conformity with the contract. The avoidance of positive liability by the factor to the debtor arises from the absence of privity of contract between the factor and the debtor; but in such a case a claim by a debtor against a factor for repayment would be based not on the contract but on the quasi-contractual principle of restitution. There appear to be no reported cases nor any other authority in which recovery against an assignee in such circumstances has been claimed.

9–34 In practice the difficulty for the factor would arise only if:

(1) he had paid against the invoice representing the transaction in question; and
(2) his client was insolvent; and
(3) his retention was insufficient to cover his recourse on the basis of the client's breach of warranty.

In such a case there can be no question of the factor being unjustly enriched by having been paid for nothing. In any case in which he would wish to resist the debtor's claim he would have paid and been unable to recover from his client. It seems possible that the debtor might claim restitution on the grounds of money paid by a mistake of fact. It seems a well established principle of English law that money paid under a mistake of fact is in most circumstances recoverable.[75] The debtor might claim that on receipt of the invoice he paid in the belief that the right goods had been despatched to him and that such a mistaken belief was induced by the legends on the very invoice.[76] If the factor would not be unjustly enriched by retaining the money paid to him, because he has paid the client and cannot recover from the client owing to the latter's insolvency, then he might attempt to rebut the debtor's claim for restitution on the grounds of a change of posi-

[74] See paras. 10–25 to 10–28 below.
[75] See, for example, *Barclays Bank Ltd.* v. *W. J. Simms Son & Cooke* [1980] Q.B. 677.
[76] For the international view of this problem see the comments on Art. 10 of the UNIDROIT Convention in para. 12–26 below.

tion. The basis of his defence would be that the debtor's payment had led him to believe that the debtor had accepted in full the obligation to pay the invoice in question and that, accordingly, he was bound to pay the client the purchase price of the debt in full. Unfortunately for the factor it appears that such a defence has not yet been formally recognised in English law.[77]

The factor's liability for credit balances

9–35 Not infrequently credit balances emerge on the accounts of debtors in the records of factors. The question of the responsibility of the factor for payment of any such credit balance to the debtor is the subject of much uncertainty and disagreement even between the factors themselves. Such uncertainty and disagreement arises because in most cases a credit balance is created by the issue by the client to the debtor, and the acceptance by the factor, of a credit note representing a value exceeding the debit balance on the debtor's account. It is clear that a credit balance created by a debtor's payment, either duplicated or mistaken as to amount, is repayable by the factor who has received the payment as money paid by mistake.

9–36 The view that the factor has no responsibility for credit balances created by the issue of credit notes is based on the doctrines of the assignee's avoidance of any liabilities under the sale contract. However, apart from the position which may arise if the credit note has been issued in recognition of total failure of consideration, there are cogent arguments in favour of the factor's liability. First, if the credit note creates a credit balance it must surely be in recognition of an earlier overpayment because a defect or deficiency in the goods or services did not emerge until after payment. It is then possible that the debtor could claim that the resulting balance represented his having paid too much in the first place by mistake of fact. His mistake was to assume that the goods or services were in order at the time when he paid; although the credit note was issued later it represented the facts in existence at the time of payment. Secondly, the debtor might claim that by a course of dealing the factor had given ostensible authority to the client to issue credit notes which adjusted the factor's own account with the debtor.

[77] Goff and Jones, *The Law of Restitution* (3rd ed., 1986), pp. 113 and 114.

7. LONG TERM CONTRACTS FOR THE SUPPLY OF GOODS OR SERVICES

9–37 The countervailing rights of the debtor against the factor as assignee, especially in relation to substantive defences[78] and equitable set-off,[79] have had the effect of restricting the field of trades and industries in which the factor may safely provide any form of factoring in which prepayments are available to the client. Such countervailing rights may detrimentally affect the factor's ability to collect the full amount of an assigned debt where such a debt arises under a continuing uncompleted contract for the supply of goods or services. The client may have sold and delivered goods or completed services under such a contract and invoiced them and, in good faith, have offered or notified to the factor the debt representing such goods or services; and the factor may have made a prepayment on account of the purchase price of the debt. If the client then fails to deliver the remainder of the goods or complete the remainder of the services for which the contract provides (for example, by reason of his insolvency or a strike or *force majeure*), the factor will in all probability then be met by a cross-claim by the debtor. The cross-claim will be for breach of the same contract as that which gave rise to the factored debt. Naturally in a continuing arrangement for factoring an occasional experience of such an uncompleted contract is unlikely to be a problem; the recourse, which is available to the factor owing to the client's breach of warranty that the debt is free from such a cross-claim, may be set off by the factor against amounts payable by him for further debts purchased from the client. The difficulty for the factor will be serious if the bulk of the client's business relates to long term contracts and the client becomes insolvent. For this reason factors tend to eschew such businesses.

Long term contracts for services

9–38 The consequences of the failure by the client to complete a contract for services depends on whether the contract is entire or divisible. Under an entire contract the debtor has no liability for payment until performance of the whole contract has been completed. A divisible contract will provide for payment for part performance. Whether a contract is divisible or entire depends on the terms of the contract itself and, if provision is made for the invoices to be issued by the supplier of services periodically, then in the absence of any specific provision in the contract the presumption may be that the contract is divisible. However, unless

[78] See para. 9–03 above.
[79] See para. 9–06 above.

the terms of the contract are examined carefully by the factor, he will not know to which type of contract the debts notified or offered to him are related.

9–39 The effect on the factor may well be as follows:

(1) If the contract is entire the debtor will not be obliged to pay any part of the invoice already issued unless the whole contract is substantially completed.[80] Even if the contract is substantially completed the debtor will be able to set off, as against the factor's claim for payment, a counterclaim for breach of contract because the claim and counterclaim arose from the same contract and are closely connected.[81]

(2) If the contract is divisible the debtor will be obliged to pay the invoice for part performance provided that the invoice relates to a separable part of the contract; but the debtor will be able to set off his counterclaim for breach of contract.[82]

The debt which is not payable by the debtor because it relates to part (but not substantially the whole) performance of an entire contract will be subject to recourse to the client who will be in breach of warranties given in the factoring agreement. For the same reason such a debt arising under a divisible contract or relating to the substantial completion of work under an entire contract, which is subject to a counterclaim for damages, may be recoursed to the client. In the one case the debt is not a legally binding obligation of the debtor and in the other is subject to a counterclaim; in both cases the client will have warranted otherwise.[83]

Contracts for the supply of goods

9–40 Where there is a contract for the sale of goods to be delivered by instalments, which are to be invoiced and paid separately, it is a question to be determined by a construction of the contract whether any defect or default in any one or more of the deliveries may give the debtor the right to repudiate the whole contract or

[80] *Bolton* v. *Mahadeva* [1972] 1 W.L.R. 1009; *Hoenig* v. *Isaacs* [1952] 2 All E.R. 176.

[81] *Government of Newfoundland* v. *Newfoundland Railway Co.* (1888) 13 A.C. 199; *Roxburghe* v. *Cox* (1881) 17 Ch. D. 520; *Business Computers Ltd.* v. *Anglo-African Leasing Ltd.* [1977] 1 W.L.R. 578.

[82] *Ibid.*

[83] See Chap. 10.

only the right to a claim for compensation.[84] However, the normal presumption, in the absence of anything to the contrary in the contract, is that each delivery according to the contract is to be invoiced and paid for separately. In this respect the factor may be somewhat better off in relation to a debt arising from a contract for the sale of goods than in relation to one arising from a contract for services. Furthermore, if the debtor has accepted one or more of the instalments of goods and not the whole quantity contracted for, the factor may well be able to rely on the Sale of Goods Act 1979 and to claim payment of the price of the goods as a part delivery accepted by the debtor.[85] However, the factor will, in relation to a contract of sale, be subject to a counterclaim by the debtor if the client wrongfully fails to deliver a further instalment.[86] The position will be exactly as described above[87] in respect of an incomplete divisible service contract.

9–41 An uncertainty that very often affects the factor's consideration of a long term contractual arrangement between a client as supplier of goods and a debtor is the practice of some purchasers by which the goods to be purchased are specified but the exact quantity (or even the price) is subject to periodic call off. Such arrangements are common among large retail chains. The specification of the product, and often its price, are agreed with the manufacturer, but the quantities to be supplied are called for direct to the manufacturer by branches as required. Whether such an arrangement constitutes a binding contract, so that failure to deliver any goods called off would give the debtor the right to set up a counterclaim against amounts payable for deliveries duly made, depends upon the degree of the uncertainty in the contract. It would seem that if the price and the quantity to be delivered were both to be agreed from time to time the arrangement could be held to be a letter of intent. In such a case it would appear that the individual calls for supply of a specific quantity at a specific price might be regarded as separate contracts; and the factor would be able to accept the debts arising from such deliveries without anxiety.

9–42 A further difficulty for the factor may arise where, although all the goods arising under an individual and separate contract have been properly delivered by the client and accepted by the debtor, the client becomes insolvent and the debtor refuses to pay in full claiming that servicing of the goods or other back-up is no longer

[84] Sale of Goods Act 1979, s.31(2).
[85] s. 30(1).
[86] Sale of Goods Act 1979, s.51(1).
[87] At para. 9–39.

available to him. Where there had been a contract for such services between the client and the debtor, it is likely that set-off of a cross-claim would be available to the debtor; even if the contract for the services were to be separate from that for the supply of the goods it is likely that they would be considered to be closely connected. If the goods are of such a nature that after sales service is implicit or usual (and the example of office equipment such as photo-copiers is sometimes mentioned in this connection) then the debtor may have a cross-claim for the absence of implied service even if it had not been the subject of a specific contract; but in relation to other goods (such as raw materials, components or non-durable consumer goods) such a presumption of after sales service is most unlikely. However, whether the service is the subject of a contract or implied, the debtor would have to formulate his cross-claim at the time when payment for the goods becomes due and, if there is no apparent defect in the goods, such a cross-claim is unlikely to be of substantial value.

Cut-off clauses

9–43 In view of these difficulties arising from the client's long term contracts with his debtors, where such contracts are a normal part of the client's business or where an individual contract of such a nature constitutes a large part of the client's business, it is advisable for the factor to stipulate that the debts arising from such a contract will be approved and eligible for prepayment only if a "cut-off clause" is included in the contract. The purpose of such a clause is to divide the contract so that each delivery may be deemed to constitute a separate contract. An example of such a clause in a contract for services would be:

> "This contract is divisible. The work performed in each month during the currency of the contract shall be invoiced separately. Each invoice for work performed in any month shall be payable by the customer in full, in accordance with the terms of payment provided for herein, without reference to and notwithstanding any defect or default in the work performed or to be performed in any other month."

Or, in a contract for the sale of goods:

> "This contract is divisible. Each delivery made hereunder:
> (i) shall be deemed to arise from a separate contract, and
> (ii) shall be invoiced separately and any invoice for a delivery shall be payable in full in accordance with the terms of payment provided for herein without reference to and notwithstanding any defect or default in the delivery of any other instalment."

Undertaking from the debtor direct

9–44 Alternatively, it may be possible for the factor to obtain from a debtor who is anxious to maintain continuity of supply from the client an undertaking on the following lines:

Re: XYZ Limited ('the Company')

> "In consideration of your continuing your factoring services for the company we hereby undertake to pay in full the amount of any invoice for goods sold to us (services completed for us) by the company and accepted by us without any deduction or set-off in relation to any claim we may have or expect to have against the company in respect of any goods (services) provided or to be provided by the company which are not the subject of the said invoice."

Chapter 10

THE FACTORING AGREEMENT—PAYMENT TO THE CLIENT BY THE FACTOR AND OTHER TERMS

10–01 In Chapter 7 it was postulated that the factor's principal requirement in the factoring agreement was that the debts which he purchases from his client should vest in him free from the rights and interests of third parties; the methods by which this is achieved was described in Chapters 7 and 8. From the client's point of view the most important provisions are those which relate to the obligations for the factor to pay him for the debts which he sells to the factor. The converse of such provisions is the protection of the factor against paying to the client more than he will ultimately collect from the debtors after a deduction for his charges.[1] The factor will be obliged to pay to such an extent if the balance owing to the client for the price of debts purchased (the factor's retention) is insufficient to absorb all the amounts subsequently to be set off by the factor for the repurchase price of debts to be recoursed; in the insolvency of the client the factor will be unsecured for the balance. These and the miscellaneous provisions peculiar to a factoring agreement are discussed in this chapter.

1. PAYMENT TO THE CLIENT AND THE FACTOR'S RETENTION

The case for a current account

10–02 Although the accounting methods and provisions for payment of the purchase price of debts as described earlier[2] vary among factoring companies it is now not unusual that the arrangements

[1] Except, in the case of an approved debt in non-recourse factoring, solely by reason of the insolvency of the debtor.
[2] See Chap. 3.

should be made by way of the credit of the purchase price to a current account and the debit thereto of all amounts paid by the factor to the client and all amounts to be charged to the client. These debits include the repurchase price of debts the subject of recourse and the amounts of credit notes (issued by the client with the authority of the factor). The provisions for payment to the client are then by way of drawing by the client against the balance on the current account subject to the maintenance of the agreed retention. If the agreement were to provide that the purchase price of each individual debt is to be paid separately, then the recovery in respect of recourse would have to be by way of set-off of individual transactions (albeit arising out of the same or a closely connected contract) rather than by way of a current account in which all transactions are merged giving rise to one debt.[3] Thus in the insolvency of the client the insolvency rules of set-off[4] will apply with the possibility of some uncertainty.

10–03 The advantage to the factor of providing for payment to the client by way of drawing against a current account was amply demonstrated in the case of *Re Charge Card Services Ltd.*[5] the importance of which to factors is such that a synopsis of part of Mr Justice Millet's judgment is set out here. The case raised two questions and the second, which is of general interest to factors, was as follows[6]:

> The liquidator of the client company challenged the right of the factor to hold (after the commencement of the winding up) a retention against further charges to arise and, more importantly, against the potential liability of the client for recourse in respect of any debts for which the factor had paid and which might remain unpaid by the debtors 120 days after the invoice date. There were two prongs to the liquidator's attack. First, the liquidator claimed that the factor's right to retain the unpaid balance of the purchase price of purchased debts, for the purpose of applying it against further amounts to become payable to the factor by the client, was a security right and a

[3] See para. 9–03 above.
[4] See paras. 9–10 and 9–11 above.
[5] [1986] 3 W.L.R. 697; [1986] 3 All E.R. 289.
[6] The first question is of interest only to a factor who is again likely to provide his services to a credit card company. It related to the possible liability of customers, who had used a credit card to settle an account, to pay the dealer when the credit card company had failed to pay him owing to its winding up. Fortunately for the factor it was decided *on the particular facts of the case* that the indebtedness of the customers to the credit card company (assigned to the factor) could be sustained. The dealer's only remedy was to prove as a creditor in the estate of the credit card company. The case went to the Court of Appeal (but only in respect of the first question) which upheld the decision of the Court of first instance.

charge on a book debt and was void for want of registration.[7] Secondly, the liquidator claimed that the rules relating to set-off in insolvency[8] did not allow the factor to set off, against the actual liability of the factor to the client for the balance of the purchase price of debts, the liability of the client company for recourse the very existence of which (in addition to its amount) was at the commencement of liquidation contingent only.

It was held that the liability of the factor to the client was not the purchase price of each debt but the balance of a current account to which the purchase price was credited and other items debited.[9] Therefore, there was no question of set-off because there were no independent obligations capable of being set off; the arrangement gave rise to a single liability—the ultimate balance on the account.[10] It was further held that the retention was security for the factor; but it was security (in the widest sense of the word), by means of a contractual arrangement, against overpayment by the factor.[11] The right to retain a balance on the current account was not a registrable charge because there was no property capable of being the subject matter of a charge; the only asset was the amount due under the agreement and this already took account of the retention.[12]

The factor was entitled under the agreement to require on notice the repurchase by the client of all debts remaining outstanding. As such notice had not been given, the repurchase price was not then available to be debited to the account and it was conceded on behalf of the factor that this was a matter of set-off. For this reason, and in case he were to be wrong regarding the retention, the judge made a thorough review of the authorities relating to the availability of set-off of a contingent claim against the estate of a bankrupt individual or company in liquidation. Following this review he held that set-off was indeed available even if the existence as well as the amount of the liability of the insolvent estate was contingent. It was further held that the retention could not be a charge in favour of the factor on the balance on the current account because it was conceptually impossible for a debt to be charged in favour of the debtor himself.

[7] Companies Act 1985, ss. 395 and 396 as then in force.
[8] See paras. 9–10 and 9–11 above.
[9] See para. 10–02 above.
[10] [1986] 3 All E.R. 289 at p. 307.
[11] *Ibid.*
[12] *Ibid.*

The decision in the case[13] has been a comfort to factors; but, since the time of the judgment it has been considered in some quarters that the provisions of the Insolvency Act 1986 and the Insolvency Rules 1986[14] have removed the availability of set-off of a contingent claim against an insolvent estate. Owing to this uncertainty it seems advisable for a factor to structure his payment obligations as the client's right to draw against the balance on a current account.

Provisions for set-off and combination of accounts

10–04 Whether the factor provides for his obligations for payment to the client by way of a current account, as described above, or for payment of the purchase price of each debt individually, it is usual to provide for the set-off of any amount owing to the factor by the client against such obligations. The set-off provisions should extend to any contingent or prospective liability and, where there is a current account between the factor and the client, it should be provided that the factor may make a reasonable estimate of any contingent liability that cannot be exactly determined and debit the current account therewith. As the factor's accounting with his client is often conducted on more than one account, provision should also be made for the combination of these accounts at the option of the factor at any time. These provisions should protect the factor against the claims of an assignee (of the factor's debt to the client) to payment of the assigned debt free from the factor's cross-claims in respect of transactions having their inception before notice of the assignment.[15]

Prohibition of assignment of the client's rights

10–05 A further protection for the factor is the usual provision in factoring agreements that the client may not assign all or any of his rights under the agreement, including his right to payment from the factor, without the consent of the factor.

[13] *Re Charge Card Services Ltd.* [1986] 3 W.L.R. 697; [1986] 3 All E.R. 289.

[14] s. 323 and r. 4.90 respectively; see also para. 9–11 above.

[15] *Mangles* v. *Dixon* (1852) 3 H.L. Cas. 702 and see also *Watson* v. *Mid Wales Railway Company* [1867] L.R. 2 C.P. 593 where the set-off was not allowed but in which the principles relating to the intervention of an assignee in a contract for set-off were indicated. See also paras. 9–16 and 9–17 above and Chap. 11.

2. WARRANTIES AND UNDERTAKINGS BY THE CLIENT

Warranty of the validity and value of debts

10–06 Among all types of agreement for the financing of debts, whereby the debts are taken by way of purchase or for security, factoring is unique in that the factor most usually is unable to rely on the debtor's acceptance of the obligation to pay. In other arrangements of a similar nature (*e.g.* leasing, block discounting or forfaiting) the financier will have available to him a document signed by or on behalf of the debtor before parting with his funds. On the other hand, the factor has perforce most usually to rely on an invoice which represents only the client's interpretation of what the debtor must pay in accordance with the contract of sale or service; although the general experience of commerce and industry is that in only a very small proportion of cases will the debtor not accept the invoice there are inevitably, in the case of most businesses, a number which are not accepted. Whether such failure by the debtor to accept the invoice is justified or not and whether the invoice is incorrect by reason of mistake, inefficient administration in the client's office or by reason of fraud the factor must protect himself.

10–07 It is no part of the factor's service to protect the client against trade disputes; and he must avoid, if possible, the payment for debts represented by overstated invoices and, if he should pay, then he must be able to recover his payment by recourse to the client. It is therefore normally provided in the factoring agreement that the client should warrant the validity and value of the debts offered and the agreement will provide that any debt, in respect of which there is a breach of such a warranty, should be subject to recourse.[16] Such warranties normally provide that:

(1) the goods which gave rise to the debt have been delivered (or the services completed) and that they conform to the contract between the client and the debtor; and
(2) that the debt is a legally binding obligation of the debtor for the amount stated in the invoice and that the debtor will accept the goods and the invoice therefor without any dispute, deduction, defence, cross-claim or set-off.

10–08 A reduction in the amount payable by the debtor may arise out of contractual arrangements between the client and the debtor even when the goods delivered or services provided and the invoice all comply with the contract of sale. It may arise from

[16] The methods of achieving repayment by the client for debts the subject of recourse are described in paras. 10–20 to 10–23 (incl.) below.

purchases by the client from the debtor[17] and this should be covered by the warranty mentioned above.[18] It may be based on an established agreement for the giving of quantity discounts based on the value of goods taken over a stated period; such a discount would be calculated at the end of the period and apply retrospectively. It is likely that the deduction would be available to the debtor against the factor as assignee in view of its close connection with the debts arising from the sales to which it related; as a result when such a discount is allowed there will be a substantial deduction from the next payment to be made to the factor. Although such deduction should be covered under the warranty relating to the value of the debt (described above) it is normally considered advisable to include in the agreement an undertaking by the client not to purchase from any debtor without first informing the factor and to disclose any contractual arrangements by which the amount of the debt may be reduced below the amount of it as notified or offered.

Warranties regarding terms in the contract of sale or service

10–09 Factoring is normally provided only for businesses that sell on short terms of payment and the factor's charges and his assessment of risks is based on the terms on which he expects the client to sell. Furthermore, the factor must ensure that the sum which he recovers from the debtor is not diminished by reason of payment in a depreciating currency or an unusually large settlement discount. As a result he will expect warranties that each debt offered or notified to him arises out of a contract which:

(1) provides for payment on terms not more liberal than have been approved by the factor; and
(2) does not provide for discounts greater than he has approved; and
(3) provides for payment in a currency approved by him.

Assignability of debts and freedom from encumbrances

10–10 It is naturally necessary that the client should warrant that the debts offered or notified are such that he has the absolute right to assign them and, in order that the factor should avoid conflicts of the type referred to in Chapter 8, the factor will expect that the client should give warranties and undertakings regarding the freedom of the debts from any encumbrance. Although the factor may be expected to make a search at the companies registry before the start of factoring, there are several types of encumbrance that

[17] For the debtor's countervailing rights in such a case see paras. 9–14 and 9–15 above.
[18] Item (2) in para. 10–07 above.

escape the requirement of registration but may affect the debts sold to the factor by the client[19]; and these may include the tracing rights of the client's suppliers whose terms include prolonged reservation of title.[20] The client should give undertakings that no encumbrances (other than as disclosed to the factor) exist at the outset, that none will be created during the currency of the factoring agreement and, in particular, that no contract for the purchase of goods will enable the supplier to have any claim on or interest in any debt arising from the onward sale of such goods; he should warrant that every debt sold to the factor will be unencumbered.[21]

Warranties in connection with variations of contracts of sale

10–11 Having sold and delivered goods in accordance with a contract of sale, correctly invoiced them and sold the resultant debt to the factor, the client may seek to vary the contract of sale. This might occur if the debtor asked the client to take some goods back and the client was disposed to agree. If this occurred on a large scale with a number of debtors, the factor might be put in a position where he would be unable to collect from the debtors all that he had paid on account of the purchased price of debts sold to him. In their arrangements with their clients factors recognise that credit notes must be issued. In every business errors occur and to a limited extent the wrong goods or faulty goods may be delivered or invoices be incorrect. However, the conscious decision to vary a contract should not be made by a client without the consent of the factor, once the debt arising out of the contract has vested in the factor. The factor will expect an undertaking from his client not to vary or cancel any contract in such circumstances.

Undertaking to co-operate in recovery proceedings

10–12 Where the debts vest in the factor by an equitable assignment and it is necessary for him to take legal proceedings for recovery it may be necessary for him to join the client or to use his name.[22] A further undertaking required from the client is that he will co-operate with the factor in recovery procedures, whether through the courts or otherwise. Furthermore, in the case of invoice

[19] See para. 8–13 above.
[20] See paras. 8–28 to 8–37 (incl.) above.
[21] It should be noted that in *E. Pfeiffer Weinkellerei-Weineinkauf GmbH & Co.* v. *Arbuthnot Factors Ltd.* [1987] B.C.L.C. 522 the factor was assisted because he relied on such a warranty and was unaware of the claims of a supplier to his client in respect of prolonged reservation of title.
[22] See para. 7–04 and Chap. 7, n. 9 above.

discounting, undisclosed factoring, agency factoring or bulk factoring, the factor requires the client to undertake to act promptly and efficiently in the collection of debts; the client, having sold the debts to the factor, is collecting them on his behalf.

Warranty to disclose

10–13 Although the credit protection element of a factoring agreement is analogous to a policy of credit insurance, a factor does not have the protection that an insurer has by reason of the insurance policy belonging to a class of contracts that are *uberrimae fidei*. Under such contracts it is assumed that one party (in the case of insurance the prospective insured) is in possession of most of the material facts regarding the subject matter of the contract; accordingly, that party is obliged to make a full disclosure of such facts. Failure to do so makes the contract voidable at the option of the other. A factoring agreement is not a contract *uberrimae fidei*. In order to place himself in a position equivalent to that of a credit insurer the factor should require a warranty from the client that, both before making the agreement, the client has disclosed any fact or matter known to the client which might have influenced the factor's decision whether or not to enter into the agreement or to approve any debt for credit or for a prepayment on account of its purchase price. The agreement should also include an undertaking by the client to disclose any further such fact or matter arising during the currency of the agreement.

3. CREDIT NOTES

10–14 Although the factor expects the client to warrant that no event will occur that will reduce the liability of the debtor to pay an amount less than that specified in the offer or notification to the factor, in the best regulated businesses such events sometimes occur. Mistakes are made in invoicing, in manufacture and in the despatch of goods; and sometimes for commercial reasons it seems requisite for the client to agree to take goods back. In the normal routine of factoring concerning, as it normally does, a continuous stream of relatively small transactions the factor will by a course of dealing allow the client to make such adjustments to the value of the debts (already owned by the factor) by the issue of credit notes to the debtor.

10–15 It is apparent that the recognition of such a right of the client by a course of dealing leaves the factor in danger of its abuse by the client. In order to protect themselves against over zealous invoicing, and the consequent issue of substantial credit notes after the factor has paid on account of the debts represented by such invoices, it is the practice of some factors to provide in their agreements that the client should issue credit notes only with the consent of the factor. Others find this practice commercially unacceptable and administratively burdensome; but even in this case it is essential that the factor should take the right in the factoring agreement to implement such an arrangement in the event that he should find that the client is misusing his authority to issue credit notes. The provision, when put into effect by notice to the client, would require the client to send the originals of credit notes to the factor who would issue them to the debtors only when he had approved them.

4. TRANSFER TO THE FACTOR OF ANCILLARY RIGHTS

10–16 There are a number of rights which are closely connected with every debt purchased by the factor. Although the debt, being the right to receive payment for goods or services supplied, is usually the principal right of the client under his contracts of sale or service, there are other important rights of the client under such contracts. These include rights of lien and to stop goods in transit, the right in certain circumstances to rescind or terminate the contract, the right to accept returned goods and in many cases the right to retain title to the goods until the debtor has paid for them.

10–17 It is usual for the factoring agreement to provide that the following should automatically be transferred to the factor on purchase of any debt:

(1) all the client's rights under the relevant contract of sale or service (except the ownership of the underlying goods);
(2) all negotiable instruments taken or available to the client in or on account of settlement of the debt;
(3) the benefit of any credit insurance policy in respect of the debt;
(4) the benefit of any guarantee or indemnity given by a third party in respect of the debtor's obligations under the contract of sale or service;
(5) the ownership of all books, computer data, records and documents on or by which the debt is recorded or evidenced.

The ownership of the last item is usually considered advisable in order to avoid a situation in which a trustee, liquidator, administrator or receiver of an insolvent client refuses access to the papers which may be required as evidence to enable the factor to collect the debts which he has purchased.

10–18 It is not advisable, in all circumstances, for the agreement to provide for the automatic transfer of ownership of goods which the client sells subject to reservation of title until payment. This would bring the factor automatically into the chain of ownership and may in some circumstances submit him to claims in respect of liability for defects in the product; as the factor would in many cases not have the opportunity to inspect every sale contract in a continuous stream of small transactions he might be unaware that the ownership of the goods had passed through his hands. In order to avoid such potential liability for the factor without his knowingly accepting it, it is advisable for the agreement not to provide for the *automatic* transfer of ownership of the goods but to provide for the right to have ownership transferred to him if he should think it requisite; this would apply to goods before title had passed to the debtor or if they had been returned. By the realisation of such goods the factor may be able to recover his funds in use in the event that a substantial proportion of the debts are irrecoverable by reason of returns of goods.

10–19 It is important that the factoring agreement should provide that the purchase price (normally the amount payable by the debtor less the factor's charges) should be payable for the sale by the client to the factor, not only of the debt itself, but also of these ancillary rights. Otherwise it could be alleged that those rights are transferred not by way of sale but by way of security; in the case of a company this could be considered to be a charge requiring registration. It should also not be overlooked that in any letter of waiver or priority agreement it should be provided that, not only the debts, but also the ancillary rights are released from the charge in respect of which the waiver is to be given.[23]

5. RECOURSE

10–20 In order to recover from the client (normally by way of debit to a current account or by way of set-off[24]) the amount of any debt (or part of a debt), which the factor cannot recover from the debtor, the factor must provide for recourse to the client in respect of such debts. The inability to recover from the debtor may be by reason of:

(1) the debtor's insolvency or the failure of the debtor to pay by a specified number of days after the due date for payment

[23] See paras. 8–44 and 8–45 above.
[24] See paras. 10–02 and 10–03 above.

(except in the case of an approved debt in a non-recourse agreement);

(2) an unauthorised deduction or discount taken by the debtor;

(3) a dispute regarding the goods or the invoice; or

(4) breach of some other warranty by the client.

10–21 The recovery from the client by recourse may be structured in the agreement by either one of two methods:

(1) by the guarantee by the client of due payment by the debtor in respect of debts the subject of recourse; or

(2) by a requirement that such debts should be repurchased at the amount specified in the relevant notification or offer.

If the recourse is by way of repurchase, the repurchase price *must* be based on the notified or offered amount (and not the amount payable by the debtor), because the former will have been the basis for the credit to the account of the client while the latter may well be less.

10–22 Where a debt is the subject of recourse by reason of the winding up or bankruptcy of the debtor *and* (1) the client is also being wound up or is bankrupt and (2) the retention is insufficient to cover the recourse, the client may be in a better position to recover the amount of the recoursed debt if the recourse is framed as a guarantee by the client rather than by way of repurchase. In the winding up or bankruptcy of a principal debtor, the creditor (in this case the factor) is not obliged to deduct, from the amount of his proof in the estate of the debtor, any payments received (whether before or after the commencement of the winding up or bankruptcy) from the guarantor (in this case the client) until the guarantor has paid 100 per cent. The reason for this rule is that the creditor's proof for the full amount of the debt does not offend against the rule against double proof in the debtor's estate for the same indebtedness; the guarantor has no right to be subrogated to any of the creditor's rights (including the right to prove in the debtor's estate for the part of the debt in respect of which he has paid) until he has discharged the guaranteed debt in full.[25] Furthermore, although the creditor is obliged to deduct from his proof against the estate of the insolvent guarantor (the client) sums received from the debtor before the submission of his proof, he is not obliged to adjust his proof in respect of sums received afterwards.[26] Therefore if the factor submits his proofs in the estates of both the debtor and the client promptly, he may receive dividends calculated on the *full amount* of the debt as specified in

[25] *Re Sass* [1896] 2 Q.B. 12; see also para. 4–37 above.

[26] *Re Amalgamated Investment & Property Co. Ltd.* [1985] 1 Ch. 349; see also para. 4–38 above.

his proofs from both estates until he has recovered, in aggregate, 100p in the pound.

10–23 It is unlikely that there are analogous principles in relation to the repurchase of a debt. However almost the same result may be achieved by providing that, on the repurchase by the client of a debt the subject of recourse, the ownership of the debt shall remain vested in the factor until the repurchase price has been fully discharged.

6. SECURING THE FACTOR'S RIGHTS AND INTERESTS TO DEBTS AND ANCILLARY RIGHTS

Assignments in statutory form

10–24 In Chapter 7 it was explained that factors do not normally take assignments of the purchased debts in statutory form[27] but rely on equitable assignments. It was also postulated that the absence of a statutory form of assignment did not detract from the factor's rights in any way because the difference is purely procedural.[28] However, as the factor may in some circumstances deem it necessary that his title to any debt should be perfected in legal form for procedural reasons, it is normally provided in the agreement that the client should execute and deliver to the factor such documents as may be necessary for this purpose. It should also be provided that the client should execute such documents and do such things as may be requisite to transfer title to any ancillary rights[29] and to any of the underlying goods in respect of which the factor may be entitled to ownership.

Creation of trusts by the client

10–25 The growing practice of buyers of goods and services to purchase on their own standard terms, which include provisions prohibiting the assignment of debts arising from such purchases, has in recent years caused factors to make special provisions for the vesting in them of the factored debts arising from such sales by their clients on such terms. The reason for such special provisions is that it is possible that an assignment in contravention of such contractual terms may be wholly void.[30] The most usual method of dealing with this problem is to include a provision within the factoring agreement itself whereby the client holds any debt,

[27] Law of Property Act 1925, s. 136.
[28] See para. 7–06 above.
[29] See para. 10–17 above.
[30] *Helstan Securities Ltd.* v. *Hertfordshire County Council Ltd.* [1978] 3 All E.R. 262 and see paras. 9–30 and 9–31 above.

which is the subject of an assignment to the factor but fails to vest absolutely in the factor, in trust for the factor. The efficacy of such a provision does not appear to have been tested and it will not prevent the purchaser (as debtor) obtaining a valid discharge by ignoring the notice of the assignment and paying the client.[31] Such a trust provision should apply also to the ancillary rights purchased by the factor.[32]

Charges on debts in favour of the factor

10–26 A method of securing the factor's rights to debts, assigned in contravention of a prohibition of assignments in the contract out of which the debts arose, is by the creation of a fixed charge, by the client in favour of the factor, on such factored debts that fail to vest in the factor. Such a charge will not be affected in any way by the prohibition of assignments because a charge, although being analogous to an assignment, unlike a mortgage does not transfer ownership of the charged asset to the chargee; the charge is purely an agreement between the chargor and the chargee by which the chargee is entitled to look to the proceeds of the charged asset for the discharge of the obligations to him of the chargor.

10–27 Such a simple form of charge may provide that all the terms of the factoring agreement will apply to the charged debts *as if* they had vested in the factor by virtue of the factoring agreement. This means that the factor may require notices to be given to the debtors instructing them to pay direct to the factor; thus the control of the debts charged is such that the charge would not only be termed as fixed but would in fact be fixed and not floating.[33] Thus also the charge would not need to include the right to appoint a receiver because the factor would have the right to collect the debts *as if* they vested in him. On the other hand it may be possible for the factor to procure the creation of a composite charge which comprised, in addition to the fixed charge on debts which fail to vest in the factor, a floating charge on all other assets of the client. The purposes of the latter would be to provide some collateral security, to enable the factor to appoint an administrative receiver[34] and to preclude the appointment of an administrator.[35]

[31] *Ibid.*
[32] See paras. 10–16 and 10–17 above.
[33] See paras. 8–15 and 8–16 above.
[34] Insolvency Act 1986, s. 29(2).
[35] Insolvency Act 1986, ss. 9(2)(a) and 9(3).

10–28 Where the factor takes a simple form of charge on debts as described above[36] and there is a charge affecting debts of the client already in place he should be sure that any letter of waiver[37] includes a release to him of the debts and ancillary rights charged as well as those purchased by him. In the case of a composite charge including a floating element and a competing charge on the same assets a priority agreement is normally essential.[38]

Provisions for and recovery of funds paid by debtor to client

10–29 Once notice of the assignment of a debt to the factor has been given to the debtor and in the absence of a prohibition of assignments in the contract giving rise to the debt, the debtor is obliged to pay the factor; payment to the client who supplied him will not give him a valid discharge. If the debtor pays to the client in these circumstances (an *indirect* payment[39]) the factor is entitled to recover the amount so paid by a second payment from the debtor; this is so whether the assignment is in statutory form[40] or equitable.[41] However, because a certain number of debtors continue to make indirect payments, even after receipt of notices of assignments, and, owing to the practice in confidential factoring or invoice discounting arrangements to appoint the client the agent of the factor to collect from the debtors, such indirect payments must be provided for in the factoring agreement. The usual provisions are that:

(1) the identical monies, cheques and other instruments representing such indirect payments must be passed on to the factor by the client immediately upon their receipt; and
(2) pending their delivery to the factor such monies and instruments are to be held by the client in trust for the factor.

In order to reinforce such trust provisions and to provide for payments by means of credit transfers direct to the client's bank account it is usual for the factor to require that the client should instruct his banker to hold in trust for and remit to the factor any such receipts. It is apparent that in purchasing the debt the factor has vested in him the right to collect it and, accordingly, the proceeds are his property; thus the trust is implicit even if it were

[36] See para. 10–26 above.
[37] See paras. 8–44 and 8–45 above.
[38] See App. 9.
[39] So called by many factors because a *direct* payment must be the payment to the person who is entitled to receive it: the factor as assignee.
[40] Law of Property Act 1925, s. 136.
[41] *Wm. Brandts Sons & Co.* v. *Dunlop Rubber Co. Ltd.* [1905] A.C. 454.

not to be explicitly provided for. The efficacy of the creation of such a trust has been upheld by the court.[42]

10–30 The factor will have no need to recover by a second payment from the debtor if he can recover from the client and in most circumstances the provisions in the factoring agreement are effective so that the remittances representing indirect payments reach the factor through the client. However, if, in breach of the trust provisions, such a remittance is paid by the client into his own overdrawn bank account and the client becomes insolvent, the factor will first look to his retention and the possibility of recoursing the debt by way of set-off against any balance of the purchase price of other debts owing to the factor.[43] In addition the factor has available to him (apart from the right to a second payment from the debtor) two other possible avenues for recovery.

10–31 First, recovery from a director of a client company who was responsible for the breach of trust may be possible. A factor was successful in one such case[44] in recovering from a solvent director of a client company in liquidation despite the absence of a personal guarantee or indemnity. In that case the director caused the client company to pay into that company's bank account a cheque made payable to the client company and sent to it by the debtor; the cheque was purportedly in settlement of a debt which had been sold to the factor. The director was held to be liable to the factor in tort. It was no defence that the director had acted on behalf of the company nor that the factor could have avoided a loss by obtaining a second payment from the debtor.

10–32 Secondly, when a client has received a payment from a debtor in respect of an assigned debt and, contrary to any trust provisions in the factoring agreement, paid the proceeds into his own bank account it may in some circumstances be possible for the factor to recover from the bank. To the extent that the money had not been paid into an overdrawn account or has not been used to honour cheques drawn on the account the factor should be able to recover from the bank through a common law claim for money had and received to the use of the factor[45] or by a proprietary claim in equity.

10–33 However, if the client has wrongfully paid the proceeds of the factored debts into his own account it is most unlikely that the money will not have been used. If it has been used *and the bank had knowledge of the trust provisions* then the bank may be liable

[42] *International Factors Ltd.* v. *Rodriguez* [1979] Q.B. 351. However, as regards a provision for the client to pass on to the factor "identical cheques" see the reference to the White Paper on Banking Services (Cmnd. 1026 (1990) para. 5.06) in para. 3–19 above.
[43] See paras. 10–01 and 10–02 above.
[44] *International Factors Ltd.* v. *Rodriguez* [1979] Q.B. 351.
[45] *Barclays Bank Ltd.* v. *Cole* [1967] 2 Q.B. 738.

as a constructive trustee of the money.[46] Where the proceeds wrongly paid into the bank or credit transfers received by the bank in respect of a factored debt have been applied against an overdraft or otherwise used to reduce the client's liability to the bank it is probable that constructive notice to the bank would be sufficient to assist the factor; but where the bank obtained no benefit, because the proceeds were used to meet cheques drawn on the bank account in accordance with the mandate, constructive notice would not suffice and, for the bank to be liable, actual knowledge would be necessary.[47] It is not clear in such circumstances if mere notice of the existence of a factoring agreement by which *every* trade debt of the customer belonged to the factor would be sufficient to constitute actual notice. The banker may well claim that he cannot be expected, in a stream of relatively small transactions, to examine every cheque paid in by his customer in order to determine whether or not it relates to a trade debt. Furthermore, the banker may be able to rely solely on the protection of section 4 of the Cheques Act 1957 which gives the banker protection in relation to the collection for a customer, in good faith, of a cheque to which the customer's title is defective. If the factor put the bank on notice that a particular cheque from a particular customer was trust money before the bank had collected the cheque and the bank disregarded the notice then there is little doubt that the bank would be liable to the factor. It is usual for factors to ensure that their client's bankers have notice of the existence and broad terms of their factoring agreements. In view of the uncertainty regarding the degree of knowledge necessary for the bank's liability to the factor for indirect payments received by it, such notice may place the bank in a difficult position in relation to a large number of relatively small transactions processed in automated modern banking procedures. As a result it is not unusual for banks to require a disclaimer in relation to these matters as a condition of giving a waiver.

Factor to have power of attorney

10–34 It may be necessary for the factor to act quickly without having to call upon his client to deal with the formalities for securing and perfecting his rights and interests. In the case of an insolvent client, an officer with authority to sign may not be available nor may the trustee, liquidator, receiver or administrator wish to cooperate. Therefore, it is normal, either within the factoring agreement itself or by a separate document, for the factor and the

[46] *Barnes* v. *Addy* (1874) 9 Ch. App. 244.
[47] *Belmont Finance Corporation Ltd.* v. *Williaims Furniture Ltd.* (No. 2) [1980] 1 All E.R. 393 and see Goode, "Some Aspects of Factoring Law" (1982) J.B.L. at p. 410.

directors and other officers of the factor to be appointed jointly and severally to be the attorney or attorneys of the client for the purpose of executing any document requisite for this purpose. In this way the factor may (for example) effect a legal assignment or assignation in his own office and give notice or intimation to the debtor without delay. Such powers normally include the authority:

(1) to institute or defend proceedings in the client's name; and
(2) to complete and endorse negotiable instruments in the name of the client where such instruments relate to factored debts.

10–35 Any such power of attorney should be stated to be irrevocable. Where an irrevocable power of attorney is given to secure a proprietary interest the power is not to be revoked:

(1) by the donor unilaterally without the consent of the donee; or
(2) by the death of the donee or, in the case of an incorporated donee, by its winding-up or dissolution.[48]

Thus, with an irrevocable power of attorney in the factoring agreement the factor may continue to perfect his title to debts, already vested in him, and to negotiable instruments after the bankruptcy, liquidation of or the appointment of a receiver to his client.

7. VALUE ADDED TAX

10–36 Factoring agreements usually provide that the value of the debts purchased by the factor should include the amount of any Value Added Tax payable to the debtor which is applicable to the goods and services giving rise to such invoices. In effect the factor is, when paying the purchase price of debts to the client, including in his payments the client's output tax. VAT may affect the factor in two other aspects of the business and may need to be provided for in the agreement.

VAT and the factor's charges

10–37 The authorities have taken a view of the substance of factoring transactions where the factor has the responsibility of administering the accounts in respect of the factored debts. As a result in such cases (which have been referred to by HM Customs and Excise as "mainline factoring") it has been accepted that the factor

[48] Powers of Attorney Act 1971, s. 4.

provides a service which is a taxable supply and the position as regards the factor's charges is as follows:

(1) value added tax at the standard rate is applied to the administration or service charges; and
(2) the discount charges, being for the provision of finance (albeit by way of early payment on account of the purchase price of the debts sold to the factor), are charges for exempt supplies.

10–38 A factor providing this type of factoring service is partially exempt and the taxable inputs must be allocated between taxable and exempt outputs (according to the regulations in force[49]); only input taxes attributable to taxable supplies by the factor will be recoverable. The regulations[50] provide for the recovery of input tax in full where it can be specifically identified as relating to a taxable outward supply and for no recovery where the input specifically relates to an exempt supply (or relates to an activity other than a taxable supply). The remainder of the inputs are to be allocated to taxable and exempt supplies proportionately or by some other method considered by the Commissioners to be fair and reasonable.

10–39 It is in most circumstances impracticable to allocate the factor's taxable inputs (such as telephone charges and computer supplies) between the administration of debtor accounts and the accounts relating to the provision of funds to the client. Accordingly virtually all the factor's input taxes need to be allocated by some method to be agreed between the factor and the Commissioners. Some factors whose business is entirely of the nature, which is referred to above[51] as "mainline," have been able to obtain agreement that the recovery should be proportionate to the number of data processing transactions for each of the activities.

10–40 All charges for all other forms of factoring, including invoice discounting and agency factoring, are exempt; and where the factor provides only such services no input tax will be recoverable. If the factor provides both types of service then he will need to reach agreement with HM Customs and Excise as to a fair and reasonable method of allocation.

[49] The Value Added Tax (General) (Amendment) (No. 2) Regulations 1987 (S.I. 1987 No. 510).
[50] *Ibid.*
[51] At para. 10–37 above.

Value Added Tax bad debt relief

10–41 Relief is available in respect of the tax element in invoices representing debts owed by insolvent debtors.[52] For this purpose insolvency includes bankruptcy of or a deed of arrangement by an individual, creditors voluntary or compulsory liquidation in the case of a company and a voluntary arrangement pursuant to the Insolvency Act 1986 in either case.[53] In the case of the appointment of an administrative receiver or administrator to a debtor company it will be considered to be insolvent for this purpose if the receiver or administrator issues a certificate that in his opinion, if it went into liquidation, there would be insufficient assets to provide for any dividend to unsecured creditors.[54]

10–42 The relief is available to the supplier of the taxable goods and services only. The factor, although having paid the client the equivalent of the output tax in his payment of the purchase price of the debt,[55] is unable to recover it if the debtor is insolvent. If the debt has been purchased by the factor with recourse to the client then the client will be obliged either to repurchase the debt or to pay the amount of it to the factor under his guarantee of due payment by the debtor. In the latter case the debt will become vested in the client by subrogation and in either case the client will be able to recover the tax. In order to provide for recovery of the tax where the debt has been purchased by the factor without recourse, it is sometimes provided that the client should repurchase any debt on the insolvency of the debtor and use his best endeavours to recover the tax. The consideration for such repurchase is the holding in trust for the factor by the client of any recoveries in respect of the debt including the tax and any dividends from the estate.

8. THE CONSUMER CREDIT ACT 1974 AND FACTORING

10–43 In order to consider the possible effect of the provisions of the Consumer Credit Act 1974 on a factor's agreement with his client and on his relations with debtors three points must be borne in mind. First, a consumer credit agreement under the Act exists

[52] Value Added Tax Act 1983, s. 22 as amended by Finance Act 1985, s. 32(1) and S.I. 1986 No. 337.
[53] Insolvency Act 1986, Pts. I and VIII.
[54] See n. 52 above. But see para. 10–54 below for recent changes.
[55] See para. 10–36 above.

where credit not exceeding £15,000[56] is provided to an individual (which includes a partnership); secondly, "creditor" includes an assignee[57]; and thirdly, the Act does not regulate a consumer credit agreement for fixed sum credit under which the number of payments to be made by the debtor does not exceed four.[58]

The effect upon the factor's relations with the client

10–44 The purchase of debts is considered not to constitute the extension of credit to the seller of the debts provided that he has no *repayment* obligation. Even if the seller (the factor's client) guarantees payment by the debtor under provisions for recourse in the factoring agreement[59] it is not considered that provision of credit is involved; in such a case the recourse is for *payment* of the debt and not for *repayment* of an advance. It is likely (but not certain) that the framing of the rights of recourse under the agreement as a repurchase (and not a guarantee)[60] would not be considered a repayment obligation in this respect. Therefore, as far as the factor's relations with his client are concerned, provided that (1) he provides his factoring or discounting services only for corporate clients or (2) his agreement provides for the purchase of debts, he does not make loans and his recourse is framed as a guarantee, the agreements will be outside the scope of the Act and accordingly will not be regulated (even if his unrecovered prepayments never exceed £15,000).

10–45 If the factor provides his services for partnerships and sole traders and his recourse is framed as a repurchase it is possible (but unlikely) that his agreement could be considered as a "personal credit agreement"[61] and fall within the scope of the Act. In such a case the credit would be considered to be "running account credit."[62] However it is most unusual in these days for a factor to enter into any agreement under which no more than £15,000 would be outstanding by way of unrecovered prepayments at any time and such an agreement would be outside the definition

[56] Consumer Credit Act 1974, s. 8(2) and Consumer Credit (Increase of Monetary Limits) Order 1983 (S.I. 1983 No. 1878).
[57] Consumer Credit Act 1974, s. 189(1).
[58] *Ibid.* s. 16(5) and s. 3(1)(a)(i) Consumer Credit (Exempt Agreements) (No. 2) Order 1977 (S.I. 1977 No. 326) 1985 (S.I. 1985 No. 757).
[59] See para. 10–21 above.
[60] *Ibid.*
[61] Consumer Credit Act 1974, s. 8(1).
[62] *Ibid.* s. 10(1)(a).

of a "consumer credit agreement" and accordingly would not be regulated.[63]

10–46 In circumstances where the funds to be provided by the factor will at some time exceed the limit this must be apparent from the outset. In this connection, the fact that the factor has not placed a prepayment limit of £15,000 or less on the client is not sufficient to take the agreement outside the scope of regulation on these grounds alone; a consumer credit agreement will be a regulated agreement if:

> "*at the time that the agreement is made* it is probable, having regard to the terms of the agreement and any other relevant considerations, that the debit balance will not at any time rise above £5000."[64]

This limit has been subsequently raised to £15,000 by statutory instrument.[65] If the agreement is to avoid regulation on the grounds of this limit it should also avoid provisions by which the charges to the client increase or other provisions favourable to the factor come into effect if that limit is exceeded.[66]

The factor's relations with debtors

10–47 Although the Act includes assignees as creditors,[67] the contracts giving rise to the factored debts will not constitute regulated agreements if they are payable, as is usual in factoring or invoice discounting, in one amount in each case.[68]

Ancillary credit business[69]

10–48 It is usually considered requisite for a factor or invoice discounter to obtain a licence for each of the following ancillary businesses[70]:

(1) Debt adjusting (generally negotiating with a creditor or the owner of goods on hire on behalf of the debtor or hirer regarding the discharge of his obligations).
(2) Debt counselling (giving advice to debtors or hirers about the liquidation of debts under consumer credit or hire agreements).

[63] See para. 10–43 above.
[64] Consumer Credit Act 1974, s. 10(3)(b)(iii).
[65] Consumer Credit (Increase of Monetary Limits) Order 1983 (S.I. 1983 No. 1878).
[66] Consumer Credit Act 1974, s. 10(3)(b)(ii).
[67] *Ibid.* s. 189(1).
[68] See n. 58 above.
[69] Consumer Credit Act 1974, Pt. X.
[70] Consumer Credit Act 1974, s. 146(6)(a) by which assignees are excluded from the exemption for regulation of this type of business.

(3) Debt collecting.

It is also considered advisable in most cases for a factor to obtain a licence for credit brokerage in view of possible introductions by their staff to other companies carrying on consumer credit or consumer hire business.

10–49 If the factor is a *credit reference agency*, then it should be licensed for that ancillary business. Whether or not it is a credit reference agency is a question of fact; and it will be such an agency if it were to collect credit information *for the purpose of* furnishing other persons with it.[71]

Factoring transactions not normally subject to regulation

10–50 The preceding paragraphs are a summary of the probable effect of the Consumer Credit Act 1974 on factoring transactions. As it appears unlikely that such transactions will be regulated under the Act no attempt has been made in this treatise to analyse or explain the provisions of the Act in more detail. If the factor's method of operation is such that his transactions are likely to be regulated he will need to obtain detailed advice.

9. MISCELLANEOUS TERMS

Inspection and production of client's records and accounts

10–51 It is usual for any factoring agreement to include provisions whereby:

(1) the client is obliged to submit to the factor copies of his annual accounts and other financial statements produced; and
(2) the factor is allowed to inspect the accounting records, together with supporting documents, of the client at the client's premises.

The provision for the submission of accounts in some cases may extend to monthly or quarterly management accounts, and to require their production if they are not otherwise produced. The provisions for the inspection of records and documents sometimes includes only such records and documents as relate to the debts sold or to be sold to the factor. They would include copy invoices, orders, proof of delivery, remittance advices and correspondence with debtors. These records and documents may be necessary for the factor as evidence of the existence of debts in his collection

[71] *Ibid.* s. 145(8).

procedures; the agreement will normally provide for their production and delivery to the factor and for the ownership of them to vest in him.[72] Some factors require the right to inspect any of the books, accounts, records and correspondence that they may in their discretion require to see and such wider provisions may be necessary for the factor to ensure that the debts sold to him are not subject to any set-off or other encumbrance.

Termination

10–52 The agreement usually provides for termination on notice of an agreed period by either side. It is also usual for the factor to provide that the agreement may be terminated immediately on notice on the occasion of events such as a serious or persistent breach by the client or the client's insolvency or its ceasing to carry on its business. The position of the factor on the appointment of a receiver or administrator in respect of a client company or its winding up or the bankruptcy of an individual client is dealt with in Chapter 11.

Repurchase of debts on client's breach or insolvency

10–53 However the factoring agreement should provide for the right of the factor to withold all payments and (at the factor's option) for the repurchase by the client of outstanding debts vesting in the factor (at a repurchase price equivalent to the amounts notified or in the original offer) when any event occurs giving him the right to immediate termination *whether or not he has exercised that right.* This last provision is necessary because it is not always considered advisable for the factor to terminate the agreement; if the business is continuing further debts may be created and be assigned to the factor. The right to require the repurchase of the debts is particularly important if the factor holds collateral security by way of guarantees or a charge on assets of a corporate client; the repurchase price of the debts will normally be a great deal more in aggregate than the unpaid balance of the purchase price owed to the client and will thus create a net actual liability to the factor on the basis of which the factor may call upon the guarantor to pay or enforce his collateral security.

Value Added Tax bad debt relief (new arrangements)

10–54 By section 11 of the Finance Act 1990 the arrangements for relief have been simplified. With effect from July 26, 1990, a business which has supplied goods or services after March 31,

[72] See para. 10–16 above.

1989, and has accounted for and paid tax on the supply will only have to show that the debt has been written off in its accounts. However, it will have to wait for two years for the relief to be available and to account for tax on any recoveries. The inability of the factor (as assignee) to recover direct (as described in paragraph 10–41 above) is not affected; and it is unlikely that, in the case of a debt incurred after July 26, 1990, and purchased by the factor without recourse, the client will be able to recover on behalf of the factor as indicated in that paragraph.

CHAPTER 11

INSOLVENCY OF THE CLIENT

11–01 In this chapter there are considered the rights and obligations of the factor both in respect of the continuation of the factoring agreement and in respect of debts already vesting in him on the occurrence of the most usual events on the insolvency of the client. These events are the appointment of an administrative receiver or administrator to a corporate client, the winding up (either compulsory or creditor's voluntary) of a corporate client or a partnership and the bankruptcy of an individual client or partnership. Also, there is considered the effect of a voluntary arrangement under Parts I and VIII of the Insolvency Act 1986 by a client.

1. RECEIVERSHIP

11–02 It is unlikely that the appointment of a receiver in relation to a specific asset of a corporate client, other than the debt owed to the client by the factor itself, will directly affect the rights and obligations of the parties to the factoring agreement; it may however be the cause of some other event that may affect them such as administrative receivership, the appointment of an administrator or winding up. The effect of the enforcement of a charge over the debt owing by the factor to the client is dealt with below[1] but, in view of the foregoing, and as the appointment of a receiver by the court or under statutory powers[2] in relation to the affairs of a client is rarely met by a factor this treatise is limited to the effect of the appointment in relation to a client company of

[1] See paras. 11–16 to 11–21 (incl.) below.
[2] Law of Property Act 1925, s. 103.

an administrative receiver out of court by virtue of the instrument of a floating charge.[3]

Administrative receivers

11–03 "Administrative receivers" are a special class of receivers created and given powers and status by the Insolvency Act 1986.[4] The right to appoint an administrative receiver is limited to the holder of a charge which, *as created*, was a floating charge[5]; the appointment must be over the whole or substantially the whole of the company's property or of what remains after the appointment of a receiver to a specific part of the property.[6] In order to have the privilege of appointing an administrative receiver (and the right to forestall the making of an administration order[7] and the appointment of an administrator[8]) it is now not uncommon for a creditor of a company, taking security on a specific asset, to include within the instrument of charge a floating charge on all other assets of the company; and sometimes, in order not to preclude the raising of secured funds elsewhere by the company, such a charge may be specified in the instrument itself as ranking behind all other prior and subsequent charges on the company's assets.

Effect of the appointment of an administrative receiver

11–04 Although the Insolvency Act 1986 has, in respect of administrative receivers, extended the duties and powers which were previously conferred on receivers and managers appointed in respect of floating charges, in many respects the case law which governed the rights and duties of the receivers and managers still applies to those of the administrative receivers. In these days the charge will in most circumstances be fixed on real property and debts and floating on other assets such as stock and work in progress.[9] The

[3] For a full review of the law relating to all types of receivers of companies reference should be made to Lightman and Moss, *The Law of Receivers of Companies*.
[4] Part III and Sched. 1.
[5] The Insolvency Act 1986, s. 29(2)(a).
[6] *Ibid.* ss. 29(2)(a) and 29(2)(b).
[7] *Ibid.* ss. 9(3) and 11 and see para. 11–26 below.
[8] *Ibid.* s. 13.
[9] For the difference between fixed and floating charges see paras. 8–14 and 8–15 above and Lightman and Moss, *The Law of Receivers of Companies*, Chap. 3.

effect of the appointment will include the following:

(1) The floating element of the charge will *crystallise*, if crystallisation has not occurred beforehand on some other event giving rise to it according to the instrument of charge. The charge will thus become fixed on all assets and attach thereto.
(2) In the absence of a resolution for the winding up of the company or of a court order to that effect, the receiver is deemed to be the agent of the company; this is so irrespective of any provision to that effect in the terms of the instrument of charge or of his appointment.[10] He is personally liable on any contracts entered into by him except where the contract itself otherwise provides.[11]
(3) His appointment does not discharge or terminate the company's normal commercial contracts. However, the other parties have no means of enforcing them against the company itself as the receiver is in possession of all the property of the company.[12] He is not liable on them nor can they be enforced against him.[13]
(4) Unlike the position in a winding up, the directors' powers do not cease and they may continue to exercise them in relation to any property or rights of which the receiver has not taken possession to the extent that they do not interfere with the receiver's rights.[14]
(5) However, over property of the company in respect of which the administrative receiver has been appointed (or where such powers would derogate from the powers of the administrative receiver) the powers of the directors of the company are suspended.[15] The administrative receiver's powers

[10] The Insolvency Act 1986, s. 44(1)(a).
[11] *Ibid.* s. 44(1)(b).
[12] But his duty to the chargee and to act with reasonable care means that, in carrying on the business of the company, he must not unreasonably damage its goodwill. See *Re Newdigate Colliery Ltd.* [1912] 1 Ch. 468 and Lightman and Moss, *The Law of Receivers of Companies*, para. 8–04.
[13] *Airline Airspares Ltd.* v. *Handley Page Ltd.* [1970] 1 Ch. 193.
[14] *Newhart Developments Ltd.* v. *Co-operative Commercial Bank Ltd.* [1978] Q.B. 814 at p. 819.
[15] *Re Emmadart Ltd.* [1979] Ch. 540.

will include the power to carry on the business[16] and to realise the assets of the company.[17] Whilst he is agent of the company his powers are limited by the Memorandum and Articles of the company but a person dealing with him in good faith and for value is not prejudiced by his acting *ultra vires*.[18]

Factor's rights on the appointment: general

11–05 The factor's rights on the appointment of a receiver to take possession of the property of a client company will depend upon the terms of the factoring agreement. Most usually the agreement will provide for one or more of the following options by the factor:

(1) to terminate the agreement forthwith by notice; or
(2) with or without termination of the agreement:
  (a) to refrain from making any further prepayments or other payments to the client until all funds in use have been recovered; or
  (b) to require that all prepayments should be repaid; or
  (c) to have all debts vesting in the factor repurchased for their full invoice value on the basis that they shall not vest in the client until the full amount of the repurchase consideration has been received by the factor.

11–06 In the usual situation in which the receiver is in possession of all the assets of the company neither (2)(b) nor (2)(c) above will be of much immediate help to the factor. In both those cases, if the factor has prepaid in respect of the outstanding debts purchased, he is likely to become a *creditor*; in the former case, to the extent that his unrecovered prepayments exceed the retention (unpaid balances owed to the client) and in the latter, to the extent that the total amount credited by him in respect of the debts exceeds the retention. The receiver will not be responsible to him and the directors will have no rights in respect of assets, with which they would need to deal, if they are to satisfy the factor's demand for repayment. In both cases, however, the factor will be in a position to make a demand on any guarantors without waiting for the final outcome—whether or not the funds in use will be fully recovered from payments by debtors.

[16] His power to do so after the commencement of any winding up of the company is not certain as he then ceases to be the agent of the company (*Gosling* v. *Gaskell* [1897] A.C. 595); for the subsequent position see para. 11–24 below.
[17] The powers are set out in Sched. 1 to the Insolvency Act 1986 and by s. 42(1) of the Act are deemed to be included in the instrument of charge by which he is appointed (whether or not they are so specified). For full details of his powers see Lightman and Moss, *The Law of Receivers of Companies*, Chap. 8.
[18] The Insolvency Act 1986, s. 42(3). *Cf.* Companies Act 1985, ss. 35, 35A and 35B introduced by Companies Act 1989, s. 108.

11–07 Whichever of the options above is available to and exercised by the factor, it is usual for the factor to be able to refrain from making further payments to the client until all funds in use have been recovered. The balance on the factor's account in favour of the client will normally be an asset subject to the charge and in the possession of the receiver[19]; accordingly, the amount ultimately payable to the client, after taking into account all recourse and any other set-off, will be payable to the receiver unless by that time he has obtained his discharge. In the event of the receiver's discharge before payment is to be made by the factor, then such payment will fall into the hands of any liquidator subsequently appointed or, in the unlikely event of a solvent company, it will be payable to the company itself.

Factor's position as regards existing debts

11–08 Assuming that the priorities have been regulated by a waiver or otherwise as described in Chapter 8, in all cases the factor's rights *in relation to the debts and related rights*[20] *vesting in him* remain unaltered on the appointment of the receiver. In particular:

(1) The factor's powers to execute legal assignments and to endorse the client's name on negotiable instruments will be unaffected, provided that the power of attorney given to him in the factoring agreement is stated to be irrevocable[21]; and

(2) Any trust provisions in the factoring agreement, by which remittances for debtors received by the client are to be held for the account of and sent to the factor, remain in effect.[22]

11–09 The factor may have available to him and may exercise the option of terminating the agreement and assigning back to the client all outstanding debts. The assignment back may arise from the nature of the factoring contract; if the contract is for recourse factoring, all the debts will have been purchased by the factor with full recourse. On the other hand the reassignment may arise from special provisions in the agreement which come into effect on insolvency as described above.

11–10 Where prepayments have been made and have not been fully recovered on the appointment of a receiver, the factor will still be interested in collecting the outstanding debts in order to recover

[19] See para. 11–16 below.
[20] See paras. 10–16 to 10–18 (incl.) above.
[21] See paras. 10–34 and 10–35 above.
[22] See paras. 10–29 to 10–33 (incl.) above.

his funds in use. However, the advantage to the factor of having the right to sell the debts back to the client is that he will no longer be responsible for any credit risk. The term in the agreement will provide that the client should repurchase the debts at the amount originally notified or at which they have been offered and this would apply notwithstanding the recovery of a lesser amount; the debts will however, *remain the factor's property until the repurchase price of all of them has been paid*. As the client has no funds with which to pay, the payment must come from the factor's collections. So, in this way, or by a direct provision in the agreement cancelling the factor's responsibility for collection or credit risk on the occurrence of insolvency (including receivership) of his client, the factor may continue to collect for his own account until he has recovered the funds he has laid out by way of prepayments. At that stage he may have no further responsibility. In the absence of provisions in the factoring agreement as described above, in the case of the full service or maturity factoring, the factor will be responsible for the ultimate collection and the credit risk on all approved accounts even after his recovery of the funds in use.

11–11 Where the arrangements for factoring have included the administration of the debtor accounts and collections and the factor has the right, as described above, to have the outstanding debts reassigned, it may well be worthwhile for the receiver to make arrangements with the factor to continue to collect and record the debts. Such an arrangement will save the receiver from the administrative burden of taking on the sales ledger accounts and effecting collection. Such arrangements may often be made with a factor for little, if anything, in the way of an additional charge in return for efficient co-operation from the receiver's staff in providing some important administrative back-up from the client's records. Examples of this back-up are:

(1) the provision of proof of delivery of goods where this is required by a debtor; and
(2) help in dealing with disputes or warranty claims relating to the goods.

No doubt the receiver will in any case appreciate that such co-operation is in his interest; the factor's recoveries are ultimately for the benefit of the estate of the client.

Position as regards existing debts not notified under agreement of the whole turnover type

11–12 Although the factor will normally have the right to terminate the agreement forthwith on the appointment of an administrative receiver to his client company,[23] such a right is not normally given to the client; the receiver, as agent of the company, will be able to terminate only on the agreed period of notice. Therefore, unless the factor himself exercises the right of immediate termination, the agreement will usually remain in existence for some months. If the receiver declines to implement the provisions of an agreement of the whole turnover type[24] then, assuming that the factor holds a valid waiver from the holder of the charge under which the receiver was appointed or if the factoring agreement was created first, the factor will be able to exercise his rights of ownership and collection of any debts (together with their related rights) which have come into existence *and been earned by performance by the client* up to the time of the receiver's appointment.[25] As such debts vest in him he may give notice to the debtors and demand payment from them whether or not the debts have been notified to him; if they have not been invoiced the factor may invoice them himself by virtue of his irrevocable power of attorney.[26]

11–13 The application of this principle (by which an agreement to assign identifiable future property operates as an actual assignment when the property comes into existence[27]) to debts arising out of contracts in existence, but not earned by performance before the appointment of the receiver, is not certain. It may be covered by the terms of a waiver. If it is not so covered, or if the charge under which the receiver was appointed was created after the factoring agreement was already in existence and, accordingly, no waiver was necessary, the position would be as follows: the client's rights under contracts of sale in existence at the time of the receiver's appointment and any debts arising out of them should vest in the factor, but any goods or other resources available to fulfil the contract would have vested in the chargee when the crystallisation of the floating charge completed an inchoate assignment to him of the stock and work in progress.[28]

11–14 There appears to be no reported case on this point in relation to receivership but in such circumstances it seems likely that the court might apply the bankruptcy principle by which assigned debts not earned by performance at the commencement of a bankruptcy

[23] See para. 10–52 above.
[24] See para. 7–13 above.
[25] *Tailby* v. *Official Receiver* (1888) 13 A.C. 523 and see para. 7–14(2) above.
[26] See paras. 10–34 and 10–35 above.
[27] *Holroyd* v. *Marshall* (1862) 10 H.L. Cas. 191; *Tailby* v. *Official Receiver* (1888) 13 A.C. 523; see also *G. & T. Earle* v. *Hemsworth R.D.C.* (1929) 140 L.T. 69 and para. 7–13 above.
[28] See *Business Computers Ltd.* v. *Anglo-African Leasing Ltd.* [1977] 1 W.L.R. 578.

belong to the insolvent estate.[29] Any debts arising out of the receiver's own contracts (before any winding up of the company) are entered into by him as agent for the company but are for the benefit of the chargee. After a winding-up order or a resolution to wind up they are entered into by him either as principal or as agent for the chargee[30]; and the resulting debts are in no way bound by the factoring agreement.

Position as regards existing debts not offered under an agreement of the facultative type

11–15 The appointment of a receiver does not terminate the company's contracts and this includes the factoring agreement (unless terminated by either party according to its terms) but the receiver is not liable on the contracts of the company existing at the date of his appointment[31] and, in the case of an administrative receiver who has taken possession of all the property of the company, the directors have not the means by which to procure the performance of the agreement.[32] As a result, on the appointment of an administrative receiver to his client, a factor with an agreement of the facultative type[33] has no remedy in the event of a refusal of the receiver to offer further debts (including those invoiced before the receiver's appointment) except a claim for breach of contract against the company itself. For this he will be unsecured. He has no rights *in rem* in relation to such debts.[34]

The receiver's rights in relation to the factor's indebtedness to the client

11–16 Arrangements by which banks and other financiers may provide finance on the security of the amounts payable by the factor to his

[29] *Re Jones ex p. Nicholls* (1883) 22 Ch. D. 782 and see Wood, *English & International Set-off*, paras. 7–173 to 7–175 (incl.). In *G. & T. Earle* v. *Hemsworth R.D.C.* (1928) 140 L.T. 69 an assignee of retention monies succeeded against the claims of a receiver but, although the retention monies did not become payable until after the appointment of the receiver, they had been earned by performance beforehand.

[30] See paras. 11–24 and 11–25 below.

[31] *Airlines Airspares Ltd.* v. *Handley Page Ltd.* [1970] 1 Ch. D. 193 and see Lightman and Moss, *The Law of Receivers of Companies*, para. 8–04.

[32] See para. 11–06 above.

[33] See para. 7–12 above.

[34] *Ibid.*

client for purchased debts under a factoring agreement (the factor's debt) are now not uncommon. In many cases the factor's debt is only the unpaid balance of the purchase price of debts after the factor has made prepayments; but in others it may be arranged for the factor to pay only on maturity or collection of each debt so that the factor's debt will be approximately the equivalent of all outstanding debts arising from the client's sales. The security may be taken by way of an assignment to the bank or financier of the factor's debt or it may be by way of a specific fixed charge on it; and in many other cases the factor's debt, being a book debt,[35] would fall within the ambit of a standard bank debenture which included a fixed or floating charge on book debts.

11–17 Following the *Charge Card Services Ltd.* case[36] and the publicity it brought to the practice of factors to hold a retention as security (in its widest sense) for recourse, there have been some attempts by receivers appointed under charges, which include a factor's debt as charged property, to seek to obtain immediate payment of that debt (including the retention) and to deny the factor the right to set off any recourse or other items to be charged to the client after the receiver's appointment. The argument in support of these attempts appears to be that, on the appointment of the receiver, the factor's debt is assigned for the benefit of the holder of the charge and that, once notice of the receiver's appointment has been given to the factor, the rights of the parties are fixed[37] and no further independent set-off will be available to the factor as debtor. If the factor's claim were to be in respect of independent transactions, this argument might prevail and the factor's position would indeed be unsafe; if the bank's security is by way of assignment (and most probably also in the case of a fixed charge[38]), it would be the notice of the assignment or of a fixed charge that would preclude further set-off.[39] This would mean that the factor would be unable safely to continue the factoring arrangements

[35] See Chap. 8, n. 37.
[36] [1986] 3 W.L.R. 697.
[37] *Roxburghe* v. *Cox* (1881) 17 Ch.D. 520 and see para. 9–15 above.
[38] See Lightman and Moss, *The Law of Receivers of Companies*, para. 16–13. In the cases relating to a debtor's rights of set-off on the appointment of a receiver to his creditor the point as to the distinction between an assignment and a charge has not been taken and they have been treated as analogous; see Goode, *Legal Problems of Credit and Security*, (2nd ed.), p. 77, n. 33.
[39] *Roxburghe* v. *Cox* (1881) 17 Ch.D. 520. and see para. 9–15 above. For this purpose it seems that actual notice would be necessary, *i.e.* not solely by reason of registration (see para. 8–12 above).

after such notice which might be received by the factor even before the start of the factoring agreement! However, all such allegations can be rebutted because there is a line of cases which are good authority for the principle that, following the assignment of a debt, any cross-claims of the debtor, which have not accrued at the time of notice of the assignment but which arise out of the same contract as that which gave rise to the debtor's actual liability and are closely connected with it, can be set off against that liability.[40]

11–18 In the case of an agreement of the whole turnover type[41] there can be no doubt about the factor's rights in this respect; the purchase of all the debts, those for which the factor has to pay and those which are the subject of potential recourse, arise from the one agreement (the factoring agreement itself) and all such transactions are inextricably interwoven.

11–19 In the case of a facultative agreement[42] also, the factor's case seems sure. It may well be considered that, as an agreement of this type does not itself give effect to assignments of the debts but provides only that they should be offered by the client, each assignment under such an agreement is the subject of a separate contract. Although there is no reported case bearing exactly on the close connection of transactions linked under the unifying influence of such a master agreement, it seems most likely that the connection in such a case would be considered to be close enough for the set-off to be allowed.[43]

11–20 In both cases, as it is usual for the factor to include within the factoring agreement provisions for the set-off of such claims, the receiver would be likely to take the debt owing by the factor to the client subject to the factor's contractual rights in this respect; it seems well established that an assignee takes subject to any agreement for set-off in respect of transactions which have their inception into before notice of the assignment.[44] Whilst owing no positive obligation to the factor, the beneficiary of the charge cannot take the benefit of the factoring agreement without the

[40] See, for example, *Young* v. *Kitchin* (1878) 3 Ex. D. 127; *The Government of Newfoundland* v. *Newfoundland Railway Co.* (1888) 13 A.C. 199; for the exercise (after the appointment of a receiver) of a right conferred by a contract of which the receiver has taken the benefit see *Barker (George) Transport Ltd.* v. *Eynon* [1974] 1 All E.R. 900.
[41] See para. 7–13 above.
[42] See para. 7–12 above.
[43] For a decision regarding equitable set-off in a case concerning a series of contracts on similar terms see "*The Angelic Grace*" [1980] 1 Lloyds Rep. 288.
[44] *Mangles* v. *Dixon* (1852) 3 H.L. Cas. 702; *Smith* v. *Parkes* [1852] 16 Beav. 115; see also Derham, *Set-Off*, p. 317 and Wood, *English & International Set-off*, paras. 16–33 *et seq*.

burden of it.[45] The holder of a charge "... could assert their position as assignees of the company's property ... only by themselves recognising and giving effect to the pre-appointment contractual rights ...."[46]

11–21 In spite of the factor's ability to rebut such allegations by receivers appointed to client companies it is advisable for the position to be clarified at the time when the factoring agreement is entered into or, in the case of a subsequent charge, when the charge is created. This may be done in the letter of waiver or acknowledgement.[47]

Summary of factor's rights

11–22 The factoring agreement remains in effect if it is not terminated according to its terms; but the receiver has no obligation in respect of it. The factor cannot enforce any rights against the company because the directors have no means to procure compliance with the terms. Subject to the priorities having been properly regulated between the factor and the chargees or if the factoring agreement has priority in relation to the debts and related rights by law[48] then the factor may in most circumstances:

(1) exercise all rights of ownership and collection in respect of debts offered to and accepted by him or notified to him (according to the type of agreement);
(2) in the case of an agreement of the whole turnover type exercise such rights in respect of debts earned by performance of its contracts by the client up to the time of the receiver's appointment; and
(3) exercise his rights of set-off in respect of recourse, charges and other amounts payable by the client under the agreement.

In relation to the set-off of independent transactions, the factor in any event should be able to claim priority over the receiver on the basis of contractual set-off if the chargee was fully aware of the terms of the agreement before the factor received notice of the charge; however this aspect should be dealt with by agreement (*e.g.* by a waiver) between the factor and the chargee when the

[45] *Barker (George) Transport Ltd.* v. *Eynon* [1974] 1 All. E.R. 900.
[46] *Ibid. per* Edmund Davies L.J. at p. 907.
[47] For a form of words which may achieve such clarification see para. 8–45 above.
[48] See Chap. 8.

factoring agreement or charge is created (whichever is later in time).[49]

Continuation of factoring by an administrative receiver

11–23 If the factoring agreement is not terminated according to its terms it will continue to be effective as regards the client company itself but the factor has no way of enforcing its terms[50] as regards:

(1) in the case of an agreement of the facultative type,[51] debts not offered to the factor before the appointment[52]; and
(2) in the case of an agreement of the whole turnover type,[53] debts not earned by performance by the client company before the appointment.[54]

If the receiver chooses to implement the agreement while he is agent of the company[55] it will continue unaffected by his appointment. However, he is unlikely to be prepared to accept any positive liability of the client in relation to debts already vesting in the factor at the time of his appointment; such positive liability will arise if the balance owing by the factor for debts purchased before the appointment is not large enough to absorb, by way of set-off, all the amounts to be charged to the client in respect of such debts (including the repurchase price of debts the subject of recourse). As a result the receiver will wish to vary the existing arrangements so that a new client account is opened in respect of debts offered or notified by him and so that any amount to be debited in respect of pre-receivership transactions is debited to the old account. As a consideration for such a change the factor should obtain an undertaking from the receiver to use his best endeavours to dispose of disputes and claims by customers in respect of goods or services provided by the client both before and after his appointment. It may well be also in the interests of the receivership to maximise the factor's recoveries in this way. The change may be made either by the creation of a new agreement between the

[49] See para. 8–44 above.
[50] See para. 11–04(3) above.
[51] See para. 7–12 above.
[52] See para. 11–15 above.
[53] See para. 7–13 above.
[54] See paras. 11–12 to 11–14 (incl.) above.
[55] *I.e.* before any winding-up order in respect of the company or a resolution to wind it up.

receiver as agent of the company and the factor (and the termination of the existing agreement) or by an amendment to the existing agreement. In the former case the receiver will be *personally* responsible for the obligations of the client under the contract unless the agreement specifically provides otherwise.[56] In the latter case the amendment to the agreement is unlikely to bring about such personal liability.

Termination of an administrative receiver's agency on winding up

11–24 An administrative receiver's agency for the company in relation to which he is appointed ceases, in the case of a winding up by the court, on the making of the winding-up order and, in the case of a voluntary winding up, on the resolution of the members.[57] He will not be the agent of the company if the company is already in liquidation at the time of his appointment.[58] If the instrument of charge in respect of which the appointment is made or the deed of appointment itself so provides he will be the agent of the chargee; he may also be held to be the chargee's agent if he acts on the chargee's instructions.[59] Otherwise he will act as principal[60] and this is very often the case when the instrument of charge and the appointment make no provision in this respect.

11–25 Where the receiver is acting either as the chargee's agent or as principal his power to deal with the property in the name of the company is not affected.[61] Whether he may then continue the business of the company otherwise than to the extent necessary for beneficial realisation of its property seems uncertain; for this reason it is not uncommon for an administrative receiver, who wishes to carry on the business of a company in liquidation, to "hive down" the assets and undertaking to a subsidiary.[62] Where an administrative receiver wishes to continue a factoring agreement while the client company is in liquidation it would be advisable for the factor either to procure a personal warranty from the receiver that he is acting as principal or confirmation of the

[56] The Insolvency Act 1986, s. 44(1)(b).
[57] The Insolvency Act 1986, s. 44(1)(a).
[58] *Ibid.*
[59] *American Express International Banking Corporation* v. *Hurley* [1985] 3 All E.R. 564.
[60] For an analysis of the significance of the difference see Lightman and Moss, *The Law of Receivers of Companies*, para. 4–11.
[61] *Sowman* v. *David Samuel Trust Ltd.* [1978] 1 W.L.R. 22.
[62] See Lightman and Moss, *The Law of Receivers of Companies*, p. 125, n. 60.

consent of the chargee as principal to the continuation of the agreement.

2. ADMINISTRATION ORDERS[63]

11–26 Mainly for the purpose of giving insolvent companies an opportunity for recovery, Part II of the Insolvency Act 1986 has created a new régime available for the administration of such companies. This is achieved by an administration order by the court, providing for the appointment of an "administrator" to an insolvent company, on the petition of the company, its directors, a creditor or creditors or all of them. The court may make the order if it considers that one of the following purposes will be achieved:

(1) the survival of the company or any part of its undertaking;
(2) the approval of a voluntary scheme of arrangement under Part I of the Act[64];
(3) a compromise or arrangement between the company and its members or creditors (or any class of either of them) under section 425 of the Companies Act 1985; or
(4) realisation of the company's assets more advantageously than in winding up.[65]

If there is an administrative receiver of the company in place when the petition is heard no order will be made unless either the receiver consents to the making of the order or the court is satisfied that the charge in respect of which he was appointed would be liable to be avoided, released or discharged[66] on the making of the order.[67]

Effect of petition for an administration order

11–27 During the period from the petition to the making of the order (or dismissal of the petition) no resolution may be passed or order made for the winding up of the company.[68] During this period, except with leave of the court:

[63] For a more detailed description see Lightman and Moss, *The Law of Receivers of Companies*, Chap. 23.
[64] See paras. 11–60 and 11–61 below.
[65] The Insolvency Act 1986, s. 8.
[66] Pursuant to The Insolvency Act 1986, ss. 238, 239 or 245.
[67] See also para. 11–03 above.
[68] The Insolvency Act 1986, s. 10(1)(a).

(1) no steps may be taken to enforce any security over the company's property nor to recover any goods in the company's possession which are the subject of hire purchase, leasing, conditional sale or reservation of title[69]; and

(2) no distress or execution may be levied and no other proceedings or legal process may be started or continued.[70]

11–28 The bar to legal process referred to in paragraph 11–27 above does not prevent during this period the presentation of a petition for the winding up of the company or the appointment of an administrative receiver or his carrying out his functions.[71] Thus, as notice of the petition has to be given the holder of a floating charge over substantially all the assets of the company,[72] such a chargee has an opportunity during this period to appoint an administrative receiver and forestall an administration order.

Effect of the order

11–29 During the period for which an administration order is in force no resolution may be passed or order made for the winding up of the company and no administrative receiver may be appointed.[73] The prohibition to steps and proceedings referred to in paragraph 11–27 above continues but with the exception that any such steps or proceedings may be allowed, not only by leave of the court, but also by the consent of the administrator.[74] An administrator is appointed with powers to do all such things as may be necessary for the management of the property and business of the company; and such powers include all the powers of an administrative receiver set out in Schedule 1 to the Act.[75] In addition the administrator may remove and appoint directors and call meetings of members or creditors.[76]

11–30 On the appointment of an administrator in relation to the affairs of a company the directors and officers of the company are prohibited from exercising any of their powers in any way as to interfere with the powers of the Administrator unless he consents

[69] *Ibid.* s. 10(1)(b).
[70] *Ibid.* s. 10(1)(c).
[71] *Ibid.* s. 10(2).
[72] *Ibid.* s. 9(2)(a).
[73] *Ibid.* ss. 11(3)(a) and 11(3)(b).
[74] *Ibid.* ss. 11(3)(c) and 11(3)(d). For a recent case in which the Court exercised its discretion in favour of lessors see *Re Atlantic Computers PLC* F.T.L.R. August 1, 1990.
[75] *Ibid.* s. 14(1).
[76] *Ibid.* s. 14(2).

thereto.[77] The administrator is deemed to act as agent of the company and a person dealing with him in good faith is not concerned to inquire whether he is acting within his powers.[78]

Effect of administration order on debts vesting in factor

11–31 The prohibition on any steps to enforce any security on any property of the company, although extended to goods and chattels leased or on hire-purchase or conditional sale or subject to reservation of title, does not extend to the factored debts. As a result the factor's rights in relation to the debts (and rights related to the debts such as guarantees, securities and negotiable instruments) already vesting in him remain unaffected. These rights will extend, in the case of an agreement of the facultative type, to debts offered to the factor before the order and accepted by him and, in the case of an agreement of the whole turnover type,[79] to debts earned by performance of the relevant contract of sale or service by the company before the time of the order (whether or not notified or invoiced).[80] The position as regards these debts will be the same as on the appointment of an administrative receiver.[81] There are no reported cases to support this view but there is nothing in the statute to impeach the factor's rights to debts vesting in him prior to the order.

11–32 An interesting question arises as regards debts, not earned by performance but to arise under contracts in existence at the time of the order, and their position in relation to a factoring agreement of the whole turnover type.[82] In theory such debts, being "in existence"[83] at the date of the order, may well vest in the factor but the means to earn them by performance would be under the control of the administrator. If the factor were to have ownership of such a debt the administrator's duty would be to refrain from providing the means for the performance of the contract to the detriment of the estate of the company. Furthermore it is likely that, if the administrator caused the company to perform the contract, the court might apply the bankruptcy principle that debts

[77] *Ibid.* s. 14(4).
[78] *Ibid.* ss. 14(5) and 14(6).
[79] See paras. 7–12 and 7–13 above.
[80] Under an agreement of the whole turnover type all future debts are bound by the agreement itself whether or not such formalities have been completed; *Holroyd* v. *Marshall* (1862) 10 H.L. Cas. 191; *Tailby* v. *Official Receiver* (1888) 13 A.C. 523.
[81] See paras. 11–08 and 11–09 above.
[82] See para. 7–13 above.
[83] *G. & T. Earle* v. *Hemsworth R.D.C.* (1929) 140 L.T. 69.

earned by performance of the trustee belong to the insolvent estate as against the claims of an assignee.[84]

Effect of the order on factor's other rights

11–33 None of the factor's other rights in relation to the debts vesting in him are affected by the order save that the administrator will owe him no positive liability[85]; nor may the factor enforce his rights in relation to any such positive liability against the company.[86] However, the agreement remains in force if it is not terminated according to its terms. As far as the balance owing to the client for the price of debts purchased allows, the factor will be able to exercise his rights of set-off. The exclusion of steps to enforce security and of proceedings against a company after an administration order has been made it does not apply to self-help by the application of equitable or contractual set-off.[87] Thus the factor will be able to exercise all his rights to withhold payments (if his agreement so provides) and to set off his debt to the company against any recourse or charges payable to him. However self-help in this connection does not extend to a counterclaim which is classed as "proceedings" and prohibited[88]; for this reason the provision for a current account (in which all debits and credits are merged giving rise to one amount owing—the balance of the account) and for a combination of accounts may well be to the factor's advantage.[89] His irrevocable power of attorney will enable him to perfect his ownership of debts vesting in him at the time of the order and of any related rights.

Continuation of the agreement after the order

11–34 If the agreement has not been terminated by either party and the administrator as agent for the company wishes to implement its terms it will continue unchanged; and the administrator, as agent for the company, may exercise the company's rights and perform its obligations in place of the directors. The position is likely in practice to be similar to that in receivership and as described in

[84] See *Re Jones ex p. Nicholls* (1883) 22 Ch. D. 782 and para. 7–14 above.
[85] Unlike the position of hire-purchase and leasing agreements under The Insolvency Act 1986, s. 11(3)(c), the Act does not treat the assignments of debts under a factoring agreement as security rights.
[86] The Insolvency Act 1986, ss. 11(3)(c) and (d).
[87] See Wood, *English & International Set-off*, para. 7–20. (Insolvency set-off as provided for in the Insolvency Rules 1986 (S.I. 1986 No. 1925) r. 4.90 will not apply because the company is not being wound up.)
[88] *Ibid.*
[89] See para. 10–02 above.

paragraph 11–23 above: as the factor cannot enforce implementation of the agreement without leave of the court the administrator is unlikely to accept responsibility for recourse in relation to debts vesting in the factor at the time of the order. As a result, if he wishes to continue to implement the agreement and the factor does not exercise his right to terminate, it is probable that an agreement will be reached to rule off the client account and start a new one.[90] However, unlike an administrative receiver, the administrator is not personally liable on any contract made or adopted by him.

3. WINDING UP OF COMPANIES REGISTERED UNDER THE COMPANIES ACTS

11–35 The winding up of companies is now regulated by the Insolvency Act 1986 and the Insolvency Rules 1986.[91] As regards the effect on a factoring agreement of the winding up of a client, which is a company registered under the Companies Acts, little has been changed from the position as it was before the coming into effect of the Act. In the following paragraphs reference is to such a company as client; unregistered companies are rarely taken on as clients by factors but the regulations relating to them are relevant to the winding up of partnerships and reference to such regulations is made later in this chapter.[92] For the purpose of this treatise the description of the procedures in and effect of winding up and bankruptcy is limited to a synopsis and to that which affects the factoring arrangements of an insolvent client. For further information reference should be made to the textbooks specialising on the subject.

The effect of winding up by the court (compulsory liquidation)

11–36 An order by the court for the winding up of a company does not terminate the company's contracts but there are no means of enforcing their continued implementation as all proceedings

[90] See para. 11–23 above. As regards a company's pre-existing contracts an administrator, whose duty is to manage the affairs of the company, is not in the same position as an administrative receiver, whose principal duty is to realise the charged property for the benefit of the person who appointed him. An administrative receiver will not be bound by a pre-existing contract if such compliance would give priority to the other party over the claims of unsecured creditors; but whether or not the Court will order such compliance by an administrator would appear to depend on the likely benefit to the company's business as a whole and the purpose for which the administration order was made. *Astor Chemicals Ltd.* v. *Synthetic Technology Ltd.* [1990] B.C.L.C. 1.

[91] S.I. 1986 No. 1925.

[92] See para. 11–54 below.

against the company are stayed except with leave of the court.[93] On the making of the order the official receiver becomes provisional liquidator[94] and the directors' powers in relation to the property and the management of the company cease. Furthermore on the making of the order *the commencement of the winding up is backdated to the date of the petition on which the order is founded* or any earlier resolution of the members for its winding up.[95] The official receiver may (or shall if so requested by a quarter in value of the company's creditors) call separate meetings of members and creditors for the purpose of choosing a person to be liquidator in his place. The liquidator (whether the official receiver or another person) takes into his custody or under his control the company's assets in order to ensure that they are realised and distributed to the persons entitled thereto according to the Act and the Rules[96]; the court may on application by the liquidator order that all or any part of the company's property shall vest in the liquidator in his official name.[97]

Effect of resolution of members of a company to wind it up (voluntary liquidation)

11–37 As in the case of compulsory liquidation the resolution of the members of a company to wind it up, whether following a declaration of solvency in relation to the affairs of the company (member's voluntary liquidation) or not (creditor's voluntary liquidation), does not terminate the company's contracts. However from the date of the resolution (the commencement of the winding up[98]) the company must cease to carry on its business except for the purpose of its beneficial winding up.[99] In a member's voluntary liquidation a liquidator is to be appointed by the members in general meeting; and on his appointment the directors' powers cease save as far as allowed by the members or the liquidator.[1] In a creditors' voluntary liquidation the liquidator is appointed by the nomination of the creditors unless they make no nomination in which case he is the person nominated by the

[93] The Insolvency Act 1986, s. 130(2).
[94] *Ibid.* s. 136(2).
[95] *Ibid.* s. 129.
[96] *Ibid.* ss. 143(1) and 144(1).
[97] *Ibid.* s. 145(1).
[98] *Ibid.* s. 86.
[99] *Ibid.* s. 87(1).
[1] *Ibid.* s. 91(2).

members.[2] On his appointment the directors' powers cease except so far as the liquidation committee (if one is appointed by the creditors) or the creditors allow.[3]

Effect of winding up on continuation of factoring agreement

11–38 As the commencement of a winding up of any type or the appointment of a liquidator does not automatically terminate the factoring agreement it will remain in full force and effect unless it is terminated according to its terms. The factor will usually have the right to terminate it forthwith but may be unwilling to do so and the liquidator on behalf of the company will need to give the requisite period of notice. However, in the case of compulsory or creditors' voluntary liquidation the factor will have no way of enforcing its continuance. In either case it would be open to the liquidator to disclaim the agreement as an unprofitable contract[4] and the factor would be in the position of an unsecured creditor in respect of any claim for damages arising from its discontinuance.[5] In practice, as in both cases the business must cease except for the beneficial realisation of the assets, it is unlikely that many further debts would be earned by performance of contracts of sale or service; as a result it is usual for factors to accept that the agreement will be discontinued except as regards their rights in relation to debts vesting in them on the appointment of a liquidator.

11–39 There appears to be no reason why a factoring agreement should not be continued on the appointment of a liquidator in members' voluntary liquidation of a client company. If the liquidator declines to implement the provisions as regards any sales made by him (or disclaims it as an unprofitable contract[6]) then the factor should have his claim for the loss which he has suffered settled in full within twelve months of the commencement of the winding up.[7] However even in a members' voluntary liquidation the business must not be carried on save for its beneficial winding up.

Effect of winding up on debts vesting in the factor

11–40 A winding-up order in relation to a client of a factor or resolution to wind it up will not affect the rights of a factor, whose

[2] *Ibid.* s. 100.
[3] *Ibid.* s. 103.
[4] *Ibid.* s. 178.
[5] *Ibid.* s. 178(6).
[6] *Ibid.* s. 178.
[7] *Ibid.* s. 89.

agreement is of the whole turnover type,[8] to the ownership of the debts vesting in him at the time of the order or resolution. These debts will include, not only those notified to him, but also all those specified in the agreement and earned by the performance of the relevant contract of sale or service by the company.[9] In respect of any such invoiced debts not notified to him he may exercise all rights of ownership, including the giving of notice to the debtors and collection, because the assignment of them took place by virtue of the factoring agreement itself and does not rely on a further act of appropriation or other formality.[10] If any debts have been fully earned by performance but not invoiced by the time of the order or resolution then the factor may invoice them by virtue of his irrevocable power of attorney.[11] The factor with this type of agreement will not be affected by the backdating of the commencement of a compulsory liquidation to the date of the petition[12] and the avoidance of dispositions of the company's property after the commencement[13] unless the factoring agreement first became effective after that time; the disposition of the debts will have been made by virtue of the factoring agreement itself.[14] Debts earned by performance by the liquidator in compulsory or creditor's voluntary liquidation will *not* vest in the factor even if they arise under contracts in existence before the liquidator's appointment.[15]

11–41 The rights of ownership of the factor, whose agreement is of the facultative type,[16] in relation to debts vesting in him *at the commencement of the winding up* will not be affected by a winding-up order in respect of his client or a resolution to wind it up. However the debts vesting in him are only those offered to him and accepted by him before that time. He has no rights of ownership at all to any debts not offered to him even if they are earned by performance of the contract of sale or service before the commencement of the winding up. Furthermore in a compulsory winding up the commencement is backdated to the date of the petition on which the

[8] See para. 7–13 above.
[9] *Holroyd* v. *Marshall* (1862) 10 H.L. Cas. 191; *Tailby* v. *Official Receiver* (1888) 13 A.C. 523.
[10] See paras. 7–13 *et seq.* above.
[11] Powers of Attorney Act 1971, s. 4.
[12] The Insolvency Act 1986, s. 129.
[13] *Ibid.* s. 127.
[14] *Holroyd* v. *Marshall* (1862) 10 H.L. Cas. 191; *Tailby* v. *Official Receiver* (1888) 13 A.C. 523.
[15] *Re Jones ex p. Nicholls* (1883) 22 Ch. D. 782 and see Wood, *English & International Set-off*, paras. 7–173 *et seq.*
[16] See para. 7–12 above.

winding up is founded or any earlier resolution to wind up[17]; and any disposition made after that time is void except as otherwise ordered by the court.[18] The disposition of debts by the client under this type of agreement takes place when they have been offered and accepted[19] as a result the factor may be in a position of having accepted and paid on account for debts offered to him after a petition for the winding up of his client and find that those debts do not vest in him; for the recovery of such payments he would be no better than an unsecured creditor unless set-off against an amount owing by him to the client is available to him. This situation could arise because a petition does not have to be advertised until seven days before the hearing[20] which could be many weeks after the date of the petition. In such circumstances it would be advisable for the factor to procure that his client makes application,[21] before the petition is heard, to the court for validation of the assignments as being in the interests of the company; the benefit to the company might be the continuation of factoring enabling the company to continue its business at least until the hearing. It is most unlikely that such an application made after a winding-up order would succeed.

Provisional liquidators

11–42 At any time after the presentation of a petition for compulsory winding up of a company and before the making of a winding up order the court may appoint the official receiver or some other fit person to be a liquidator of the company provisionally.[22] The functions of the provisional liquidator will be such as the court may confer on him[23] and his powers may be restricted by the court.[24] The effect upon the factoring agreement of such an appointment will be the same as the appointment of a liquidator following a winding-up order[25] unless the court makes some special restriction in the liquidator's powers in relation to it. The appointment will not affect the rights of the factor to debts then vesting in him and the backdating of the commencement of the winding up (which

[17] The Insolvency Act 1986, s. 129.
[18] *Ibid.* s. 127.
[19] See para. 7–12 above.
[20] The Insolvency Rules 1986 (S.I. 1986 No. 1925) r. 4.11.
[21] Under The Insolvency Act 1986, s. 127.
[22] *Ibid.* s. 135.
[23] *Ibid.* s. 135(4).
[24] *Ibid.* s. 135(5).
[25] See para. 11–38 above.

affects factors whose agreements are of the facultative type[26]) cannot be effective until a winding up order is made.

4. BANKRUPTCY OF AN INDIVIDUAL CLIENT

11–43 The bankruptcy of an individual is regulated by Part IX of the Insolvency Act 1986 and is brought about by a bankruptcy order made by the court on the petition of a creditor or creditors, of the individual or of the supervisor of or any person bound by a voluntary arrangement by the individual.[27] The bankruptcy commences on the date of the order and continues until the discharge of the individual.[28] Upon the making of a bankruptcy order the official receiver becomes receiver and manager of the bankrupt's estate[29] and upon the appointment of a trustee (either the official receiver[30] or an insolvency practitioner appointed by the creditors[31]) the bankrupt's estate vests in the trustee.[32]

Effect of bankruptcy on continuation of factoring agreement

11–44 The bankruptcy of an individual does not terminate or destroy the individual's contracts so that, unless the factoring agreement with the individual who becomes bankrupt is terminated by either party according to its terms, it will remain in effect. However, the factor has no way of enforcing its continuation because any action taken would be for damages for breach of the agreement and any such action would be likely to be stayed by the court[33]; and, furthermore, the trustee by notice may disclaim the agreement as an unprofitable contract.[34] In respect of any such claim for damages the factor will be no better than an unsecured creditor.

Effect of bankruptcy of client on debts vesting in factor

11–45 The rights of the factor to the debts vesting in the factor on the making of a bankruptcy order are the same as those which apply in the case of a winding-up order of a company client as described

[26] See para. 11–41 above.
[27] The Insolvency Act 1986, s. 264.
[28] *Ibid.* s. 278.
[29] *Ibid.* s. 287.
[30] *Ibid.* ss. 293(2) and 293(3).
[31] *Ibid.* ss. 293(1) and 294.
[32] *Ibid.* s. 306.
[33] *Ibid.* s. 285.
[34] *Ibid.* s. 315.

above.[35] The factor whose agreement is of the whole turnover type[36] will be able to claim all debts earned by performance of the client before the bankruptcy order[37] and will be able to exercise his rights of ownership and collection of such debts even if not notified to him or invoiced. However, debts earned by performance of services or the delivery of goods by the official receiver (as receiver and manager) or the trustee (whether the official receiver or an insolvency practitioner), even if they arise out of contracts in existence before the commencement of bankruptcy, vest in the estate of the bankrupt and not the factor.[38]

11–46 The determination of which debts will vest in the factor, whose agreement is of the facultative type,[39] on the bankruptcy of his client is less straightforward. Certainly he will not have ownership of any debt not offered to and accepted by him before the official receiver becomes receiver and manager of his client's estate on the making of the bankruptcy order unless (which is unlikely) the official receiver or a subsequently appointed trustee continues to implement the factoring agreement. Dispositions of property of the bankrupt between the day on which the petition for bankruptcy is presented and the vesting of the estate in the trustee on his appointment are void except:

(1) to the extent that such disposition is made with the consent of or is ratified by the court; or
(2) the transaction took place before the commencement of bankruptcy (the date of the order) and was entered into by the other party in good faith and for value without notice that the petition had been presented.[40]

As a result of the foregoing it seems likely that the factor with a facultative type of agreement will lose the ownership of any debt offered to him after he has notice of the petition for the bankruptcy of his client. This provision should not affect the factor with an agreement of the whole turnover type unless the agreement had not become effective before the date of the petition. Debts that are earned by delivery of goods or the performance of services up to the commencement of the bankruptcy (the date of the order)

[35] See para. 11–40 above.
[36] See para. 7–13 above.
[37] *Holroyd* v. *Marshall* (1862) 10 H. L. Cas. 191; *Tailby* v. *Official Receiver* (1888) 13 A.C. 523.
[38] *Re Jones ex p. Nicholls* [1883] 22 Ch. D. 782. See also para. 7–14(2) above.
[39] See para. 7–12 above.
[40] The Insolvency Act 1986, s. 284.

are bound and vest in the factor by virtue of an agreement of this type itself.[41]

11–47 A factor with an agreement of the whole turnover type which constitutes a general assignment of book debts of a sole trader or partnership is likely to lose the ownership of all debts in existence at the date of the presentation of a petition for the bankruptcy of the sole trader or partners if he has not ensured registration of the agreement within seven days of its execution under the Bills of Sale Act 1878.[42] An agreement of the facultative type under which the individual debts are offered to and accepted by the factor would not be caught by this provision in view of the exclusion of "debts due at the date of the assignment from specified debtors" from the definition of a general assignment.[43]

5. EFFECT OF CLIENT'S INSOLVENCY ON OTHER RIGHTS OF FACTOR

11–48 The effect of the winding up of a company client and of the bankruptcy of an individual client on the factor's other rights is similar. Provided that his power of attorney is stated to be irrevocable it will remain unaffected by the insolvency of the client; and, as far as it is practicable, he will be able to continue to use the client's name in order to procure compliance with the obligations of the client as regards the debts in respect of which his rights of ownership are not impeached by the insolvency of his client as described above. The factor will thus be able to execute, on behalf of the client as assignor, assignments of such debts in accordance with the statute,[44] to sue in the client's name and to resolve merchandise disputes with debtors. Furthermore, in view of the assignment to the factor of all rights under the relevant supply contracts along with the debts,[45] he will be able to exercise any lien on goods the subject of such supply contracts and to recover any goods of which the ownership has not passed from the client to the debtor.

[41] See para. 7–13 above.
[42] The Insolvency Act 1986, s. 344 and see paras. 7–16 and 7–17 above.
[43] *Ibid.* s. 344(3)(b).
[44] Law of Property Act 1925, s. 136.
[45] See para. 10–17 above.

Effect of the client's insolvency on set-off provisions

11–49 In both winding up and bankruptcy of the client the statutory provisions for set-off[46] take effect to replace any equitable, common law or contractual set-off available to the factor. Although set-off is not a security right the factor needs to rely upon it for his security (in the widest sense of the word) in the insolvency of his client and it is then to the statutory provisions, and not those in his agreement, that he must look. In particular it is important that he should be able to retain any balance owing to the client's estate, as it appears at the commencement of bankruptcy or winding up, and to set off against it any of the client's obligations for recourse that may subsequently arise. Such claims against the client, which the factor requires to set off, are likely to be contingent only at the commencement of the client's insolvency. The question of set-off of contingent claims against an insolvent estate had long been a matter of doubt. It was settled in favour of the factor in *Re Charge Card Services Ltd.*[47]; but following the enactment of the Insolvency Act 1986 some uncertainty of the right of a debtor to set off a contingent claim in the insolvency of his creditor has again emerged.

11–50 It is important that the factor should ensure that the provisions in his agreement for retention of amounts owing to the client and for recourse[48] take into account the statutory provisions for set-off in force; no matter how widely the set-off provisions in his agreement they will be of no effect when he most needs them—in the insolvency of his client.[49]

6. TRANSACTIONS AT AN UNDERVALUE

11–51 In the winding up or administration of a company and in the bankruptcy of an individual the Insolvency Act provides that the liquidator, administrator or trustee, as the case may be, may apply to the court to restore the position to what it would have been if the company or individual had not entered into a "transaction at an undervalue."[50] Such transactions include gifts and transactions under which the insolvent company or individual receives either no consideration or significantly less than it or he has provided in

[46] Insolvency Rules 1986 (S.I. 1986 No. 1925) r. 4.90 and The Insolvency Act 1986, s. 323 respectively and see paras. 9–10 and 9–11 above.
[47] [1986] 3 W.L.R. 697 and see paras. 10–02 and 10–03 above where this aspect of the factor's rights in the insolvency of the client is dealt with more fully.
[48] See paras. 10–20 *et seq.* above.
[49] See paras. 9–10 and 9–11 above.
[50] The Insolvency Act 1986, s. 238 and s. 339 respectively.

return[51]; and the provisions apply to gifts made to and such transactions entered into, whilst the company or individual is insolvent (or if the company or individual becomes insolvent by reason of the transaction),[52] within two years before the "onset" of the insolvency in the case of a company and five years of the petition in the case of an individual.[53] In the case of an individual, transactions within two years of the petition may be caught even if the individual was not insolvent at the time.[54] The "onset" of the insolvency is a new term used in the Act and it means the commencement of winding up[55] or, in the case of an administration or a winding up immediately following an administration, the presentation of a petition for an administration order.[56] However the court will make no order in respect of any transaction at an undervalue entered into by a company if it is satisfied that it was entered into in good faith for the purpose of carrying on the business of the company and, at the time, there were grounds for belief that it would benefit the company.[57]

7. PARTNERSHIPS

11–52 The difficulty of dealing briefly with the position arising on the insolvency of a client which is an English partnership is due partly to the absence of a distinct legal personality of a partnership. In law the factor, whose client is an English partnership, has a contract with each of the individual partners. The position is further complicated by a radical change in the rules governing the insolvency of partnerships brought about by a most complex piece of subordinate legislation: The Insolvent Partnerships Order

[51] *Ibid.*
[52] In the case of a company the Act refers to the company being "unable to pay its debts" which is defined in s. 123. In the case of an individual insolvency means inability to pay debts or a shortfall in the value of assets as compared with liabilities; see The Insolvency Act 1986, s. 341(3). In both cases the transaction will be caught if the company or individual becomes insolvent by reason of the transaction itself; The Insolvency Act 1986, s. 240(2)(b) and s. 341(2)(b).
[53] The Insolvency Act 1986, s. 240 and s. 341 respectively.
[54] *Ibid.* s. 341.
[55] See paras. 11–36 and 11–37 above.
[56] The Insolvency Act 1986, s. 240(3).
[57] *Ibid.* s. 238(5).

1986.[58] The new rules bring in a new concept of the winding up of an insolvent partnership and this concept no doubt owes its origins to the difficulty of dealing with the insolvency of a partnership of many partners across international borders when some of the partners are insolvent and some not. There appear to be four courses which may be taken in the case of an insolvent partnership:

(1) winding up of the partnership without the bankruptcy of any partner;
(2) winding up of the partnership combined with bankruptcy of two or more partners;
(3) bankruptcy of partners without the winding up of the partnership; and
(4) bankruptcy of one or some of the partners (but not the others) without the winding up of the partnership.

11–53 It is often the case (though rarely met by a factor) that one or more of the partners is a registered company and in that case reference to the winding up of a partner or partners should be substituted for bankruptcy in the options referred to in the preceding paragraph. The factor's rights will not be affected where there is no winding up and one or more of the partners remains solvent (item (4) above); the factoring agreement should have provided for the joint responsibility of the partners and the solvent partner or partners will remain responsible to the factor. However, the bankruptcy of any partner will in most cases bring about the dissolution of the partnership and the position in such an event is described below.[59]

Winding up of the partnership (items (1) and (2))

11–54 The rules[60] provide for the treatment of a partnership as an unregistered company for the purposes of winding up and, with certain exceptions which are not relevant to the effect of the winding up on the position of the partnership's factor, all the provisions of the Act and the Companies Act 1985 regarding winding up apply to unregistered companies.[61] Accordingly the rights of the factor in relation to the continuation of the agreement, to the debts vesting in him and his other rights (including set-off) are the same as those which would apply if his client had

[58] S.I. 1986 No. 2142.
[59] See para. 11–57 below.
[60] The Insolvent Partnership Order 1986 (S.I. 1986 No. 2142).
[61] The Insolvency Act 1986, s. 221.

been a registered company in compulsory liquidation.[62] It will often be the case that concurrent bankruptcy proceedings are taken against some or all of the partners as individuals; but in the winding up of a partnership it is to the winding up procedure that the factor must look to determine his rights.

Bankruptcy of all the partners without the winding up of the partnership

11–55 Part 4 of The Insolvent Partnership Order 1986 provides for insolvency proceedings against all the individual partners of an insolvent partnership without involving the winding up of the partnership.[63] These proceedings, which are by way of a petition for the bankruptcy of all of them by all of them jointly, may be taken when all the partners are individuals and none of them is a limited partner. The petition requires all the partners to concur in its presentation. The procedure does not involve the winding up of the partnership as an unregistered company and the trustees of the individual estates administer the partnership property.

11–56 In the case of bankruptcy of all the partners of a client of a factor, the factor's rights as regards the agreement, the debts vesting in him and set-off and retention are the same as those applicable in the bankruptcy of an individual client.[64]

Dissolution of a partnership

11–57 Subject to express agreement to the contrary on the death or bankruptcy of any partner a partnership will automatically be dissolved.[65] Furthermore, in the absence of special provisions, a partner may retire only by a dissolution of the firm. If the partnership agreement provides for its continuation then, subject to the exercise by the factor of any provision in the factoring agreement for the factor to terminate it immediately, it will continue and the outgoing partner or his estate will be liable for any obligation to the factor until he is released; this is the effect of the absence of a distinct legal personality in a partnership. Any incoming partner will not be bound by the factoring agreement unless he so agrees[66]; it is usual for a factor to provide in the factoring agreement that the existing partners should procure the execution by any incoming partner of a deed binding him to the terms of the agreement. Such arrangements are usually made by a novation including a power of attorney from the new partner.

[62] See paras. 11–36 *et seq.* above.
[63] S.I. 1986 No. 2142.
[64] See paras. 11–43 *et seq.* above.
[65] Partnership Act 1890, s. 33.
[66] *Ibid.* s. 17(1).

11–58 If the partnership is dissolved either automatically as described above or by an agreement between the partners, the factoring agreement, being an agreement between the factor and each of the individual partners, does not terminate automatically and all the former partners will remain jointly and severally liable to the factor. The dissolution will therefore not affect the factor's rights in relation to the debts vesting in him at the time of the dissolution nor will it affect his rights of retention and set-off; if his power of attorney is stated to be irrevocable he will be able to use the firm name to procure the performance of the client in respect of the debts vesting in him.

11–59 After the dissolution of a partnership the authority of each partner to bind the firm continues so far as may be necessary to wind up the affairs of the partnership and to complete contracts in existence at the time of dissolution.[67] If any partner has become bankrupt his ability to bind the firm ceases[68] but his estate remains liable for the partnership's obligations. It would therefore appear that the factoring agreement may continue (unless terminated according to its terms) as regards debts arising from contracts of sale or service in existence at the time of the dissolution. Following a dissolution the factor may obtain a good discharge by paying to any one of the partners what is due to a client which comprised a partnership.[69]

8. VOLUNTARY ARRANGEMENTS

11–60 The Insolvency Act has provided for procedures by individuals[70] and companies[71] who wish to compromise with their creditors. These procedures are less formal, and should be less expensive, than the formalities for an arrangement by a company under the Companies Act 1985[72] or for the bankruptcy of an individual. The procedure is similar but not identical whether the arrangement is to be made by a company or an individual; in each case the arrangement is based on a "proposal" in which an insolvency practitioner must be named as "nominee" who, if the arrangement is made, becomes the "supervisor" of the arrangement. The supervisor acts under the supervision of the court and may apply to the court for directions. In the case of a company the proposal may be made by the directors or, where a company is being wound up,

[67] *Ibid.* s. 38 and see *I.R.C.* v. *Graham's Trustees* S.L.T. 46 (H.L.).
[68] *Ibid.*
[69] Payment to any one of joint creditors discharges a debt; *Powell* v. *Brodhurst* [1901] 2 Ch. D. 160.
[70] Pt. VIII.
[71] Pt. I.
[72] ss. 425–430.

by its liquidator or, after an administration order, by the administrator. In the case of an individual the proposal may be made by the debtor or his trustee in bankruptcy or the official receiver. In each case the proposal is put to a meeting of creditors and, if approved, it becomes effective. The supervisor must notify the court who in the case of winding up or administration or bankruptcy may stay such proceedings.

11–61 Unlike the position in winding up or bankruptcy the property of the subject of the arrangement remains vested in the company or individual and, in the case of a company, the directors' powers are not affected except as provided for in the arrangement. The position regarding the contracts of the subject of the arrangement will depend on the terms of the arrangement itself and, where a company or individual, is a party to a factoring agreement it would be usual for the proposal to provide for its continuance or otherwise. However, the factor's and the client's rights and obligations in respect of debts vesting in the factor at the time when the arrangement becomes effective, should be unaffected except as provided for in the factoring agreement.

CHAPTER 12

SPECIAL CONSIDERATIONS FOR INTERNATIONAL FACTORING

12–01 In domestic factoring the relations between the three parties, the client, the debtor and the factor, are governed by one legal system and the legal framework of the relations in England and Wales has been described in previous chapters. However, in international factoring, the law of at least two countries may affect any of these relations; it may be more than two because a factor may be situated in a country that is neither that of the client nor the debtor.

1. MATTERS AFFECTING THE FACTOR'S RIGHTS TO FACTORED DEBTS

Conflicts of law

12–02 Which law is to be applied to each of the undermentioned matters is of concern to the factor and, unfortunately, the answers are not, in most circumstances, clear. The matters for consideration are:

(1) the validity of the assignment as between the factor and the client and the law to be applied in resolving a dispute between the factor and his client or between the factor and a correspondent factor in a different jurisdiction (to whom debts have been sub-assigned);
(2) the factor's rights to the assigned debts when a person has been appointed to administer the property and business of an insolvent client;
(3) the validity of the assignment as against any third party seeking to attach the debt; and
(4) the validity of the assignment as between the factor and the debtor and the countervailing rights of the debtor.

12–03 Before dealing with the aspects of the law which are of concern to a factor in the consideration of his ability to recover the funds laid out by way of prepayments, one general point has to be made. It was at one time thought that a debt (being intangible) had no locality but the courts have now evolved rules for determining the situation of intangibles. *Choses in action* are generally considered as situate in the country in which they are recoverable or can be enforced; this means that a simple contract debt must be situate in the country where the debtor has his place of business for that is where it may normally be enforced.[1] "The general rule is clear that the debt is situate where the debtor resides. . . ."[2] But this is the general rule only and it may in some circumstances be negatived by the terms of the contract out of which the debt arose and if the debt is not yet due for payment it may have no locality because it cannot then be enforced.[3] A study of the authorities on this subject shows it to be one of great difficulty and much uncertainty and that generalisation may lead to wrong conclusions in particular cases. The facts of the cases that can arise have been described as "bewildering permutations and combinations."[4] A factor buying a series of individual debts of moderate amounts is in no position to determine his probable rights in relation to all the conflicts that may arise in each case (particularly where his rights depend on the proper law of the contract giving rise to the purchased debt); the factor should, therefore, have regard to the precautions mentioned below. At least, he should be aware of the risks if he, for commercial reasons, decides to forego these precautions.

Validity of assignments as between factor and client

12–04 In general the capacity of the client to assign and the validity of the assignment as between the factor and his client and all matters of a contractual nature arising between them will be governed by the proper law of the contract (*i.e.* the factoring agreement).[5] This means the system of law by which the factor and the client intended the factoring agreement to be governed. In any well drawn agreement this will be clearly expressed and it will not be necessary that it should be inferred from the circumstances surrounding the formulation of the agreement. The same principles should apply to any sub-assignment to a correspondent factor and to relations between a factor and his correspondent; but in that case the proper law may be difficult to determine when the parties

[1] See Dicey & Morris, *The Conflicts of Laws* (11th ed., 1987), p. 908.
[2] *Per* Upjohn J. in *Re Claim by Helbert Wagg & Co Ltd* [1956] 1 Ch. 323 at p. 342.
[3] *Re Claim by Helber Wagg & Co. Ltd.* [1956] 1 Ch. 323.
[4] Collins, "Floating Charges, Receivers and Managers and the Conflict of Laws" (1978) I.C.L.Q. 691 at p. 696.
[5] See Dicey & Morris, *The Conflicts of Laws* (11th ed., 1987), pp. 961–964.

operate under an international code of practice and not a bilateral agreement.

However, as will be seen from the succeeding paragraphs, it does not necessarily follow from the effectiveness of the assignments as contractual rights under the proper law of the factoring agreement that the factor will be entitled to obtain recognition abroad. For example, in the United States the use of an assignment as "security" (in the widest meaning of the expression) will only gain recognition if it is perfected by registration in the state in which the assignor (the client) has its principal place of business; where that place is in a territory where no registration is possible (*e.g.* England) then the assignment must be perfected by notice to the debtor.[6]

Validity of the assignments in insolvency of client

12–05 As regards the validity of the assignment of a debt on the insolvency of the client, the usual view is that the assignment must be valid in accordance with the law of the country in which the client is domiciled. For a company in the United Kingdom this is considered to be the country in which the registered office is located, because it is under the law of that country that the insolvency would be regulated.[7] However, while the administration of the property which has passed to the trustee or liquidator is so governed, the question as to:

(1) what foreign property passes; and
(2) subject to what encumbrances such property passes;

may be governed by the law of the country where the debt is situate or by the proper law of the contract giving rise to the debt (whichever is appropriate in the circumstances of the case).[8]

12–06 From the foregoing it seems possible that an English liquidator of an English client of a factor might claim to apply the law of the country where the debtors were located and to include the debts owing by such debtors in the client's estate. In such an event the liquidator's claim might be upheld if the law of the debtors' country did not recognise the validity of the assignments. Such failure to recognise the assignments might arise (for example) because the formalities relating to notice had not been complied with before the commencement of the liquidation or the law of that country did not recognise assignments of future debts without individual written assignments (under an agreement of the whole

[6] U.C.C., s. 9–103.
[7] *Re Anchor Line (Henderson Bros.) Ltd.* [1937] Ch. 483.
[8] See Dicey & Morris, *The Conflicts of Laws* (11th ed., 1987), p. 1112.

turnover type).[9] An example of the application of the law of the debtor's country in the consideration of the effectiveness of assignments in the insolvency of the client was in the *Tay Valley* case.[10] In that case counsel for all parties agreed that the question should be governed by Scots law, because most of the debtors were Scottish, notwithstanding that the factoring agreement provided that it should be governed by English law.

12–07 The English courts have normally considered that the appointment of an administrative receiver gives effect to an assignment of the property of the company in receivership to the chargee.[11] In the case of a client in receivership any conflict between the factor and the receiver would be considered as between two assignees and probably determined as indicated below.

Conflicts between the factor and a creditor of the client seeking to attach a factored debt

12–08 The validity and effect of an attachment of a debt (the equivalent of a garnishee order) is governed by the law of the country in which the debt is situate.[12] This means that, if the formalities of the assignment to the factor do not comply fully with the requirements of that law, he may well lose the debt to a judgment creditor of the client who attaches the debt according to those formalities. This would also apply if the attachment took place after the assignment or even after the notice of that assignment to the debtor.

12–09 An example of the difficulty that may face a factor in this respect occurred as long ago as 1900. In that case[13] priority was given to an unsecured creditor of an English company in receivership when the creditor had attached a debt owing to that company by a French debtor, notwithstanding that the debt fell within the ambit of a floating charge in relation to which a receiver had been appointed. After the receiver's appointment the creditor, holding a dishonoured acceptance of the company, complied with the formalities of French law for the attachment of the debt. Unlike the position under English law, the earlier crystallisation of the charge, in the absence of the required formalities for an assignment in France, did not have the effect of vesting the debt in the chargee under French law. The conflict between the receiver and the creditor was decided by an English court which applied the *lex situs* of the debt to the third party's claim. In such a conflict the

[9] See para. 7–13 above.
[10] *Tay Valley Joinery Ltd* v. *C.F. Financial Services Ltd.* 1987 S.L.T 207; and see para. 7–25 above.
[11] See, for example, *Business Computers Ltd.* v. *Anglo-African Leasing Ltd.* [1977] 1 W.L.R. 578.
[12] See Dicey & Morris, *The Conflicts of Laws* (11th ed., 1987), p. 966.
[13] *Re Maudslay, Sons & Field* [1900] 1 Ch. 602.

appointment of a receiver is considered to effect an assignment to the chargee of the company's property[14] and the charge may be considered to be analogous to a factoring agreement. In view of the growth of cross-border trading it is not unlikely that an insolvent client may have creditors and debtors in the same overseas country in which case the law of that country would undoubtedly be applied to such a conflict.

The priority of competing assignments:

12–10 The rule in *Dearle* v. *Hall*[15] (by which priority is given to the first whose notice has been received by the debtor provided that the former acted in good faith) has no influence outside those countries which have adopted English law or based their own laws on it. In some jurisdictions priority goes to the assignee whose assignment is first in time. It is on this basis that in Germany the right of a seller, who has sold to the factor's client on condition that title to the goods and proceeds remain reserved to the seller, would prevail over the factor's title to the proceeds (as factored debts) unless the latter had purchased them without recourse.[16]

12–11 The law governing such conflicts cannot be the proper law of the assignment (*i.e.* the law by which the factoring agreement is governed) because the competing assignments may have been made and be governed by the laws of different countries; where there is competition there is no reason why the law of one or other should be applied. Such a conflict must be governed by the law of the country in which the debtor has his business or that in which the debt may be enforced. Such difficulties may be aggravated by the difficulty in ensuring that there is no earlier assignment in countries where registration or other publicity is not required for the perfection of such assignments.

The validity of the assignment as between the factor and the debtor and the debtor's countervailing rights

12–12 It seems that the obligation of the debtor to recognise the assignment and his countervailing rights against the assignee will be governed by the proper law of the debt which would in most cases be the law governing the contract of sale.[17] The importance of this to the factor will be apparent as soon as the factor attempts to collect from a foreign debtor. At that stage there may be claims by the debtor that he has no obligation to pay the factor (for example because the law of his country recognises a ban on the

[14] See n. 11 above.
[15] (1823) 3 Russ 1.
[16] See BGH WM 1977, 1198; 1982, 37 and 1350.
[17] See Dicey & Morris, *The Conflicts of Laws* (11th ed., 1987), p. 959.

assignment in the contract of sale) or that on account of some countervailing or restitutionary right (unknown in English law) he is not obliged to pay. In the case of a ban on assignments, the usual safeguards used in England (*i.e.* trust provisions or charges[18]) may not be recognised in other countries.

Precautions to be taken by the factor

12–13 Whether the factoring is confidential or with notices to the debtors all the difficulties mentioned above must be taken into account and precautions taken to keep the risks to a minimum. The absence of notice at the outset by using invoice discounting aggravates the difficulties in a situation where the factor has to give notice to the debtors and himself carry out the collections. At the minimum the following precautions are necessary:

(1) All underlying contracts of sale by the client should be governed by English law.
(2) Each assignment from the client to the factor should be valid according to the law of country of the relevant debtor (in addition to being valid under the law of the client's country) and the formalities relating thereto should be complied with.

Use of two factor system to alleviate the problems

12–14 It is commonly thought that by the use of the two factor system[19] all those problems will be overcome. The general view is that the export factor[20] will ensure that his rights to the debts are valid as regards his relations with the client and in its insolvency and the import factor[21] will ensure that the debt is validly assigned as regards his ability to collect free from third party claims. However, it is doubtful if the import factor would accept responsibility if the circumstances were similar to those described in the *Maudslay* case[22] mentioned above with the substitution of the export factor for the debenture holder. However, the two factor system at least gives the export factor the opportunity to be advised regarding the formalities of the law of the countries in which the debtors are situated. These formalities vary widely.

[18] See paras. 10–25 to 10–28 above.
[19] An arrangement by which the client's factor, having purchased debts from the client, sub-assigns them to a correspondent factor in the debtors' countries and by which the latter will be responsible for the collection and credit risks. See Chap. 6.
[20] Who purchases the debt from the client.
[21] Normally located in the debtor's country and to whom the debt is sub-assigned.
[22] See para. 12–09 and n. 13 above.

Direct relations between an English factor and a client outside England and Wales

12–15 If an English factor wishes to provide his services direct,[23] including a prepayment facility, to a client outside England and Wales he must be sure that, on the insolvency of his client, the debts which he has purchased and for which he has paid on account remain vested in him and cannot be claimed by the insolvent estate; otherwise he will be unable to recover the prepayments made. He must therefore ascertain the formalities for perfection of the assignments, valid in the insolvency of his client, in the country of his client. For example, an English factor, who used for a client in the United States a standard factoring agreement (with all the safeguards described in previous chapters of this book) would not be protected against claims to the factored debts by a trustee in bankruptcy in the United States unless the factor had filed the agreement, as a security interest, in the state in which the client had its chief executive office.[24] From this it seems clear that, in order to be protected both in the insolvency of his client and against third party claims to the factored debts, a factor providing factoring services for cross-border sales of a foreign client (as in the case of an English client) should ensure that his agreement is valid for these purposes in both the country of the client and that of the debtors.

2. STAMP DUTY CONSIDERATIONS IN INTERNATIONAL FACTORING

12–16 In the factoring of transactions across national borders, where the two factor system is used, the factor in the client's country will effect a sub-sale of the debts purchased from the client to a factor in the debtor's country. The application of stamp duty to documents evidencing assignments seems to arise only in those jurisdictions which follow English or Scottish law; it is therefore understandable that the associations of factors,[25] which have co-ordinated the development and promulgated the administrative rules of the two factor systems, have not in general been influenced by stamp duty considerations. As a result the sub-sales between the client's factor and the correspondent factor in the debtor's country are often effected by assignments evidenced by documents peculiar to an individual group of transactions. In the

[23] *I.e.* not through an export factor in the client's country.
[24] U.C.C., ss. 9–102, 9–103 and 9, Pt. 4.
[25] Or "chains" as they are usually named.

paragraphs which follow the incidence of stamp duty on these transactions is discussed.

Export transactions

12–17 The sub-sale by an English factor to an overseas factor will normally relate to a debt owing by a debtor overseas created by an export sale by the English factor's United Kingdom client. Although a conveyance made in the United Kingdom of property situated abroad is liable to be stamped,[26] agreements for the sale of of any "estate or interest" in such property are excepted from the liability to duty.[27] The general rule is that the debt is situate where the debtor resides[28]; and for the purposes of the application of stamp duty it has been established that a debt, the enforcement of which must be by proceedings abroad, is "property locally situate out of the United Kingdom."[29] It appears, therefore, that, if an English factor who sells the export debts purchased from his client to a correspondent factor abroad frames his document relating to the transfer of ownership as an *agreement* to assign, he may well escape stamp duty on the document. The agreement to assign, if expressed to take effect under English law and to give effect to the assignment on the happening of a specific event (*e.g.* on the entry of the transaction in the records of the correspondent factor) should effect the transfer of ownership in equity on that event. In order to satisfy the law relating to assignments in the debtor's country the English factor would undertake to perfect his correspondent factor's ownership of the debts if this should be required.

Import factoring

12–18 Where an English factor acts as correspondent factor for a foreign factor (an export factor) whose client is selling to debtors in the United Kingdom, the sub-assignments of the debts owing by the United Kingdom debtors will normally be evidenced by documents executed by the export factor in his own country. If there is no incidence of stamp duty in that country on the transactions or documents then the documents need no stamp whilst they remain there; but (subject to the exemptions by reason of the amount of

[26] See Nock, *Monroe and Nock on the Law of Stamp Duties*, para. 1–32 and Stamp Act 1891, s. 14(4).
[27] Stamp Act 1891, s. 59.
[28] See para. 12–06 above.
[29] *English, Scottish and Australian Bank* v. *I.R.C.* [1932] A.C. 238.

the consideration[30]) they will become liable as soon as they arrive in the United Kingdom.[31] They must then be stamped within 30 days of their arrival. It seems that the duty may be avoided by the retention of the document by the export factor; if the English factor requires the document for evidential purposes he will then have to call for it and, if by reason of the amount of the consideration of the assignment and any linked transactions it is liable, it must be stamped.

Alternatively the English factor may be able to persuade the export factor to use, for the transactions between the two factors in respect of each client, an agreement of the whole turnover type.[32] Such an arrangement should include an undertaking to perfect the English factor's ownership of the debts if this is requisite; and, in order to avoid delay in the execution of an assignment in statutory form[33] when proceedings are to be taken for debt recovery, the English factor should take a power of attorney from the export factor.

3. UNIDROIT

12–19 The International Institute for the Unification of Private Law, more commonly known as UNIDROIT, was set up by the Italian government under the auspices of the League of Nations with the object of promoting the harmonisation of commercial law. It is now financially supported by about 50 countries. The Council of the Institute, which is situated In Rome,[34] decided in 1974 to include within its work programme for the period 1975 to 1977 a study of the subject of assignments of debts in general and of the contract of factoring in particular. Following a preliminary study and the replies to a questionnaire sent to interested parties, including national factoring associations, it set up a restricted study group of academics and practitioners. The study group considered that owing to the great differences of legal systems the study should in the first place be restricted to the desirability of promulgating rules for factoring only of transactions across national borders. It was felt, however, that the adoption of such rules by national governments would eventually influence legislation for domestic transactions. It was also considered undesirable to formulate a standard factoring contract for use between any factor and his client because the relationship of the factor with

[30] See paras. 7–07 to 7–11 (incl.) above.
[31] See Nock, *Monroe and Nock on the Law of Stamp Duties*, para. 1–59.
[32] See para. 7–13 above.
[33] Law of Property Act 1925, s. 136.
[34] Via Panisperna 28.

his client, although for international factoring falling within the framework of the proposed rules, should be a matter of freedom to contract between the parties.

12–20 At the outset it was appreciated that, although the mechanics of factoring in its various forms are conceptionally fairly simple, the converse is true of the law under which factoring arrangements operate in many countries. Furthermore, these problems are aggravated by the wide variations in the legal systems and national laws.

12–21 The study was followed by meetings of an enlarged study group and later of "government experts," being in most cases representatives of justice or trade ministries of national governments. These were held during the years 1981 to 1987. At these meetings a draft convention, formulated by the study group, was discussed and amended in the light of comments and representations called for by the national governments from interested parties in their own countries. The draft convention was finally considered by a Diplomatic Conference of representatives of 55 countries held in Ottawa in May 1988 and hosted by the Government of Canada. The conference made some further amendments to the draft and then adopted it. The convention known as "The Unidroit Convention on International Factoring" was deposited with the Government of Canada and was open for signature and accession from the end of the conference until December 31, 1990.

Definition of "factoring" under UNIDROIT

12–22 The convention as finally drafted provided a narrow definition of factoring in order to avoid encroaching on other forms of financing of *choses in action*. To be a "factoring contract" and covered by the convention a contract must have three characteristics.[35] First, it must provide for the assignment to the factor of debts arising from contracts of sale or service other than goods bought primarily by the customers for their personal, family or household use. Although factoring is concerned principally with trade debts only, it was thought that to define it as restricted to such would have the effect of excluding many debts normally included in factoring contracts; examples of these are debts owing by professional people, universities and government departments. Secondly, it must provide for the factor to perform at least two of the following functions[36]:

(1) finance including loans and advance payments;

[35] See App. 5, Art. 1, para. 2.

[36] The word "services" in the original draft was replaced by "functions" because it was pointed out that the factor performs most of the functions of factoring for himself as owner of the debts and not as a serivce for his client.

(2) maintenance of debtor accounts;
(3) collection of debts;
(4) protection against default by debtors.

Thirdly, the contract must provide for notices of the assignments to be given to debtors.

Application of the UNIDROIT convention

12–23 The convention is limited in its application to factoring of debts arising from sales between persons whose places of business are in different states; and it will apply when both those states and the state of the factor are contracting states (*i.e.* states which have acceded to the convention) or when both the sale contract and the factoring contract are governed by the law of a contracting state.[37] However, the application of the convention *as a whole* may be excluded by agreement between the factor and the client or between the client and the debtor.[38] In the latter case the exclusion will apply only to debts arising after the factor has been given notice of it; if this were not so, the factor might be misled into accepting responsibility for debts on the basis of protection of the convention where there was no such protection. The convention also recognises the two factor system by the application of the rules to a subsequent assignment by the factor and it avoids the need for two notices of assignment in respect of each debt in that system[39]; notice of the sub-assignment by a factor to a correjespondent factor will serve also as notice of the assignment by the client to his factor.[40]

Substantive rules of the UNIDROIT convention

12–24 The convention provides *inter alia* as regards the validity of assignments:

(1) the effectiveness of agreements to assign future debts and debts of a particular character in bulk[41] (agreements of the whole turnover type[42]);

[37] Art. 2(1).
[38] Art. 3.
[39] Art. 11(1).
[40] Art. 11(2).
[41] Art. 5.
[42] See para. 7–13 above.

(2) the effectiveness of provisions in factoring contracts for the transfer to the factor of rights deriving from the contract of sale including rights to the underlying goods[43];

(3) the obligation of the debtor to pay the factor and the discharge of the debtor on such payment if he has received notice of the assignment given by the client or by the factor with the client's consent provided that the debtor is not at the time aware of a third party's prior right.[44]

For this last provision to apply the notice must reasonably identify the debts to which it relates and the *factor* to whom payment is to be made; it must also relate to debts arising under contracts of sale then in existence. Therefore under the convention an introductory letter[45] will have no effect in respect of future debts.

12–25 As regards the countervailing rights of the debtor, the convention provides that (i) the debtor may set up against the factor all defences arising out of the contract to which the debt claimed by the factor related and (ii) any right of set-off existing at the time when he received notice of the assignment.[46] These provisions are broadly in line with the law as it is known in England and described in this book.

12–26 The convention also deals with the rights of the debtor in relation to recovery from the factor in the event of failure of the client fully, promptly and satisfactorily to perform the contract of sale or service; the uncertainty in relation to this matter under English law has been described above.[47] Under the convention[48] late or defective performance or total failure to perform by the client will not entitle the debtor to recover from the factor. There are however two exceptions to the rule: the debtor will be entitled to recover from the factor (to the extent of the debtor's right to recover from the client) a sum paid to the factor when the latter has not discharged his obligation to pay the client for the debt in question or when the factor has made payment for it in the knowledge of the client's default.

Prohibitions of assignments in contracts of sale

12–27 The most controversial provision in the convention, which was initially inserted at an early meeting in Rome, was based on the

[43] Art. 7.
[44] Art. 8.
[45] See paras. 8–08 to 8–10 (incl.) above.
[46] Art. 9.
[47] See paras. 9–33 *et seq.* above.
[48] Art. 10.

provision in the Uniform Commercial Code of the United States[49] by which a prohibition of the assignment of a debt in a contract of sale is not effective as regards the rights of an assignee of the debt. Such a provision was commended by a number of representatives in the meetings of government experts on the grounds that it would assist small exporting businesses to counter the greater bargaining power of large and powerful buyers by enabling the exporters to finance their export sales on open credit often insisted upon by the buyers. A number of others objected to the provision on the grounds that it interfered with the rights of buyer and seller freely to contract. It was pointed out to the objectors that the provision would not make the contract term ineffective and that, if it was breached by a seller's assignment of the resulting debt to a factor, the buyer would retain the usual remedies available to him such as a right to damages for breach of contract. However, no general agreement was reached and only after considerable discussion was a compromise solution accepted by all the parties. By this compromise, the Convention provided[50] that an assignment should be effective notwithstanding an agreement between the client and the debtor prohibiting such assignment; however it also provided that an assignment in contravention of such an agreement would not be effective as regards the debtor if at the time of the contract of sale his place of business were to be in a contracting state which had made a declaration that this provision should not apply to debtors within its borders.[51]

Limitation of scope of UNIDROIT convention

12–28 It is to be noted that the rules themselves are somewhat limited in their application. They do not cover domestic factoring arrangements nor do they govern arrangements between factors and their clients. In particular no attempt was made to propose substantive rules for regulating priorities; this was held to be impossible without impinging on national laws relating to the regulation of companies, bankruptcy, banking and the registration and publicity of security rights. Futhermore, owing to the widely differing national views on the subject, not least between those whose concepts are based on common law and those who live under a civil code system, it was not even possible to formulate rules as to which law should apply in given circumstances: that of the debtor's country or that of the client's. Again the provision, by which contracting states may opt out of the making effective of assignments where there is a prohibition in the contract of sale, may

[49] ss. 9–318(4). See also paras. 9–30 and 9–31 above.
[50] Art. 6(1).
[51] Arts. 6(2) and 18.

severely limit the effectiveness of Article 6; based on experience in the United States the general adoption of this Article would have provided a reassurance for factors to provide their services with more confidence for the general benefit of smaller exporters and the encouragement of international trade. The fact that not even a "conflict of laws" rule could be formulated is an indication that the uncertainties regarding this aspect described at the start of his chapter have not been exaggerated.

APPENDIX 1

INDEX OF FACTORING VOLUME GROWTH

For:
Total world (base = 1980 in USD)
Total FCI (base = 1980 in USD)
14 major FCI countries (base = 1980 in local currency)

	1980	1981	1982	1983	1984	1985	1986	1987	1988	1989
World	100	103	103	113	120	143	175	235	270	319
		+ 3%	= %	+ 10%	+ 6%	+ 19%	+ 22%	+ 34%	+ 15%	+ 18%
FCI	100	100	96	106	108	159	207	304	350	445
		= %	− 4%	+ 10%	+ 2%	+ 47%	+ 30%	+ 47%	+ 15%	+ 27%
Austria	100	138	131	129	132	133	138	153	166	176
		+ 38%	− 5%	− 1%	+ 2%	+ 1%	+ 4%	+ 11%	+ 9%	+ 6%
Belgium	100	95	122	160	201	229	274	279	324	401
		− 5%	+ 28%	+ 31%	+ 26%	+ 14%	+ 20%	+ 2%	+ 16%	+ 24%
Canada	100	105	102	91	95	120	137	144	138	185
		+ 5%	− 3%	− 11%	+ 4%	+ 26%	+ 14%	+ 5%	− 4%	+ 34%
Denmark	100	95	126	140	170	159	163	166	205	286
		− 5%	+ 33%	+ 11%	+ 21%	− 7%	+ 3%	+ 2%	+ 23%	+ 40%

Finland	100	144	185	230	273	316	305	320	372	399
		+44%	+28%	+24%	+19%	+16%	−4%	+5%	+16%	+7%
France	100	147	195	211	240	248	294	379	480	585
		+47%	+33%	+8%	+14%	+3%	+19%	+29%	+27%	+22%
Germany	100	115	110	115	120	133	161	184	177	191
		+15%	−5%	+5%	+4%	+11%	+21%	+14%	−4%	+8%
Italy	100	207	396	600	958	1,475	1,935	2,920	4,076	5,890
		+107%	+91%	+51%	+60%	+54%	+31%	+51%	+40%	+44%
Japan	100	112	103	202	213	172	180	173	258	259
		+12%	−9%	+98%	+5%	−23%	+5%	−4%	+49%	=
Netherlands	100	105	116	155	188	228	262	278	346	372
		+5%	+10%	+34%	+21%	+21%	+15%	+6%	+24%	+8%
Norway	100	127	145	160	192	211	253	326	264	208
		+27%	+14%	+10%	+20%	+10%	+20%	+29%	−19%	−27%
Sweden	100	109	124	128	120	121	103	86	94	81
		+9%	+14%	+3%	−7%	+1%	−17%	−20%	+9%	−16%
U.K.	100	104	120	152	196	255	313	395	522	643
		+4%	+15%	+27%	+29%	+30%	+23%	+26%	+32%	+23%
U.S.A.	100	108	106	117	132	132	141	157	160	165
		+8%	−2%	+10%	+13%	=%	+7%	+11%	+2%	+3%

SOURCE: Factors Chain International

APPENDIX 2

GRIFFIN FACTORS LIMITED: CURRENT ACCOUNT AND DISCOUNTING ACCOUNT

A SUBSIDIARY OF MIDLAND BANK plc

21 FARNCOMBE ROAD WORTHING SUSSEX BN11 28W
TELEPHONE WORTHING 205181 (STD 0903) TELEX 87102

YOUR COMPANY LTD
WILMINGTON ROAD
WORTHING
WEST SUSSEX
BN2R 3ST

Supplier Statement

ACCOUNT NUMBER 1234

AS AT 31 JAN 89
(TAX POINT AS ABOVE)

PAGE No. 1

VAT REGISTRATION No. 376 7764 93

	DISCOUNTING ACCOUNT						CURRENT ACCOUNT		
VALUE DATE	DEBIT ENTRIES	CREDIT ENTRIES	BALANCE	RATE %	DISCOUNTS/DEDUCTIONS	DESCRIPTION	DEBIT ENTRIES	CREDIT ENTRIES	BALANCE
1 JAN			43,636.10	13.00		BROUGHT FORWARD			23,912.02CR
1 JAN	5,500.00		49,136.10	13.00		PAYMENT	5,500..00		18,412.02CR
5 JAN		2,646.98	46,489.12	13.00		PAYMENTS FROM CUSTOMERS			
8 JAN	600.00		47,089.12	13.00		PAYMENT	600.00		17,812.02CR
12 JAN						INVOICES RECD - BATCH 4567		6,168.20	23,980.22CR
13 JAN		10,355.28	36,733.84	13.00		PAYMENTS FROM CUSTOMERS			
15 JAN	7,500.00		44,233.84	13.00		PAYMENT	7,500.00		16,480.22CR
16 JAN						INVOICES RECD - BATCH 4707		3,561.19	20,041.41CR
20 JAN		928.40	43,305.44	13.00		PAYMENTS FROM CUSTOMERS			
22 JAN		2,483.39				PAYMENTS FROM CUSTOMERS			
22 JAN	3,200.00		44,022.05	13.00		PAYMENT	3,200.00		16,841.41CR
26 JAN						INVOICES RECD / BATCH 4095		1,850.23	18,691.64CR
27 JAN		1,199.56	42,822.49	13.00		PAYMENTS FROM CUSTOMERS			
28 JAN		11,285.76	31,536.73	13.00		PAYMENTS FROM CUSTOMERS			
29 JAN	5,700.00		37,236.73	13.00		PAYMENT	5,700.00		12,991.64CR
31 JAN	150.53					ADMIN CHARGE AT 1.300%	150.53		
31 JAN	22.58					VAT ON ADMIN CHARGE AT 15.000%	22.58		
31 JAN	470.72		37,880.56			DISCOUNTING CHARGE AT 13.000%	470.72		12,347.81CR

MEMBER OF FACTORS CHAIN INTERNATIONAL

TOTAL DISCOUNTS/ DEDUCTIONS DURING THIS PERIOD: 0.00

TOTAL INVOICES THIS PERIOD: 11,579.62

TOTAL CREDIT NOTES THIS PERIOD: 0.00

SUPPLIER STATEMENT: PURCHASE PRICE PAYABLE ON COLLECTION DATE

ACCOUNT NUMBER 1234 AS AT 31 JAN 89 PAGE No. 1

(TAX POINT AS ABOVE)

VAT REGISTRATION No. 376 7764 93

	DISCOUNTING ACCOUNT						CURRENT ACCOUNT		
VALUE DATE	DEBIT ENTRIES	CREDIT ENTRIES	BALANCE	RATE %	DISCOUNTS/DEDUCTIONS	DESCRIPTION	DEBIT ENTRIES	CREDIT ENTRIES	BALANCE
1 JAN			43,636.10	13.00		BROUGHT FORWARD			23,912.02CR
1 JAN	5,500.00		49,136.10	13.00		PAYMENT	5,500..00		18,412.02CR
5 JAN		2,646.98	46,489.12	13.00		PAYMENTS FROM CUSTOMERS			
8 JAN	600.00		47,089.12	13.00		PAYMENT	600.00		17,812.02CR
12 JAN						INVOICES RECD - BATCH 4567		6,168.20	23,980.22CR
13 JAN		10,355.28	36,733.84	13.00		PAYMENTS FROM CUSTOMERS			
15 JAN	7,500.00		44,233.84	13.00		PAYMENT	7,500.00		16,480.22CR
16 JAN						INVOICES RECD - BATCH 4707		3,561.19	20,041.41CR
20 JAN		928.40	43,305.44	13.00		PAYMENTS FROM CUSTOMERS			
22 JAN		2,483.39				PAYMENTS FROM CUSTOMERS			
22 JAN	3,200.00		44,022.05	13.00		PAYMENT	3,200.00		16,841.41CR
26 JAN						INVOICES RECD / BATCH 4095		1,850.23	18,691.64CR
27 JAN		1,199.56	42,822.49	13.00		PAYMENTS FROM CUSTOMERS			
28 JAN		11,285.76	31,536.73	13.00		PAYMENTS FROM CUSTOMERS			
29 JAN	5,700.00		37,236.73	13.00		PAYMENT	5,700.00		12,991.64CR
31 JAN	150.53					ADMIN CHARGE AT 1.300%	150.53		
31 JAN	22.58					VAT ON ADMIN CHARGE AT 15.000%	22.58		
31 JAN	470.72		37,880.56			DISCOUNTING CHARGE AT 13.000%	470.72		12,347.81CR

TOTAL DISCOUNTS/ DEDUCTIONS DURING THIS PERIOD: 0.00

TOTAL INVOICES THIS PERIOD: 11,579.62

TOTAL CREDIT NOTES THIS PERIOD: 0.00

APPENDIX 3

CALCULATION OF AVAILABILITY - FULL FACTORING

****

REQUESTED BY ON 25/05/90 AT 10.56

****

SUPPLIER AVAILABILITY: 1234 YOUR COMPANY LIMITED

PRE/PAYMENT AVAILABILITY

TOTAL OUTSTANDING	88032.37	INVOICES TODAY	0.00
(2) CREDIT BALANCES	1142.27CR		
TOTAL DR BALANCES	89174.64	*RETENTIONS*	
UNAPPROVED	2092.25	100%	2092.25
APPROVED	87082.39	20%	17416.48
(4) TOTAL DISPUTED	636.46		
UNAPPROVED	174.38	0%	0.00
APPROVED	462.08	80%	369.66
(1) SOLICITORS' A/CS	984.20		
UNAPPROVED	984.20		
APPROVED	0.00		
		TOTAL	19878.39
APPROX CURRENT a/c BALANCE	23228.18		
LESS RETENTIONS	19878.39		
NATIONAL AVAIL-ABILITY	3349.79	FUNDS IN USE	65946.46
PAYMENT TODAY	0.00		

Notes:

1 The number in brackets shown opposite some of the categories denotes the number of accounts in that category.

2 In this case a full retention is made in respect of all "unapproved" debts (*i.e.* not approved for credit) consequently there is no further retention to be made for the unapproved debts which are disputed.

3 In respect of approved disputed debts a retention of 80 per cent is made because 20 per cent retention is included in the general retention in respect of approved debts.

4 Similarly no further retention is necessary in respect of debts in the hands of solicitors in this case: if they are unapproved, a full retention has already been made and, if they are approved, the factor is responsible for the credit risk.

DEBTS PURCHASED ACCOUNT STATEMENT

AS AT 30 JUN 90 IN ACCOUNT WITH 01234
(i) (ii)
ENGINEERINEERING LIMITED
(iii)
THE INDUSTRIAL ESTATE
ANYTOWN
BRITAIN (iv)

TRADING IN STERLING
(v)

RECEIVED (vi)	NUMBER (vii)	MATURES (viii)	DESCRIPTION (xi)	VALUE DEBIT	VALUE CREDIT
			BROUGHT FORWARD		74959.45
25JUN90	26470	13SEP90	INVOICES NOTIFIED		7371.83
28JUN90	15031		INVOICES MATURED	6989.51	
28JUN90	15032		INVOICES MATURED	147.49	
			CARRIED FORWARD BALANCES		75194.28

REPORT CONTENTS

(i)	The date to which the account refers
(ii)	Your unique number issued by us
(iii)	Your name
(iv)	Your address
(v)	The name of the currency to which all values on this account refer
(vi)	The date on which an item was received by us or sent to you
(vii)	Our reference number
(viii)	The date on which a Notification Schedule of Invoices matures
(ix)	A description of each transaction

SUPPLIER'S CURRENT ACCOUNT STATEMENT

AS AT 30 JUN 90 IN ACCOUNT WITH 01234
(i) (ii)
ENGINEERINEERING LIMITED
(iii)
THE INDUSTRIAL ESTATE
ANYTOWN
BRITAIN (iv)

TRADING IN STERLING
(v)

DATE (vi)	REF (vii)	DESCRIPTION (viii)	DEBIT	CREDIT	VALUE BALANCE
			brought forward		44590.49
25JUN90	10462	FACTORING CHARGE ON 26476	132.69		44723.18
25JUN90	10462	VAT CHARGE ON 26476	19.90		44743.08
28JUN90	15031	INVOICES MATURED		6989.51	37753.57
28JUN90	15032	INVOICES MATURED		147.49	37606.08
30JUN90	144000	PREPAYMENT	12160.00		49766.09
30JUN90		DISCOUNT CHARGE	632.02		50398.10
30JUN90		RETROSPECTIVE DISCOUNT	4.01		50402.11
30JUN90	04311	DEBTOR DISCOUNT ALLOWED	83.16		50485.27
30JUN90	124713	DEBTOR DISCOUNT DISALLOWED		4.27	50481.00
30JUN90	24890	CREDIT NOTES NOTIFIED	206.88		50687.88
			CARRIED FORWARD		50687.88

REPORT CONTENTS

(i) The date to which the account refers
(ii) Your unique number issued by us
(iii) Your name
(iv) Your address
(v) The name of the currency to which all values on this account refer
(vi) The date of the transaction
(vii) Our reference number
(viii) A description of each transaction

APPENDIX 5

UNIDROIT CONVENTION ON INTERNATIONAL FACTORING

THE STATES PARTIES TO THIS CONVENTION,

CONSCIOUS of the fact that international factoring has a significant role to play in the development of international trade,

RECOGNISING therefore the importance of adopting uniform rules to provide a legal framework that will facilitate international factoring, while maintaining a fair balance of interests between the different parties involved in factoring transactions,

HAVE AGREED as follows:

CHAPTER I—SPHERE OF APPLICATION AND GENERAL PROVISIONS

Article 1

1.—This Convention governs factoring contracts and assignments of receivables as described in this Chapter.

2.—For the purposes of this Convention, "factoring contract" means a contract concluded between one party (the supplier) and another party (the factor) pursuant to which:

(a) the supplier may or will assign to the factor receivables arising from contracts of sale of goods made between the supplier and its customers (debtors) other than those for the sale of goods bought primarily for their personal, family or household use;
(b) the factor is to perform at least two of the following functions:

- — finance for the supplier, including loans and advance payments;
- — maintenance of accounts (ledgering) relating to the receivables;
- — collection of receivables;
- — protection against default in payment by debtors;

(c) notice of the assignment of the receivables is to be given to debtors.

3.—In this Convention references to "goods" and "sale of goods" shall include services and the supply of services.

4.—For the purposes of this Convention:

(a) a notice in writing need not be signed but must identify the person by whom or in whose name it is given;
(b) "notice in writing" includes, but is not limited to, telegrams, telex and any other telecommunication capable of being reproduced in tangible form;
(c) a notice in writing is given when it is received by the addressee.

Article 2

1.—This Convention applies whenever the receivables assigned pursuant to a factoring contract arise from a contract of sale of goods between a supplier and a debtor whose places of business are in different States and:

(a) those States and the State in which the factor has its place of business are Contracting States; or
(b) both the contract of sale of goods and the factoring contract are governed by the law of a Contracting State.

2.—A reference in this Convention to a party's place of business shall, if it has more than one place of business, mean the place of business which has the closest relationship to the relevant contract and its performance, having regard to the circumstances known to or contemplated by the parties at any time before or at the conclusion of that contract.

Article 3

1.—The application of this Convention may be excluded:

(a) by the parties to the factoring contract; or
(b) by the parties to the contract of sale of goods, as regards receivables arising at or after the time when the factor has been given notice in writing of such exclusion.

2.—Where the application of this Convention is excluded in accordance with the previous paragraph, such exclusion may be made only as regards the Convention as a whole.

Article 4

1.—In the interpretation of this Convention, regard is to be had to its object and purpose as set forth in the preamble, to its international character and to the need to promote uniformity in its application and the observance of good faith in international trade.

2.—Questions concerning matters governed by this Convention which are not expressly settled in it are to be settled in conformity with the general principles on which it is based or, in the absence of such principles, in conformity with the law applicable by virtue of the rules of private international law.

CHAPTER II—RIGHTS AND DUTIES OF THE PARTIES

Article 5

As between the parties to the factoring contract:

(a) a provision in the factoring contract for the assignment of existing or future receivables shall not be rendered invalid by the fact that the contract does not specify them individually, if at the time of conclusion of the contract or when they come into existence they can be identified to the contract;
(b) a provision in the factoring contract by which future receivables are assigned operates to transfer the receivables to the factor when they come into existence without the need for any new act of transfer.

Article 6

1.—The assignment of a receivable by the supplier to the factor shall be effective notwithstanding any agreement between the supplier and the debtor prohibiting such assignment.

2.—However, such assignment shall not be effective against the debtor when, at the time of conclusion of the contract of sale of goods, it has its place of business in a Contracting State which has made a declaration under Article 18 of this Convention.

3.—Nothing in paragraph 1 shall affect any obligation of good faith owed by the supplier to the debtor or any liability of the supplier to the debtor in respect of an assignment made in breach of the terms of the contract of sale of goods.

Article 7

A factoring contract may validly provide as between the parties thereto for the transfer, with or without a new act of transfer, of all or any of the supplier's rights deriving from the contract of sale of goods, including the benefit of any provision in the contract of sale of goods reserving to the supplier title to the goods or creating any security interest.

Article 8

1.—The debtor is under a duty to pay the factor if, and only if, the debtor does not have knowledge of any other person's superior right to payment and notice in writing of the assignment:

(a) is given to the debtor by the supplier or by the factor with the supplier's authority;
(b) reasonably identifies the receivables which have been assigned and the factor to whom or for whose account the debtor is required to make payment; and
(c) relates to receivables arising under a contract of sale of goods made at or before the time the notice is given.

2.—Irrespective of any other ground on which payment by the debtor to the factor discharges the debtor from liability, payment shall be effective for this purpose if made in accordance with the previous paragraph.

Article 9

1.—In a claim by the factor against the debtor for payment of a receivable arising under a contract of sale of goods the debtor may set up against the factor all defences arising under that contract of which the debtor could have availed itself if such claim had been made by the supplier.

2.—The debtor may also assert against the factor any right of set-off in respect of claims existing against the supplier in whose favour the receivable arose and available to the debtor at the time a notice in writing of assignment conforming to Articles 8(1) was given to the debtor.

Article 10

1.—Without prejudice to the debtor's rights under Article 9, non-performance or defective or late performance of the contract of sale of goods shall not by itself entitle the debtor to recover a sum paid by the debtor to the factor if the debtor has a right to recover that sum from the supplier.

2.—The debtor who has such a right to recover from the supplier a sum paid to the factor in respect of a receivable shall nevertheless be entitled to recover that sum from the factor to the extent that:

(a) the factor has not discharged an obligation to make payment to the supplier in respect of that receivable; or
(b) the factor made such payment at a time when it knew of the supplier's non-performance or defective or late performance as regards the goods to which the debtor's payment relates.

CHAPTER III—SUBSEQUENT ASSIGNMENTS

Article 11

1.—Where a receivable is assigned by a supplier to a factor pursuant to a factoring contract governed by this Convention:

(a) the rules set out in Articles 5 to 10 shall, subject to sub-paragraph (b) of this paragraph, apply to any subsequent assignment of the receivable by the factor or by a subsequent assignee;
(b) the provisions of Articles 8 to 10 shall apply as if the subsequent assignee were the factor.

2.—For the purposes of this Convention, notice to the debtor of the subsequent assignment also constitutes notice of the assignment to the factor.

Article 12

This Convention shall not apply to a subsequent assignment which is prohibited by the terms of the factoring contract.

CHAPTER IV—FINAL PROVISIONS

Article 13

1.—This Convention is open for signature at the concluding meeting of the Diplomatic Conference for the Adoption of the Draft Unidroit Conventions on International Factoring and International Financial Leasing and will remain open for signature by all States at Ottawa until December 31, 1990.

2.—This Convention is subject to ratification, acceptance or approval by States which have signed it.

3.—This Convention is open for accession by all States which are not signatory States as from the date it is open for signature.

4.—Ratification, acceptance, approval or accession is effected by the deposit of a formal instrument to that effect with the depositary.

Article 14

1.—This Convention enters into force on the first day of the month following the expiration of six months after the date of deposit of the third instrument of ratification, acceptance, approval or accession.

2.—For each State that ratifies, accepts, approves, or accedes to this Convention after the deposit of the third instrument of ratification, acceptance, approval or accession, this Convention enters into force in respect of that State on the first day of the month following the expiration of six months after the date of the deposit of its instrument of ratification acceptance, approval or accession.

Article 15

This Convention does not prevail over any treaty which has already been or may be entered into.

Article 16

1.—If a Contracting State has two or more territorial units in which different systems of law are applicable in relation to the matters dealt with in this Convention, it may, at the time of signature, ratification, acceptance, approval or accession, declare that this Convention is to extend to all its territorial units or only to one or more of them, and may substitute its declaration by another declaration at any time.

2.—These declarations are to be notified to the depositary and are to state expressly the territorial units to which the Convention extends.

3.—If, by virtue of a declaration under this article, this Convention extends to one or more but not all of the territorial units of a Contracting State, and if the place of business of a party is located in that State, this place of business, for the purposes of this Convention, is considered not to be in a Contracting State, unless it is in a territorial unit to which the Convention extends.

4.—If a Contracting State makes no declaration under paragraph 1, the Convention is to extend to all territorial units of that State.

Article 17

1.—Two or more Contracting States which have the same or closely related legal rules on matters governed by this Convention may at any time declare that the Convention is not to apply where the supplier, the factor and the debtor have their places of business in those States. Such declarations may be made jointly or by reciprocal unilateral declarations.

2.—A Contracting State which has the same or closely related legal rules on matters governed by this Convention as one or more non-Contracting States may at any time declare that the Convention is not to apply where the supplier, the factor and the debtor have their places of business in those States.

3.—If a State which is the object of a declaration under the previous paragraph subsequently becomes a Contracting State, the declaration made will, as from the date on which the Convention enters into force in respect of the new Contracting State, have the effect of a declaration made under paragraph 1, provided that the new Contracting State joins in such declaration or makes a reciprocal unilateral declaration.

Article 18

A Contracting State may at any time make a declaration in accordance with Article 6(2) that an assignment under Article 6(1) shall not be effective against the debtor when, at the time of conclusion of the contract of sale of goods, it has its place of business in that State.

Article 19

1.—Declarations made under this Convention at the time of signature are subject to confirmation upon ratification, acceptance or approval.

2.—Declarations and confirmations of declarations are to be in writing and to be formally notified to the depositary.

3.—A declaration takes effect simultaneously with the entry into force of this Convention in respect of the State concerned. However, a declaration of which the depositary receives formal notification after such entry into force takes effect on the first day of the month following the expiration of six months after the date of its receipt by the depositary. Reciprocal unilateral declarations under Article 17 take effect on the first day of the month following the expiration of six months after the receipt of the latest declaration by the depositary.

4.—Any State which makes a declaration under this Convention may withdraw it at any time by a formal notification in writing addressed to the depositary. Such withdrawal is to take effect on the first day of the month following the expiration of six months after the date of the receipt of the notification by the depositary.

5.—A withdrawal of a declaration made under Article 17 renders inoperative in relation to the withdrawing State, as from the date on which the withdrawal takes effect, any joint or reciprocal unilateral declaration made by another State under that article.

Article 20

No reservations are permitted except those expressly authorised in this Convention.

Article 21

This Convention applies when receivables assigned pursuant to a factoring contract arise from a contract of sale of goods concluded on or after the date on which the Convention enters into force in respect of the Contracting States referred to in Article 2(1)(a), or the Contracting State or States referred to in paragraph 1(b) of that article, provided that:

(a) the factoring contract is concluded on or after that date; or
(b) the parties to the factoring contract have agreed that the Convention shall apply.

Article 22

1.—This Convention may be denounced by any Contracting State at any time after the date on which it enters into force for that State.

2.—Denunciation is effected by the deposit of an instrument to that effect with the depositary.

3.—A denunciation takes effect on the first day of the month following the expiration of six months after the deposit of the instrument of denunciation with the depositary. Where a longer period for the denunciation to take effect is specified in the instrument of denunciation it takes effect upon the expiration of such longer period after its deposit with the depositary.

Article 23

1.—This Convention shall be deposited with the Government of Canada.

2.—The Government of Canada shall:

(a) inform all States which have signed or acceded to this Convention and the President of the International Institute for the Unification of Private Law (Unidroit) of:
   (i) each new signature or deposit of an instrument of ratification, acceptance, approval or accession, together with the date thereof;
   (ii) each declaration made under Articles 16, 17 and 18; the withdrawal of any declaration made under Article 19(4);
   (iv) the date of entry into force of this Convention;
   (v) the deposit of an instrument of denunciation of this Convention together with the date of its deposit and the date on which it takes effect;

(b) transmit certified true copies of this Convention to all signatory States, to all States acceding to the Convention and to the President of the International Institute for the Unification of Private Law (Unidroit).

IN WITNESS WHEREOF the undersigned plenipotentiaries, being duly authorised by their respective Governments, have signed this Convention.

DONE at Ottawa, this twenty-eighth day of May, one thousand nine hundred and eighty-eight, in a single original, of which the English and French texts are equally authentic.

APPENDIX 6

FACTORS CHAIN INTERNATIONAL

CODE OF INTERNATIONAL FACTORING CUSTOMS (IFC)

Promulgated by Factors Chain International
(latest revision June 1990)

General provisions

Article 1

The parties taking part in international factoring transactions are:

the seller; the party who invoices for the supply of goods or the rendering of services and whose accounts receivable are factored by the Export Factor.

the debtor: the party who is liable for payment of the accounts receivable arising from the supply of goods or rendering of services.

the Export Factor: the party who factors the seller's accounts receivable under an agreement to that effect.

the Import Factor: the party who agrees to collect the accounts receivable invoiced by the seller and assigned to the Export Factor, and who, subject to these customs, is bound to pay such accounts receivable assigned to him for which he has assumed the credit risk.

Article 2

(a) All disagreements arising between an Export Factor and an Import Factor in connection with international factoring transactions shall be settled under the Rules of Arbitration of Factors Chain International provided that both are members of Factors Chain International at the time of the request for arbitration.
(b) Any such disagreements may be so settled if only one of the parties is a member of Factors Chain International at the time of the request for arbitration provided that the other party accepts such arbitration.
(c) The award shall be final and binding.

Article 3

The Export Factor agrees to use his best efforts to ensure that the seller assists in fulfilling these customs as far as transactions from the seller are concerned.

Article 4

The transactions to be covered by this Code shall be limited to accounts receivable arising from sales on credit terms of goods and/or services provided by sellers who have agreements with an Export Factor to or for debtors located in a country in which an Import Factor provides a factoring service. Excluded are sales based on letter of credit, cash against documents or any kind of sales for cash.

Article 5

An agreement in writing made between an Export Factor and an Import Factor which conflicts with, differs from or extends beyond the terms of this Code, shall take precedence over and supersede any other or contrary condition, stipulation or provision in the Code relating to the subject matter thereof, but in all other respects shall be subject to and dealt with as part of this Code.

Assumption of credit risk

Article 6

Requests for approval, containing the information to enable the Import Factor to appraise the credit risk, may refer to individual transactions or lines for current transactions. The Import Factors

must, without delay, and not later than 14 days from receipt of the request, advise the Export Factor of his decision.
If within the said period, the Import Factor cannot make a decision he must, at the earliest, and before the expiry of the period, advise the Export Factor hereof, possibly with a further statement about the facts upon which such a decision is to be based and when it can be made.

Article 7

The assumption by the Import Factor of the credit risk on accounts receivable assigned to him is conditional upon his approval of such accounts receivable.
Each such approval shall be given by cable or telephone (either one subsequently confirmed in writing) or by telex or letter.
Unless otherwise agreed the approval shall apply (up to the amount approved) to the following accounts receivable owed by the debtor:

(a) those on the IF's records on the date of the approval
(b) those arising from shipments made on or after the date of the request for approval

and shall be conditional in each case, upon the receipt by the Import Factor of the copy of the invoice and other documents as stipulated in Article 10 without undue delay and in any event before the due date of the account receivable.

Article 8

(a) Approval in full or in part of an individual transaction binds the Import Factor to assume the approved credit risk, provided that the goods are placed in transit to or to the order of the debtor whether by common carrier or seller's own transport ("shipment") not later than the time of shipment stated in the request for approval.
Approval of a line for current transactions binds the Import Factor to assume the credit risk on accounts receivable up to the approved amounts for shipments made before cancellation of the line in accordance with this Article.

(b) If the Import Factor obtains adverse credit information before shipment he shall have the right to cancel the approval of the individual transaction or the line for current transactions. Such cancellation must take place by cable or telephone (either one subsequently confirmed in writing) or telex.
Upon receipt of such notice of cancellation from the Import Factor, the Export Factor shall immediately notify the seller

and such cancellation shall be effective as to shipments made after the seller's receipt of such notice.
On or after the sending of any such notice of cancellation to the Export Factor, the Import Factor shall have the option to send such notice also direct to the seller; but he shall inform the Export Factor of such action.
The Import Factor shall have the right to the cooperation of the seller to stop any goods in transit and thus minimise the Import Factor's loss.
The Export Factor undertakes to give the Import Factor all assistance possible in such circumstances.

(c) The Import Factor may cancel a credit line for reasons other than adverse credit information on such terms as may be agreed with the Export Factor.

Article 9

Subject to the provision in the last paragraph of this Article the Export Factor must offer to the Import Factor all accounts receivable sold to the Export Factor by the seller. In particular when the Import Factor has given an approval all subsequently created accounts receivable of that seller in respect of the same debtor must be assigned to the Import Factor, even when the accounts receivable are only partly approved or not approved at all. When the Import Factor is not prepared to approve the credit risk on further individual transactions or when the Import Factor decides to cancel the credit line, the obligation for the Export Factor continues to exist until all approved accounts receivable have been paid or otherwise provided for, in other words, until the IF is "out of risk."
After cancellation of the contract between the EF and the seller, further assignments of accounts receivable to the IF cannot be expected.
The Export Factor may withhold from the Import Factor accounts receivable in respect of any debtor (other than such a debtor as is referred to in the foregoing paragraph) for which the Import Factor is not prepared to assume a substantial part of the credit risk or is prepared to do so only at a factoring commission unacceptable to the Export Factor.

Article 10

The Import Factor must receive as proof of any account receivable assigned to him an exact copy of the invoice issued to the debtor, and at the request of the Import Factor any or all of the following documents:

(a) evidence of shipment such as non-negotiable copy of the bill of lading or of any other acceptable shipping document showing that the goods have actually been despatched;
(b) evidence of fulfillment of contract of sale and/or service where applicable;
(c) any other documents which have been requested before shipment.

The Import Factor may at any time require that the original documents evidencing title including the negotiable shipping documents and/or insurance certificate are forwarded through him.

Article 11

Accounts receivable or parts thereof, which are not within approved lines and which do not relate to an approved transaction, shall be on a collection basis only, but the Import Factor will use his best endeavours to collect such accounts receivable promptly and in full provided that:

(a) he shall obtain the consent of the Export Factor before incurring costs and/or expenses (other than the Import Factor's own administrative costs) relating to the collection of such receivables;
(b) such costs and/or expenses shall be the responsibilities of the Export Factor; and
(c) he shall not be responsible for any loss and/or costs which are attributable to any delay in the giving of such consent by the Export Factor.

Article 12

In the case of credit granted to the debtor by the seller in excess of a line approved by the Import Factor, the Import Factor's obligations under Article 13 shall relate to the amount(s) first falling due at any time up to the approved amount.

While the line remains in force, accounts receivable (or parts thereof) in excess of the line will succeed amounts within the line which are paid by or credited to the debtor. The succession of such accounts receivable (or parts thereof) shall take place in the order in which they are due for payment and shall be limited at any time to the amounts then so paid or credited.

The right of succession ceases when the line is cancelled and thereafter any payment or credit may be applied by the Import Factor in satisfaction of approved accounts receivable in priority to unapproved accounts receivable. If, however, the credit relates to an unapproved account receivable and the Export Factor establishes to the satisfaction of the Import Factor that the credit arose solely because of the seller's mistake, made in good faith, the credit shall be applied to such unapproved accounts receivable.

Obligation to pay

Article 13

(a) Except as provided in Article 14:
  (i) the Import Factor shall bear the risk of loss arising from the failure of the debtor to pay in full any approved account receivable on the due date in accordance with the terms of the relevant contract of sale or service; and
  (ii) to the extent that any such account receivable shall not be paid by or on behalf of the debtor by the 90th day after the due date as described above the Import Factor shall on such 90th day make payment to the Export Factor ("payment under guarantee").
  (iii) For the purposes of (a)(i) and (ii), payment by the debtor shall mean payment to any one of the Import Factor, the Export Factor, the seller or the seller's agent.

(b) Unless otherwise agreed, when any payment is made by the debtor to the Import Factor in respect of any account receivable (or part thereof) the Import Factor shall pay to the Export Factor an equivalent sum promptly after collection, except to the extent of any previous payment in accordance with (a)(ii).

(c) Except as provided in (d), if the Import Factor does not initiate a payment to the Export Factor according to the foregoing requirements, the Import Factor shall:
  (i) be liable to pay to the Export Factor interest calculated for each day from the date on which such payment shall be due until actual payment at twice the 90 day LIBOR rate quoted on such due date in the relevant currency; and
  (ii) reimburse the Export Factor with the equivalent of any currency exchange loss suffered by him and caused by the delay in payment.

If there shall be no LIBOR quotation for the relevant currency, twice the lowest lending rate for such currency available to the Export Factor on such date shall apply.

(d) If as a result of circumstances beyond his control the Import Factor is unable to make any such payment when due:

(i) he shall give immediate notice of that fact to the Export Factor;
(ii) he shall apply to the Export Factor interest at a rate equivalent to the lowest lending offer rate available to the Export Factor in the relevant currency calculated for each day from the day when his payment shall be due until actual payment.

Article 14

(a) If a debtor raises a defence, counterclaim or set-off ("dispute") and if the EF receives notice of such dispute within 270 days after the due date of the invoice to which the disputed account receivable relates, the IF shall not be required to make payment of the amount withheld by the debtor by reason of such dispute.
(b) Upon being notified of a dispute the IF shall immediately send to the EF a dispute notice containing all details and information known to him regarding the account receivable and the nature of such dispute.
(c) Upon receipt of such dispute notice the account receivable shall be deemed to be unapproved notwithstanding any previous approval. If such dispute is raised after payment under guarantee the IF shall be entitled to reimbursement of the amount withheld by the debtor by reason of such dispute.
(d) The IF shall again accept as approved such disputed account receivable to the extent that the dispute is settled in favour of the seller within 365 days after the receipt of the dispute notice by the EF provided that:
(i) the EF and the seller have acted to ensure that the dispute was settled as quickly as possible and
(ii) the IF has been kept fully informed about the status of negotiations or proceedings at regular intervals.

If, however, during such 365 day period, the debtor becomes officially insolvent or makes a general declaration or admission of his insolvency, the IF shall remain at risk until the dispute has been settled.

(e) In case a settlement in favour of the seller occurs more than 75 days after the original due date of the relevant invoice, the IF shall have 14 days to collect from the debtor and, if not successful, he must pay the EF as if it were a normal payment under guarantee.

In case a settlement occurs before a 75 day period has passed since the original due date, the IF's obligations shall be as described in Article 13.

In either case, late payment by the IF will be subject to the same obligations as described in Article 13.

(f) The IF shall co-operate with and assist the EF in settlement of any dispute.

(g) If the EF and/or the seller do not act in accordance with paragraph (d) of this Article, the IF shall have the right to reassign to the EF the disputed account receivable.

It shall be presumed that such reassignment is justified if the EF does not communicate with the IF within 60 days of receipt of the dispute notice by the EF.

(h) (i) If the EF has substantially breached any provision of this Code, the IF shall not be required to make payment under guarantee to the extent that the IF has been prejudiced in his appraisal of the credit risk and/or has been prevented from obtaining payment from or on behalf of the debtor as a result of such substantial breach. The burden of proof in this paragraph rests with the IF.
If the IF has made payment under guarantee the IF shall be entitled to reimbursement of the amount paid.

(ii) A substantial breach of Article 15(a) and (b) that results only from a dispute shall not be subject to the provisions of this paragraph and shall be covered by the provisions of (a) to (g) of this Article.

(iii) The provisions of this paragraph shall not prejudice the rights of the IF relating to the assumption of credit risk and/or payment under guarantee provided for elsewhere in this Code.

(iv) A substantial breach must be asserted within 365 days after the due date of the invoice to which it relates.

(i) The EF shall promptly reimburse the IF under paragraphs (c) and (h) of this Article, such payment shall include interest from date of payment under guarantee to date of reimbursement as calculated in accordance with Article 13 (d) (ii).

Representations, warranties and additional obligations of the Export Factor and the Import Factor

Article 15

The Export Factor warrants and represents for himself and on behalf of his seller

(a) that each account receivable represents an actual and bona fide sale and shipment of goods or provision of service made in the regular course of business and in conformity with the description of the seller's business and the terms of payment (with a permissible occasional variation of 100 per cent. or 45 days whichever period is shorter) contained in the pertinent information upon which such approval was granted;

(b) that the debtor is liable for the payment of the amount stated in each invoice in accordance with the terms without defence or claim;

(c) that the original invoice bears notice that the account receivable to which it relates has been assigned and is payable only to the Import Factor as its owner or that such notice has been given otherwise in writing before the due date of the invoice, any such notice of assignment being in the form prescribed by the Import Factor;

(d) that both have the unqualified right to assign and transfer to the Import Factor full ownership of each account receivable including any interest and other costs relating to such account receivable which are recoverable from the debtor;

(e) that he will inform the Import Factor of any indirect payment received by the seller or himself; and

(f) that he is factoring all the accounts receivable arising from sales as defined in Article 4 of any one seller to any one debtor for which the Import Factor has given approvals and that, as long as the Import Factor is on risk, he will recognise his obligation to inform in general or if requested in detail the Import Factor about the existence of the excluded transactions as defined in Article 4.

In the event of a breach of this warranty the Import Factor shall be entitled to recover from the Export Factor

(i) the commissions and/or charges as agreed for that seller on the accounts receivable withheld, and

(ii) compensation for other damages, if any.

Article 16

(a) By reason of the assignment to the Import Factor of full ownership of each account receivable, the Import Factor shall have the right of bringing suit and otherwise enforcing collection either in his own name or jointly with that of the Export Factor and/or that of the seller and the right to endorse debtor's remittances for collection in the Export Factor's name or in the name of such seller, and the Import Factor shall have the benefit of all rights of lien, stoppage in transit, and all other rights of the unpaid seller to goods which may be rejected or returned by debtors.

(b) If any cash, cheque, draft, note or other instrument in payment of any accounts receivable assigned to the Import Factor hereunder is received by the Export Factor or any of his sellers, the Export Factor must immediately inform the Import Factor of such receipt. It shall be held in trust by the Export Factor or such seller on behalf of the Import Factor and shall—if requested by the Import Factor—be duly endorsed and delivered promptly to him.

(c) If the sales contract contains a prohibition of assignment the Import Factor shall have the same rights as set forth in paragraph (a) of this Article as agent for the Export Factor and/or seller.

Article 17

Whenever a debtor has failed to pay his indebtedness to the Import Factor in accordance with Article 13, and such indebtedness includes unapproved amounts:

(a) the Import Factor shall have the right to full repayment from the Export Factor of any advance payment made to the Export Factor in respect of any unapproved account receivable owing by that debtor; and

(b) any subsequent monies received by the Import Factor resulting from a general distribution from the estate of the debtor in respect of accounts receivable assigned by the Export Factor or the relevant seller shall be shared between the Import Factor and the Export Factor proportionally to their interests in the indebtedness.

Article 18

(a) If, before approval of any account receivable, the Import Factor shall have advised the Export Factor that special documentation relating to the assignment of that account receivable is required for the enforcement of its payment to the Import Factor, the Export Factor undertakes to obtain such documentation at the request of the Import Factor.

(b) The Import Factor may re-assign any such account

receivable, which he has approved, and may recover from the Export Factor any amount paid in accordance with Article 13(a) in respect of it if the Export Factor shall fail to provide such documentation in relation to that account receivable within 14 days of the receipt of the Import Factor's request, or

(c) The Import Factor may similarly reassign any account receivable and may recover from the Export Factor any amount paid in accordance with Article 13(a) in respect of it if the Import Factor has been prevented from obtaining a judgement in respect of that account receivable in the courts of the debtor's country by reason only of a term relating to jurisdiction in the contract of sale between the seller and the debtor which gave rise to that account receivable.

Article 19

The Export Factor undertakes to assist the Import Factor to the best of his ability in obtaining any document that may assist the Import Factor in his recovery of amounts paid under his obligation to pay and which has not previously been requested.

Article 20

Each of the Import Factor and the Export Factor warrant that each will inform the other immediately of any fact or matter which comes to his attention and which may adversely affect the collection of any account receivable or the credit worthiness of any debtor.

Validity of assignment

Article 21

It is hereby agreed between Export Factor and Import Factor that the law applicable to the assignment to the Import Factor shall be the law of the Import Factor's country.
Accordingly the Import Factor is obliged to inform the Export Factor about the wording of the notice of assignment and the procedure of the assignment.
If the Export Factor requests an assignment enforceable against third parties, the Import Factor is obliged to act accordingly as far

as he is able to do so in accordance with the applicable law, at the expense of the Export Factor.

Indemnification

Article 22

As between the Export Factor and the Import Factor, the Export Factor shall pay all duties, forwarder's fees, storage and shipping charges and such other expenses that are the responsibility of the seller under the contract of sale. The Export Factor shall likewise be responsible for the payment of all expenses of collection, attorney's fees and other charges relating to the enforcement, settlement or other disposition of claims arising from accounts receivable assigned to the Import Factor which remain unpaid otherwise than as described in Article 13 (a). The Import Factor shall not take any action likely to incur other than routine expenses without the prior consent of the Export Factor.

Article 23

(a) In rendering his services, the Import Factor shall be deemed to be acting on behalf of the Export Factor and shall have no responsibility whatsoever to the Export Factor's sellers.

(b) The Export Factor shall indemnify the Import Factor and hold him harmless against all suits, claims, losses or other demands which may be made or asserted against the Import Factor:

(i) by any such seller by reason of any action that the Import Factor may take or fail to take and

(ii) by any debtor in relation to the goods and/or services, the invoices or the underlying contracts of such seller,

provided that in either case the Import Factor's performance in his action or failure to act is reasonable and in good faith.

(c) The Export Factor shall reimburse the Import Factor for all costs, damages and expenses (including legal fees) suffered or incurred by the Import Factor by reason of any of the matters for which the indemnity is given in (b).

Advance payments

Article 24

Advance payments on accounts receivable assigned to the Import Factor may be made on the request of the Export Factor and at the discretion of the Import Factor on such terms and conditions as are bilaterally agreed.

Time limits

Article 25

The time limits set forth in this Code shall be understood as calendar days. Where a time limit expires on a Sunday or on any other public holiday or on days which are not working days of the Export Factor or the Import Factor, the period of time in question is extended until the first following working day with the factor concerned.

Accounts, reports and remuneration

Article 26

(a) The Import Factor shall account at least once a month to the Export Factor with respect to all transactions and such monthly accounts shall be deemed approved and accepted by the Export Factor except to the extent that written exceptions are taken by the Export Factor within a reasonable amount of time.

(b) The Export Factor shall be entitled to rely upon all information and reports submitted by the Impact Factor provided that such reliance is reasonable and in good faith.

(c) The Import Factor shall be entitled to commissions and/or charges for his services on the basis of the structure as promulgated by the FCI Council from time to time. These commissions and/or charges must be paid promptly, in any case not later than 10 days after receipt of the "commission statement." Late payment shall incur interest in accordance with Article 13.

Infringement of the Code

Article 27

If any of the parties infringes the provisions of this Code, the party becoming aware of such infringement shall notify the Secretariat who will investigate the case and possibly make a protest. Should the Secretariat establish that there is a question of gross infringement, or repeated infringements, the Secretariat must bring the case before the Executive Committee which may in the ultimate case decide upon cancellation of the membership.

Amendments in the Code

Article 28

If one or more of the Articles of this Code should be or become invalid, either fully or partly, the parties shall be governed by what they would have agreed if they had foreseen the invalidity or uncertainty of such article(s).

APPENDIX 7

A DIAGRAMMATICAL COMPARISON OF FULL FACTORING WITH THE TWO FACTOR SYSTEM

(1) FULL FACTORING (Domestic):

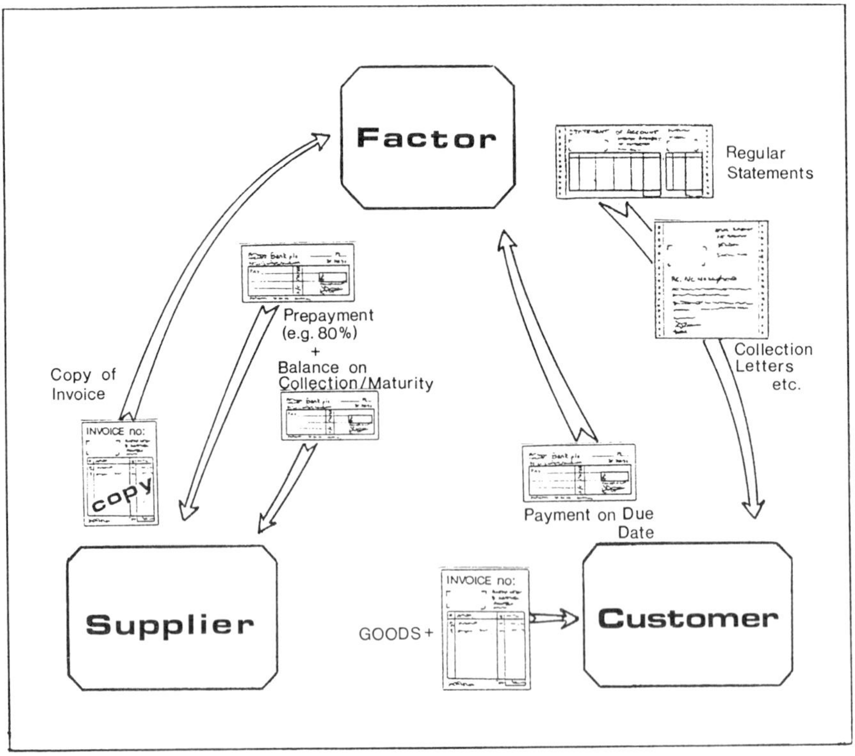

(2) THE TWO FACTOR SYSTEM (International):

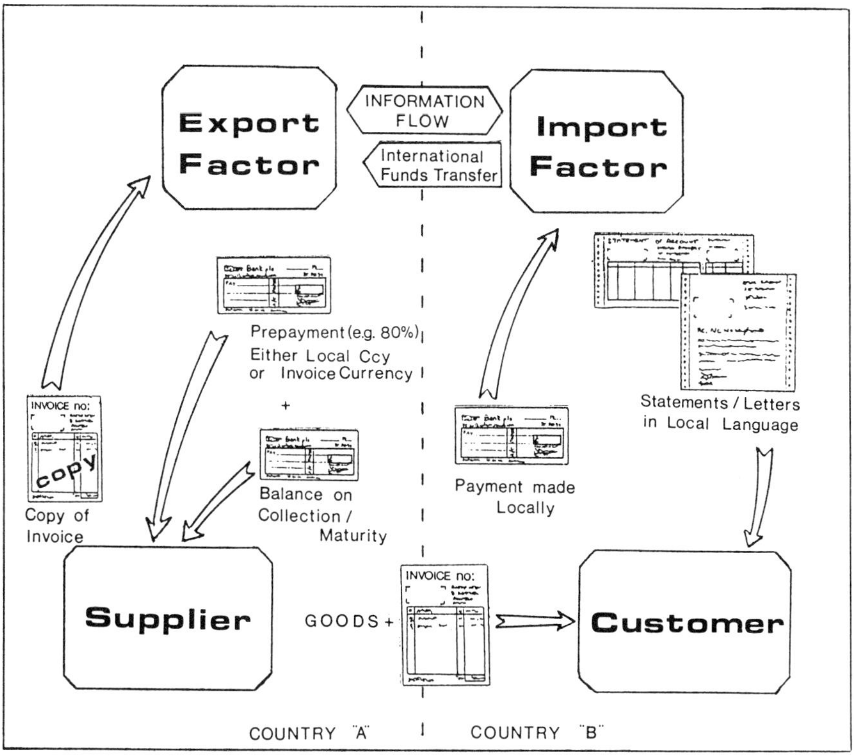

APPENDIX 8

DEED OF AGREEMENT FOR THE FACTORING OR DISCOUNTING OF DEBTS

1. PARTIES:

(1) VENTURE FACTORS PLC. of Amberley House Harlands Road Haywards Heath West Sussex ("the Factor") whose registered office is 3 Lombard Street London EC3V 9DT;

(2) The person ("the Client") named in section 1 of the schedule ("the Schedule") annexed to and forming part of this Agreement.

2. DATE:

This agreement shall be deemed to be made (i) if the Client is a body corporate on the date on which it is executed by or on behalf of the Client or (ii) if the Client is not a body corporate on the date on which it is executed by the Factor.

3. DEFINITIONS AND INTERPRETATION:

(1) In this Agreement except where the context otherwise requires:

(i) The singular shall include the plural and vice versa and any of the three genders shall include the other two;

(ii) references to "the Factor" shall include the Factor's successors and assigns; references to clauses (except where otherwise specified) are to clauses of this Agreement; references to any statute shall be deemed to include any statutory modification or re-enactment thereof or any part thereof;

(iii) the expressions specified in the appendix annexed to and forming part of this Agreement shall have the meanings assigned to them therein;

(iv) the headings to clauses are for ease of reference only and shall not affect or limit the meaning or extent of any clause; and

(v) expressions which in or for the purpose of proceedings outside England and Wales have no precise counterpart in the jurisdiction in which those proceedings are to take place shall have the meaning of the closest equivalent expression in such jurisdiction.

(2) This Agreement shall be construed and take effect according to English law and the Client submits to the jurisdiction of the English courts without prejudice to the right of the Factor to take proceedings in the courts of any state in which the Client carries on business or has assets.

4. TRANSFER OF OWNERSHIP OF DEBTS:

(1) The Client shall sell and the Factor shall purchase all Debts incurred or to be incurred by any Debtor of the class or description specified in section 2 of the Schedule which shall be in existence at the Commencement or which shall come into existence at any time thereafter before termination of this Agreement. The ownership of every such Debt in existence at the Commencement shall vest in the Factor at the Commencement and of every such Debt coming into existence thereafter shall vest in the Factor upon such Debt coming into existence.

(2) Upon the vesting in the Factor of any Debt pursuant to clause 4(1) there shall also vest in the Factor the ownership of all the Related Rights pertaining to such Debt and the Factor shall at any time after such sale also have the right to have transferred to it any Goods included in the Sale Contract giving rise to such Debt (otherwise than when the ownership of such Goods is vested in the Debtor).

5. PERFECTION OF FACTOR'S TITLE:

The Client shall at any time at the request of the Factor and at the expense of the Client execute and deliver to the Factor a formal written assignment (with the applicable stamp duty endorsed thereon) of any Debt or Related Rights purchased by the Factor. The Client shall hold in trust for the Factor and separately from the Client's own property any Debt or Related Rights or Transferred Goods purchased by the Factor of which the ownership shall fail to vest in the Factor for any reason.

6. PURCHASE PRICE AND NOTIFICATION OF DEBTS:

(1) The Purchase Price of each Debt (together with its Related Rights and any Transferred Goods pertaining to such Debt)

purchased by the Factor shall be equivalent to the amount (including any tax or duty) payable by the Debtor in respect of such Debt according to the relevant Sale Contract after there has been deducted therefrom (i) any discount allowance or other deduction allowed or allowable by the Client to the Debtor and (ii) the factoring fee and discount charge in respect of such Debt (as provided for in clause 9(1)) and (iii) in the case of a Currency Debt bank and other charges incurred by the Factor in collecting and converting the proceeds into Sterling.

(2) The Client shall promptly notify the Factor of each Debt sold to the Factor in such manner and with such particulars and documents evidencing the Debt as the Factor may from time to time require as soon as the relevant Goods have been Delivered or if so required by the Factor at any other time. No Notification shall include any Debt previously notified.

(3) If in relation to any Debt the Client is unable to give to the Factor every one of the warranties and undertakings contained in this Agreement then the Client shall notify such Debt to the Factor separately from other Debts and clearly mark the relevant Notification to that effect.

7. CLIENT ACCOUNTS; CREDIT OF PURCHASE PRICE; PAYMENT BY THE FACTOR:

(1) Upon receipt by the Factor of a Notification relating to any Debt the Factor shall credit its Purchase Price to the Debts Purchased Account. For administrative convenience the Factor may in its absolute discretion make any such credit before deduction of any of the items to be deducted in computing such purchase price as provided for in clause 6(1) and may consequently debit such item to any account of the Client at any time thereafter.

(2) The Factor shall transfer the amount credited to the Debts Purchased Account pursuant to clause 7(1) in respect of each Debt to the credit of the Current Account on the Transfer Date. The Factor may debit to the Current Account all amounts payable by the Client to the Factor (whether arising under this Agreement or otherwise) including any contingent or prospective liability of the Client to the Factor in accordance with clause 10.

(3) At any time after 24 hours following receipt of a Notification by the Factor relating to any Approved Debt (subject to the provisions of clauses 7(5) to 7(7) inclusive) the Factor shall at the request of the Client make a Prepayment to the Client in respect of such Debt. The Factor may at any time in its absolute discretion make a Prepayment in respect of any notified Debt. The amounts of all such Prepayments shall be debited to the Current Account. Solely for the purposes of this clause a Debt shall be deemed to be

an Approved Debt notwithstanding that it is of the nature or description specified in section 4 of the Schedule if it otherwise would rank as an Approved Debt.

(4) Subject to the provisions of clause 7(5) within one working day of receiving a request from the Client so to do the Factor shall pay to the Client the whole or any part of the balance standing to the credit of the Client on the Current Account.

(5) The Factor shall not be obliged to make any payment (including any Prepayment) to the Client:

(a) whilst any petition for the bankruptcy or winding up of the Client or for an administration order in relation to the Client pursuant to the Act or any proposal for a voluntary arrangement in relation to the Client pursuant to the Act is pending; or

(b) if the effect of that payment would be to make the credit balance in favour of the Client after a combination of all the accounts in the Client's name in the Factor's records less than the Minimum Balance whether or not such accounts have been so combined.

(6) The Factor shall not be obliged to make any Prepayment if the effect of it would be that the aggregate amount of all Prepayments made in respect of Debts owing by any one Debtor would be in excess of the percentage specified in section 6 of the Schedule of the aggregate amount of all Outstanding Debts.

(7) At any time when the Factor shall have the Right of Immediate Termination the Factor may withhold all Prepayments and shall have the right to the repayment by the Client of any Prepayments previously made and unrecovered promptly on the demand of the Factor.

(8) Any payment (including any Prepayment) to be made by the Factor hereunder shall be made by cheque sent by post to the Client or to any bank account of the Client or by such other means of transmission as the parties may agree in writing.

(9) The Factor shall send to the Client a statement of its accounts with the Client once in each month or at such other intervals as may be agreed. Such statement shall be deemed correct and shall be binding on the Client except for manifest errors or errors in law or any error notified by the Client to the Factor within 14 days of its despatch.

8. DEBTS PAYABLE OTHERWISE THAN IN STERLING:

(1) Unless otherwise agreed by the Factor at the request of the Client the Purchase Price of every Currency Debt shall be paid in Sterling and shall be computed by reference to the spot selling rate

of the relevant currency quoted in London by Barclays Bank PLC on the date when payment for such Debt is received by the Factor.

(2) For the purpose of calculating the Factoring Fee in respect of any Currency Debt and for making a provisional credit of the Purchase Price the Factor may apply such selling rate ruling on the date when the Notification relating to the Debt is received by the Factor and thereafter make such adjustment as may be necessary to accord with clause 8(1).

(3) On Recourse of any Currency Debt the repurchase price shall be computed by reference to the rate applied in crediting the Purchase Price to the Current Account.

9. FACTORING FEES AND DISCOUNT CHARGES:

(1) The Factoring Fees and Discount Charges to be deducted in computing the purchase price of Debts shall be as follows:

(a) in respect of every Debt purchased by the Factor a Factoring Fee equivalent to such percentage as is specified in section 7 of the Schedule (or such other percentage as may be agreed by the parties in writing) of the notified value of such Debt before the deduction of any discount or other allowance allowed or allowable at any time to the Debtor; and

(b) in respect of each Debt in relation to which a Prepayment is made, a Discount Charge equivalent to the rate per annum specified in section 8 of the Schedule calculated daily with monthly rests on the amount of such Prepayment from the date on which it is made until it has been fully recovered by the Factor.

(2) For the purposes of clause 9(1)(b) any amount debited to the Current Account (except by reason of Recourse) shall be deemed to be and shall be treated as a Prepayment and for administrative convenience the Factor may calculate and debit such Discount Charges in aggregate each month by applying the rate referred to in clause 9(1)(b) to the total of Outstanding Debts at the end of each day after deducting therefrom the aggregate of the amounts of credit balances on Debtor accounts in the Factor's records and (i) after further deducting any credit balance in favour of the Client on a combination of the accounts of the client in the Factor's records or (ii) after adding any debit balance therein.

(3) In respect of each Unapproved Debt which remains outstanding after the number of days specified in section 9(a) of the Schedule following the last day of the month in which the relevant invoice is dated there shall be payable by the Client to the Factor a supplementary fee equivalent to such percentage as is specified in

section 9(b) of the Schedule of the notified value of such Debt (or the amount thereof unpaid) on the last day of each month on which it remains outstanding. Any such supplementary fee shall be debited to the Current Account on the date on which it becomes payable.

(4) If the aggregate amount of Factoring Fees in respect of Debts of which Notifications shall be received by the Factor in any year commencing on the Commencement or any anniversary thereof shall be less than the minimum sum specified in section 10 of the Schedule then the Client shall pay to the Factor an additional factoring fee equivalent to the difference between the sum so specified and the said aggregate amount. Such additional factoring fee shall be calculated provisionally for each period of three months and debited to the current account at the end of each such period with any necessary adjustment at the end of each year. In the event of termination of this agreement otherwise than on an anniversary of the Commencement the minimum amount to be so applied to the final period shall be such proportion of the amount specified in section 10 of the Schedule as the final period bears to one year.

10. SET-OFF AND COMBINATION OF ACCOUNTS:

(1) The Factor shall be entitled to set off, against any amount payable by the Factor to the Client, the amount of any actual or contingent liability or prospective liability of the Client to the Factor (whether arising in or by contract tort restitution assignment or breach of statutory duty and whether arising under this Agreement or otherwise) and where the amount of any such liability cannot be immediately ascertained the Factor shall be entitled to make a reasonable estimate thereof.

(2) The Factor may in its absolute discretion without notice or other formality combine any two or all the accounts maintained in the Factor's records in the name of the Client. At any time when the Factor shall have Right to Immediate Termination all such accounts shall be deemed to have been combined. Any balance owing to the Factor as a result of such combination of accounts shall be paid by the Client to the Factor in sterling forthwith upon demand.

11. WARRANTIES AND UNDERTAKINGS OF THE CLIENT:

(1) In addition to and without prejudice to any other undertaking given elsewhere in this agreement the Client warrants and undertakes (as applicable):

(a) that save as disclosed by the Client to the Factor in writing no disposition charge trust or other encumbrance (whether created by the Client or otherwise) affects or may affect any of the Debts or Related Rights or Transferred Goods sold to the Factor and that no supplier to the Client has or may have any claim to any such Debt or Related Rights whether by equitable tracing right or otherwise;

(b) that prior to entry into this Agreement the Client has disclosed to the Factor every fact or matter known to the Client which the Client knew or should reasonably have known might influence the Factor in its decision whether or not to enter into this Agreement or to accept any person as surety for the Client's obligations to the Factor or as to the terms of the Agreement or as to the making of any Prepayment or the designation of any Debt as an Approved Debt and to disclose promptly to the Factor any such fact or matter of which the Client becomes aware during the currency of this Agreement including (without prejudice to the generality of the foregoing) any change or prospective change in the constitution or control of the Client or of any such surety or any prospective security right to be created by the Client affecting any of its assets;

(c) immediately after the sale of any Debt to the Factor to make an appropriate entry in the Client's records of account regarding such sale and in all cases in which the Client acts as agent of the Factor pursuant to clause 13(3) to ensure that all accounts and records relating to Debtors are clearly marked that the Debts so recorded thereon have been sold to the Factor;

(d) to indemnify the Factor against all costs and expenses (including legal costs and fees) incurred by the Factor in enforcing or attempting to enforce payment and collection of all Unapproved Debts and in settling or compromising any disagreement with a Debtor (whether justified or not); and

(e) to pay to the Factor all costs and expenses incurred by the Factor (except the Factor's own administrative costs) in entering into this Agreement and in enforcing the terms thereof.

(2) The inclusion of any Debt in a Notification (other than a Notification pursuant to clause 6(3)) or any report made to the Factor pursuant to clause 13(3) shall be deemed to constitute a warranty by the Client that:

(a) the Client has the unqualified right to sell the Debt and its Related Rights to the Factor;

(b) the Goods have been Delivered and the Debt is a legally binding obligation of the Debtor to the extent of the amount notified and has arisen from a Sale Contract made in the ordinary course of the Client's business as specified in section 11 of the Schedule which:

   (i) provides for the invoice to be expressed and payment to be made in a currency specified in section 12 of the Schedule on terms not more liberal than those specified therein;

   (ii) is subject to the law of a country specified therein; and

   (iii) is otherwise as approved by the Factor;

   and the Client will not vary or attempt to vary any of the terms of any such Sale Contract without the prior written consent of the Factor;

(c) the client has no obligations to the Debtor other than under any Sale Contract and there exists no agreement between the Client and the Debtor for set-off or for abatement or whereby otherwise the amount of the Debt specified in the Notification may be reduced except in accordance with the terms of the Sale Contract as approved by the Factor herein;

(d) the Client is not in breach of any of its obligations under the relevant Sale Contract and that the Debtor will accept the goods and the invoice therefor (or if the Debtor is or shall become insolvent that the person having the duty to administer the estate of the Debtor will accept proof of Debt for the unpaid balance thereof) without any dispute or claim whatsoever; and

(e) the Debtor has an established place of business and is not an Associate.

12. DISAGREEMENTS, CREDIT NOTES AND RECOURSE:

(1) If (notwithstanding the warranties and undertakings given by the Client in relation to any Debt) a disagreement should arise between the Client and the Debtor relating to the Debtor's liability to pay in full the notified amount of any Debt (less any discount or allowance approved by the Factor herein) the Client shall forthwith notify the Factor of such disagreement.

(2) The Client undertakes:

(a) to use its best endeavours promptly to settle every such disagreement subject to the right of the Factor itself to settle or compromise any such disagreement or to require that the Client should settle or compromise it on such terms as the Factor may in its absolute discretion think fit; and

(b) promptly to perform all further and continuing obligations of the Client to the Debtor under any Sale Contract giving rise to a Debt sold to the Factor and to give evidence to the Factor of such performance and to agree that in the event of the failure of such performance the Factor may itself perform such obligations at the expense of the Client; and the Client shall be bound by anything done by or at the direction of the Factor pursuant to this clause.

(3) The Client shall promptly advise the Factor in such manner and with such documents as the Factor may require of all credit notes issued to Debtors. The Factor shall have the right by notice to the Client to require that:

(a) as from the date of such notice no credit note for any Debtor should be authorised or issued by the Client without the Factor's consent and
(b) for this purpose the originals of all credit notes which the Client wishes to issue shall be sent to the Factor for despatch to the Debtors after the giving of such consent.

(4) The Factor shall have Recourse:

(a) in respect of every Debt which ranks as an Unapproved Debt by reason of a breach of warranty or undertaking given by the Client to the Factor as soon as such breach occurs;
(b) in respect of every Debt which is the subject of a separate Notification pursuant to clause 6(3) at any time after receipt by the Factor of such Notification;
(c) in respect of every Debt which comprises solely discount or any other deduction wrongly claimed or deducted by the Debtor or which is the subject of such disagreement as is described in clause 12(1) on the sixtieth day after the making of such deduction or claim or the arising of such disagreement;
(d) in respect of every other Unapproved Debt on the day next following that on which it is due for payment by the Debtor; and
(e) in respect of every Debt which the Debtor (or if the Debtor is insolvent the person who has the duty to administer the Debtor's estate) claims to be unable to pay by reason of any law or rules or regulations having the force of law (other than arising solely from the Debtor's insolvency) as soon as such claim is made.

The ownership of every Debt (together with any Related Rights and Transferred Goods pertaining thereto) the subject of

Recourse shall remain vested in the Factor until the repurchase price has been fully discharged.

(5) With every advice of a credit note pursuant to clause 12(3) and immediately on notice of any Recourse the Client shall furnish the Factor with a cheque drawn on a London clearing bank in favour of the Factor for the amount of the credit note or the repurchase price of the Debt the subject of the Recourse as the case may be. On receipt of advice of any credit note or the notice of any Recourse the amount thereof shall be debited to the Current Account and on collection of any such cheque from the drawee the amount of the cheque shall be credited to the Current Account.

(6) Following the vesting of the ownership of any Debt in the Client by reason of Recourse the Factor shall credit to the Current Account the amount of any recovery made by the Factor arising from the enforcement or realisation of any Related Rights or Transferred Goods pertaining to such Debt.

13. NOTICES TO AND COLLECTION FROM DEBTORS:

(1) The Client undertakes to give to each Debtor and prospective Debtor notice in the form prescribed by the Factor and in the manner specified in section 13 of the Schedule (or as otherwise required by the Factor) that the Debt has been purchased by and is payable only to the Factor.

(2) Whilst the ownership of any Debt remains vested in the Factor (except where the provisions of clause 13(3) apply) the Factor shall have the sole right to enforce payment of and collect such Debt and to institute defend or compromise proceedings in its own name or the name of the Client in such manner and upon such terms as it may in its absolute discretion think fit. The Client shall cooperate in such enforcement collection or proceedings and in the recovery of any Goods the ownership of which has not passed to the Debtor and shall use its best endeavours to ensure that payment by the Debtor is made solely to the Factor.

(3) Where it is specified in section 13 of the Schedule that no notices shall be given or if reference to "Agent" is made in the said section:

(a) the Factor hereby appoints the Client as agent of the Factor for the purpose of administering the accounts of Debtors and enforcing payment of and collecting Debts and the Client accepts such appointment and undertakes to act promptly and efficiently in carrying out such tasks; and
(b) the Client shall furnish the Factor by such date in each month as the Factor may direct with such copies of the

records and such reports and statements showing the position of the accounts of Debtors as the Factor may require.

(4) The factor may at any time by notice to the Client withdraw any such agency in which event the Client shall forthwith give the notices prescribed in clause 13(1) in such form and manner as the Factor may direct and the provisions of clause 13(2) shall thereafter apply in full.

(5) The Client shall forthwith deliver to the Factor (or if so required by the Factor direct to a bank account designated by the Factor) the identical monies cheque or other instrument comprising any payment received by the Client in or on account of the discharge of any Debt purchased by the Factor and shall meanwhile hold the said monies cheque or instrument in trust for the Factor.

14. CREDIT LIMITS AND ALLOCATION OF PAYMENTS:

(1) Any Credit Limit may in the Factor's absolute discretion be increased reduced or cancelled by the Factor by oral or written notice to the Client at any time and any such change shall take immediate effect except that no reduction or cancellation shall affect any Debt arising from Goods Delivered before the receipt by the Client of notice of such cancellation or reduction.

(2) Where two or more Debts are owing by the same Debtor they shall be treated as falling within any Credit Limit relating to that Debtor in the order in which they are respectively due for payment by the Debtor.

(3) If the aggregate of Outstanding Debts owing by any Debtor exceeds the Credit Limit relating to that Debtor at any time before cancellation of such Credit Limit then to the extent that any Debt within the Credit Limit shall be paid or otherwise satisfied then the next Debt in the order referred to in clause 14(2) shall fall within it.

(4) When Approved and Unapproved Debts are owing by the same Debtor (except as provided in clause 14(5)) the Factor shall have the right to appropriate any payment by the Debtor or any credit or allowance granted by the Client to the Debtor in satisfaction of any Approved Debt in priority to any Unapproved Debt owing by that Debtor notwithstanding any contrary appropriation by the Debtor.

(5) Following the Onset of Insolvency of any Debtor any dividend or other benefit received by either the Factor or the Client in reduction of any Debt owed by such Debtor shall be divided between the Factor and the Client. The Factor shall be

entitled to such proportion of the dividend or benefit as the total of Approved Debts owed by the Debtor bears to the total of all such Debts as at the Onset of Insolvency. The Client's share of any such dividend or other benefit received by the Factor shall be credited to the Current Account.

(6) The Client shall not disclose to the Debtor or any third party the amount of or absence of any credit limit or reasons therefor and shall indemnify the Factor for all losses costs claims and demands arising out of breach of this requirement.

15. CREDIT BALANCES:

The Client hereby irrevocably authorises the Factor to make payment on account of or in settlement of any credit balance appearing on the account of any Debtor in the records of the Factor whether such credit balance arises from the issue of a credit note by the Client or otherwise.

16. RECOVERY OF VALUE ADDED TAX:

(1) For the purpose of recovering any value added tax included in any Debt owing by a Debtor as at the Onset of Insolvency of that Debtor the Client shall (if so required by the Factor) repurchase such Debt and use its best endeavours to recover such tax. The Client irrevocably authorises the Factor in the name of the Client

(a) to submit proof of debt in the estate of such Debtor and/or
(b) to obtain from the person who has the duty to administer the estate of the Debtor any certificate that may be necessary for the purpose of such recovery.

(2) If any Debt repurchased pursuant to clause 16(1) shall be an Approved Debt then the repurchase price shall be nil and the Client shall hold in trust for the Factor and immediately pay to the Factor (or in the Factor's absolute discretion the Factor may debit the Current Account with) the amount of any such tax recoverable and of any dividend or other benefit received in reduction of such Debt.

(3) If any such repurchased Debt shall be an Unapproved Debt then the repurchase price shall be the amount specified in the Notification relating thereto or the unpaid balance thereof.

17. CLIENT'S ACCOUNTS AND RECORDS:

(1) Whether or not the Client is a body corporate it shall provide for the Factor:

(a) a signed copy of its audited balance sheet and accounts for each year or accounting reference period (as defined in the Companies Act 1985) ending during the currency of this Agreement within six months of the end of such period; and
(b) such other accounts or statements of its financial position or affairs as the Factor may at any time require.

(2) The Client shall promptly furnish the Factor (at the Client's expense) with such of the books records or documents included in the Related Rights or copies of them and copies of any other records or documents of the Client as the Factor may at any time require.

(3) Any official or duly authorised representative or agent of the Factor may at any time enter upon any premises at which the Client carries on business and inspect and/or take copies of any such records or documents (at the Client's expense) and/or remove any books records or documents included in the Related Rights.

18. POWER OF ATTORNEY:

The Client hereby irrevocably appoints the Factor and the Directors and the Company Secretary and every other officer for the time being of the Factor jointly and each of them severally to be the Client's attorney in the name of the Client to execute such deeds or documents and to complete and indorse such instruments and to institute or defend such proceedings and to perform such other acts as the Factor may consider requisite in order to perfect the Factor's title to any Debt Related Rights or Transferred Goods and to secure performance of any of the Client's obligations under this Agreement.

19. COMMENCEMENT AND TERMINATION:

(1) This Agreement shall commence on the Commencement and unless it is terminated pursuant to clause 19(2) shall continue for the minimum period prescribed in section 15 of the Schedule and thereafter until the expiry of the period (specified in section 16 of the Schedule) of notice of termination given by either party to the other.

(2) On the occurrence of any of the following events the Factor shall have the right by notice to the Client to terminate this Agreement forthwith or at any time thereafter:

(a) The Client's Insolvency or its calling any meeting of its creditors;

(b) A petition for an administration order pursuant to the Act in relation to the Client (being a body corporate) or a resolution of its members for its winding up;
(c) The dissolution of any partnership comprising the Client;
(d) The Client's income or assets or any part thereof being seized under any execution legal process or distress for rent or the making or threat of a garnishee order on any person indebted to the Client;
(e) The occurrence of any of the events referred to in paragraphs (a) to (d) inclusive of this clause in relation to any person who has given a guarantee or indemnity in respect of the Client's obligations under this Agreement or the death of any such person or the termination or attempted termination of any such guarantee or indemnity;
(f) Any breach of any covenant or undertaking given by any person in reliance upon which the Factor entered into or continued this Agreement or the withdrawal or attempted withdrawal of any waiver or release given to the Factor in relation to any security right affecting any asset of the Client;
(g) The cessation or threatened cessation of the Client's business; or
(h) Any material or persistent breach of any of the Client's obligations under this Agreement.

(3) On the giving of notice by the Factor pursuant to clause 19(2) the Factor shall have immediate Recourse in respect of all Outstanding Debts but so that the ownership of none of such Debts shall vest in the Client until the repurchase price of all such Debts has been received by the Factor.

(4) Subject to the provisions of clauses 7(6) and 19(3) termination of this Agreement shall not affect the rights and obligations of either party in relation to Debts which are in existence on the date of termination and such rights and obligations shall remain in full force and effect until duly extinguished.

20. EXCLUSION OF OTHER TERMS AND PRESERVATION OF THE FACTOR'S RIGHTS:

(1) This Agreement (including the Appendix thereto and the Schedule and any special conditions set out therein) contains all the terms agreed between the Factor and the Client to the exclusion of any agreement statement or representation made by or on behalf of the Factor prior to the making of this Agreement whether orally or in writing. Except to the extent provided for herein no variation of this Agreement or of any term thereof shall

be valid unless it is in writing and signed on behalf of the Factor by a Director or the Company Secretary and on behalf of the Client (being a body corporate) by a Director or the Company Secretary of the Client or (not being a body corporate) by every person named as Client herein.

(2) The Factor's rights under this Agreement shall not be affected in any way by the granting of time or indulgence by the Factor to the Client or to any other person nor by any failure or delay in the exercise of any right or option under this Agreement or otherwise.

21. CONSTITUTION AND PLURALITY OF CLIENT:

(1) If the Client comprises two or more persons:

(a) references to the Client in clauses 7(5) and 19(2) shall be deemed to be references to any one or more of them;

(b) all undertakings and warranties given herein shall be deemed to have been given by every one of them;

(c) their liability hereunder shall be joint and several and the Factor may release or compromise with any one or more of them without affecting its rights against the others; and

(d) the Factor may in its absolute discretion treat any notice to or demand on any one or more of them as notice to or demand on them all and any notice to the Factor by any one or more of them as notice by them all.

(2) If the Client comprises a partnership all the persons who have executed this Agreement warrant that all the present partners of such partnership are named herein.

(3) Except as provided in clause 19(2) this Agreement and all the terms thereof shall remain in full force and effect notwithstanding any change in the constitution of the Client whether by death retirement addition or otherwise.

22. ASSIGNMENT OR DELEGATION BY CLIENT:

The Client shall not be entitled to assign any of its rights or delegate any of its obligations under this Agreement without the prior written consent of the Factor.

23. NOTICES:

Any notice or demand required or permitted to be served or made by the Factor shall be validly served or made if handed (in the case of a body corporate) to any officer of the Client (or if the Client is not a body corporate) to any of the persons comprising the Client or if sent by telex or facsimile transmission or by post or delivered to the registered office of the Client or to its address stated herein or to its address last known to the Factor or to any address at which the Client carries on business. Notices and demands served personally shall take effect upon such service and notices sent and demands made by post shall be conclusively deemed to have been received within seventy-two hours of the time of posting and notices sent and demands made by telex or facsimile shall be deemed to have been received upon their transmission.

APPENDIX TO THE AGREEMENT

DEFINITIONS:

"the Act"

The Insolvency Act 1986;

"Approved Debt"

Any Debt which is (when aggregated with all other Outstanding Debts owing by the same Debtor) for the time being within a Credit Limit established in accordance with clause 14 and in relation to which the Client is not in breach of any obligation under this Agreement and which is not a Debt of the nature or description contained in section 4 of the Schedule;

"Associate"

An associate as defined in section 184 of the Consumer Credit Act 1974 of the Client or a director or shareholder or employee of the Client;

"Commencement"

The date of Commencement of this Agreement as specified in section 14 of the Schedule;

"Credit Limit"

A limit established by the Factor in its absolute discretion in relation to any Debtor for the purpose of determining which Debts owing by such Debtor may be classified as Approved Debts;

"Currency Debt"

Any Debt which is represented by an invoice expressed otherwise than in sterling or is payable otherwise than in sterling in the United Kingdom in accordance with the Sale Contract giving rise to it;

"Current Account"

An account maintained by the Factor in the name of the Client for the recording of transactions between the Factor and the Client pursuant to this Agreement;

"Debt"

Any obligation incurred by a Debtor under a Sale Contract and where the context so admits a part of a Debt;

"Debtor"

Any person who incurs any obligation to the Client under a Sale Contract or who may incur such an obligation under a prospective Sale Contract;

"Debts Purchased Account"

An account maintained in the records of the Factor in the name of the Client for the purpose of recording the Purchase Price of Debts (together with any Related Rights and Transferred Goods pertaining thereto);

"Delivered"

In the case of goods, despatched to or to the order of the Debtor from a place in the United Kingdom and, in the case of services, completed;

"Discount Charge"

The discount charge (if any) to be deducted in computing a Purchase Price in accordance with clause 9(1)(b) and dealt with in accordance with clause 9(2);

"Factoring Fee"

The fee to be deducted in computing the Purchase Price of every Debt purchased by the Factor in accordance with clause 9(1)(a);

"Goods"

Any goods (and where the context so admits any services) the subject of a Sale Contract;

"Insolvency"

(i) In the case of an individual: bankruptcy or sequestration;
(ii) in the case of a partnership: winding up by the court or bankruptcy or sequestration;
(iii) in the case of a corporate body: winding up by the court or voluntary winding up by reason of its inability to pay its debts or the appointment of an administrator pursuant to the Act or of a receiver of any part or all of its income or assets; and
(iv) in any case: any informal or voluntary arrangement (whether or not in accordance with the Act) with or for the benefit of the general body of creditors of the individual partnership or body corporate;

"Minimum Balance"

The amount which at any time is equivalent to the aggregate of the amounts of the following:

(i) all outstanding Unapproved Debts as shown in the records of the Factor;
(ii) all liabilities of the Client to the Factor which may be debited to the Current Account pursuant to clause 7(2) but which have not been so debited; and
(iii) such percentage of the outstanding Approved Debts (as shown in the records of the Factor) as is the remainder after deducting from 100 per cent. the percentage specified in section 5 of the Schedule;

"Notification"

A notification of a Debt by the Client to the Factor pursuant to clause 6(2) and "notified" shall be construed accordingly;

"Onset of Insolvency"

(i) In the case of sequestration or bankruptcy or winding up by the court: the date of the sequestration award or the bankruptcy or winding up order respectively;
(ii) in the case of voluntary winding up: the date of the effective resolution for winding up by members of the body corporate;
(iii) in the case of the appointment of a receiver or administrator: the date of his appointment; and
(iv) in the case of an arrangement the date when it is made;

"Outstanding Debt"

Any Debt which has been included in a Notification and which remains vested in the Factor and unpaid and "outstanding" shall be construed accordingly;

"Prepayment"

A payment made by the Factor to the Client on account of any Purchase Price (before the Transfer Date thereof) up to the percentage specified in section 5 of the Schedule of the amount of such Debt as notified;

"Purchase Price"

The amount payable by the Factor to the Client pursuant to clause 6(1) for each Debt (together with any Related Rights and Transferred Goods pertaining thereto) purchased by the Factor;

"Recourse"

The right of the Factor to require the Client to repurchase a Debt (together with any Related Rights and Transferred Goods relating thereto) purchased by the Factor at a repurchase price equivalent to the amount of such Debt as notified;

"Related Rights"

(i) All the Client's rights under the Sale Contract giving rise to a Debt;
(ii) the benefit of all guarantees indemnities insurances and securities given to or held by the Client in relation to such Debt;
(iii) all cheques bills of exchange and other instruments held by or available to the Client in relation to such Debt; and
(iv) the ledgers computer data records and documents on or by which such Debt is recorded or evidenced;

"Right of Immediate Termination"

The right of the Factor to terminate this Agreement forthwith by notice in the circumstances described in clause 19(2) whether or not the Factor shall have exercised that right;

"Sale Contract"

A contract for the supply of Goods by the Client;

"Transfer Date"

The day specified in section 3 of the Schedule on which any Purchase Price is to be transferred to the Current Account pursuant to clause 7(2);

"Transferred Goods"

Any Goods in respect of which the Factor shall have exercised its right pursuant to clause 4(2);

"Unapproved Debt"

A debt which is not an Approved Debt.

THE SCHEDULE

(forming part of an agreement for the factoring or discounting of Debts between Venture Factors PLC. and the person named in section 1 hereof)

1. (a) Name and trading address of Client:

(b) In the case of a partnership or sole trader the full names and residential addresses of the partners or principal:

(c) In the case of a company its place of incorporation and

registered number: (clause 1)

2. Debtors for inclusion (clause 4(1)):
3. Transfer Date (clause 7(2)): The date on which payment for the Debt is received in the bank account of the Factor or (in respect of any Approved Debt) any earlier Onset of Insolvency of the Debtor:
4. Debts within Credit Limits which are not Approved Debts (clause 7(3) and Definition of Approved Debt):

5. Prepayment percentage (clause 7(3) and definition of Prepayment):	%
6. Prepayment concentration on single Debtor – percentage (clause 7(6):	%
7. Factoring Fee (exclusive of value added tax) (clause 9(1)(a)):	%
8. Discount Charge (clause 9(1)(b)):	% over the Base Rate of Barclays Bank Plc for the time being in force.
9. Supplementary Fee (exclusive of value added tax) (clause 9(3)):	
(a) Number of days:	
(b) Percentage rate:	%

10. Additional Factoring Fee (exclusive of value added tax)—minimum (clause 9(4)):
11. Nature of Client's Business (clause 11(2)(b)):
12. Client's Sale Contract (clause 11(2)(b)):
    (a) Currency:
    (b) Terms of payment:
    (c) Governing law:
13. Notices to Debtors and Collection Arrangements (clauses 13(1) and 13(3)):
14. Commencement (clause 19(1)):
15. Minimum Period (clause 19(1)):
16. Period of Notice of Termination (clause 19(1)):

17. Special Conditions:

IN WITNESS WHEREOF the Parties have executed this Deed in the manner described below:—

SIGNED and DELIVERED as a	)	
DEED by VENTURE FACTORS	)	
PLC	)	....
acting by	)	Director
a director and	)	
its sectetary [a director]	)	....
on the .... day of	)	Director
.... 19....	)	

Corporate Client

SIGNED and DELIVERED as a	)	
DEED by	)	
Limited	)	....
acting by	)	Director
a Director and	)	
its sectetary [or a director]	)	....
on the .... day of	)	Director
.... 19....	)	

Sole Trader or Partnership Client

SIGNED and DELIVERED as a)
DEED by ....)
....) ....
....)
on the .... day of) ....
.... 19.... in the)
presence of:—) ....

....)
a solicitor of the Supreme Court of)
Judicature the effect of the assignment)
contained herein having been)
explained by me to the said ....)
....)
....)
before execution thereof.)
)
.... Solicitor)

Copyright: Wilde and Partners, Solicitors, London.

APPENDIX 9

AGREEMENT FOR PRIORITIES

1. PARTIES: (1) ("the Bank")

(2) Limited of

("the Factor")

(3) Limited (a company registered in England and Wales with the number) of ("the Company")

2. DATE:

3. DEFINITIONS:

(1) In this Deed except where the context otherwise requires, the singular shall include the plural and vice versa and the following expressions shall have the meanings assigned to them below:

"The Factoring Agreement"	The proposed agreement, in the form set out in the First Annexe hereto, for the factoring or discounting of receivables between the Factor and the Company.
"The Bank's Charge"	The charge executed by the Company in favour of the Bank represented by an instrument dated in the Bank's standard form.
"The Factor's Charge"	The charge to be made between the Company and the Factor in accordance

with the Factor's standard form as set out in the Second Annexe hereto.

"The Bank's Debt"	The aggregate amount of principal interest charges and other sums and liabilities from time to time owing or incurred by the Company to the Bank and secured by the Bank's Charge.
"The Factor's Debt"	The aggregate amount of principal interest charges and other sums and liabilities from time to time owing or incurred to the Factor and secured by the Factor's Charge, in particular but without prejudice to the generality of the foregoing, any liability of the Company to the Factor in respect of recourse in accordance with the provisions of the Factoring Agreement.
"Excepted Receivables"	(i) Receivables and associated rights not covered by the factoring agreement (ii) receivables and associated rights coming into existence after the Factor shall have received notice that the Bank has withdrawn its consent and waiver in accordance with sub-clause (3) of clause 4 hereof and (iii) receivables and associated rights repurchased by the Company from the Factor and revested in the Company.

(2) Any expression used herein, which is defined in Clause 3 of the Factoring Agreement, shall have the meaning assigned to it therein.

(3) Reference to any clause or sub-clause shall mean a reference to a clause or sub-clause in this Agreement.

4. THE BANK'S CONSENT AND WAIVER:

(1) The Bank hereby agrees, subject to the provisions of sub-clause (3) hereof, that:

(a) notwithstanding any restriction contained in the Bank's Charge or any other charge or encumbrance affecting the receivables made or which may hereafter be made in favour of the Bank the Company is at liberty to enter into the Factoring Agreement;

(b) as regards the receivables and associated rights which shall be purchased by the Factor pursuant to the Factoring Agreement, all such receivables and associated rights shall be free from any trust, charge or other security held or to be held by the bank over the property of the Company; and

(c) the consent and waiver given herein shall extend to any agreement which is supplemental to the agreement or is made by way of variation or replacement thereof so long as a copy of such agreement is given by the Factor to the Bank.

(2) For avoidance of doubt it is hereby confirmed that:

(a) Any amount owing or which shall become due from the Factor to the Company by virtue of the Factoring Agreement, subject to the Factor's rights under the Factoring Agreement whether actual or contingent, shall be and remain subject to the Bank's Charge; and

(b) Any Excepted Receivable shall be and remain subject to the Bank's Charge and the Factor's Charge in accordance with the rights of the parties as set out in Clause 5 hereof.

(3) The Bank reserves the right to withdraw the foregoing consent and waiver by notice to the registered office of the Factor and any such withdrawal shall not affect the Factor's right to any receivable or associated right which shall vest in the Factor before receipt by it of such notice.

5. PRIORITIES:

Subject to the provisions of clause 7(3),

(i) any sum of money arising from the realisation of any of the receivables or associated rights, with the exception of the Excepted Receivables, shall be applied to the satisfaction of the Factor's debt in priority to the Bank's debt and

(ii) any sum of money arising from the realisation of any other of the property and assets charged by the Bank's Charge or by the Factor's Charge or by both of them (including the excepted receivables) shall be applied to the satisfaction of the Bank's debt in priority to the Factor's debt.

Neither the Bank's priority nor the Factor's priority shall be affected by any fluctuations in the amounts from time to time due owing or incurred by the Company to the Bank or by the existence from time to time of any credit balance on any current or other account.

6. EXCHANGE OF INFORMATION:

Until the termination of the Factoring Agreement and the discharge of all the Company's obligations thereunder to the Factor or the discharge of the Bank's Charge (whichever shall be the earlier) the Bank and the Factor shall be at liberty from time to time to disclose to each other information concerning the Company and its affairs in such manner and to such extent as the Bank and the Factor shall from time to time desire and no action shall lie on the part of the Company in regard thereto.

7. CRYSTALLIZATION:

(1) Save (i) as provided in the Factoring Agreement and (ii) as regards the receivables and associated rights (other than the Excepted Receivables), the Factor shall not without the written consent of the Bank first obtained exercise its power of sale over any of the assets of the Company or otherwise have recourse to such assets except through a Receiver of the Company.

(2) In the event of either the Bank or the Factor being desirous of appointing a Receiver they shall consult together with a view to agreeing upon a suitable person to be appointed as such Receiver provided that nothing contained in this clause shall prevent either the Bank or the Factor appointing a Receiver of the Company when it deems it necessary to make such appointment.

(3) All monies received by any such Receiver under whichever of the Charges such Receiver is appointed shall be applied first in payment of his remuneration and the costs of realisation secondly in providing for the matters specified in the first three paragraphs of sub-section 8 of Section 109 of the Law of Property Act 1925, thirdly in or towards the payment of any debts or other imposts which are by statute made payable in preference to the monies secured by the Bank's Charge and the Factor's Charge to the extent to which such debts or imposts are made so payable and fourthly in or towards satisfaction of the money and liabilities secured by the Bank's and the Factor's Charges in accordance with the terms of this Agreement.

8. MISCELLANEOUS PROVISIONS:

(1) Nothing contained in this Agreement shall bind either the Bank or the Factor to make any advance or to give credit or to grant banking or other facilities to the Company.

(2) Until the termination of the Factoring Agreement and the discharge of all the Company's obligations thereunder to the Factor or the discharge of the Bank's Charge (whichever shall be the earlier) neither the Bank or the Factor shall permit the Company to create any charge ranking in priority to its respective charge.

(3) The Factor hereby acknowledges the right of the Bank to production of the Factor's Charge and to delivery of copies thereof.

(4) The Bank hereby acknowledges the right of the Factor to production of the Bank's Charge and to delivery of copies thereof.

9. UNDERTAKING BY COMPANY

As a party to this Deed the Company acknowledges the agreement as to priorities between the Bank and the Factor and undertakes to be bound by the provisions of hereof.

IN WITNESS whereof
of   in the
exercise of the power conferred upon him by a Power of Attorney dated the   day of   19   has hereunto set the name of the said   Bank p.l.c. to and signed this Deed in the presence of the person named below and   Limited and   Limited have executed this Deed the day and year first above written:—

SIGNED AND DELIVERED by the)
above named)
as Attorney) ....
and in the name of the above named)
Bank p.l.c.)
in the presence of:) by ....

Signature of Witness ....
Name of Witness ....
Address of Witness ....
....

SIGNED AND DELIVERED by	)	....
Limited	)	Director
acting by a director and its secretary	)	....
[or two directors]	)	Director/Secretary
	)	
SIGNED AND DELIVERED by	)	....
Limited	)	Director
acting by a director and its secretary	)	....
[or two directors]	)	Director/Secretary

APPENDIX 10

GLOSSARY OF TERMS

(* = *Usage in the United States*)

Account debtor. * Debtor.

Account receivable. * Debt *(q.v.)*.

Administration charge. An *ad valorem* charge made by the factor (often by deduction from the purchase price of debts) calculated on the amount of each debt purchased by the factor. The charge is made to compensate the factor for taking over certain administrative functions and/or the risk of bad debts.

Advance or advance payment. A prepayment *(q.v.)*.

Ageing. The analysis of outstanding debts by reference of their due dates.

Aged balance report. A schedule of outstanding debts analysed by reference to their due dates.

Agency factoring. Factoring disclosed to the debtors but with the sales accounting and collection functions retained by the client.

Approved. In relation to a debt:
(i) in the case of non-recourse factoring, not subject to recourse to the client by reason of the financial inability of the debtor to pay the debt; and/or
(ii) in the case of most forms of factoring (except maturity), eligible for a prepayment on account of its purchase price.

Assignment notice. The written instruction to the debtor to pay the factor normally placed on the face of each invoice issued by the client other than in invoice discounting or undisclosed factoring.

Associate. A person connected with the client by reason of common control or relationship.

Availability. The amount payable, at any one time, by the factor to the client for or on account of the purchase price of debts sold to the factor.

Back-to-back factoring. The provision of factoring services to a debtor in order to provide security for the approval of the debtor's indebtedness arising from the sales of another client.

Balance payment. Payment, of the purchase price of a debt purchased by the factor, on the due date for payment of the purchase price (the maturity date or collection date *(q.v.)*) after deducting any prepayment *(q.v.)* made in respect of that purchase price.

Batch. A bundle of copy invoices accompanying a notification *(q.v.)*.

Bulk factoring. Agency factoring *(q.v.)*.

Chain. An international association of correspondent factors.

Charge back. An amount payable by the client to the factor in respect of a debt the subject of recourse and debited to the client's account with the factor.

Client. A business with which the factor has entered into a factoring agreement.

Collection date. The date on which the factor has received payment (by way of cleared funds) for a debt.

Collection only. In relation to a factoring agreement, an arrangement whereby the factor is responsible to pay the purchase price only on the collection date with no prepayments.

Collection report. A periodic report by the factor to the client of payments received from debtors.

Commission. Administration charge *(q.v.)*.

Confidential factoring. Factoring (either with or without recourse), without notices of the assignments to the debtors, whereby the client administers the sales ledger and collects as agent for the factor. See also "invoice discounting," "non-notification factoring" and "undisclosed factoring."

Correspondent factor. A factor who is prepared to act as an import factor *(q.v.)* or an export factor *(q.v.)* under the two factor system *(q.v.)*.

Credit approval. The approval of a debt in non-recourse factoring whereby the credit risk *(q.v.)* in relation to that debt is accepted by the factor without recourse to the client.

Credit limit. A limit established by the factor in relation to a debtor within which outstanding debts are deemed to be approved.

Credit line. Credit limit *(q.v.)*.

Credit risk. The risk of the inability of the debtor to pay for a debt, purchased by a factor, solely by reason of financial inability to pay.

Current account. An account between the factor and the client for the recording of some or all of the transactions between them (according to the accounting system in use).

Customer. Debtor *(q.v.)*.

Dated invoices. Invoices to which forward dating *(q.v.)* has been applied.

Debit back. Charge back *(q.v.)*.

Debtor. A person who is or may become indebted to a client under a contract or prospective contract for the sale of goods or the provision of services. *A business concern for which a financial facility is provided; *e.g.* a client.

Debts purchased account. An account maintained by the factor on which are recorded the value of all unmatured debts purchased by the factor. (This applies in a particular system of accounting referred to in Chapter 3).

Debt turn. The average period of credit taken by the debtors of a client.

Direct export factoring. The provision of factoring services to a client for his exports without the use by the factor of correspondent factors in the countries of the debtors.

Direct import factoring. The provision of factoring services by a factor in the country of the debtors to an exporter in another country without the intervention of a correspondent factor in that country.

Disapproved. In relation to a debt: unapproved *(q.v.)*..

Disclosed invoice discounting. Another term (possibly more apt) for agency factoring *(q.v.)*.

Discount/Discounting charge. The charge made by a factor (often as a deduction in calculating the purchase price of debts) for the provision of prepayments *(q.v.)*.

Discount tolerance letter. A letter from the client to the factor at the outset of factoring whereby the client agrees to the factor's allowing (at the client's expense) settlement discounts taken out of time up to agreed limits of time and amount.

Dispute. The failure of the debtor to accept the goods or services and the invoice the subject of a debt purchased by the factor for any reason whatsoever.

Dispute notice. A written notice from the factor to the client (or, in the two factor system *(q.v.)*, from the import factor to the export factor) advising the latter of a dispute.

Domestic factoring. The factoring of debts arising from sales of a client to debtors in the same country.

Drop-in. A provision in non-recourse factoring whereby a debt (or a part of a debt) in excess of a credit limit may fall within it to the extent that an item within the limit is paid or credited.

Early payment. Prepayment *(q.v.)*.

Eligible debt. A debt in relation to which the factor has presribed that the client may draw a prepayment on account of the purchase price.

Export factor. A factor (normally in the country of his client) providing factoring for exports and using the two factor system *(q.v.)*.

Facultative agreement. An agreement which provides for each debt to be offered by the client to the factor who may exercise his discretion as to whether or not to accept it.

Forward dating of invoices. A means by which the client allows an additional period of credit to the debtor; the client dates his invoice "as" a date later than that on which it is issued and the normal due date is calculated from such later date.

Full factoring (or full service factoring). A factoring arrangement whereby the factor takes on the administrative functions of the sales ledger and collection from debtors, relieves the client from bad debts and provides finance by way of prepayments.

Funds in use. The aggregate amount, at any one time, of prepayments and amounts charged to the client by the factor unrecovered by payments from the debtors.

Import factor. A correspondent factor (normally in the country of the debtors) who is prepared to take sub-assignment of debts owing by such debtors and consequently be responsible for collection and/or the credit risk.

Indirect payment. A payment made by a debtor to the client for a debt purchased by the factor contrary to a notice of the assignment of that debt.

Ineligible debt. A debt in relation to which the factor is not prepared to make a prepayment on account of the purchase price (for example, by reason of a breach of warranty by the client in relation to the debt or by reason of its being in excess of a limit prescribed by the factor in relation to the debtor).

Initial payment. Prepayment *(q.v.)*.

Interfactor agreement. An agreement between correspondent factors whereby they mutually agree to act as import and export factors in accordance with a code of practice.

Introductory letter. A letter sent to each of the debtors by a client at the start of factoring (on a disclosed basis) for the purpose of explaining the factoring arrangements and instructing the debtor to pay the factor for all supplies by the client until further notice.

Invoice discounting. Confidential factoring *(q.v.)* normally with recourse.

Maturity date. The due date for payment of the purchase price of a debt purchased by the factor after the deduction of any prepayment made in respect of that debt. It is normally the end of the maturity period *(q.v.)* in relation to each debt.

Maturity factoring. A factoring arrangement whereby payment of the purchase price of each debt is made on the maturity date *(q.v.)* often without any provision for prepayments. The term is sometimes used for an arrangement for payment of the whole of the purchase price of each debt on the collection date *(q.v.)* without any prepayments; in such a case the factoring is to relieve the client from administrative functions and bad debts.

Maturity period. The number of days after invoice date (or the end of the month in which the invoice is dated or the date of the receipt by the factor of copy invoices) fixed by reference to a historical average period of credit taken by debtors. The period is the basis for fixing a maturity date *(q.v.)*.

Minimum balance. Retention *(q.v.)*.

Non-notification factoring. Confidential factoring *(q.v.)*.

Non-recourse factoring. Full factoring *(q.v.)* or any variation by which the factor has no right of recourse in respect of approved debts unpaid by reason only of the financial inability of the debtor to pay.

Notification. A report by the client to the factor of the coming into existence of debts (already purchased by the factor pursuant to a whole turnover type of agreement *(q.v.)*) often by the submission of copy invoices. The expression is sometimes also used to denote notice to a debtor of the assignment of his indebtedness.

Old line factoring.* Full factoring *(q.v.)*; *i.e.* traditional factoring.

Open account credit. Credit not covered by a bill of exchange or promissory note.

Open item sales accounting. A system of accounting by which the balance owing is broken down into the individual invoices remaining outstanding and unallocated payments and credits.

Payment report. A periodic report from a factor to his client (or from an import factor to an export factor) of payments received from debtors since the last such report.

Permitted limit. Credit limit *(q.v.)*.

Prepayment. A payment, made by the factor to the client on receipt of a notification *(q.v.)* or schedule offer *(q.v.)*, on account of the purchase price of the debts included in the notification or offer.

Receivable. Debt *(q.v.)*.

Record Account. Another term for a debts purchased account *(q.v.)*.

Recourse. The right of the factor to be guaranteed the due payment of a purchased debt by the debtor or tohave an unpaid debt repurchased by the client.

Refactoring charge. An additional administration charge *(q.v.)* made by some factors in respect of any debt, which is subject to recourse and remains unpaid after a specified period, in consideration for the factor's not exercising his right of recourse.

Retention. A minimum credit balance in favour of the client retained by the factor on the account (or a combination of accounts) of the client held by the factor. The retention is held to provide for the set-off of amounts payable to the factor by the client, particularly for the repurchase price of debts the subject of recourse.

Schedule of offer. A list of invoices constituting an offer (under a facultative type of agreement *(q.v.)*) to the factor by the client of the debts represented by the invoices.

Seller, Client *(q.v.)*.

Service charge. Administration charge *(q.v.)*.

Shipping limit. A limit of deliveries prescribed by the factor per specified period (often per month) for the purpose of determining which debts are approved for credit or eligible for prepayment *(q.v.)*.

Single factor system. A modification of the two factor system *(q.v.)* by which the correspondent factor becomes responsible for collection only when difficulties arise.

Supplier. Client *(q.v.)*.

Switch on. Take on *(q.v.)*.

Switch on letter. Introductory letter *(q.v.)*.

Take on (or take-over). The entering of the debts purchased by the factor and outstanding at the date of the commencement of a factoring agreement into the records of the factor and the start of the practical arrangements for factoring.

Take on (or take-over) debts. Debts purchased by the factor and outstanding at the start of factoring.

Two factor system. A system by which the client's factor sub-assigns export debts to correspondent factors in the countries of the debtors and by which the latter are responsible for collection and the credit risk in relation to such debts as are approved.

Unapproved. In relation to a debt: subject to recourse and (particularly in the case of any form of factoring with recourse in relation to *all* debts) not eligible for prepayment *(q.v.)*.

Undisclosed factoring. Confidential factoring *(q.v.)* normally on as non-recourse factoring *(q.v.)*.

Whole turnover agreement. An agreement which itself provides for the assignment to the factor of all existing and future debts (or all of a class of debts) of the client without any further act of transfer of the individual debts.

INDEX